Law, Text, Terror

The relationship between law and terrorism has re-emerged recently as a pressing issue in contemporary jurisprudence. Terrorism appears to take law to its limit, whilst the demands of counter-terrorism hold the cause of justice in contempt. At this point the case for engaging alternative intellectual approaches and resources is compelling. Ian Ward argues that through a closer appreciation of the ethical and aesthetical dimensions of terror, as well as the historical, political and cultural, we can better comprehend modern expressions and experiences of terrorism. For this reason, alongside juristic responses to modern expressions of terrorism, this book examines a variety of supplementary literary texts as well as alternative intellectual approaches; from the drama of Euripides and Shakespeare, to the rhetoric and poetry of Burke and Shelley, the literary feminisms of Lessing and Rame, and the narrative existentialism of Conrad, Coetzee, Dostoevsky and DeLillo.

Ian Ward is Professor of Law at Newcastle University. He has written extensively in the associated areas of public law, legal theory and international order, and has held visiting positions at universities in Canada, the US, France, Italy and Finland.

The Law in Context Series

Editors: William (University College London),
Christopher McCrudden (Lincoln College, Oxford) and
Bronwen Morgan (University of Bristol).

Since 1970 the Law in Context series has been in the forefront of the movement to broaden the study of law. It has been a vehicle for the publication of innovative scholarly books that treat law and legal phenomena critically in their social, political and economic contexts from a variety of perspectives. The series particularly aims to publish scholarly legal writing that brings fresh perspectives to bear on new and existing areas of law taught in universities. A contextual approach involves treating legal subjects broadly, using materials from other social sciences, and from any other discipline that helps to explain the operation in practice of the subject under discussion. It is hoped that this orientation is at once more stimulating and more realistic than the bare exposition of legal rules. The series includes original books that have a different emphasis from traditional legal textbooks, while maintaining the same high standards of scholarship. They are written primarily for undergraduate and graduate students of law and of other disciplines, but most also appeal to a wider readership. In the past, most books in the series have focused on English law, but recent publications include books on European law, globalisation, transnational legal processes, and comparative law.

Books in the Series

Anderson, Schum & Twining: *Analysis of Evidence*
Ashworth: *Sentencing and Criminal Justice*
Barton & Douglas: *Law and Parenthood*
Beecher-Monas: *Evaluating Scientific Evidence: An Interdisciplinary Framework for Intellectual Due Process*
Bell: *French Legal Cultures*
Bercusson: *European Labour Law*
Birkinshaw: *European Public Law*
Birkinshaw: *Freedom of Information: The Law, the Practice and the Ideal*
Cane: *Atiyah's Accidents, Compensation and the Law*
Clarke & Kohler: *Property Law: Commentary and Materials*
Collins: *The Law of Contract*
Cranston: *Legal Foundations of the Welfare State*
Davies: *Perspectives on Labour Law*
Dembour: *Who Believes in Human Rights?: The European Convention in Question*
de Sousa Santos: *Toward a New Legal Common Sense*
Diduck: *Law's Families*
Elworthy & Holder: *Environmental Protection: Text and Materials*
Fortin: *Children's Rights and the Developing Law*
Glover-Thomas: *Reconstructing Mental Health Law and Policy*

Goldman: *Globalisation and the Western Legal Tradition: Recurring Patterns of Law and Authority*

Gobert & Punch: *Rethinking Corporate Crime*

Harlow & Rawlings: *Law and Administration*

Harris: *An Introduction to Law*

Harris, Campbell & Halson: *Remedies in Contract and Tort*

Harvey: *Seeking Asylum in the UK: Problems and Prospects*

Hervey & McHale: *Health Law and the European Union*

Holder & Lee: *Environmental Protection, Law and Policy*

Kostakopoulou: *The Future Governance of Citizenship*

Lacey, Wells & Quick: *Reconstructing Criminal Law*

Lewis: *Choice and the Legal Order: Rising above Politics*

Likosky: *Transnational Legal Processes*

Likosky: *Law, Infrastructure and Human Rights*

Maughan & Webb: *Lawyering Skills and the Legal Process*

McGlynn: *Families and the European Union: Law, Politics and Pluralism*

Moffat: *Trusts Law: Text and Materials*

Monti: *EC Competition Law*

Morgan & Yeung: *An Introduction to Law and Regulation, Text and Materials*

Norrie: *Crime, Reason and History*

O'Dair: *Legal Ethics*

Oliver: *Common Values and the Public–Private Divide*

Oliver & Drewry: *The Law and Parliament*

Picciotto: *International Business Taxation*

Reed: *Internet Law: Text and Materials*

Richardson: *Law, Process and Custody*

Roberts & Palmer: *Dispute Processes: ADR and the Primary Forms of Decision-Making*

Scott & Black: *Cranston's Consumers and the Law*

Seneviratne: *Ombudsmen: Public Services and Administrative Justice*

Stapleton: *Product Liability*

Tamanaha: *The Struggle for Law as a Means to an End*

Turpin & Tomkins: *British Government and the Constitution: Text and Materials*

Twining: *Globalisation and Legal Theory*

Twining: *Rethinking Evidence*

Twining & Miers: *How to Do Things with Rules*

Ward: *A Critical Introduction to European Law*

Ward: *Law, Text, Terror*

Ward: *Shakespeare and Legal Imagination*

Zander: *Cases and Materials on the English Legal System*

Zander: *The Law-Making Process*

Law, Text, Terror

IAN WARD

CAMBRIDGE UNIVERSITY PRESS

Cambridge, New York, Melbourne, Madrid, Cape Town, Singapore, São Paulo, Delhi

Cambridge University Press
The Edinburgh Building, Cambridge CB2 8RU, UK

Published in the United States of America by Cambridge University Press, New York

www.cambridge.org
Information on this title: www.cambridge.org/9780521740210

© Ian Ward 2009

First published 2009

Printed in the United Kingdom at the University Press, Cambridge

A catalogue record for this publication is available from the British Library

ISBN 978-0-521-51957-1 hardback
ISBN 978-0-521-74021-0 paperback

Contents

Preface

Concerns come and go, just as interests wax and wane. And there is absolutely nothing new about terrorism and political violence; as we shall see time and again in the following chapters. But, for reasons which are only too tragically obvious, we are at present inordinately concerned about the presumed threat of terrorism. And few subjects can claim a greater interest, both in the wider public as well as the narrower legal academy. More and more law schools offer courses in terrorism and counter-terrorism law, more and more students study the subject, more and more legal academics claim it to be an ongoing research interest. Unsurprisingly, the number of scholarly books and articles on the subject has increased quite markedly in the years since September 2001. Most, though not all, tend to focus on the perceived merits, or more likely demerits, of contemporary state-based responses to terrorism. At the same time, beyond the closer concerns of the lawyer and legal academic, there is of course a similarly burgeoning scholarship on associated aspects of terrorism history and politics, aesthetics and culture. Occasionally these scholarships engage; but not that often. The purpose of this book is to strengthen this engagement, in the hope that both the student of law and the student of terrorism and counter-terrorism will gain from a closer mutual appreciation. The vitality of inter-disciplinary and contextual engagement is perhaps the defining feature in contemporary legal studies. Nowhere is the case for such an engagement more obviously vital than in the often elusive relation of terrorism, counter-terrorism and law.

The original impetus for the material that follows came in the form of an invitation to give a public lecture on the subject of law, literature and terrorism at Swansea University in spring 2005. I should thank Melanie Williams in particular for the invitation to do so. This lecture, much revised, appears as Chapter 5. It has also appeared in volume 4 of *Law, Culture and the Humanities*. My thanks are due to the editor and publishers for permission to reprint a slightly amended version here. A similar debt of appreciation is due to the editors and publishers of *Law and Humanities*, for permission to reproduce material, in Chapter 2, that appeared in volume 1 of their journal. Again, I owe a particular debt of gratitude to Paul Raffield for a number of helpful observations on this material, and for his kind invitation to give a plenary address on the subject of 'Macbeth and the Terrorists' at his 'Shakespeare and the Law' conference held at Warwick University in summer 2007. Various other draft chapters were presented in various states of disarray at various other workshops and conferences over the last few years. My thanks, in general form, go to the many who took the trouble to listen and to make comments.

Ian Ward

August 2008

Introduction: Law, text, terror

On 11 September 2001, two hijacked planes crashed into the Twin Towers in New York killing three thousand. A terrorist organisation, hitherto largely unknown outside security circles, claimed responsibility. Nineteen 'martyrs' of Al-Qaeda had carried out the attack. It was designed to bring nihilistic violence to the forefront of the American psyche, and that of its allies. It was designed to terrify, to obsess us, to lead us, perhaps, into abandoning centuries of jurisprudence, to abandoning our faith in the powers of reason, and the political ideas of liberty, tolerance and justice. It succeeded.[1] And it was designed to hurt. It hurt, most obviously, those who suffered loss, the families and friends of victims of the initial strike. But it was also designed to hurt a potentially infinite number of others; all those who would become victims of the counter-terrorist response which, or so it was fervently hoped by those who planned the events of 9/11, would be launched.

And, once again, it has. Seduced by our political leaders, betrayed by our own deeper insecurities, we have developed a peculiar 'tolerance of nonsense'.[2] And so, in pursuit of something termed a 'war on terror', and with scant regard to any associated provisions of international law, US and British forces have invaded two far-away Islamic countries, Afghanistan and Iraq, laying waste to both.[3] Anarchy has ensued. Collateral violence has been spawned in much of the rest of the region, most obviously Pakistan, Lebanon and various former Soviet republics. Thousands of allied military personnel have died, tens of thousands of Afghans and Iraqis, Pakistanis and Palestinians, Chechens and Kurds. We will never know the exact number; just as we will never know the exact number of women raped, and children maimed.

---

[1] See M. Amis, *The Second Plane* (Jonathan Cape, 2008), 7, reaching precisely the same conclusion. If a criterion of success rests in the extent to which we have allowed ourselves to be terrified far beyond reason, then the mission to destroy the Twin Towers was an unalloyed success.

[2] See Amis, *Plane*, 198, for this assertion.

[3] For a comment on the 'chain of events' which has unfolded following 9/11, see A. Chaskalson, 'The Widening Gyre: Counter-Terrorism, Human Rights and the Rule of Law', *Cambridge Law Journal*, 67 (2008), 72.

The 'war on terror' continues. So does the terror. Whilst this is not, at first instance, a book about the 'war on terror' or 9/11, it can now only be read in this immediate context.[4] Any study of terrorism is written in the shadows of this 'gigantic abreaction', as Jean Baudrillard rather fantastically calls it.[5] We live in a long shadow, and we write in it too. This book, the more particular aspiration of which is to explore the historically and conceptually fraught relation of law, literature and terrorism, cannot escape this shadow. Terrorism is evasive, maddeningly so. Its primary strategy is dissimulation. It seeks to entrance us, so that we might be deluded into thinking it is something much more than it really is.[6] Susan Faludi has recently written about the 'terror dream' in which contemporary America continues to 'walk', and the 'kind of cultural hypnosis' which appears to have afflicted us all.[7] And, critically, it evades definition. And it seems to evade the law; or at least so our political leaders would have us believe. And we, or a substantial number of us it seems, are willing to accept this. We are terrified, not just by the rhetoric of terrorism, but by the rhetoric of counter-terrorism too. We shall revisit this rhetoric in the first part of this Introduction, before doing so again in subsequent chapters.

This is, then, a book about terrorism, and about counter-terrorist strategy, about the relation of law and terror, the limitations of the former, the elusiveness of the latter. But more precisely still, it is about the extent to which the related tensions that exist in the jurisprudential discourse of terrorism might be better comprehended in an interdisciplinary context framed by the particular relation of literature, terror and justice. The possibilities which this particularly inter-disciplinary strategy presents will be introduced in the final part of this Introduction. First, however, we need to get a better sense of the nature of the discourse of 9/11, and the impact it has had upon current debates surrounding the extent to which law can or cannot respond to the challenges it presents. We live, we are told, in an 'age of terror'. We certainly live in an age when we are supposed to be terrified. But what, really, does this mean?

The age of hysteria

The rhetoric of terrorism and counter-terrorism, post-9/11, is all-consuming. It seeks to persuade us that our lives will never be the same again.[8] Terrorism is

---

[4] For a similar suggestion, see D. Held, 'Violence, Law, and Justice in a Global Age', *Constellations*, 9 (2002), 79.

[5] J. Baudrillard, *The Spirit of Terrorism* (Verso, 2003), 4–5, 73–4.

[6] Amis presents two statistics, both equally shocking, and equally revealing. 85% of American troops currently engaged in Iraq believe that Saddam Hussein was responsible for the attack on the Twin Towers. 42% think it was, in fact, the US government itself. Cited in Amis, *Plane*, at 139–40.

[7] S. Faludi, *The Terror Dream: Fear and Fantasy in Post-9/11 America* (Metropolitan Books, 2007), 2. Amis plays with an associated metaphor, suggesting that 9/11 'loosened the ground between reality and delirium'. See his *Plane*, at 206.

[8] Rhetoric 'designed', as Eric Hobsbawn puts it pithily, 'to make the flesh of the citizens creep rather than help fight terror'. See his *Globalisation, Democracy and Terrorism* (Little Brown, 2007), 150–1.

an ultimate expression, something which in its aesthetic form Enlightenment *philosophes* presented as the sublime. We shall encounter such expressions in Chapter 1. Ours is an 'Age of Terror', because we are told it is, and because we tend to believe the rhetoric; one which, we are further assured, post-9/11, lays waste to all the cosy complacencies of liberal democratic politics, and its law.[9] It is part of a wider descent into an age of 'global anarchy'.[10] Ours is, therefore, also a 'new' terrorism, far more terrifying than any terrorism that has gone before.[11] We should be terrified, the logic proceeds, we are right to be terrified. The future is bleak.

It finds a harrowing depiction in J.G. Ballard's novel *Millennium People*. Of all the contributions to the emergent post-9/11 'genre', Ballard's portrayal of our shared fate, terrorist and counter-terrorist alike, as 'apostles' of a 'new kind of alienation', best captures the intensely pessimistic mood of so many who presently presume to chart our future.[12] Of all the terrors that a terrorist act insinuates, the possibility that it conceals nothing at all, that it is wholly devoid of meaning, is perhaps the most terrifying of all.[13] Martin Amis touches upon the same supposition when he suggests that the 'age of terror' might, in time, also be remembered as an age of 'superboredom, rounding out and complementing the superterror of suicide-mass murder'.[14] The familiar Conradian metaphor has never resonated more terrifyingly. The 'heart of darkness' has finally possessed the middle-class psyche, and is to be found, as Ballard puts it, not in late nineteenth-century Africa, but in early twenty-first-century Twickenham and Chelsea Quays.[15] For many, like Ballard, Conrad is not just the chronicler of modern terrorism, but also its most prescient prophet. We shall revisit these particular chronicles and prophesies in Chapter 5.

---

[9] See W. Bradford, '"The Duty to Defend Them": A Natural Law Justification for the Bush Doctrine of Preventive War', *Notre Dame Law Review*, 79 (2004), 1365.

[10] See B. Barber, *Fear's Empire: War, Terrorism and Democracy* (Norton, 2004), 87, adding at 92, that 'terror is the apotheosis of international anarchy'.

[11] For sceptical commentaries on the extent to which contemporary experiences of Al-Qaeda terrorism are somehow distinctively 'new', still less any more terrifying than previous instances of terrorist activity, see I. Duyvesteyn, 'How New is the New Terrorism?' *Studies in Conflict and Terrorism*, 27 (2004), particularly 449–51, and M. Stohl, 'Old Myths, New Fantasies and the Enduring Realities of Terrorism', *Critical Studies on Terrorism*, 1 (2008), 11–14.

[12] J. Ballard, *Millennium People* (HarperCollins, 2004), 136.

[13] Something which, of course, imports the ever more frantic desire to fantasise some kind of meaning. See B. Durodie, 'Fear and Terror in a Post-Political Age', *Government and Opposition*, 42 (2007), 430, 441.

[14] Amis, *Plane*, 77, and also 108, 'whatever else terrorism' has 'achieved in the past few decades', it has 'certainly brought about a net increase in boredom'. The latter observation is couched in the context of airport security checks, but retains, for very obvious reasons, a wider resonance.

[15] Ballard, *Millennium People*, 84. The Conradian theme finds its most acute expression in the comments of his Nietzschean protagonist Gould. 'In his despairing and psychopathic way', Ballard concludes, at 292, 'Richard Gould's motives were honourable. He was trying to find meaning in the most meaningless times, the first of a new kind of desperate man who refuses to bow before the arrogance of existence and the tyranny of space-time'.

Meanwhile, all we can do for now is await the irresistible and 'devastating storm' of 'megaterrorism' that approaches.[16] Terrorism, we are advised, is now 'all-invasive', affecting all our lives, either directly, for the tragic few, or indirectly, for the rest of us.[17] The 'grammar of political terror' has changed. Ideology has gone, and in its place can be found an 'apocalyptic kind' of 'transcendental nihilism'; a future which again finds an acute expression in Ballard's novel, a prospective history that can only be defined by necessarily random 'meaningless acts'.[18] The apocalyptic fascinates us, the apparent potential of 'hyperterrorism' and 'technoscience' to obliterate us all.[19] And so we live in an age of terror, not because we are likely to be obliterated, but because we are entranced by the possibility, however remote.[20] And so we wait, thrilled and terrified in equal measure; for as Alfred Hitchcock shrewdly observed, 'There is no terror in a bang, only in the anticipation of one'.[21]

We are also, very clearly, living an age of hyperbole. 9/11, Amis opines, represents a 'massive geohistorical jolt, which will reverberate for centuries'.[22]

---

[16] W. Lacqueur, *The New Terrorism: Fanaticism and the Arms of Mass Destruction* (Oxford University Press, 1999), 282.

[17] So concluded Xavier Raufer, writing before 9/11. See his 'New World Disorder, New Terrorisms: New Threats for Europe and the Western World', *Terrorism and Political Violence*, 11 (1999), 30, and 37, observing that terrorist threats are, in their modern form, 'a lot more than fuzzy silhouettes in hazy far-away lands'. Charles Webel cites research in the *New England Journal of Medicine* which revealed the extent to which the impact of 9/11 had caused serious degrees of stress and anxiety amongst the wider population of America. Of those interviewed, 44% suggested that they experienced 'substantial symptoms' of 9/11-related stress, 90% admitted to suffering some degree of stress. See C. Webel, *Terror, Terrorism and the Human Condition* (Palgrave, 2004), 6–7.

[18] Ballard, *Millennium People*, 139–40.

[19] See J. Schell, *The Unconquerable World: Power, Nonviolence and the Will of the People* (Penguin, 2003), 5; M. Cusimano, 'Globalization, Ethics, and the War on Terrorism', *Notre Dame Journal of Law, Ethics and Public Policy*, 16 (2002), 66, 77; Raufer, 'New World Disorder', 30–51; and T. Homer-Dixon, 'The Rise of Complex Terrorism', *Foreign Policy* (Jan/Feb 2002), 52–62, emphasising the fact that the Twin Towers collapsed in approximately 15 seconds each, a tribute, albeit a perverse one, to the destructive capacity of modern technology. Speaking to the relation of modern terrorism and technology, Benjamin Barber puts it succinctly. Without the internet and global credit card facilities, bin Laden would have been 'reduced to throwing stones at local sheiks'. See his 'Democracy and Terror in the Era of Jihad and McWorld' in K. Booth and T. Dunne (eds.) *Worlds in Collision: Terror and the Power of Global Order* (Palgrave, 2002), 249.

[20] For a commentary on the extent to which we fail to comprehend just how remote is the danger of experiencing a terrorist attack, see R. Jackson, 'Constructing Enemies: Islamic Terrorism in Political and Academic Discourse', *Government and Opposition*, 42 (2007), 419, concluding that the possibility can be most accurately termed 'minuscule', and also J. Zulaika and W. Douglass, 'The Terrorist Subject: Terrorism Studies and the Absent Subjectivity', *Critical Studies on Terrorism*, 1 (2008), 30–1, noting the statistic that we are, each of us, as likely to die from the impact of a falling asteroid as we are as a result of a terrorist bomb.

[21] In L. Freedman, 'Terrorism as Strategy', *Government and Opposition*, 42 (2007), 320. For a recent affirmation of this simple truth, one which deploys a cinematic metaphor, see A. Guelke, 'Great Whites, Paedophiles and Terrorists: the Need for Critical Thinking in a New Age of Fear', *Critical Studies on Terrorism*, 1 (2008), 21–3. Fear is something that producers, terrorist or counter-terrorist, 'produce'.

[22] Amis, *Plane*, 22.

The 'fates of each one of us, our species as a whole' might 'depend' on our 'collective ability, or inability, to come to terms with terror' and terrorism.[23] It is the 'defining issue of our age'.[24] The 'spirit of the laws', moreover, itself is at stake.[25] Rarely given to understatement, Jean Baudrillard announces that the 'Whole play of history and power is disrupted by this event', and so too are the 'conditions of analysis'. 9/11 has awakened the 'terroristic imagination that dwells in all of us'; a supposition which is intended to insinuate a common reaction against the twin tyrannies of US hegemony and globalisation.[26] We are condemned, he comments, without any apparent sense of irony, to live in an age of fantastical 'hysteria'.[27]

Certainly the target of 9/11 was not coincidental.[28] The cultural context aligns with the economic. The Islamic terrorist, Baudrillard continues, is an 'antibody' of globalisation.[29] 9/11, we are told, represents the 'dark side of globalization', its mutant 'offspring', a glimpse, moreover, of a forbidding future.[30] John Gray invokes the spectre of a coming age of 'Hobbesian anarchy'.[31] Amis contemplates

---

[23] See Webel, *Terror*, 2, and also 99.

[24] A. Dershowitz, *Why Terrorism Works: Understanding the Threat, Responding to the Challenge* (Yale University Press, 2002), 11–12. A similar question is articulated by Dominic McGoldrick at the outset of his *From '9–11' to the Iraq War 2003*, (Hart, 2004), 1–2.

[25] H. Koh, 'The Spirit of the Laws', *Harvard International Law Journal*, 43 (2002), 23–4.

[26] Baudrillard, *Spirit of Terrorism*, 4–5, 73–4. A similar insinuation can be found in Slavoj Zizek's suggestion that such violence is necessary in order to shake people 'out of their ideological numbness, their hypnotic consumerist state'. See his *Welcome to the Desert of the Real* (Verso, 2002), 9.

[27] Baudrillard, *Spirit of Terrorism*, 33.

[28] See M. Rasmussen, 'A Parallel Globalization of Terror: 9–11, Security and Globalization', *Cooperation and Conflict*, 37 (2002), 324, suggesting that the World Trade Centre had become 'a scale model of a globalized world, and the fact that the twin towers fell represented the vulnerability of the world order defined by globalization'. And also Amis, *Plane*, 4–5, engaging the same supposition.

[29] Baudrillard, *Spirit of Terrorism*, 3, 11–2, 21, 37, 87–91.

[30] The critical literature here is considerable. See variously A. Heller, '9/11, or Modernity and Terror', *Constellations*, 9 (2002), 55; J. Urry, *Global Complexity* (Polity, 2003), 7–8; Jacques Derrida's comments in 'A Dialogue with Jacques Derrida' in G. Borradori (ed.), *Philosophy in a Time of Terror: Dialogues with Juergen Habermas and Jacques Derrida* (Chicago University Press, 2003), 96–7; F. Megret, 'Justice in Times of Violence', *European Journal of International Law*, 14 (2003), 332; Rasmussen, 'Parallel Globalization', 327; W. Sofsky, *Violence: Terrorism, Genocide and War* (Granta, 2003), 150; and also C. Douzinas, 'Postmodern Just Wars: Kosovo, Afghanistan and the New World Order' in J. Strawson (ed.), *Law After Ground Zero* (Glasshouse, 2002), particularly 20–1, 32. For a compelling, if controversial, account of a post-modern world order, see B. de Sousa Santos, *Towards a New Common Sense: Law, Science and Politics in Paradigmatic Transition* (Routledge, London, 1995).

[31] J. Gray, *Al-Qaeda: and What it Means to be Modern* (Faber and Faber, 2003), 1–2, 21, 73–5, 84. A similar sentiment can be found in R. Cooper, *The Breaking of Nations: Order and Chaos in the Twenty-First Century* (Atlantic Books, London, 2003), vii–ix, 70. The Hobbesian allusion finds an obvious echo in the distinction between the idealistic Europeans and the pragmatic Americans which lies at heart of Robert Kagan's analysis of contemporary international relations. See his *Paradise and Power: America and Europe in the New World Order* (Atlantic Books, 2003), particularly 55–7, 73–6.

a 'day of de-Enlightenment'.[32] '9/11' has itself become a semiotic, a symbol of this rupture, a 'day', to use the language coined by the US National Commission on Terrorism, 'of unprecedented shock and suffering'.[33] According to Norman Mailer, '9/11 is one of those events that will never fade out of our history, for it was not only a cataclysmic disaster but a symbol, gargantuan and mysterious, of we know not what, an obsession that will return through decades to come'.[34] At a deeper, no less troubling level, the collapse of the Twin Towers is taken to be a semiotic for the 'abject nature of our dying culture', a bolt of lightning that revealed all the 'profound fissures and cleavages' that threaten to tear our world asunder.[35] 'Something terrible happened on September 11', an agonised Jacques Derrida opines, and in the end we 'don't know what'.[36] But we are not short of opinions, particularly scary ones.

Politicians, of course, live by hyperbole. President Bush warned of a 'lengthy campaign' against terrorism, one that will dictate whether 'civilisation' can defeat the forces of 'evil'. It will be the defining battle for 'progress and pluralism, tolerance and freedom'.[37] In similar tones former German Chancellor Schroeder confirmed that 9/11 represented a 'declaration of war against all of civilization'.[38] The idea of an apparently indefinite 'war' against terrorism has taken hold.[39] 'We are at war, and it is a world war' according to one senior US military official.[40] America must engage a 'new set of totalitarian enemies' intones Vice-President Cheney.[41] 'Either you are with us, or you are with the terrorists', the President warned the world nine days later. There were no longer any 'shades of grey'.[42] In his State of the Union address to Congress in early 2003, Bush famously described an 'axis of Evil, aiming to threaten the peace of the World'. And somewhere between the co-ordinates of the axis could be

---

[32] Amis, *Plane*, 13.

[33] Quoted in C. Walker, 'Prisoners of "War All The Time"', *European Human Rights Law Review*, 1 (2005), 50.

[34] N. Mailer, *Why Are We At War?* (Random House, 2003), 4.

[35] See Baudrillard, *Spirit of Terrorism*, 64, and also F. Dallmayr, 'Lessons of September 11', *Theory, Culture & Society*, 19 (2002), 137.

[36] Derrida, 'Dialogue', 87. A similar sentiment is articulated by Ulrich Beck, in 'The Terrorist Threat: World Risk Society Revisited', *Theory, Culture & Society*, 19 (2002), at 39.

[37] In McGoldrick, *From 9–11*, 11.   [38] In Rasmussen, 'Parallel Globalization', 333.

[39] See J. Fitzpatrick, 'Speaking Law to Power: The War Against Terrorism and Human Rights', *European Journal of International Law*, 14 (2003), at 244, commenting on the 'truly unprecedented' nature of this claim. A similar sentiment is articulated by David Williams, who muses on a 'growing appreciation of the seemingly endless drift of terrorist activity into the future', in 'The United Kingdom's Response to International Terrorism', *Indiana International and Comparative Law Review*, 13 (2003), at 683.

[40] In R. Jackson, *Writing the War on Terrorism: Language, Politics and Counter-Terrorism* (Manchester University Press, 2005), 9. See G. Achcar, *The Clash of Barbarisms: The Making of the New World Disorder* (Saqi, 2006), 27, ridiculing such a suggestion.

[41] In Jackson, *Writing*, 46.

[42] In Jackson, *Writing*, 86–7. For critical commentary, see Barber, *Fear's Empire*, 17–18, and C. Merill, 'A Kind of Solution', *Virginia Quarterly Review*, 80 (2004), 68–9. For the Schmittian echo, see Zizek, *Desert*, 109–11.

found the terrorists, 'them', the 'other'. The world must choose, Bush re-asserted, either to be 'with us or against us'.[43]

Perspective can help; but not that much.[44] Statistics are cold.[45] Three thousand died on 9/11; more American troops have since died in Iraq in the futile pursuit of an illusory 'war on terror', and still more will follow.[46] There were fifty times as many victims of the tsunamis in the Indian Ocean in 2004. Each year, 3,000 American women are killed by abusive husbands.[47] Each day, around the world, more than 20,000 die of starvation.[48] In Africa alone 3,000 children die each day from malaria.[49] But there is nothing particularly fascinating or thrilling about drowning or starving, and no one seems particularly inclined to go to war against easily preventable diseases. In a world of impressions and rhetorical frenzy, cold facts are of limited value. Hyperbole devours perspective.[50] The discourse of terrorism today is an apocalyptic one; both terrorists and counter-terrorists prefer it that way.[51]

History provides further context.[52] We shall in ensuing chapters encounter similar hyperbole stretching back to classical Greece. More contemporary history provides a further, and slightly different, context. A decade earlier, we had been advised that a 'new world order' heralded an age of 'perpetual peace'. The great Enlightenment prophesies, Kantian or Hegelian by turn, were supposed to have come to pass, at long last. The 'end of history', famously, was

---

[43] In K. Hayward and W. Morrison, 'Locating Ground Zero: Caught Between Narratives of Crime and War' in Strawson, *Ground Zero*, 153.

[44] As Zulaika and Douglass observe, America is a country where in excess of 100,000 are murdered each year, and where, between 1974 and 1994, more people died each year of bee-stings than as a result of any terrorist-related events. See J. Zulaika and W. Douglass, *Terror and Taboo: The Follies, Fables and Faces of Terrorism* (Routledge, 1996), 6.

[45] For a suggestive set of such statistical comparators, see S. Marks, 'Branding the War on Terror: Is There a New Paradigm of International Law?', *Michigan State Journal of International Law*, 14 (2006), 73.

[46] See J. Gray, *Black Mass: Apocalyptic Religion and the Death of Utopia* (Penguin, 2007), 157.

[47] See C. MacKinnon, *Are Women Human? And Other International Dialogues* (Harvard University Press, 2006), 260–1, and also 274, referring to a 'systematic slaughter built into everyday life'.

[48] See T. Honderich, *Terrorism for Humanity: Inquiries in Political Philosophy* (Pluto, 2003), 23–4, 54–6.

[49] A disease which, in strictly medical terms, is easily preventable. For this statistic, see P. Hoffman, 'Human Rights and Terrorism', *Human Rights Quarterly*, 26 (2004), 953.

[50] Walter Lacqueur suggests that 'perhaps no other topic in our time has provoked such violent emotions'. See his *No End to War* (Continuum, 2004), 8.

[51] For this accusation, see Zulaika and Douglass, *Terror*, 30, and also T. Kapitan, 'The Terrorism of "Terrorism"' in J. Sterba (ed.), *Terrorism and International Justice* (Oxford University Press, 2003), 53.

[52] The literature here is again vast. See, for example, Sterba, 'Introduction' in Sterba, *Terrorism*, 2–3; Webel, *Terror*, 16–17; B. Ackerman, *Before the Next Attack: Preserving Civil Liberties in an Age of Terrorism* (Yale University Press, 2006), 170; W. Lacqueur, *Terrorism* (Weidenfeld & Nicolson, 1977), 3–22; Megret, 'Justice', 328; C. Bassiouni, 'Legal Control of International Terrorism: A Policy-Oriented Assessment', *Harvard International Law Journal*, 43 (2002), 83; Hoffman, 'Human Rights', 932–3; and most recently Guelke, 'Great Whites', 18–21.

announced.[53] In his 1991 State of the Union address, the first President Bush described a 'new world order – where diverse nations are drawn together in common cause, to achieve the universal aspirations of mankind: peace and security, freedom and the rule of law'. It was, the President confirmed, a very 'big idea'.[54] Indeed.

Unfortunately, a decade later the optimism has rather vanished.[55] The pessimist is vindicated. 'Violence', we are told, is 'the result of our specific humanity', moments of peace merely transient interludes.[56] The decade anticipated by Francis Fukuyama's fantastical provenance has proved to be no less brutal than most of its predecessors, a decade of extremes; to quote Derrida, of extreme 'violence, inequality, exclusion, famine'.[57] We are presently trapped amidst an age of unprecedented violence, one that is stripping to the bones all our pretences to reason, progress and civilisation.[58] Terrorism is a 'metaphor' for the 'revolutionary' challenges of globalisation, its apparent vitality 'emblematic' of shattered hopes, an expression of the 'paradox of humanitarianism drowned in human disaster'.[59] The irony is immediate; the abrupt end of the 'end of history'. The 'most devastating act of terrorism in history' represents the symbolic moment when modernity itself 'ended'.[60]

In the perception of many, far too many, particularly outside America, the 'new world order' has morphed into a new US imperialism, whilst terrorism, especially the terrorism of militant Islam, has emerged as a virulent allergic response.[61] Responses to 9/11 merely serve to confirm this suspicion.[62] Most obvious is the National Security Strategy, or 'Bush Doctrine', an expression of

---

[53] Most famously of all by Francis Fukuyama. See *The End of History and the Last Man* (Penguin, London, 1992), xi–ii, 13–18.

[54] See H. Koh, 'On American Exceptionalism', *Stanford Law Review*, 55 (2003), 1498–9, and also I. Ward, *Justice, Humanity and the New World Order* (Ashgate, 2003), 73.

[55] Paradoxically, the 'end' of such naïve optimism had been long foretold, finding an original expression in Albert Camus's observation, in 1946, that 'our time marks the end of ideologies, that is, absolute utopias which in reality destroy themselves'. See R. Jacoby, *The End of Utopia: Politics and Culture in an Age of Apathy* (Basic Books, 1999), xi, 3, 155–8. For similar conclusions, see D. Archibugi and I. Young, 'Envisioning a Global Rule of Law' in Sterba, *Terrorism*, 160–1, and Hobsbawn, *Globalisation*, 83–9, 124–9. The suggestion was also famously echoed in Martin Heidegger's proclamation that philosophy itself had come to an 'end'. See M. Heidegger, 'The End of Philosophy and the Task of Thinking' in D. Krell (ed.), *Basic Writings* (Harper & Row, 1972), 374–8, 387–91.

[56] Sofsky, *Violence*, 7.   [57] J. Derrida, *Specters of Marx* (Routledge, 1994), 85.

[58] Sofsky, *Violence*, 61, 65.

[59] See G. Hart, *The Fourth Power: A Grand Strategy for the United States in the Twenty-First Century* (Oxford University Press, 2004), 5–7, 19–20, 65–6, 109; Douzinas, 'Kosovo', 20; and also Zulaika and Douglass, *Terror*, 186, 228.

[60] See G. Borradori, 'Introduction' in Borradori, *Philosophy*, 1–20, and also Jonathan Schell commenting that the 'burning towers of 2001 eclipsed the broken wall of 1989', in his *World*, at 6.

[61] See A. Soueif, *Mezzaterra: Fragments from the Common Ground* (Anchor, 2004), 10–11 articulating the common Islamic view that the rhetoric of the 'new world order' was always intended to be a mask for a 'new American century'. For a caustic critique of US imperialism, and the myth of 'Pax Americana', see Hobsbawn, *Globalisation*, 54–61.

[62] For the particular impact of 9–11, see Archibugi and Young, 'Envisioning', 160–1.

US 'exceptionalism', and the quasi-legal authority for the 'war against terror'.[63] Arguments regarding the legal efficacy of this 'war' continue, just as do those which test the novelty of the unilateralism of which it is an expression.[64] The Bush administration has tended to pronounce a more visceral justification.[65] Thomas Friedman puts it bluntly. Regardless of the legal shadow-boxing, post 9/11, the US 'needed to hit someone in the Arab-Muslim world', to flex a little muscle and vent a little spleen.[66] Looking back more than a year after 9/11, the *Washington Post* was prosaic. 'All you need to know' was that 'there was a before 9/11, and there was an after 9/11'. And, it continued, 'After 9/11 the gloves came off'.[67] It was a time, as the *Chicago Tribune* confirmed, when it was 'Ok to let boys be boys again'; untrammelled by the twin restrictions of uppity women and irritating human rights conventions.[68]

Opposition to the 'war on terror' has been louder, though not always much louder, in Europe. The 'American administration is now a bloodthirsty wild animal', Harold Pinter declaims, 'Bombs are its only vocabulary'.[69] A counter-terrorist strategy of 'shock and awe' is representative of a further descent into a pervasive global 'barbarism'.[70] Baudrillard is again acerbic. Americans, he

---

[63] State Department Policy Director Richard Haass preferred the phrase '*a la carte* multilateralism', in P. Sands, *Lawless World: America and the Making and Breaking of Global Rules* (Penguin, 2005), 20. Either way, the 'war against terror' is not, of course, the only expression of this *a la carte* approach to foreign policy. Precedents can be found in a refusal to lend support to the Kyoto Protocol, the Anti-Ballistic Missile Treaty or the Test-Ban Treaty, or the International Criminal Court. A notorious example of the US's equivocal attitude to international law can be found in its response to the judgement of the International Court of Justice in the *Nicaragua* case. As far back as 1994, then Secretary of State Albright confirmed that the US would, henceforth, act multilaterally where possible, unilaterally where 'necessary'. For a commentary on Albright's observation, see T. Franck, 'The Use of Force in International Law', *Tulane Journal of International and Comparative Law*, 11 (2003), 10–11. See also Miriam Sapiro, 'Iraq: the Shifting Sands of Preemptive Self-Defence', *American Journal of International Law*, 97 (2003), 599, suggesting that the doctrine rose 'like a phoenix from the ashes' after 9/11.

[64] See M. Walzer, *Arguing About War* (Yale University Press, 2004), xiv, 88–91, 137–8, 160, seeking to present a theoretical justification for the war against terror as a 'just war'. Such wars, Walzer asserts, must be limited, and directed against credible threats, and fought in aid of legal and moral principle. Accordingly, he is prepared to sanction the Afghan war in these terms, but not the Iraqi. For the suggestion that unilateralism has always characterised US foreign policy, see also Barber, *Fear's Empire*, 75, 79.

[65] See Barber, *Fear's Empire*, 114, noting that no one in the Bush administration has ever invoked a 'just war' defence.

[66] In A. Paulus, 'The War Against Iraq and the Future of International Law: Hegemony or Pluralism?', *Michigan Journal of International Law*, 25 (2004), 695. Martin Amis deploys the same metaphor, commenting on the appearance of President Bush as a 'man in the bar who isn't going anywhere until he has had his fist fight'. See his *Plane*, 151.

[67] Quoted in J. Steyn, 'Guantanamo Bay: The Legal Black Hole', *International and Comparative Law Quarterly*, 53 (2004), 8. And the purses opened too. During the following two years, over $100 billion was spent, in part funding the salaries of 40,000 employees in a revamped Department of Homeland Security. See Jackson *Writing*, 15.

[68] See Faludi, *Dream*, 77.

[69] In Mailer, *Why*, 43, also quoting the similar observation of John le Carre, that the US has 'entered one of its periods of historic madness'.

[70] See Barber, *Fear's Empire*, 21, and Achcar, *Barbarisms*, 67, 104–5.

suggests with a deceptive simplicity, have 'fomented all this violence', and have thus brought about their own trauma. Terror has assumed its inherently 'asymmetrical' form. At some level, he insinuates, whilst 'we can say that they did it ... we wished for it'.[71] Preferring to recast the blame in conceptual terms, Ulrich Beck is similarly unsentimental. The 'horrible pictures' burnt into our collective memories of 9/11 'contain a message: a state can neo-liberalise itself to death'.[72]

Jacques Derrida dances more nimbly around the sentimentality. But the conclusion is much the same. 'My unconditional compassion, addressed at the victims of September 11, does not prevent me from saying aloud: with regard to this crime, I do not believe that anyone is politically guiltless'.[73] There is an obvious ethical edge here; one to which we will return in due course. Indeed, we shall encounter similar sentiments, similar anxieties, throughout subsequent chapters; ever more intense the greater the shock and the awe, and the more readily the very principles which are supposed to be under threat from terrorists, such as liberty, democracy and the rule of law, appear to be compromised by the so-called 'war on terror'.

The limits of law

All this matters, not just because it sets the tone for current discussions of terrorism, but because it establishes the necessarily depressive mood within which jurists presently stumble towards some kind of legal response. Not everyone is depressed, of course. There is a tangible sense of excitement in President George W. Bush's declaration, 'I don't care what the international lawyer says we are going to kick some ass'. Ours, he confirms, is a world 'without rules'; a view, and a metaphor, which found ready echo and favour across the Atlantic in London.[74] There would be no more 'siding with the arseholes', as Under-Secretary of Defence Feith confirmed, revealing a less than respectful view of the legal profession.[75] The sentiment finds a more sombre echo in the advice of the US Ambassador for War Crimes, that ours is a 'changed world', one which

---

[71] Baudrillard, *Spirit of Terrorism*, 5, 9, 15. For a similar sentiment, from within America, see N. Chomsky, *9–11*, (Seven Stories Press, 2002), 12, 61 and *Hegemony or Survival: America's Quest for Global Dominance* (Penguin, 2003), 51–61, suggesting that 9/11 can be seen, accordingly, as a 'blowback' against decades of US-sponsored terrorism across the globe. A similar tone can be discerned in Ariel Dorfman's *Other Septembers, Many Americas: Selected Provocations 1980–2004*, (Pluto, 2004), xii–vi and 8–14. It can also be seen in Kenneth McKenzie's observation, quoted in Achcar, *Barbarisms*, at 157, that anti-US terrorism might be cast as the 'revenge of the Melians'. We shall encounter the Melians again in shortly.

[72] Beck, 'Terrorist Threat', 47.   [73] In Zizek, *Desert*, 57.

[74] In Sands, *Lawless World*, 174 and McGoldrick, *9–11*, 87. For the London echo, articulated most immediately by Prime Minister Blair, in his 2005 declaration 'Let no one be in any doubt, the rules of the game are changing', see C. Walker, 'The Treatment of Foreign Terror Suspects', *Modern Law Review*, 70 (2007), 427.

[75] Quoted in P. Sands, *Torture Team: Deception, Cruelty and the Compromise of Law* (Penguin, 2008), 126.

forces 'us to re-examine our traditional notions of security, our understanding of our attackers, and our approaches to bringing the perpetrators to justice'.[76] The official line is that the 'war on terror' announces a 'new paradigm' in international law, and a new age.[77]

Critics of the pretences of international law feel vindicated as, of course, do critics of modern legalism itself.[78] There is a wider intellectual context here; one which is described by post-modern critics of liberal legalism. According to these critics, the striking inability of international or indeed domestic law to account satisfactorily for the experience of terrorism is merely a semiotic for a deeper 'crisis' of liberal legalism.[79] Chatter about human rights and universal values, we are told, is just that; chatter.[80] International legality, one leading British newspaper concluded, has become a 'gigantic irrelevance'.[81] Harold Koh reflects on the fact that so many lawyers 'seem to have concluded that somehow the destruction of four planes and three buildings has taken us back to a state of nature in which there are no laws or rules'. The very 'spirit of the laws' appears to have been abandoned; just as the terrorists hoped it would be.[82] Lord Steyn fears that the 'horror' of 9/11 has crushed all the optimism which a newly envisaged age of human rights had brought a decade earlier.[83] International law is 'shattering', and terrorism is doing most of the shattering.[84]

The Bush Doctrine gestured towards some kind of quasi-jurisprudential justification, presuming that the 'struggle against global terrorism is different from any other war in our history', thus making it necessary to abandon the 'reactive posture' of classical international law, and replace it with a right to

---

[76] In McGoldrick, *9–11*, 21. Philippe Sands agrees, suggesting that 9/11 provided an 'added spur' to US policy-makers who anyway wished to recast international order. See his *World*, xiii.

[77] See generally, Marks, 'Branding the War', 71–119.

[78] M. Koskenniemi, *The Gentle Civilizer of Nations: The Rise and Fall of International Law* (Cambridge University Press, 2002), 515.

[79] See, for example, C. Douzinas and R. Warrington, *Justice Miscarried: Ethics, Aesthetics and the Law* (Harvester Wheatsheaf, 1994), 1, 14, and more recently M. Williams, *Empty Justice: One Hundred Years of Law, Literature and Philosophy* (Cavendish, 2002), xxiii, 1–3, 185–7, 218.

[80] See also M. Flory, 'International Law: an Instrument to Combat Terrorism' in R. Higgins and M. Flory (eds.), *Terrorism and International Law* (Routledge, 1997), 30, and more recently, post 9–11, C. Greenwood, 'International Law and the "War Against Terrorism"', *International Affairs*, 78 (2002), 301.

[81] *Sunday Telegraph* leader, from 29 February 2004, quoted in Sands, *World*, 180. For a similar commentary on the 'obsolete' nature of contemporary international law, see Borradori, Preface, x–xi.

[82] Koh, 'Spirit', 23, and also 'Exceptionalism', *Stanford Law Review*, 55 (2003), 1496, 1527, adding that 'we have almost literally left the light and entered the shadows of a new age of global pessimism', one that will require an 'epochal transformation' to reverse.

[83] Steyn, 'Black Hole', 6.

[84] For this speculation, see A. Cassese, 'Terrorism is Also Disrupting Some Crucial Legal Categories of International Law', *European Journal of International Law*, 12 (2001), 993, and also J. Stromseth, 'Law and Force After Iraq: A Transitional Moment', *American Journal of International Law*, 97 (2003), 628–9, and Sands, *World*, 21, concluding that 9/11 was the 'catalyst for the systematic disregard of established international rules'.

take preventive measures against any perceived 'threat'.[85] According to its adherents, the Doctrine, which represents not a threat to international law but the 'best hope' for its 'continued viability' merely resuscitates the right to 'anticipatory self-defence' founded in classical natural law theory.[86] Any fragments of legality which are sought for the present Iraq war tend, accordingly, to be grasped in this fashion.[87] The 'war on terror', former US Attorney-General John Yoo duly concludes, is an appropriate response to 'rogue states' that support 'terrorism'.[88] In the light of the various wars against terror, in Iraq and elsewhere, international lawyers as prominent as Ruth Wedgwood are inclined to agree, advising that it might now be best to see 'legality' as a 'question of degree, rather than an all-or-nothing choice'.[89]

The uglier side of this rhetorical slippage can be discerned in contemporary debates regarding the utility of torture. The notorious Yoo and Bybee Memoranda, written by senior Justice Department legal advisors, sought to justify various measures taken by US military and intelligence personnel which might ordinarily have fallen foul of international torture and human rights conventions.[90] The Memoranda, as Philippe Sands has recently shown, are the product of an unedifying politics of evasion and deceit, not to mention arrogance, flippancy and cruelty. When asked to formally approve a technique of

---

[85] Such a 'right' might take the form of a preventive war, or the targeted assassination of suspected terrorist leaders. For a discussion, see W. Bradford, '"The Duty to Defend Them": A Natural Law Justification for the Bush Doctrine of Preventive War', *Notre Dame Law Review*, 79 (2004), 1423–6; M. Bothe, 'Terrorism and the Legality of Pre-emptive Force', *European Journal of International Law*, 14 (2003), 236–8; J. Fitzpatrick, 'Speaking Law to Power: The War Against Terrorism and Human Rights', *European Journal of International Law*, 14 (2003), 245, 247–8; and also D. Kretzmer, 'Targeted Killing of Suspected Terrorists: Extra-Judicial Executions or Legitimate Means of Defence?', *European Journal of International Law*, 16 (2005), 171–212.

[86] Advocates of this approach to the doctrine of pre-emption tend to present the UN Charter as a suitably organic document, one that can justify a radical rethinking of what kind of pre-emption might be considered lawful. A 'living document deliberately designed by its founders to have the capacity to meet new threats to peace and security', according to Jane Stromseth, in 'A Transitional Moment', at 633. See also Sapiro, 'Iraq', 599–607; J. Yoo, 'International Law and Iraq', *American Journal of International Law*, 97 (2003), 563–4, 575; R. Wedgwood, 'The Fall of Saddam Hussein: Security Council Mandates and Preemptive Self-Defence', *American Journal of International Law*, 97 (2003), 577–8, making much of an implicit 'procedural dynamism' in the Charter.

[87] The defence of action justified by 'continual breach' of Resolutions depends upon an organic sense of UN law; on a particular construction of a series of UN Resolutions, beginning with 678, which in 1991 limited the time during which Iraq would have to comply with UN conditions articulated in Resolution 660, and 687 which then iterated a whole series of further conditions which accompanied the cease-fire at the end of the Kuwait war. Resolution 1441, in September 2002, then cited 'material breach' and condemned continued Iraqi 'non-compliance' with these existing Resolutions. Whether it impliedly sanctioned war is the matter of greatest controversy. For critical commentaries on this convoluted construction, see T. Franck, 'What Happens Now? The United Nations After Iraq', *American Journal of International Law*, 97 (2003), 610–14, and also Sands, *World*, 177–8, 184–5, 186–203.

[88] Yoo, 'Iraq', 575.   [89] Wedgwood, 'Saddam Hussein', 581.

[90] Most obviously the Geneva Convention Against Torture. The Memo sought to argue that those suspected members of Al-Qaeda captured in Afghanistan and elsewhere, being 'unlawful combatants', fell outside the provisions of the Convention. See Sands, *Torture Team*, 40, 78–9.

forced standing for up to four hours at a time, Defence Secretary Rumsfeld famously observed 'I stand for 8–10 hours a day. Why is standing limited to 4 hours?'[91] Small wonder that accounts of systematic torture and ritualised humiliation, in Guantanamo, Abu Ghraib and elsewhere, are so easily dismissed.[92]

Such measures, apparently, are vital. The Bush Doctrine announces the age of 'exceptionalism', where America will pick and choose the moments when it might conform to the dictates of international law, and when it will not. The messianic mood, a mood which we will investigate in rather greater depth in later chapters, was captured by former Secretary of State Madeleine Albright, 'If we have to use force it is because we are America. We are the indispensable nation. We stand tall. We see further into the future'.[93] The more sceptical detect in the rhetoric of successive Secretaries of State and successive Presidents an 'imperial grand strategy' of rather longer imagining, dedicated to destroying the crumbling edifice of international law.[94] In this vein, it is suggested that the 'war on terror' symbolises the ongoing and symbolic 'degradation' of international law; a degradation that can be just as readily discerned in the earlier bombings of Libya in 1986, or Belgrade in 1999.[95] According to Bill Bowring, the US response to 9/11 has seen the UN Charter finally and most overtly

[91] See generally Sands, *Torture Team*, quoting Rumsfeld at 7, and discussing the 'slippery' evasion of administration lawyers at 22–6.

[92] See E. Saar and V. Novak, *Inside the Wire* (Penguin, 2005), for a general account of Guantanamo, and more particularly 94–5, 234–5, 224–8 and 243–4, for more specific instances of torture and international condemnation. See also M. Begg, *Enemy Combatant* (Free Press, 2006), 152–8, and also M. Minow, 'What is the Greatest Evil?', *Harvard Law Review*, 118 (2005), 2134–5; D. Amann, 'Guantanamo', *Columbia Journal of Transnational Law*, 323–5; and D. Rose, *Guantanamo: America's War on Human Rights* (Faber and Faber, 2004), 1–2, 5–6, 50–3, 60–1, 65–7, 70–3, 90–104, for graphic accounts of the various degradations suffered by detainees during their transportation to Guantanamo, and their residence. The Gonzales memorandum is given in M. Ratner and E. Ray, *Guantanamo: What the World Should Know* (Arris, 2004), 117–23. Another government memorandum, the Bybee memorandum, notoriously, sought to redefine torture, limiting it to only the most brutal of assaults, those the pain from which might 'rise to the level of death, organ failures, or the permanent impairment of a significant bodily function', see Rose, *Guantanamo*, 24. See also the account provided by two released detainees, Shafiq Rasul and Asif Iqbal to the Senate Armed Services Committee in Ratner and Ray, *Guantanamo*, 150–4. For a further account of the prohibition of torture in international law in general, see Sands, *World*, 160, 205–10.

[93] In R. Blackburn, 'The Imperial Presidency, the War on Terrorism, and the Revolutions of Modernity', *Constellations*, 9 (2002), 9.

[94] The term 'imperial grand strategy' was originally advanced by John Ikenberry, and has been taken on vigorously by Chomsky. See his *Hegemony*, Chapter 2. A similar allusion to US imperialism, and its possible role in the crisis of international law, can be found in McGoldrick, *9–11*, 129. For similar observations see Blackburn, 'Imperial Presidency', 3–11, suggesting that the imperialism that was let loose post-9/11 was the product of a long imagining. For a discussion of the notorious *Nicaragua* judgement, which many cite as a presaging the imagining, see R. Higgins, 'The General International Law of Terrorism' in Higgins and Flory, *Terrorism and International Law*, 20, and Chomsky, *9–11*, 40–5.

[95] See McGoldrick, *9–11*, 16, and also Megret's conclusion, in 'Justice', 345.

'jettisoned in the name of the war against terrorism'.[96] In the age of terror, it seems, classical liberal conceptions of the rule of law or individual human rights are of limited currency.[97]

This is to be regretted.[98] There is little to be gained by a return to a global state of nature. Moreover, if there is to be any kind of resolution to the 'war on terror', sooner or later we are going to need the doctrines, the principles and the institutions of international law once again. They are easy to destroy, but far more difficult to rebuild.[99] And, as Michael Walzer concurs, ultimately, 'hegemony, unlike empire, rests on consent'.[100] And there is, perhaps, even more to be lost by the abrogation of domestic principles of legality. Neglect for the rule of law, and the rights of others, is corrosive; betokening, perhaps, not just a deeper unease, but a conscious desire to nurture a 'climate of fear'.[101] The call to crusade, something that we will investigate in greater depth in Chapter 2, replaces a faith in law.

Certainly, the idea of a 'war on terror' presents myriad problems for the international lawyer.[102] Indeterminacy is pervasive, and lawyers fear indeterminacy. There is, for a start, temporal indeterminacy. If there is no end to terrorism, and there is never likely to be a definitive one, then it is not obvious if, or when, the war against it will end either.[103] Certainly terrorist wars are never

[96] B. Bowring, 'The Degradation of International Law?' in Strawson, *Ground Zero*, 15.

[97] See A. Carty, 'The Terrors of Freedom: the Sovereignty States and the Freedom to Fear', and R. Talbot, 'The Balancing Act: Counter-terrorism and Civil Liberties in British Anti-terrorism Law', both in Strawson, *Ground Zero*, at 54–5 and 134, respectively, addressing, in turn, the compromised nature of liberal legalism in international and British domestic counter-terrorism strategies. On the latter issue, UK counter-terrorist legislation, see also D. Bonner, 'Managing Terrorism While Respecting Human Rights? European Aspects of the Anti-Terrorism, Crime and Security Act 2001', *European Public Law*, 8 (2002), 497–524.

[98] As is firmly argued by Philip Hoffman, in his 'Human Rights', particularly 933–4, suggesting that the 'war on terrorism' is a far greater threat to the 'human security' across the globe than any 'terrorist bombing'.

[99] Steyn, 'Black Hole, 7. A similar line is taken in Stromseth, 'Iraq', 628–42, stressing, like many, the need for UN Charter law to evolve in line with changing circumstances.

[100] Quoted in Paulus, 'War', 731. Eric Hobsbawn reaches the same conclusion, in his *Globalisation*, at 158–9. So does Gary Hart, suggesting that contemporary America stands at an 'imperial precipice', its 'war on terror' merely a 'metaphor' for the absence of a coherent 'grand strategy' with which it might address the challenges of a 'new revolutionary age' of globalisation. In the absence of such a strategy, he adds, America all too easily finds itself engaged in messy 'brawling, however well intentioned, in another man's ally', a conclusion that has obvious pertinence in the context of the Iraq war. See Hart, *Power*, vii, 3–5, 11–14, 40, 109, 143, 150, 157–61.

[101] See Salman Rushdie,' The Ministry of False Alarms', *Virginia Quarterly*, 80 (2004), 5. For a further invocation of the American 'problem', see Koh, 'Exceptionalism', 1489 and 1524–5, citing Fareed Zakaria's original use of the term, and also M. Cox, 'September 11th and US Hegemony – Or Will the 21st Century be American Too?', *International Studies Perspectives*, 3 (2002), 54, 67, and S. Babb, 'Fear and Loathing in America: Application of Treason Law in Times of National Crisis and the Case of John Walker Lindh, *Hastings Law Journal*, 54 (2003), 1722.

[102] For the suggestion that the idea of 'war' against terror is a jurisprudential 'misnomer', see Cassese, 'Terrorism', 993 and also Greenwood, 'International Law', 305–6.

[103] See Dershowitz, *Terrorism*, 6, and also Rees, *Terrorists*, 66–7, noting President Bush's affirmation that the 'war against terror' 'will not end until every terrorist group of global reach has been found, stopped and defeated'. For a broader critique of the idea, concluding that we are indeed

short.[104] The essential 'vacuity of content and range' that lies behind the notion of a 'war' against terror is further reinforced by the sense that terrorism is an experience to be contained, rather than an event to be defeated.[105] And then there is conceptual indeterminacy. How, as it is so often asked, 'do you wage war on an abstract noun?'[106] Conceptual indeterminacy revisits the pervasive problem of definition, the critical absence of what Walter Lacqueur terms a 'magic formula' for defining terrorism.[107] Any attempt at 'specific' definition, Lacqueur adds, is 'bound to fail, for the simple reason that there is not one but many different terrorisms'; some insurrectionary, some issue-based, some ideologically grounded, some focused on perceived nationalist grievances.[108] Perhaps, as Noam Chomsky would have us believe, terrorism is just 'what our leaders declare it to be'.[109] Perhaps, as Baudrillard concludes, terrorism just has 'no meaning'.[110]

Maybe. Terrorism is indeed a 'definitional quagmire'.[111] Reduced to the level of banality, Israeli Premier Ariel Sharon declaimed that 'terrorism is terrorism is terrorism anywhere in the world'.[112] But such simplicity serves no purpose. It certainly does nothing to stop terrorists committing acts that demand some kind of jurisprudential response. And it does not stop jurists agonising over what this response should be.[113] Broader definitions of terrorism tend to focus

immersed in what can only be an 'endless war', see O. Gross, 'What Emergency Regime?' *Constellations*, 13 (2006), 76.

[104] See M. Burleigh, *Blood and Rage: A Cultural History of Terrorism* (HarperCollins, 2008), 479–80.

[105] See P. Fitzpatrick, 'Enduring Right' in Strawson, *Ground Zero*, 41, and also, Gray, *Al-Qaeda*, 116 and Hoffman, 'Human Rights', 940.

[106] See McGoldrick, *9–11*, 28, and more generally J. Waldron, 'Terrorism and the Uses of Terror' *Journal of Ethics*, 8 (2004), 5–6, arguing for the importance of asking the question, even if it is appreciated that there can be no determinate answer.

[107] Lacqueur, *War*, 139. In the words of Khachig Tololyan 'terrorism is in fact such a complex conjunction of socio-cultural, psychological and political factors that a conceptually satisfying schema of terrorism is likely to remain elusive, at least for the time being'. See K. Tololyan, 'Cultural Narrative and the Motivation of the Terrorist', *Journal of Strategic Studies*, 10 (1987), 217. Two decades later it is just as elusive. For a discussion of the particular jurisprudential implications of this problem see Higgins, 'Terrorism', 14–19, and also C. Blakesley, 'Ruminations on Terrorism and Anti-Terrorism Law and Literature', *University of Miami Law Review*, 57 (2003), 1072–86. For a broad, and relatively recent, discussion of the ethical and political implications of conceptual indeterminacy, see C. Coady, 'Terrorism and Innocence', *Journal of Ethics*, 8 (2004), 37–42.

[108] Lacqueur, *Terrorism*, 46. See also Kapitan, 'Terrorism', 48; Bassiouni, 'Terrorism', 84–6; and M. Ignatieff, *The Lesser Evil: Political Ethics in an Age of Terror* (Edinburgh University Press, 2005), 83. Others ponder the possibility that terrorism might be construed to include vivisectionist letter-bombs, or the firing of church-halls by white supremacists. Claudia Card puts it pithily, if darkly; the National Coalition of Burned Churches is alive today, and its 'concerns are not lightning or faulty wiring'. See C. Card, 'Making War on Terrorism in Response to 9/11' in Sterba, *Terrorism*, 179. For an overview of the possibilities, see R. Leeman, *The Rhetoric of Terrorism and Counter-Terrorism* (Greenwood Press, 1991), 1–2.

[109] Chomsky, *Hegemony*, 110. [110] Baudrillard, *Spirit of Terrorism*, 57.

[111] Guelke, 'Great Whites', 18. For a similar reflection, see A. Chaskalson, 'Counter-Terrorism, Human Rights and the Rule of Law', *Cambridge Law Journal*, 67 (2008), 76.

[112] In V. Held, 'Terrorism and War', *Journal of Ethics*, 8 (2004), 59–60.

[113] For, as he concludes, 'Language moulds thought, and thought precipitates action'. See Kapitan, 'Terrorism', 61.

on the nature of the deed, the characteristics of coercion and disregard for human life, and the experience of trauma. Igor Primoratz's definition is renowned. 'Terrorism', he declares, 'is intimidation with purpose: the terror is meant to cause others to do things they would otherwise not do. Terrorism is coercive intimidation'.[114] Chomsky concedes that 'coercion' might provide the root of a working definition.[115] Ted Honderich hazards something to do with 'violence, illegality and scale'.[116] All, in passing, admit a further and critical truth of history; understood on these terms, terror is far more often inflicted by states upon individuals than by groups of individuals upon states. It is not, of course, a history that the modern state likes to write.

Official definitions tend to seek refuge in coercion and violence, and the comfort of similar vagueness. The US Army manual isolates the 'calculated use of violence or threat of violence to attain goals that are political, religious or ideological in nature', and which is effected 'through intimidation, coercion or instilling fear'. Legislative definitions in the UK, most obviously that provided in the 2000 Terrorism Act, are similar. Section 1 of the Act identifies 'the use or threat' of violence which is 'designed to influence the government or to intimidate the public', and which is 'made for the purpose of advancing a political, religious or ideological cause'. The common denominator in such definitions is the presumption that terrorism must be comprehended as an event. Act-based definitions inevitably focus on events. So do perpetrator-based definitions.[117] But neither resolves the associated problems of definition and consistency. All in all it is a bit of a mess. Certainly progress towards some kind of international law of 'terrorism' remains unconvincing.[118]

In lieu of definition, there is a tendency to list and proscribe groups and kinds of action. The General Convention on Terrorism eschews definitions, preferring instead the enumeration of kinds of 'criminal and unjustifiable' actions.[119] Anti-terrorist legislation in various jurisdictions including the UK and the US invariably comes with an appendix of proscribed terrorist groups, with whom

---

[114] I. Primoratz, 'What is Terrorism?', *Journal of Applied Philosophy*, 7 (1990), 129–30.

[115] Chomsky, *9–11*, 57. So does Carl Wellman. See his 'On Terrorism Itself', *Journal of Value Inquiry*, 13 (1990), 250–8.

[116] Honderich, *Terrorism*, 15.

[117] See C. Gearty, 'Terrorism and Morality', *European Human Rights Law Review*, 4 (2003), 379–82 discussing the categorisation of individual terrorists, and also Zulaika and Douglass, *Terror*, 100–3.

[118] For a sober commentary on the state of international terrorist 'law', see A.-M. Slaughter and W. Burke-White, 'An International Constitutional Moment', *Harvard International Law Journal*, 43 (2002), 11. For a strident argument in favour of a specific Terrorism Convention, see Bassiouni, 'Terrorism', 101.

[119] For a discussion of this approach, see J.-M. Sorel, 'Some Questions About the Definition of Terrorism and the Fight Against its Financing', *European Journal of International Law*, 14 (2003), 368–70. The European Union Framework Decision on Terrorism also includes a list of eight identifiably terrorist 'acts', ranging from hostage taking to 'major economic loss' to 'disrupting the supply of water'. See S. Peers, 'EU Responses to Terrorism', *International and Comparative Law Quarterly*, 52 (2003), 228–9.

even association is often enough to establish guilt. European Union anti-terrorist provisions are almost exclusively cast in terms of lists of proscribed 'groups' whose assets might be seized. Aside from the rather lame nature of this response, the problem with such lists is their obvious tendency to proscribe guilt by association.[120]

The redefinition of existing areas of law is another strategy. Thus terrorist events might be addressed within humanitarian law, with terrorist groups, such as Al-Qaeda, categorised as 'irregular' forces.[121] The problem, of course, is that the present 'war on terror' makes no attempt to situate itself within existing laws of war. We shall encounter this particular issue in Chapter 6, when we take a look at the myriad implications of Guantanamo Bay. Neither terrorism nor the war against it can be comprehended within the definition of an 'international armed conflict' as understood by the jurisprudence of the Geneva Conventions.[122] Technically, the US is at war with no one. And neither is Al-Qaeda.[123]

An alternative might be the use of international criminal law. Such a strategy would help to defray accusations that the 'war on terror' is imperial. The possibility of using the new International Criminal Court (ICC) has its supporters.[124] But it also has its doubters, wary of making too much of an area of law that is, at present, little more than 'bits and pieces of overlapping norms' with no overarching jurisprudential coherence.[125] The use of ad hoc tribunals, such as those which were established under the auspices of the UN in the wake of the Balkan and Rwandan wars is a further possibility; one to which we will return in Chapter 3. The kinds of 'crimes against humanity' that the tribunals considered, and which are also recognised in the ICC Statute, can be described within the existing laws of war. But they do not have to be. And neither does the jurisprudence of genocide.[126] The idea that terrorism might be a crime against humanity has gained the approbation of such luminaries as the UN

---

[120] See K. Roach and G. Trotter, 'Miscarriages of Justice in the War Against Terror', *Pennsylvania State University Law Review*, 109 (2005), 996, and also Marks, 'Branding the War', 86.

[121] D. Meltzer, 'Al-Qaida: Terrorists or Irregulars?' in Strawson, *Ground Zero*, 82.

[122] McGoldrick, *9–11*, 31–6. See also Megret, 'Justice', 336–41.   [123] See Zizek, *Desert*, 107.

[124] See M. Drumbl, 'Judging the 11 September Terrorist Attack', *Human Rights Quarterly*, 24 (2002), particularly 333–8, 348–53, 357–8, arguing along the way for a tribunal that would include Islamic jurists. For defences of the international criminal court or international tribunals as the most appropriate for dealing with instances of transnational terrorism, see also Megret, 'Justice', 323–4; C. Greenwood, 'International Law and the "War Against Terrorism"', *International Affairs*, 78 (2002), 317; C. Much, 'The International Criminal Court and Terrorism as an International Crime', *Michigan State Journal of International Law*, 14 (2006), 121–38; and perhaps most stridently, R. Goldstone and J. Simpson, 'Evaluating the Role of the International Criminal Court as a Legal Response to Terrorism', *Harvard Human Rights Journal*, 16 (2003), 15–16.

[125] Bassiouni, 'Terrorism', 90.

[126] See S. von Schorlemer, 'Human Rights: Substantive and Institutional Implications of the War Against Terrorism', *European Journal of International Law*, 14 (2003), 272–4.

Secretary-General Kofi Annan, and the UN High Commissioner for Human Rights, Mary Robinson, together with an array of international lawyers.[127]

The use of domestic courts also has its adherents. Terrorists who commit criminal acts would be treated as criminals, a strategy which would have the added merit of denying the fetishistic aspirations of the terrorist. Killing would simply be treated as that; nothing more spectacular or glorious.[128] But it would also deny the unarguable case that, in many instances, there is a political root, and a transnational aspiration, to terrorist acts; both of which are rarely present in ordinary conceptions of, or procedures in, domestic criminality.[129]

The possibilities are then various. But none, once again, is compelling. And the sense of confusion is pervasive. Perhaps we would, as Rosalyn Higgins suggests, be better off just giving up the chase. Terrorism, she declares, is a 'term without legal significance'. Instead it has become a 'convenient way of alluding to activities, whether of States or of individuals, widely disapproved of and in which either the methods used are unlawful, or the targets protected, or both'.[130] Vaughan Lowe is equally sceptical as to whether there is a 'need' for a 'law' of terrorism.[131] And this may well be true. It will be argued throughout this book that a measure of scepticism is a vital tool in any attempt to penetrate the discourses of terrorism and counter-terrorism. But there is a real problem here too, a problem of rhetorical and conceptual confusion blinding the harsh reality of cities destroyed and lives lost.

Doubts with regard to the perceived need or desirability of a law of terrorism should not detract from the validity of a jurisprudential response to terrorist violence. The limitations of existing legal responses, more particularly the apparent limitations of existing legal institutions, must not imply that we should abandon the cause of justice, or that we should meekly accept that we must, for however long, live in a 'world without rules'. A world in which justice is administered not by lawyers, but by ass-kicking politicians, will not be a happy one.[132] As President Eisenhower noted, half a century ago, 'there will be no peace without law'.[133] For this reason, the real 'test' of 9/11 will not be who wins a 'war against terror', but who wins the war for law and for justice.[134]

---

[127] See Cassese, 'Terrorism', 994–5. Another variation on the theme might see terrorism recast within a law of 'civilian inviolability', wherein any act directed against civilians would be subject to sanction before international or domestic courts. For this suggestion, see Slaughter and Burke-White, 'Moment', particularly 13–21.

[128] An observation emphasised by Christopher Greenwood, in 'International Law', 302, and also 308. The view also finds favour with Michael Burleigh, in his *Blood and Rage*, at 450.

[129] See Kapitan, 'Terrorism', 60.   [130] Higgins, 'Terrorism', particularly 13–14, 28.

[131] V. Lowe, 'The Iraq Crisis: What Now?', *International and Comparative Law Quarterly*, 52 (2003), 864.

[132] Indeed, it is altogether more likely to be a rather 'nasty one' suggests Ahdaf Soueif. See her *Mezzaterra*, 93.

[133] Adding 'And there can be no law if we were to invoke one code of international conduct for those who oppose us, and another for our friends'. Presidential address of 31 October 1956, quoted in Barber, *Fear's Empire*, 237. For a similar view, see Schell, *World*, 354.

[134] See Koh, 'Spirit', 26, 29; Franck, 'Iraq', 620, urging that, now more than ever, the international jurist must 'stand tall for the rule of law', and also Lowe, 'Iraq Crisis', 862–4.

Poethics and poetics

The case for a 'critical' terrorist studies has, in recent years, been pressed with increasing vigour. It is driven, not just by a desire to counter hyperbole with perspective, but also by a sense that there is much to be gained by pursuing a consciously contextual and interdisciplinary agenda.[135] At its heart is a particular desire to 'humanise', to seek to comprehend not just events, but those who perpetrate and suffer their consequences; a desire which, as we have already noted, our political leaders would prefer us not to share.[136] In doing so, as Anthony Burke has confirmed, its primary aspiration is 'fixed in a critical *telos* of justice'.[137] To this end, critical terrorist studies will further provide a place where 'fragmented voices can converge'.[138] In this it will, like indeed any critical intellectual venture, be most obviously discursive and textual in its aspiration.

This book is intended to be a contribution to this emergent 'critical' approach to terrorism. It is also intended to be a still closer contribution to an equally distinctive jurisprudential genre, one which is readily identifiable with the aspiration of 'law and literature'. In a recent summation of this movement, Kieran Dolin has confirmed that all 'law is inevitably a matter of language'.[139] It is an assertion that echoes Robert Cover's renowned injunction, 'No set of legal institutions or prescriptions exists apart from the narratives that locate it and give it meaning'.[140] The relation of law with literature is not, in these terms, an intellectual option. Law is literature.

It is an insight which has, for obvious reasons, enjoyed considerable support amongst various disciples of the rather wider 'critical legal studies' and law and society movements.[141] One of the most textually sensitive 'crits' Allan Hutchinson provides an eloquent statement, one which further appreciates the necessary presence of history in the emergent 'law and literature' venture:

> We are never not in a story. History and human action only take on meaning and intelligibility within their narrative context and dramatic settings. There are many stories being imagined and enacted, but we can only listen to them and comprehend them within the vernacular contexts of other stories. Our conversations about these narratives are themselves located and scripted in

---

[135] Perhaps the most immediate evidence of this emergent genre is the arrival of a new journal entitled *Critical Studies on Terrorism*. For an overview of the aspirations of critical terrorism studies, see the collection of essays in the inaugural edition of the journal in April 2008, especially Stohl, 'Old Myths, New Fantasies and the Enduring Realities of Terrorism', J. Burke, 'The End of Terrorism Studies', and K. Booth, 'The Human Faces of Terror: Reflections in a Cracked Looking-glass', at 5–16, 37–49 and 65–79, respectively. See also J. Gunning, 'A Case for Critical Terrorism Studies', *Government and Opposition*, 42 (2007), 363–93.

[136] See Gunning, 'Studies', 377–8, 384.   [137] Burke, 'End', 43.

[138] See Gunning, 'Studies', 384. Burke makes the same point, in 'End', at 42.

[139] K. Dolin, *A Critical Introduction to Law and Literature* (Cambridge University Press, 2007), 2.

[140] R. Cover, 'Foreword: Nomos and Narrative', *Harvard Law Review*, 97 (1983), 4.

[141] For an overview, see M. Constable, *Just Silences: The Limits and Possibilities of Law* (Princeton University Press, 2005), 50–3.

deeper stories which determine their moral force and epistemological validity. There is no truth nor knowledge outside the dramatic context and idiom of history. All conversations occur within history.[142]

Scholars engaged more directly still in the 'law and literature' enterprise tend to accept a supervening intellectual demarcation; between law 'as' literature, and law 'in' literature, that is between an appreciation that law is a form of literature, and the deployment of law in literary form.[143] We shall encounter both forms at various points in subsequent chapters.

The art of description inheres its own dangers, of course, foremost of which is stasis, the temptation simply to portray, to use literature to depict injustice, or a lack of voice perhaps. The radical edge comes with the projection of how things might be and it is here that the embrace of texts which we might, for reasons of convenience, term non-legal carries its obviously ethical as well as political import. This more proactive ambition can be found in the idea of literary 'strategies' originally suggested by Richard Weisberg.[144] In this sense the now well-established insights, that law is a textual expression, and that literary texts deploy law in metaphorical or indeed non-metaphorical form, is taken further. The engagement of law and literature is intended to do something more, to realise, to construct, even, an alternative jurisprudential narrative. In this book, it will be suggested that a 'law and literature' perspective can facilitate a better understanding of an issue which classical jurisprudence seems largely unable to comprehend. That issue is terrorism.

But what, more precisely, can a 'law and literature' strategy do in this or indeed any other context? The chapters that follow are premised on the idea that there are three identifiable strategies. Again, the demarcation should be understood to be one that is driven as much by convenience, for in truth, as we shall see, they overlap one another constantly. Taken together they compose a kind of physiognomy of sensibilities; a way in which we, as citizens and jurists, might learn to listen more perceptively, and compassionately, learn to speak more confidently, and learn to look and perceive more acutely. Ultimately, they coalesce around the need, urgent at present, to raise voices, for there can be no justice without a reciprocal capacity to speak and to listen.[145]

First, therefore, a better appreciation of the textual or literary form of law can help us to identify the intensely aesthetic nature of terrorism and counter-terrorist strategies, and the equally intensely rhetorical forms which their

---

[142] A. Hutchinson, *Dwelling on the Threshold: Critical Essays on Modern Legal Thought* (Carswell, 1988), 13.

[143] For a recent discussion of the basic demarcations in 'law and literature', see Dolin, *Law and Literature*, Chapter 1. For a more critical commentary, suggesting rather different demarcations, see J. Baron, 'Law, Literature, and the Problems of Interdisciplinarity', *Yale Law Journal*, 108 (1999), particularly 1059–71.

[144] R. Weisberg, *Poethics and Other Strategies of Law and Literature* (Columbia University Press, 1992).

[145] For a recent and powerful assertion of this, see Constable, *Just Silences*, 177.

engagement takes.[146] Any 'war on terror', like indeed any collateral 'war on law', is irreducibly rhetorical, a game of feints and delusions. Political rhetoric seeks to numb our senses, to reduce us to passive receptors. Terrorist rhetoric does this, as does terrorist iconography and aesthetic. And the same is true of counter-terrorist rhetoric. Both seek to terrify us into abrogating our rational and aesthetic senses. Here 'law and literature' can make us more perceptive as well as nurture our scepticism. We will come across examples of this kind of rhetoric in the first two chapters in particular. In Chapter 1, we will examine what can be credibly presented as the first piece of counter-terrorist polemic in modern political literature, Edmund Burke's *Reflections on the Revolution in France*. The subject of Chapter 2 will be the anti-Jesuit scares of late sixteenth- and early seventeenth-century England, and more precisely their necessarily equivocal presentation in Shakespeare's *Macbeth*.

In both cases we will therefore encounter examples of rhetoric that were devised as a strategic response to a perceived threat to the state. It will become immediately obvious that, for both the counter-terrorist and the terrorist, language is a vital weapon in any imagined 'war'. And it will be equally apparent that its success is measured in terms of our passive acceptance of it. It will, in passing, become equally apparent that the distinction between terrorist and counter-terrorist, a distinction very often pressed, perhaps paradoxically by both parties, is a tendentious one. This tension, as we shall see, runs through Shakespeare's treatment of 'equivocation'. It will also be seen in rather more strident form in Chapter 1, in Percy Shelley's brusque critique of state terrorism.

This appreciation of rhetoric and dissimulation leads us to our second 'strategy'. Literature provides a supplement. In an immediate form, it provides a supplementary chronicle of events. This is sometimes termed the 'narrative' ambition of law and literature.[147] One of the most debilitating limitations that legalism imposes on the quest for justice is textual constraint. Legal cases, legal judgements, pieces of legislation, even constitutions, seek to delimit what is law, and what therefore, in terms of legal justice, counts.[148] And what goes missing, so often, is the human voice. So determined to preserve its own integrity legalism retains a profound suspicion of testament. This is as true for terrorism as it is for any legal event or experience. Literature addresses this critical failure.[149] It retrieves those 'voices' which, as Ariel Dorfman put it, otherwise remain 'hidden, at the bottom of the rivers of silence of humanity'.[150] In its various forms, such supplementary chronicles can provide what Richard Jackson, in the more immediate context of Truth Commissions, has termed a 'kind of public narrative' of political violence and injustice.[151]

---

[146] For the invocation of a more particular jurisprudential 'poetics', see A. Gearey, '"Tell the Truth, but Tell it Slant": A Poetics of Truth and Reconciliation', *Journal of Law and Society*, 31 (2004), 38–59.

[147] See Baron, 'Problems of Interdisciplinarity', 1065–6.   [148] See Hutchinson, *Dwelling*, 21.

[149] On this point, see Dolin, *Law and Literature*, 10.   [150] Dorfman, *Other Septembers*, 232.

[151] See Jackson, *Writing*, 1, 188.

In more prosaic terms, alternative texts, whether or not they proclaim themselves to be fictive, testamentary or indeed legal, tell stories. An appreciation of the value of such stories is not just desirable, in the sense of allowing us to gain a broader comprehension of how victims of terror, or indeed perpetrators, think and feel. It is also vital, necessary to a proper understanding of what law is. Allan Hutchinson puts it thus:

> The life of law is not logic or experience, but a narrative way of world-making. The styling, staging and phrasing of the law structure the world in particular and partial ways... Like all tales, legal stories gain meaning and significance from the selective emphasis on certain features of always complex and frequently ambiguous experience... More importantly still, it is the stories themselves that come to comprise the reality of our experience. In this sense, legal stories mediate our engagement in the world and with others: they provide the possibilities and parameters of our own self-definition and understanding.[152]

Again, such an approach finds a particular resonance with legal scholars keen to re-describe law as a social construct, a lived experience, and keen too to stress the extent to which a 'legal consciousness' must be understood as a discursive and textual phenomenon. As Patricia Ewick and Susan Silbey have more recently confirmed, it is 'through our storytelling' that 'we (re)create the commonplace experience of law'.[153] The 'contours' of law, accordingly, are described by 'numerous actors, involved in diverse projects, employing different legitimating discourses, material resources, and political power'.[154] And, most importantly, the contours are always changing. A whole range of different voices and different narratives go together to form a good society with a proper sense of justice.

Of course, there is a catch here. The constraints of law are clinical, but effective, and without them the question of authenticity becomes pressing. A legal court, like a governmental statute, proclaims its own veracity, and, by and large, we accept this. There is no such quality-control for extra-legal texts. This is, at once, both the virtue and the vice. The lack of constraint liberates, but at the same time places a responsibility on us, the audience.[155] Whilst a chronicle might presume truth, we must always retain our scepticism of the presumption. But it will be a constructive scepticism, for at the heart of this book is a strong commitment to the value of stories in the pursuit of justice, and to literary and other testamentary forms as a vital supplement to the practices of law and legalism.

To this end, we shall, in subsequent chapters, encounter various examples of such chronicles. Chapter 3 will present striking examples of such stories and

---

[152] Hutchinson, *Dwelling*, 14.
[153] See P. Ewick and S. Silbey, *The Common Place of Law: Stories from Everyday Life* (Chicago University Press, 1998), 244, and more generally 34–9, 241–4.
[154] Ewick and Silbey, *Common Place*, 19, 223, 226.
[155] For a comment on this danger, and the need for 'disciplining rules' of interpretation, see O. Fiss, 'Objectivity and Interpretation', *Stanford Law Review*, 34 (1982), 739.

chronicles in the context of alternative strategies for achieving reconciliation and justice in the aftermath of political violence. These instances of violence, and these alternative strategies, are set within the contextual frames of the Balkan wars and the Truth Commissions of South Africa. Of course, it might be countered that the forms of political violence perpetrated and suffered in these contexts were not really terrorist. But that would depend upon our willingness to buy into one of the central planks of counter-terrorist rhetoric; that terrorism can only be conducted by 'others', by outlaws, by those who exist beyond the state. And, following Shelley, we will already have confirmed that this is one of the most debilitating of mythologies. States terrorise their citizens, and those who they deem 'other'. And for those terrorised, the terror is just as great.

We shall also encounter examples of this strategy, of literary supplements, elsewhere in this book. We shall, for example, encounter it in Chapter 4, the subject of which is the peculiar status of the woman terrorist. We will quickly see that the peculiarity of this status is, in large part, the product of a broader peculiarity which pervades, not just terrorist discourse, but gender discourse itself. At the heart of the former is the frequently observed absence of women. Where, it is so often suggested, are the women? They can be discerned, more often as victims than perpetrators. But the terrorist discourse, more broadly conceived, seems to be a strikingly male one. The reason is simple, and then not so simple. The woman terrorist is absent, not because there are no women terrorists, still less because they do not experience terror, but because the discourse is masculine, composed more often than not by men, by male politicians, male judges, male terrorists. What is lacking, therefore, is voice; a lack which is all too familiar to those engaged more widely in the study of women and the law. And what is needed to remedy this lack is chronicles, testaments of terror and terrorism. In Chapter 4 we will encounter precisely such testaments, some fictive, such as Euripides *The Bacchae* and *The Women of Troy*, some not, and some that can be best situated twixt and between, such as Franca Rame's monologues on the peculiar relation of women and political violence.

We shall also encounter supplementary chronicles in the final chapter, where the subject matter is legal responses to the 'war on terror', and more particularly the 'black hole' of Guantanamo. Here we will encounter a genre of verbatim drama, a genre which has been devised in its current form as a precise response to the perceived lack of narrative accountability in our post-9/11 world. As we shall see, this dramatic genre, composed as a splicing together of various verbatim statements articulated by political and non-political actors, is conceived in terms of presenting, in textual and dramatic form, an alternative court of law. Indeed, given the extent that the war on terror is conceived to be an extra-legal experience, it is perhaps better understood less as an alternative, more as the only court of law.

Chronicle and supplement, then, contribute voice to our physiognomy of 'law and literature'. And because they do, they again make us better listeners. At the same time, these texts, as we shall also see, speak to a further aspect of this physiognomy, a further strategy of 'law and literature'. This is the strategy of 'poethics' or what is sometimes termed 'humanist' law and literature.[156] It is our third strategy; one designed to make us see more and feel more, to see more acutely and feel more sensitively. It speaks to the kind of sentiment articulated half a century ago by Albert Camus. 'Because dialogue is no longer possible', Camus suggested, we can no longer discern 'beauty in the world and in human faces'.[157]

The same physiognomic metaphor is deployed with similar eloquence by Richard Weisberg. 'Stories about the "other"', he advises, 'induce us to *see* the other, and once we do so, we endeavour consistently to understand the world from within the other's optic'.[158] The same ambition underpins much contemporary legal humanist scholarship. We shall examine this closely in Chapter 5, the subject of which is the depiction of nineteenth- and early twentieth-century anarcho-nihilist terrorism in the novels of Joseph Conrad, Feodor Doestoevski and J.M. Coetzee. It will be suggested that what binds these depictions, more than anything, is a determination to explore the human experience of terrorism; not just the suffering of the victims of terrorism, but the suffering of the perpetrators too. Whilst the rhetoric of terrorism strives to convince us, at all times, of the momentous, even apocalyptic, nature of particular terrorist events, the poethics of terrorism seeks to impress upon us, as a counter, the intensely ordinary nature of its experience.[159]

The same argument will, of course, insinuate itself across the other chapters of this book. It will be detected, very obviously in those chapters which examine the alternative forms of testament presented before and alongside the International Criminal Tribunal for Yugoslavia, as well as the various texts which seek to articulate a female terrorist discourse. And it will be encountered once again in the final chapter, in the context, not just of verbatim chronicle, but also the emergent genre of '9/11 fiction'.

Writing at once to the general aspiration of 'law and literature' as well as the more precise desire to raise the female voice in legal studies, Maria Aristodemou has emphasised the ultimate aspiration of such strategies, the potential literature enjoys to better inform a new jurisprudential 'ethics' of 'otherness'. 'No writing', she affirms, 'ever takes place outside the mirroring love of, and for, others'.[160]

---

[156] For an exploration of 'humanist' law and literature, see Baron, 'Problem of Interdisciplinarity', 1063–4, and at greater length, I. Ward, 'Universal Jurisprudence and the Case for Legal Humanism', *Alberta Law Review*, 38 (2001), 941–58.

[157] A. Camus, *Between Hell and Reason* (Wesleyan University Press, 1991), 117–18.

[158] Weisberg, *Poethics*, 46.

[159] On the need to appreciate that all victims 'bleed and grieve in the same way', see Burleigh, *Blood and Rage*, x.

[160] M. Aristodemou, *Law and Literature: Journeys from Her to Eternity* (Oxford University Press, 2000), 295. See also 2, 225.

The mirroring metaphor speaks once again to the idea of physiognomy.[161] But it takes it a critical step further. It suggests that a better appreciation of others will nurture in us a better appreciation of ourselves, and our responsibilities. It speaks, very obviously, to ethics, and more particularly still perhaps to the distinctive ethical aspiration of jurisprudential deconstruction. In this spirit, the need for us to reinvest a 'human rights imaginary' based on a fundamental re-conception of justice as the construct of intimate 'human relationships' is vigorously argued by Costas Douzinas.[162] Drucilla Cornell likewise couches such a jurisprudence as something 'driven by an ethical desire to enact the ethical relation', meaning the 'aspiration to a non-violent relation to the Other, and to otherness more generally, that assumes responsibility to guard the Other against the appropriation that would deny her difference and singularity'.[163] For both Douzinas and Cornell, the prelude to reinvesting a deconstructionist ethics is a proper appreciation of our lives as textual and discursive constructs.

Poethics, in like tone, is devised as a strategy that can make us better understand law. But that is only a first step; for what really matters, what literature can really help us to do, is better understand our lives as ethical persons. By raising voices a narrative jurisprudence fashions this possibility. It can take us beyond the confines of law and into the realms of ethics and human relations. In his seminal study of the modern condition, written nearly half a century ago, *Man for Himself*, Erich Fromm urged us to reinvest moral philosophy with a core belief in the power of love and compassion:

> To love one's neighbour is not a phenomenon transcending man; it is something inherent in and radiating from him. Love is not a higher power which descends upon man, nor a duty which is imposed upon him; it is a power by which he relates to the world and which makes it truly his.[164]

If poethics can reinvest in us a proper appreciation of Fromm's insight, it might perhaps help to raise jurisprudence from the mood of pessimism which the experience of terrorism appears to have confirmed, even promoted. It presents us with an ethics that does not need to concern itself with abstruse metaphysics, but which, for precisely this reason, can revitalise a sense of hope and justice.

It is against pessimism, and the lure of abrogating our faith in ideas of law and justice, that the chapters in this book are written. It is against silence too. As Ulrich Beck observes, for an enduring moment, a worryingly long one, 9/11 stood 'for the complete collapse of language', the 'implosion of the Twin Towers' followed by 'an explosion of silence'.[165] A deeper poetical understanding of the

---

[161] It is also deployed by Melanie Williams, in her *Empty Justice*, at xxiv, suggesting that literature allows us to hold 'a mirror to ourselves'.

[162] C. Douzinas, *The End of Human Rights: Critical Legal Thought at the Turn of the Century* (Hart, 2000), 341.

[163] D. Cornell, *The Philosophy of the Limit* (Routledge, 1992), 62.

[164] E. Fromm, *Man for Himself* (Routledge, 1990), 14.

[165] Beck, 'Terrorist Threat', 39. See also Faludi, 339, commenting likewise regarding that 'terrible period when it seemed pointless to talk about anything else, but so hard to know what to say'.

experience of terrorism, and the ethical charge it demands, will confirm in us an appropriately sceptical contempt for those who urge the need for a jurisprudence of 'ass-kicking', just as it should promote in us an equivalent distrust of those who are so keen to preclude or constrain what we might, following Richard Rorty, term the terrorist 'conversation'.[166]

A poethical or humanist jurisprudence will, in turn, help us to revitalise our determination to counter the challenges of terrorism, not with fantastical wars against imaginary enemies, but with something called justice. In more immediately jurisprudence terms, it will help us to come to terms with an event which, whilst it may not be quite so momentous as our more excitable commentators and political leaders would have us believe, is, for better or worse, likely to retain a dominant place in jurisprudential debate for decades to come. At the same time, and on a rather more immediate, but certainly no less vital, level, it can also make us think and make us care. In this, it can give us a sense of common responsibility, of participation in strategies which are designed, not to win mythic wars, but to counter real horror and real suffering.[167]

---

[166] For Rorty's invocation of a politics of 'conversation', see his *Contingency, Irony, and Solidarity* (Cambridge University Press, 1989), 5–6, 60–1.

[167] See Gunning, 'Studies', 392–3, closing with a similar injunction, to pursue a critical intellectual agenda precisely because the human stakes are so high.

1

Terror and the sense sublime

We live in apocalyptic times; apparently.[1] Ours is a terrifying age, or so we are told, time and again. In his State of the Union address in January 2002, President George W. Bush sagely advised his awed audience that:

> Thousands of dangerous killers, schooled in the methods of murder, often supported by outlaw regimes, are now spreading throughout the world like ticking time bombs, set to go off without warning.[2]

We should be troubled by this; not by the thought that there are thousands of these killers wandering the streets, but by the presumption that we should believe such nonsense.[3] As Benjamin Barber argues, the pressing of a 'war on terror', and the myriad imperial jaunts that it entails, depends upon embedding a sense of 'fear' in the collective mind of America and its allies.[4]

Bush's observations, raising images of streets packed with explosive-carrying terrorists, resonate with the closing passages of Joseph Conrad's novel *The Secret Agent*; a novel to which we shall return in Chapter 5. At the close of his novel, Conrad leaves his reader with the image of a demented professor busy making bombs and scurrying round the streets of London with them strapped to his person, 'like a pest in the street full of men'.[5] Conrad, as we shall see, wanted his audience to be troubled. But he also knew that he was fantasising. Bush, however, was not speaking in a spirit of irony. He believed it.[6]

---

[1] For the discussion of apocalyptic allusions in post-9/11 political rhetoric, see M. Ruthven, *A Fury for God: The Islamist Attack on America* (Granta, 2002), 32–3.

[2] In R. Jackson, *Writing the War on Terrorism: Language, Politics and Counter-Terrorism* (Manchester University Press, 2005), 110.

[3] Edward Said long ago advised of the need to be wary of those who would presume to exploit our anxieties in such a way, aiming to convince us that there are such global conspiracies abroad. See E. Said, 'The Essential Terrorist' in E. Said and C. Hitchens (eds.), *Blaming the Victims: Spurious Scholarship and the Palestinian Question* (Verso, 1988), 157–8.

[4] See B. Barber, *Fear's Empire: War, Terrorism and Democracy* (Norton, 2004), 17–18.

[5] J. Conrad, *The Secret Agent* (Penguin, 2004), 227. For a commentary on the 'terrifying simplicity' of the professor's 'madness', see S. Kim, 'Violence, Irony and Laughter: The Narrator in *The Secret Agent*', *Conradiana*, 35 (2003), 84–5. For a discussion of the novel and its literary context, see T. Eagleton, *Holy Terror* (Oxford University Press, 2005), 91–8, and 121–7.

[6] Though Salman Rushdie is quick to accuse the Bush administration of a wilful nurturing of a 'climate of fear'. See S. Rushdie, 'The Ministry of False Alarms', *Virginia Quarterly Review*, 80 (2004), 5.

We have, of course, come across this kind of rhetoric before. The ringing declarations of January 2002 find an echo in the President's similar invocations of a 'lengthy campaign' against terrorism, one that will dictate whether 'civilisation' can defeat the forces of 'evil', and his advice that the 'war against terror' will be a war for 'progress and pluralism, tolerance and freedom'.[7] They resonate too with Prime Minister Blair's constant warning that our 'whole way of life' is threatened with extinction.[8] And we have come across the intellectual hyperbole too; the suggestion that we are living in an age of hyper or mega-terrorism, that 9/11 is a semiotic of our 'dying culture', an expression of the 'terrorist imagination that dwells in all of us'.[9] The order of the day is hysteria; of precisely the kind that the terrorists pray for.[10] Terrorism sells copy. Our media is every bit as entranced.[11] And so are we. We seem to crave the experience of terror, even as it terrifies us.[12] As Ariel Dorfman has confirmed, 'We have created a planet where what matters most, what sells most, what entertains most is the spectacular. And violence has become the spectacle to end and outsell all spectacles'.[13]

[7] In D. McGoldrick, *From 9–11 to the Iraq War 2003: International Law in an Age of Complexity* (Hart, 2004), 11. We have already encountered German Chancellor Schroeder's equally fantastical rhetoric, that 9/11 represented a 'declaration of war against all of civilization', cited in M. Rasmussen, 'A Parallel Globalization of Terror: 9–11, Security and Globalization', *Cooperation and Conflict*, 37 (2002), 333.

[8] See R. Johnson, 'Defending Ways of Life: The (Anti-)Terrorist Rhetorics of Bush and Blair', *Theory, Culture and Society*, 19 (2002), 211–12.

[9] J. Baudrillard, *The Spirit of Terrorism* (Verso, 2002), 4–5, 64, 73–4. See also Jason Burke's comments regarding a terrorism that is 'new and different, complex and diverse, dynamic and protean and profoundly difficult to categorise', in his *Al-Qaeda: The True Story of Radical Islam* (Penguin, 2004), 1.

[10] Charles Webel chronicles instances of witnesses of 9/11 who remain mentally and emotionally scarred, including those who are subject to repeated hallucinations. See C. Webel, *Terror, Terrorism and the Human Condition* (Palgrave, 2004), 75–80, and also 86–7. The fact that many such hallucinations involved images of Osama bin Laden 'floating in the sky' above the smouldering ruins of the Twin Towers, echoes similar observations chronicled amongst those who milled around the Mall and Buckingham Palace in the hours and days which followed news of the death of Princess Diana. On this occasion, instead of bin Laden, the afflicted claimed to see cloud formations of Diana's profile.

[11] For a caustic critique of the role of the media in the 'age of terror', see T. Kapitan, 'The Terrorism of Terrorism' in J. Sterba (ed.), *Terrorism and International Justice* (Oxford University Press, 2003), 47, 61. For similar observations, see J. Butler, *Precarious Life: The Powers of Mourning and Violence* (Verso, 2004), 39–40, and 150–1, and also G. Achcar, *The Clash of Barbarisms: The Making of the New World Disorder* (Saqi, 2002), 37, accusing the media of joining the 'war effort', and perhaps most stridently, John Pilger, in *Tell Me No Lies: Investigative Journalism and its Triumphs* (Vintage, 2005), at xxiii, decrying the extent to which western media appears to have been duped on a hitherto 'unrecognisable scale'.

[12] See D. Rapoport, 'The International World as Some Terrorists Have Seen It: A Look at a Century of Memoirs', *Journal of Strategic Studies*, 10 (1987), 33, 40–1.

[13] A. Dorfman, *Other Septembers, Many Americas: Selected Provocations 1980–2004*, (Pluto, 2004), 253. We will encounter Don DeLillo's novel *Mao II* in Chapter 6, in which the protagonist, Bill, muses much on precisely this theme.

We also know that perspective can temper hyperbole; that half a million Iraqi children died during the first Gulf War and its aftermath, and that thousands more have died in the present war.[14] But we also know that these are the statistics that tend to be forgotten. For ours is not just an age of hypocrisy, but of calculated amnesia.[15] And of paranoia; a paranoia which, as Richard Hofstadter noted half a century ago, tends to pervade the discourse of terrorism.[16] Alongside the much-vaunted, if oddly elusive, weapons of mass destruction must be placed a different WMD, the writings of mass deception. Within weeks of 9/11, Hollywood moguls were being entertained at the White House, in the hope that they might help craft an effective communication strategy for the 'war on terror'. Watch John Wayne in *The Searchers*, it was suggested, and try to be like him. By lucky, or perhaps unlucky, coincidence, it was anyway one of the President's favourites. Articulating the rhetorical culture of the Wild West, or at least the Wild West envisaged by post-war Hollywood, the President and his army went hunting the 'evil folk'.[17] Before we can comprehend the real challenges of terrorism, and the law which is enacted in pretence of countering it, we have to hack our way through the wedded detritus of pictographic fantasy and linguistic dissimulation.[18] And we must tread carefully. We must, as Norman Mailer advises, have our 'crap-detectors' programmed to full alert; for crap, as we shall see, abounds.[19]

[14] The figure, given by UNICEF, includes those who died during the war, and also during the decade of UN-imposed sanctions that followed. The efficacy of the UN policy is commonly questioned. A 'medieval-style siege', according to John Pilger, 'sanctions of mass destruction', according to Gilbert Achcar. See Pilger, *Lies*, xv, and also 531–2, and Achcar, *Barbarisms*, 30–1. The immediate allusion is to a rigorous policy of sanctions against Iraq following the first Gulf War, which was approved, after considerable US and UK pressure, by the UN. See also Judith Butler in *Precarious Life*, 34–5, suggesting that there is something morally awry in a grievance that is so selective, that is so overwhelmed by the fate of those who died in the Twin Towers, but so underwhelmed by those who died during its prehistory.

[15] For the reference to an 'era of supreme hypocrisy', see Achcar, *Barbarisms*, 155.

[16] Characterised by a determination to effect a 'curious leap of the imagination' at critical points in the 'recital of events'. See R. Hofstadter, *The Paranoid Style in American Politics and Other Essays* (Alfred Knopf, 1966), 37.

[17] Though it vied for popularity amongst Bush's inner cadre of security advisors with the more recent espionage series *24*, the 'hero' of which is notorious for his scant interest in legal niceties. For a discussion of the Hollywood moguls and their recommendation, see S. Faludi, *The Terror Dream: Fear and Fantasy in Post-9/11 America* (Metropolitan Books, 2007), 6–7. For an equally despairing commentary on the influence of *24* and similar series of that ilk, see P. Sands, *Torture Team: Deception, Cruelty and the Compromise of Law* (Penguin, 2008), 89, quoting Homeland Security Secretary John Chertoff affirming admiringly, 'That is what we do every day, that is what we do in government, that's what we do in private life when we evaluate risks'.

[18] For recognition of this need, see C. Gearty, 'Rethinking Civil Liberties in a Counter-Terrorist World', *European Human Rights Law Review* (2007), 111–19.

[19] D. Burrell, 'Narratives Competing for Our Souls' in Sterba, *Terrorism*, 88, 93, and N. Mailer, *Why Are We At War?* (Random House, 2003), 4.

Virtual terror

9/11, as we have already noted, has become an icon; cherished, paradoxically, by both terrorist and counter-terrorist.[20] The 'image consumes the event', colonising the collective memory of a generation.[21] 9/11 is no longer a mere tragedy, an event in which 3,000 innocents were slaughtered. It is an image of our own innermost terrors, our sense of impotence and mortality, our 'theatre of cruelty' indeed.[22] Violence, as Baudrillard observes, is often 'banal'. But symbolic violence is devastating. It never leaves us. Time and again, we see the same planes crash into the same buildings, the same victims leap to their death.[23] Seyla Benhabib deploys a phrase which will resonate even more with the subject of the next chapter, the unhealthy relation of theology and terror. 9/11, she suggests, represents an 'unholy' coming together, a 'sublime combination of high tech wizardry and moral and political atavism'.[24]

As we shall see in Chapter 6, the impact of 9/11 was such that, in the short run at least, we seemed to lose our capacity, even our will, to speak. Sat before his keyboard, Martin Amis famously confessed to a feeling of 'gangrenous futility'.[25] It was, as Susan Faludi confirms, a 'terrible' moment, one in which no one seemed to know what to 'say'.[26] If our capacity to rationalise was momentarily lost it is hardly surprising. The imagery surpasses the rational, becoming alternatively virtual and sublime. Alluding to the stunning imagery of 9/11, Malise Ruthven refers to our 'hypnagogic state lying somewhere between dream and wakeful fancy'.[27] Faludi depicts a 'terror dream'.[28] Slavoj Zizek refers to a 'process of virtualization', where the spectacle assumes its own 'reality'.[29] Ahdaf Soueif concurs; the destruction of the Twin Towers describes the dreaming of a 'nightmare into reality'. For decades, she

---

[20] See M. Amis, *The Second Plane* (Jonathan Cape, 2008), 4–6, Rasmussen, 'Globalization', 342, and also Baudrillard, *Spirit of Terrorism*, 43–7 and 52 discussing the 'symbolic potency' of the event. As Ruthven notes, the image of Osama bin Laden has assumed pretty much the same iconic status, again cherished by both terrorist and counter-terrorist alike. See his *Fury*, 305.

[21] See Baudrillard, *Spirit of Terrorism*, 27, and also 28–9, and also F. Dallmayr, 'Lessons of September 11', *Theory, Culture & Society*, 19 (2002), 137.

[22] Baudrillard, *Spirit of Terrorism*, 30. See also Amis, *Plane*, 195–6, commenting on the semiotic of 9/11, one that 'sounds snappy and contemporary and wised-up'.

[23] See Baudrillard, *Spirit of Terrorism*, 29–30, 34.

[24] S. Benhabib, 'Unholy Wars', *Constellations*, 9 (2002), 35.

[25] Amis, *Plane*, 12. See also *Guardian Review*, 19 May 2007, 4, citing the similar sentiments of Jay McInerney and Ian McEwan.

[26] Faludi, *Dream*, 339.   [27] Ruthven, *Fury*, 1–2.

[28] The metaphor is deployed throughout *Dream*. For an initial justification, see 2–6.

[29] Zizek, *Desert*, 9–11, 16. See also F. Megret, 'Justice in Times of Violence', *European Journal of International Law*, 14 (2003), 330–1; M. Cusimano, 'Globalization, Ethics, and the War on Terrorism', *Notre Dame Journal of Law, Ethics and Public Policy*, 16 (2002), 66, 77; X. Raufer, 'New World Disorder, New Terrorisms: new Threats for Europe and the Western World', *Terrorism and Political Violence*, 11 (1999), 30–51; and T. Homer-Dixon, 'The Rise of Complex Terrorism', *Foreign Policy* (Jan/Feb 2002), 52–62. For similar sentiments, see also Gary Hart, *Power: A Grand Strategy for the United States in the Twenty-First Century* (Oxford University Press, 2004), 5–7, 19–20, 65–6, 109.

observes, generations of Americans had spent their Saturday afternoons, if not watching John Wayne westerns, savouring Bruce Willis and Mel Gibson fighting swarthy Arab terrorists in cinemas from New York to Nevada.[30] The reality and the fantasy become ever more difficult to detach.

Both Damien Hirst and Karl Heinz Stockhausen courted controversy in describing the destruction of the Twin Towers as a 'work of art'.[31] The attack was intended to be spectacular, to paint a picture, however gruesome and terrifying. The determination 'to remake the world by spectacular acts of terror' is a defining characteristic of contemporary terrorism.[32] The 9/11 acts were just the most obviously spectacular of all.[33] In one of his justificatory videos, bin Laden himself emphasised that the targets of 9/11 were particular 'icons' of US 'military and economic power'.[34] In his post-9/11 novel, *The Reluctant Fundamentalist*, Mohsin Ahmed testifies to the success of the strategy. Whilst admitting that his reaction betokens a momentary failure of compassion, Ahmed's Pakistani waiter Changez confesses to an inability to suppress a smile on seeing images of the attack; 'I was caught up in the symbolism of it all, the fact that somebody had so visibly brought America to its knees'.[35]

[30] A. Soueif, *Mezzaterra: Fragments from the Common Ground* (Anchor, 2004), 65.

[31] The observation was, for obvious reasons, controversial, not least insofar as it appeared to be somehow unsympathetic, perhaps even tending to glorify the event. Such a response, however, is more visceral than sensible. As Malise Ruthven has suggested 'public indignation does not diminish the force of the observation'; in 'the video age the literalness of the image replaces the density of language'. See Ruthven, *Fury*, 31. See also K. Hayward and W. Morrison, 'Locating Ground Zero: Caught Between the Narratives of Crime and War' in J. Strawson, *Law After Ground Zero* (Glasshouse, 2002), 144. For a similar sentiment, see J. Habermas, 'Dialogue' in G. Borradori (ed.), *Philosophy in a Time of Terror: Dialogues with Juergen Habermas and Jacques Derrida* (Chicago University Press, 2003), 28. The broad insinuation, that 9/11 was a piece of art, finds an echo in Terry Eagleton's recent appraisal of terrorists as nihilists and thus 'supreme artists, conjuring into existence a nothingness so pure that it beggars all other artefacts, with their inevitable blemishes and imperfections'. See his *Holy Terror*, 119.

[32] J. Gray, *Al-Qaeda and What it Means to be Modern* (Faber and Faber, 2003), 22.

[33] See W. Sofsky, *Violence: Terrorism, Genocide, War* (Granta, 2003), 181–2, observing that the 9/11 targets were 'an emblem of the great international metropolis, the monument of the world market, the hubris of an urban culture that has built its edifices to God-like heights'.

[34] See A. Houen, *Terrorism and Modern Literature: From Joseph Conrad to Ciaran Carson* (Oxford University Press, 2002), 3, and also M. Cox, 'September 11th and US Hegemony – Or Will the 21st Century be American Too?' *International Studies Perspectives*, 3 (2002), 53–4, emphasising the symbolic import of the destruction of the Twin Towers. The 'perfect embodiments', as Jean Baudrillard puts it, of the hatred which so much of the globe feels towards the US. See Baudrillard, *Spirit of Terrorism*, 6. For similar suggestions, that the 'root' of 9/11 is a simple hatred of the US, see Ruthven, *Furry*, 29–30 and also B. Cordes, 'When Terrorists Do the Talking: Reflections on Terrorist Literature', *Journal of Strategic Studies*, 10 (1987), 163–4, emphasising the extent to which terrorist activities have, down the centuries, tended to be expressions of anti-imperial or post-colonial resentment. In this context, perhaps, a hatred of the US becomes more comprehendible. Judith Butler quotes Arundhati Roy's resonant observation, that bin Laden and Al-Qaeda were 'sculpted from the spare rib of a world laid waste by America's foreign policy'. See Butler, *Precarious Life*, 10.

[35] His following observation has an added, if different, prescience. Anticipating the horror that such a comment will have on his American conversant, Changez asks, 'Do you feel no joy at the video-clips – so prevalent these days – of American munitions laying waste the structures of your enemies?' See M. Ahmed, *The Reluctant Fundamentalist* (Hamish Hamilton, 2007), 73.

Understood in these terms, the destruction of the Twin Towers resonates with the 'propaganda by deed' terrorism of the Russian nihilists during the last decades of the late nineteenth century; a species to which we shall return in Chapter 5.[36] Spectacle is everything. Terrorism is theatre.[37] There is no point, as one senior Al-Qaeda spokesman put it, in terrorist 'volunteers' killing, and being killed, 'in silence'.[38] Publicity is the oxygen that the terrorist craves; and the counter-terrorist too. Their mutual relation, and their 'symbiotic' relationship with the media, is the pivot around which modern terrorist discourse revolves.[39] Hijacked planes are intended to be spectacular events; perhaps the most spectacular of all. So too the filming of terrified kidnap victims pleading for their lives and then being beheaded on tape has a ritualistic, as well as repellent, quality. It has been suggested that one of the characteristics of militant Islamic terrorism is a fetish for ritualised cruelty.[40] Perhaps. But it is not an exclusive characteristic. Abu Ghraib destroyed this convenient ascription.[41] 'Shock and awe' was intended to be spectacular; to impress those of us who watched it unfold in the living rooms of London and Washington, and to terrify those who shivered in anticipation in the cellars of Basra and Baghdad.[42] Terror is no less terrifying for being 'virtual'. It is the experience that terrifies. And a terror that becomes normalised, a 'banal' terror, as Baudrillard puts it, can be just as terrifying, a 'living' terror.[43]

---

[36] As we shall see, it was within this context that Conrad set his novel *The Secret Agent*. See also Ruthven, *Fury*, 127, and also 207 quoting George Sorel, who declared that, in promoting the cause of revolutionary fascism, 'use must be made of a body of images which, by intuition alone, and before any considered analyses were made, is capable of evoking as an undivided whole the mass of sentiments which corresponds to the different manifestations of the war undertaken by Socialism'.

[37] See Brian Jenkins's observations, quoted in P. Rees, *Dining with Terrorists* (Macmillan, 2005), 19, and also M. Stohl, 'Old Myths, New Fantasies and the Enduring Realities of Terrorism', *Critical Studies on Terrorism*, 1 (2008), 8–9.

[38] Quoted in J. Burke, 'Theatre of Terror', the *Observer*, 21 November 2004, Review, 2.

[39] See Houen, *Terrorism*, 11–13, and also A. Kubiak, *Stages of Terror: Terrorism, Ideology, and Coercion as Theatre History* (Indiana University Press, 1991), 1–2, 157, and also Soueif, *Mezzaterra*, 72, making reference to a western media 'shivering deliciously in anticipation' of the copy that will be sold as the 'war on terror' develops.

[40] W. Lacqueur, *No End to War* (Continuum, 2004), 44–5.

[41] See J. Pugliese, 'Abu Ghraib and its Shadow Archives', *Law and Literature*, 19 (2007), 247–76, exploring the ritualised, especially sexual, nature of the abuse suffered by Iraqi prisoners, male and female, in Abu Ghraib. It represents, Pugliese argues, a 'geocorpography of torture', one that resonates with an inherited 'imperial-fascist aesthetics' which can be traced through much of American history.

[42] As Ted Koppel, former ABC newscaster, observed, 'without television, terrorism becomes rather like the philosopher's hypothetical tree falling in a forest; no one hears it fall, and therefore it has no reason for being'. And counter-terrorism too. Quoted in J. Zulaika and W. Douglass, *Terror and Taboo: The Follies, Fables and Faces of Terrorism* (Routledge, 1996), 7. See also Ruthven, *Fury*, 27.

[43] See Baudrillard, *Spirit of Terrorism*, 10, 81, confirming that 'we now live in a state of perpetual terror'. See also Jackson, *Writing*, 94–5, 112–14, and Christopher Blakesley, 'Ruminations on Terrorism and Anti-Terrorism in Law and Literature', *University of Miami Law Review*, 57 (2003), 1045, musing on the idea of a 'banal' terror.

Here amidst the miasma of imagery and iconography terrorism starts to look rather different. And the challenges change too.[44] For terrorism is not, as Terry Eagleton has recently observed, 'political in any conventional sense of the term'.[45] Very quickly it becomes apparent that terrorism is an innately narrative and rhetorical experience, a function of myriad stories and discourses, metaphors and mythologies. And this means that terrorism is culturally 'embedded'; something that can only be understood within the context of immediate narratives.[46] Terrorists, and counter-terrorists, are thoroughly immersed in forms of artistic expression, generally witting, occasionally not. The expressions might be grotesque, but they remain artistic in that they intend to convey impressions.[47]

The discourse of terrorism is one of 'collective enchantment', one of 'secrecy, masks and hidden agendas', of what Edward Said terms 'fantasies and fixations'.[48] It possesses, as Michel Foucault confirms, a 'magical aspect'. The politics of violence, pursued as it is by terrorist and counter-terrorist alike, seeks to 'dazzle', to 'fascinate, terrorize and immobilize' in equal measure.[49] In such an enchanted ring it becomes possible to compass fake terrorist attacks, as the Macedonian government did, in a bid to curry the approbation of the US.[50] Terror begets terror, myth breeds more myth, and history gets to be constantly rewritten.[51] At the same time, cast in such a mythical dimension, the discourse of terrorism remains radically, and virulently unstable, a myriad competition of discursive strategies and narratives, a 'barrage', as Gilbert Achcar puts it, 'of vicious polemical artillery'.[52]

[44] For, as Christian Bourguet has emphasised, the issue of terrorism must always be comprehended on a 'plane of symbols'. Quoted in Pilger, *Lies*, 594. See also Kapitan, 'Terrorism', 48–51.

[45] Eagleton, *Holy Terror*, vi.

[46] According to Khachig Tololyan one of the chief failings of so much critical commentary on terrorism is that it tends to the analytical and universal, presuming certain core characteristics that might be uncovered. The reality is quite the reverse, and it is for this reason that a narrative approach offers itself as the more credible strategy. See K. Tololyan, 'Culture Narrative and the Motivation of the Terrorist', *Journal of Strategic Studies*, 10 (1987), especially 217–20.

[47] See W. Lacqueur, *Terrorism* (Weidenfeld & Nicholson, 1977), 219.

[48] Quoted in Pilger, *Lies*, 597. See also R. Leeman, *The Rhetoric of Terrorism and Counter-Terrorism* (Greenwood Press, 1991), 13–17, 52–5, and Zulaika and Douglass, *Terror*, 82–3, 186–90, 210–12, 226.

[49] A model which, he concluded, must, if humanity is to progress, be abandoned. See M. Foucault, *Society Must Be Defended* (Penguin, 2003), 68, 72, 265, 270.

[50] The counter to the fake attack entailed the murder of a group of illegal immigrants. See A. Roberts, 'Righting Wrongs or Wronging Rights? The United States and Human Rights Post-September 11', *European Journal of International Law*, 15 (2004), 734.

[51] Burke, *Al-Qaeda*, 20. As Sofsky concludes, 'illusions are the engines that propel' violence. See his *Violence*, 171.

[52] Achcar, *Barbarisms*, 23. The 'war on terror', suggests Ahdaf Soueif, is best understood as a 'battle of the images'. See her *Mezzaterra*, 73, and also Jackson, *Writing*, 183, commenting on the particular virulence of rhetorical exchanges in the present 'war on terror'. For a general commentary on the importance of the rhetorical and discursive engagements, see Rapoport, 'Memoirs', 40–1 and also Butler, *Precarious Life*, 82–3, discussing the various 'speech act' strategies of terrorist and counter-terrorist. See also Tololyan, 'Narrative', 218–19, 222–3 and 231, stressing the complexity of relations between 'master-narratives' and their myriad constituent 'micro-narratives'. As an example of this

The 'terrorist' aspires to fetishism, to fabricate a mythic image of transcendental heroism, even goodness.[53] The Russian nihilist Stepniak wrote that the terrorist should be regarded as 'noble, terrible, irresistibly fascinating, for he combines in himself the two sublimities of human grandeur: the martyr and the hero'.[54] Such, of course, frames the myth of the suicide-bomber; a myth that seems fanatical, but which also inheres its own peculiar rationality.[55] A death that is ritualised seems, somehow, to make sense; at least to an impressionable, generally young and ill-educated, putative martyr.[56] In this context, whether it makes sense to the Enlightenment rationalist matters rather less.[57] Terrorist confessions and chronicles are written precisely to nourish this kind of dramatic and ritualised fetishism.[58] Terrorist literature is commonly characterised by a determination to establish legitimacy; suicide and martyrdom represent an extreme example of such justificatory narratives.[59] Such narratives become, perhaps inevitably, also discourses of denial. The attempt to establish legitimacy, to justify acts of extreme political violence, entails a complementary denial of responsibility.[60] And justification too; the expression of presumed theological, political, cultural or economic grievances.[61] Such grievances might or might not be valid. It rarely matters. It is a testament to the effectiveness of terrorist rhetoric that so many, around so much of the world, believe the rhetoric, and subscribe to the mythology.[62]

The engagement of terrorist and counter-terrorist, as Lawrence Freedman has recently confirmed is a 'battle of narratives', and the immediate counter-

compelling 'intertextuality', Tololyan suggests an Armenian terrorist whose motivation might be framed by a geo-political master-narrative regarding Armenian independence, but which is itself the construct of various micro-narratives emanating from a 'network of churches, schools, athletic unions, youth and student groups'.

[53] For a compelling account of ETA's attempts to craft such a narrative, see Zulaika and Douglass, *Terror*, 37–44.

[54] From his *Underground*, quoted in Houen, *Terrorism*, 57. Stepniak was chiefly notorious for executing the assassination of the Russian General Mesentzoff in 1878.

[55] See Ruthven, *Fury*, 28, observing that 'while brutal both for the perpetrators and the victims, the suicide-bombing tactic is not irrational', and also 101–2, commenting that, alongside religious zeal, the 'fury' that possesses the Islamic suicide-bomber can also be rationalised in terms of political, social and economic 'despair', and 132–3, concluding that events such as 9/11 should, thus, be understood 'not as a gesture of Islamic heroism, but of Nietzschean despair'.

[56] On the walls of Hamas Kindergarten can be found the injunction 'The Children are the Holy Martyrs of Tomorrow'. Cited in Lacqueur, *War*, 94. See also Eagleton, *Holy Terror*, 90–3, M. Ignatieff, *The Lesser Evil: Political Ethics in an Age of Terror* (Edinburgh University Press, 2005), 131, and also Sofsky, *Violence*, 31, suggesting that the 'festival of violence' which encapsulates martyrdom 'fulfils an ancient yearning: the dream of absolute power, of absolute freedom and wholeness, the dream of a return to paradise'.

[57] See Lacqueur, *War*, 71, and more recently J. Gray, *Black Mass: Apocalyptic Religion and the Death of Utopia* (Penguin, 2007), 177, suggesting that, seen within the context of the particular history of Enlightenment utopianism, modern terrorism, either secular or theological, is entirely rational.

[58] Such testimonies have been termed 'auto-propagandist', see Cordes, 'Literature', 155–6. See also Leeman, *Rhetoric*, 14–15, and Rapoport, 'Memoirs', 50–5.

[59] Cordes, 'Literature', 157, 161.   [60] Cordes, 'Literature', 150–1.

[61] Lacqueur, *Terrorism*, 219–23.   [62] Lacqueur, *Terrorism*, 223–4

terrorist strategy is to attempt to retrieve this narrative; on the one hand to destroy the myth of the terrorist as hero, and on the other to present a counter-discourse.[63] It must, first, be a counter-discourse of defiance. The 'terrorist' never wins we are told repeatedly; even if history suggests that more often than not they either win hands down, as in France in 1790 or Palestine in 1948, or at the very least secure considerable political concessions, as in Northern Ireland in 1998.[64] At this point, of course, the maligned campaign of terrorist atrocities tends to be recast as a national struggle for liberation, whilst its pursuers undertake the mandatory rhetorical makeover, transformed from murderous terrorist to lauded freedom fighter.[65]

Meanwhile, the heroes of counter-terrorism parade themselves, loud and vital, in the living-rooms of their terrified compatriots. In the days immediately following 9/11, everyone went in search of new superheroes, and ended up instead with paler imitations of latter-day Jimmy Stewarts. Former President Clinton raced back from Australia in order to be seen amidst the carnage, and most importantly before his successor; only to find that Mayor Giuliani had got there first and already sequestered the front pages. The rapidity of Clinton's return lead to bitter rejoinders from an affronted administration which assumed that, as a matter of decorum, their President should have been the first to be seen on prime-time television emoting amidst the rubble.[66] But no one was inclined to wait as Air Force One went back and forth across the skies of North America waiting for the President and his advisors to decide what to do.[67]

Second, it must be a discourse of demonisation.[68] As Ariel Dorfman observes, down the centuries 'generals and politicians have always known

---

[63] As Richard Jackson argues, 'the practice of counter-terrorism is predicated on and determined by the language of counter-terrorism'. See his *Writing*, at 8. For similar conclusions, see also Hayward and Morrison, 'Ground Zero', 151–2, and Leeman, *Rhetoric*, 2–5. For Freedman's observations, see his 'Terrorism as a Strategy', *Government and Opposition*, 42 (2007), 316–17.

[64] See Stohl, 'Old Myths', 10–11, dispelling the rhetorical assumption that terrorism is futile. As Stohl affirms, terrorism may be an inhuman strategy, but only very rarely is it futile. More often than not, a terrorist organisation secures some kind of concession.

[65] As Leila Khaled observed, prior to their campaign of hijackings in 1970, no one had paid much attention to starving Palestinian refugees. Thereafter everyone knew about their fate, and the liberal editorials, political summits and peace plans flowed. In V. Held, 'Terrorism and War', *Journal of Ethics*, 8 (2004), 69. For a rather jaundiced commentary on this process of conceptual re-calibration, see M. Burleigh, *Blood and Rage: A Cultural History of Terrorism* (HarperCollins, 2008), 150–1, focusing particularly on colonial wars of liberation, and again at 345 referring to the 'divine injustice' of the Good Friday agreement of 1998, which purported to end the Northern Irish 'Troubles'.

[66] See Hayward and Morrison, 'Ground Zero', 151–2 and also Faludi, *Dream*, 49–50.

[67] The fact that the President had, on being told that hijacked planes had struck New York and destroyed the Twin Towers, continued to finish reading *My Little Pony* to a class of school children, and then allowed himself, for the next few hours, to be flown around America in Air Force One, whilst his advisors tried to work out what was happening, did attract early mutterings of disappointment. Surely a real Wild West hero might have acted with rather greater decisiveness, and courage? But the grander narrative, and a sympathetic media, served to quiet such mutterings.

[68] Gray, *Black Mass*, 117–18.

that it is easier to kill an enemy whom one can portray as a demon'.[69] In an immediate sense, the rabid Islamic fundamentalist could be slotted into the space vacated a decade earlier by the menacing Communist fundamentalist.[70] But the theological edge makes a difference. The emergent 'Islamic terrorist' discourse frames a deeper fear, a deeper hate. Over 6,000 speeches given by administration officials in the two years following 9/11 reinforced the image of the Islamic terrorist as the 'paradigm of inhuman bestiality', someone who dwelt in the 'darkness'.[71] Former Secretary of State Baker asserted that America had been attacked by 'animals', and it was not intended to be a merely metaphorical insinuation.[72] Attorney-General Ashcroft proffered a similarly stark demarcation, between the 'civil and the savage'.[73] And, as we shall see in the next chapter, alongside the demonisation of the bestial could be found the demonisation of the infidel. The 'animals' that had attacked America also believed in the wrong prophet and the wrong faith.

Third, it must be a discourse of fear, and justification.[74] It is a Faustian pact; states need terrorists, just as terrorists crave states to terrorise.[75] They need a citizenry that is 'transfixed by fear', one that craves protection, even at the cost of sacrificing its most basic political liberties and social goods.[76] In the weeks that followed 9/11, 'moms and dads' were urged to hold 'their children closer and maybe for a moment longer'.[77] And the need is all the greater in the absence of any alternative bogey that can be deployed to terrify the masses.[78] The danger is great, terrifying indeed; only trust in government can deflect the terrorist

---

[69] A. Dorfman, *Other Septembers*, 57. For an equally astute commentary on demonisation, see Robert Fisk's observations in Pilger, *Lies*, 275–6.

[70] See Johnson, 'Ways of Life', 216.

[71] For an overview of this strategy, see Jackson, *Writing*, 48–9, 61–2, 75–6, and also 'Constructing Enemies: Islamic Terrorism in Political and Academic Discourse', *Government and Opposition*, 42 (2007), 407–12. See also Zizek, *Desert*, 33–4; Johnson, 'Ways of Life', 221; T. Seto, 'The Morality of Terrorism', *Loyola of Los Angeles Law Review*, 35 (2002), 1261; and also M. Stohl, 'Old Myths', 7–9.

[72] In Jackson, *Writing*, 48.

[73] In Jackson, *Writing*, 49. For a condemnation of such ascriptions as a form of 'playground ethics', see Achcar, *Barbarisms*, 28.

[74] See Kapitan, 'Terrorism', 53, and also Barber, *Fear's Empire*, 33, 36–7, stressing the extent to which the twin policies of US 'exceptionalism' and a 'war on terror' are dependent upon maintaining the mass of American citizens in a state of suspended terror. America, Barber suggests, has become the 'capital of fear's spreading empire'.

[75] See N. Chomsky, *Hegemony of Survival: America's Quest for Global Dominion* (Penguin, 2004), 115–20; Jackson, *Writing*, 117; and also Zulaika and Douglass, *Terror*, 234–5.

[76] D. Burrell, 'Narratives Competing for Our Souls' in Sterba, *Terrorism*, 95. Jackson reaches a similar conclusion, accusing government officials, in the US and the UK, of being 'engaged in the deliberate construction of a world of unimaginable dangers and unspeakable fears'. See *Writing*, 120. So does Rushdie, in 'Ministry', 5–7.

[77] See Johnson, 'Ways of Life', 218.

[78] Slavoj Zizek has recently argued that the 'west' has constructed a 'war on terrorism' as the most obvious, and most convenient, successor to the Cold War. See S. Zizek, 'Are We in a War? Do We Have an Enemy?' *London Review of Books*, 24 (2002). The suspicion that the mythology of terrorism is invariably deployed in order to ensure the continued presence of a common 'other' is sadly familiar. See Said, 'Essential Terrorist', 149.

threat. 'Trust' and 'threat'; two more words which laced counter-terrorist rhetoric on both sides of the Atlantic in the months and years which followed 9/11.[79] Half a century ago, President Roosevelt famously advised that the only thing a free society needs to fear is 'fear itself'.[80] We should remain sceptical of those who would terrify us, who would have us believe that the terrorism inflicted by 'others' threatens our very way of life. It does not. The instruments of counter-terrorism, however, just might.

The rhetorical struggle is, then, a treacherous one, engaged in a linguistic environment, to borrow Derrida's phrase, of 'semantic instability'.[81] The 'first symptom of the barbarization of thought', as Ahdaf Soueif reminds us, 'is the corruption of language'.[82] And few discourses are more readily corrupted than the terrorist; a discourse which, by definition, represents a 'distortion in communication'.[83] The problem is that we, the audience, are the third party to this corrupted discourse.[84] We have to try to make some sense of all this, pick our way through the heroes and anti-heroes, the mythologies and the realities.[85] We have to try to work out what 'insurgents' are, and what they do, when they are terrorists and when they are not. We are left to muse on the pretended distinctions between 'coercive interrogation' and torture, to ponder the differences between lawful and 'unlawful' combatants, when rendition is ordinary and when it is 'extraordinary'.[86]

And it is not easy. For a start, we are not supposed to engage our own imaginations too much. Interaction with the terrorist 'other' is violation of a taboo.[87] We are supposed to be terrified. We are not supposed to do anything that might lead us to understand, still less sympathise, with this 'other'. Our engagement in the discourse of terror is supposed to be passive.[88] The 'language of terrorism', as Conor Gearty concludes, 'has become the rhetorical servant of the established order, wherever it might be, and however heinous its own activities are'.[89] It is not to be questioned; merely accepted.

---

[79] In Jackson, *Writing*, 100–13   [80] Quoted in Barber, *Fear's Empire*, 50.

[81] In J. Derrida, 'Dialogue' in Borradori, *Philosophy*, 105.

[82] Soueif, *Mezzaterra*, 15.   [83] Habermas, 'Dialogue', 35.   [84] Leeman, *Rhetoric*, 20–1.

[85] Robert Fisk puts it nicely as he muses on possible inversions of counter-terrorist rhetoric, 'Surely, if you could leap from being a terrorist to an insurgent with a little hop, skip and a jump, you could become a freedom-fighter'. Quoted in Rees, *Dining*, 4.

[86] See A. Chaskalson, 'Counter-Terrorism, Human Rights and the Rule of Law', *Cambridge Law Journal*, 67 (2008), 75, citing UNHCR chief Mary Robinson's caustic dismissal of a counter-terrorist rhetoric of 'Orwellian euphemisms', and likewise pondering a political discourse which has increasingly resembled that preferred by Lewis Carroll's Humpty Dumpty, where words can mean anything the speaker wants them to.

[87] Zulaika and Douglass, *Terror*, x.

[88] See Barber, *Fear's Empire*, 234, noting that the 'empire of fear is a realm without citizens, a domain of spectators, of subjects and victims whose passivity means helplessness and whose helplessness defines and sharpens the fear'.

[89] See C. Gearty, 'Terrorism and Morality', *European Human Rights Law Review* (2003), 380, and also 'Civil Liberties', particularly 111 and 116–19 reinvesting the same argument.

Purified by terror and pity

Once again, of course, we have been here before. 9/11 has an intellectual, and aesthetic, progenitor. Two centuries ago, Europe was similarly terrified and troubled, titillated and thrilled; on the one hand by the apparently apocalyptic events in France during the revolution and the Great Terror that followed, and on the other by the associated intellectual furore that erupted over the implications of a radical and violent politics that was as much about the spectacular and the sublime as it was the limits of reason.[90] The modern terrorist, and the counter-terrorist, as John Gray has recently confirmed, are both 'disciples' of Maximilian Robespierre and his fellow Jacobin zealots.[91]

At the grand Festival of Supreme Being, held at the Champ de Mars in Paris in 1794, Robespierre had offered the violence of the Terror as a sacrifice to the 'cult of sensibility'.[92] 'The true priest of the Supreme Being', he declared to his presumably bemused, if awed, audience, 'is Nature itself; its temple is the universe; its religion virtue; its festivals the joy of a great people assembled under its eyes to tie the sweet knot of universal fraternity and to present before it the homage of pure and feeling hearts'. The purgation of terror, he went on to imply, was an expression of nature, of a politics of feeling, ultimately, at an extreme, of a politics of the sublime.[93] Its self-styled champions revelled in the very idea of being instigators of terror.[94] And so the blood flowed.

And, as it did, attitudes across Europe, and particularly across the Channel, changed too. Initial enthusiasm for the cause of 'liberty, equality, fraternity' gave way to horror. The Beast of the Apocalypse was abroad, or so countless pulpits up and down England declaimed. The heroes of liberty were quickly recast as emissaries of the anti-Christ, the progenitors indeed of the modern terrorist. Edmund Burke had celebrated the revolution of 1789 as a most 'wonderful Spectacle'. A year later, in his *Reflections on the*

---

[90] As Terry Eagleton comments, 'terrorism and the modern democratic state were twinned at birth'. In *Holy Terror*, at 1. Percy Shelley was troubled by precisely this realisation, readily admitting that the French Revolution was, accordingly, the 'master theme of the epoch in which we live'. See C. Duffy, *Shelley and the Revolutionary Sublime* (Cambridge University Press, 2005), 124. For a discussion of this wider intellectual context, one which finds its roots in earlier Enlightenment studies of the relation of reason and feeling, such as Adam Smith's *Theory of Moral Sentiments* and David Hume's *Treatise of Human Nature*, see I. Ward, 'The Echo of a Sentimental Jurisprudence', *Law and Critique*, 13 (2002), 107–16.

[91] Gray, *Black Mass*, 27, adding at 36, that the 'role of the Enlightenment in twentieth-century terror remains a blind spot in western perception'. In *Blood and Rage*, Michael Burleigh confirms, at 71, the extent to which the image of the Jacobin terrorist inspired successive generations of nineteenth century radicals.

[92] Borrowing very obviously from Rousseau.

[93] Cited and discussed in S. Schama, *Citizens: A Chronicle of the French Revolution* (Penguin, 1989), 831–6. The idea of terror as purgation is also discussed in Gray, *Black Mass*, 26–8, 70.

[94] As described by Ruthven, in *Fury*, at 281.

Revolution in France, he published the first canon of the modern counter-terrorist polemic.[95]

At the heart of *Reflections* could be found Burke's notorious depiction of the rape of Marie Antoinette; or at least the rape of her bedroom.[96] On the morning of 6 October 1789, Burke recounted, 'after a day of confusion, alarm, dismay, and slaughter', the king and queen had lain down for a 'few hours of respite, and troubled, melancholy repose'. They were out of luck, for:

> From this sleep the queen was first startled by the voice of a centinel at her door, who cried out to her, to save herself by flight – that this was the last proof of fidelity he could give – that they were upon him, and he was dead. Instantly he was cut down. A band of cruel ruffians and assassins, reeking with his blood, rushed into the chamber of the queen, and pierced with an hundred strokes of bayonets and poniards the bed, from whence this persecuted woman had but just time to fly almost naked, and through ways unknown to the murderers had escaped to seek refuge at the feet of a king and husband, not secure of his own life for a moment.[97]

Burke and his contemporaries viewed the invasion of Versailles, with much the same horror as we contemplate 9/11 or 7/7.[98] The unthinkable had happened. It might have happened most immediately to others, but it was experienced, so Burke imputed, by all right-thinking English men and women.[99]

---

[95] Burke's initial enthusiasm was shared by Charles Fox, who declared, 'How much the greatest event it is that ever happened in the world and how much the best'. For his and Burke's expressions of welcome, see I. Ward, *A State of Mind? The English Constitution and the Popular Imagination* (Sutton, 2000), 133–5. Expressions of enthusiasm were not, of course, limited to certain Englishmen or Frenchmen. Far away in Prussia, Immanuel Kant wrote, 'But I maintain that this revolution has aroused in the hearts and desires of all spectators who are not themselves caught up in it a sympathy which borders almost on enthusiasm, although the very utterance of this sympathy was fraught with danger. It cannot therefore have been caused by anything other than a moral disposition with the human race'. In H. Reiss (ed.), *Kant: Political Writings* (Cambridge University Press, 1991), 182.

[96] According to Isaac Kramnick, Burke's *Reflections* 'reach their literary, emotional, and theoretical crescendo in the passages Burke devotes to the queen'. See his *The Rage of Edmund Burke: Portrait of an Ambivalent Conservative* (Basic Books, 1977), 31. The 'stripping' of the queen is also presented by Tom Furniss, as the central moment in the *Reflections*. See his *Edmund Burke's Aesthetic Ideology: Language, Gender and Political Economy in Revolution* (Cambridge University Press, 1993), Chapter 6. More recently, Andrew Stauffer has referred to the passage as the 'lightning-rod' for popular debates regarding the French Revolution, in his *Anger, Revolution and Romanticism* (Cambridge University Press, 2005), 44.

[97] E. Burke, *Reflections on the Revolution in France* (Penguin, 1986), 164. For a commentary on the rape imagery in Burke's account of Marie Antoinette's flight, see Furniss, *Aesthetic Ideology*, 154–7, and also Kramnick, *Rage*, 151–5.

[98] Burke was certainly not alone in exploiting the iconic potential framed by the fall of Versailles. A suitably excitable version was printed in *The London Times* on 12 October. It was later deployed by Alfred Cobban in his seminal *A History of Modern France* (Penguin, 1957), vol. I, 161–2. For an account of the extent to which Burke's fantastical account embedded itself in English Jacobin historiography, see Furniss, *Aesthetic Ideology*, 139–40.

[99] A textual battlefield, as Furniss puts it. See his *Aesthetic Ideology*, 141. Eagleton refers to a necessary and 'salutary stiffening of the sublime', in *Holy Terror*, at 54. Richard McLamore similarly emphasises the extent to which Burke was aware of the need to engage a textual and discursive counter-terrorist strategy. See his '"To Forge a New Language": Burke and Paine', *Prose Studies*, 16 (1993), 179–92.

In composing his *Reflections* on the Terror, Burke was, of course, engaging a far wider debate regarding the politics of the sublime.[100] In his earlier *Philosophical Enquiry*, he had contrasted the metaphysical idea of the sublime, as that which is 'fitted in any sort to excite ideas of pain' or 'terror', with the beautiful, which excites feelings of 'pleasure'.[101] The disposition of the mind, he added, is governed by these two 'simple ideas', pain and pleasure.[102] They describe the political aesthetic; not just the nature of political judgement, but also the reception of political injunctions. In this way, the success or failure of politics can be understood in terms of the success or failure of its aesthetic, and the political imagination, and discourse, which it frames. In his *Reflections*, Burke referred to this as the 'moral constitution of the heart'.[103]

Events in revolutionary France merely served to convince Burke of the acuity of his intellectual prophecies, not just those that cast politics as a matter of aesthetics as well as reason, but also those that spoke to the related ideas of the 'false sublime' and the sublime of negativity. The French Revolution was presented as an exemplar of the 'false sublime'; a perverted sublime which, rather than approaching a metaphysical or natural majesty, had been perverted by crude political ideology and common bloodlust.[104] At the same time, it just as readily confirmed his belief that the idea of the sublime was critically bifurcated; the positive sublime being an expression of the beneficent power of nature, the negative sublime being an expression of the malevolent forces of fear and terror.

And deep down was the persistent fear that the latter sublime was the dominant, even the purest representation.[105] In his *Philosophical Enquiry*, Burke had observed:

> There is no spectacle we so eagerly pursue, as that of some uncommon and grievous calamity; so that whether the misfortune is before our eyes, or whether they are turned back to it in history, it always touches with delight.[106]

---

[100] Much of the debate oscillated around the issue of whether the sublime was driven by a divine or a natural metaphysics. Second generation romantics such as Shelley or Keats inclined strongly to the latter option, which became commonly known as the British 'school'. Those of Burke's generation, including Burke himself, tended to be more ambivalent, recognising the inevitability of nature as a prime mover in describing the individual, and political, imagination, but eschewing the more radical atheistic implications. For a recent discussion of this dilemma, see Duffy, *Shelley*, 13–23, 29–30, 33–7.

[101] E. Burke, *A Philosophical Enquiry* (Oxford University Press, 1990), 36–7, 53–4, 113.

[102] Burke, *Enquiry*, 30–1. For commentaries, see Furniss, *Aesthetic Ideology*, 17–40, and also N. Wood, 'The Aesthetic Dimension of Burke's Political Thought', *Journal of British Studies*, 4 (1964), 42–6, 62–3.

[103] Burke, *Reflections*, 176.

[104] For a discussion of Burke's anxiety regarding the 'false sublime' of the French Revolution, and its particular democratic expression, see Furniss, *Aesthetic Ideology*, 115–16, 122.

[105] The idea has been revisited more recently by Judith Butler, in *Precarious Life*, xviii–xix, and also Duffy, *Shelley*, 13–14, discussing the extent to which Percy Shelley, whose political aesthetic we shall encounter shortly, was troubled by Burke's concentration on terror as a supreme expression of the negative sublime.

[106] Burke, *Enquiry*, 43.

According to Paul Crowther, the Burkean 'existential sublime' is characterised by a particular interest in the violent, even nihilistic, aspects of human emotion.[107] The Great Terror represented the purest expression of this existential, intensely nihilistic strain of sublimity. To use contemporary parlance, revolutionary France translated the existential sublime into a politics of 'shock and awe'.[108]

The romantic imagination clung to the hope that the sublime represented a form of self-affirmation otherwise denied by the constraints of reason. Wordsworth, as we shall see, clung with a particular fervour to this possibility. Burke was not so haunted. But he was troubled by the idea that politics and morality might be assumed to be a matter of reason alone. The visceral sense, he realised, was a vital complement to the political and the rational.[109] This, of course, takes politics to the edge of language.[110] But not necessarily beyond it. Whilst language might constrain the sublime, even degrade it, it also serves to facilitate its comprehension. The politics and the 'pleasure' of 'resemblance' is everything.[111] We can, in simple terms, comprehend horror, even as we feel it. For this reason, the aesthetics of the sublime has a political and indeed ethical aspect. And it can, accordingly, be deployed as a political instrument; perhaps crudely, certainly in prejudice.[112] 'Eloquence and poetry', Burke observed, are 'more capable of making deep and lively impressions' than any other art or science, for it is only through the 'pictures' they paint that skilled politicians can harness the 'contagion of our passions'.[113]

Reflections on the Revolution in France was composed in precisely this spirit; a supreme example of the 'existential sublime'. The French Revolution was a kind of drama, a 'monstrous tragic-comic scene'.[114] And Burke's response was to present a countervailing theatre of the absurd.[115] The paradox is, of course, immediate, and Burke was fully aware of it. A master at playing with emotions, his depiction of Marie Antoinette and her bedroom was intended, as its author confessed in correspondence, to wring tears from his readers.[116] At the same

---

[107] P. Crowther, *Critical Aesthetics and Postmodernism* (Oxford University Press, 1993), 128–9. For a similar commentary, see Furniss, *Aesthetic Ideology*, 119–22, 161–2.

[108] See Butler, *Precarious Life*, 148–9.   [109] See Furniss, *Aesthetic Ideology*, 29–31.

[110] For a discussion within the immediate context of terrorism, see Eagleton, *Holy Terror*, 42, and also 44, suggesting that the 'sublime is any power which is perilous, shattering, ravishing, traumatic, excessive, exhilarating, dwarfing, astonishing, uncontainable, overwhelming, boundless, obscure, terrifying, enthralling, and uplifting'.

[111] Burke, *Enquiry*, 18.

[112] For a commentary on this aspect of the politics of the sublime, see Crowther, *Postmodernism*, 153–4, 163–4. For a more specific discussion regarding the ethical implications, albeit within a more immediately Kantian context, see P. Crowther, *The Kantian Sublime: From Morality to Art* (Oxford University Press, 1989), 91, 121–2, 172–4, and also *Art and Embodiment: From Aesthetics to Self-Consciousness* (Oxford University Press, 1993), 186–7.

[113] Burke, *Enquiry*, 152, 158, 160–1. For a commentary on this aspect of Burke's idea of a political aesthetic, see Furniss, *Aesthetic Ideology*, 89–112.

[114] Burke, *Reflections*, 92.

[115] See Furniss, *Aesthetic Ideology*, 128–32 discussing this dramatic strategy.

[116] It certainly caused 'to draw tears from me', or so Burke claimed. In Furniss, *Aesthetic Ideology*, 160.

time, Burke was equally terrified of the capacity of language to terrorise.[117] He summoned all his literary skills to manage a popular political imagination that he dreaded, and which he strove might and main to neutralise.

In attacking those who had sought to enthuse his compatriots with a zeal for liberty and revolution, Burke confessed the full, and terrifying, potential that resided in human sensibility. Commenting specifically on the events of 1789, and invoking the 'spectator' theory made famous by the likes of David Hume and Adam Smith, he sought to distinguish 'natural' sympathies, of the kind that should be felt by all those who read of the misfortunes that befell Marie Antoinette's bedroom, from hypocritical ones, of the kind felt by those who invaded it:

> Why do I feel differently... because it is natural that I should; because we are so made as to be affected at such spectacles with melancholy sentiments upon the unstable condition of mortal prosperity, and the tremendous uncertainty of human greatness; because in those natural feelings we learn great lessons; because in events like these our passions instruct our reason; because when kings are hurl'd from their thrones by the Supreme Director in this great drama, and become the objects of insult to the base, and of pity to the good, we behold such disasters in the moral, as we should behold a miracle in the physical order of things. We are alarmed into reflexion (as it has long since been observed), are purified by terror and pity; our weak unthinking pride is humbled, under the dispensations of a mysterious wisdom.[118]

The affinity between the virtual drama of politics and the real drama of the theatre is immediate. 'Some tears', Burke added, 'might be drawn from me, if such a spectacle were exhibited on stage', but 'I should be truly ashamed of finding in myself that superficial, theatric sense of painted distress, whilst I could exult over it in real life'.[119] The inversion of reality and virtuality is acute.[120]

Whilst Burke's *Reflections* was undoubtedly the most compelling, it was certainly not the only contemporary example of anti-terror rhetoric, and it was not the only one that flirted with the more elusive temptations of the metaphysical sublime. A similar, if rather more oblique expression could be found in William Wordsworth's *Lines Composed a Few Miles Above Tintern Abbey*. Wordsworth, of course, like Burke, had displayed an unreserved enthusiasm for the revolutionary 'dances of liberty', at least for a while. His epic *The Prelude* was composed as a vast confession to this grand error, to the 'visitings of imaginative power' that had momentarily possessed him, to the belief that in the moment of violence and revolution a sublime and 'benignant spirit was abroad', one that 'would not be withstood'.[121]

---

[117] For an appreciation of Burke's critical dilemma, see Furniss, *Aesthetic Ideology*, 93–5.
[118] Burke, *Reflections*, 175.   [119] Burke, *Reflections*, 175.
[120] And a peculiar propensity of the French, he insinuated. See Burke, *Reflections*, 89, and also 137, famously contrasting the steadiness of the English constitution, and its 'mind'.
[121] W. Wordsworth, *Prelude*, in *Complete Poetical Works* (Oxford University Press, 1936), bk.ix, 20, at 561.

Tintern Abbey represented a decisive abrogation. Henceforth, the politics of dissent, Wordsworth averred, would be an aesthetic politics, one written in tune with nature, and which resonated with images of beauty and the sublime. As Hazlitt noted of Coleridge's similar sentiments, this would be a politics of poetic musing and of the 'soul'.[122] At the heart of *Tintern Abbey* is a 'sense sublime', of 'tranquil restoration', and the 'warmer love' of humanity.[123] If terror is an expression of the sublime, so is 'that serene and blessed mood / In which the affections gently lead us on', and which can herald the healing 'feelings too / Of unremembered pleasure', the 'little nameless, unremembered acts / Of kindness and of love' which confirm a 'good man's life'.[124]

As Tom Paulin has confirmed, *Tintern Abbey* is definitive of a tradition of English radical dissent that struggled with the terrifying implication of Milton's 'angry Jove', and which strove, like Burke indeed, to somehow extract a greater, more beneficent, 'sense sublime' from the virtual experiences of the Great Terror.[125]

Alongside Wordsworth's *Lines* and Burke's *Reflections*, can be placed a third, very different, text, Percy Shelley's *The Mask of Anarchy*. Written in response to the 'Peterloo massacre' of 1819, an occasion when a radical meeting in a field outside Manchester was broken up by a charge of hussars, leaving eleven dead and four hundred injured, Shelley's *Mask* presented a rather different view of terror and tyranny.[126] The government sought to portray the massacre as a necessary measure to counter incipient anarchism. Shelley demurred. The real terrorists, he rejoined, were those hussars who ran amok, those magistrates who authorised the slaughter, and those politicians who stood behind them.[127]

It was indeed 'Anarchy' that appeared outside Manchester, but it was the anarchy of state terror. It came up from behind:

---

[122] For Hazlitt's commentary on Coleridge's lectures on revolutionary politics and the sublime, see *Selected Writings* (Penguin, 1982), 43–65.

[123] W. Wordsworth, *Lines Composed Above Tintern Abbey* ll.30, 95, 154, in *Poetical Works*, at 164–5. The poem was a particular favourite of Percy Shelley's precisely because it offered the possibility of a politics of tranquillity and philosophical reflection. See Duffy, *Shelley*, 104. For a discussion of Wordsworth's particular experience, and the centrality of *Tintern Abbey* in the development of his political sympathies, see Ward, *State of Mind*, 156–60.

[124] Wordsworth, *Lines*, ll.28–35,and 41–2.

[125] See T. Paulin, *Crusoe's Secret: The Aesthetics of Dissent* (Faber and Faber, 2005), 22–3, 31–2, 41, and also 156–7 and 164–7, discussing Milton, and Hazlitt's belief that images of English dissent were cast by received memories of such 'heroic orators'. Burke acknowledged precisely the same presence. See Furniss, *Aesthetic Ideology*, 102.

[126] The term 'Peterloo' was in part a reference to St. Peter's Fields, where the meeting was convened, and in part an ironic illusion to Waterloo, the battle so patriotically lauded just four years earlier. For a discussion of the context of 'Peterloo' and Shelley's response, see Ward, *State of Mind*, 164–7.

[127] For a recent commentary on the *Mask*, stressing its affinity with biblical notions of revelation, and the innate theatricality contained in the alignment of 'mask' and 'masque', see Stauffer, *Anger*, 128–9, 132.

On a white horse, splashed with blood;
He was pale even to the lips,
Like Death in the Apocalypse
And he wore a kingly crown;
And in his grasp a sceptre shone;
On his brow this mark I saw-
I am God, and King, and Law.[128]

Whilst he despised the pretences of 'Law', Shelley cherished the idea of justice. The final stanzas of the *Mask* were written as a paean to the principles of justice contained in the common law; principles that were now masked by a disingenuous rhetoric of counter-terrorism.[129] This idea, that law inheres a measure of terror, and thus of the sublime, was, of course, fully appreciated by Burke, and by others who sought to excavate the aesthetic root of radical Enlightenment politics.[130]

The association of state and terror is not one that our political leaders like us to contemplate. Terrorists, we are constantly reminded, operate outwith the state.[131] History, of course, suggests otherwise; as Shelley well knew. All states have their origins in moments of political violence, and the inculcation of terror is the primary means by which they endeavour to maintain their authority.[132] They terrify us with the threat of violence, either from within the organs of the state, or without; and when they are not terrorising us, they are terrorising each other. *The Mask of Anarchy*, like Burke's *Reflections*, was composed in this belief.[133]

In *The Revolt of Islam*, his own particular poetic commentary on the French Revolution, Shelley lauded a politics that was rooted both in a respect for

---

[128] P. Shelley, *The Mask of Anarchy* ll.30–7, in P. Shelley, *Complete Poetical Works* (Oxford University Press, 1971).

[129] See ll.230–3, 'Thou are Justice – ne'er for gold / May thy righteous laws be sold / As laws are in England – thou / Shields't alike the high and low', and also ll.331–5, 'The old laws of England – they / Whose reverend heads with age are gray, / Children of a wider day; / And whose solemn voice must be / Thine own echo – Liberty!'

[130] See Eagleton, *Holy Terror*, 48–52, describing the contemporary aesthetic of terror as the masculine component of law, and sympathy as its female counter. For a broad discussion of the politics of the sublime in English romanticism, see Duffy, *Shelley*, particularly 13–23.

[131] For an intelligent discussion of the derivation of state terrorism, see Sterba, 'Introduction', 2–4, and also Lacqueur, *Terrorism*, 6–20.

[132] As Lacqueur reminds us, state terror has 'been responsible for a thousand times more misery than all the actions of individual terrorism taken together'. See his *The Age of Terrorism* (Little Brown, 1987), 146. For a similar sentiment see James Sterba, 'Introduction', 11, suggesting that history, ancient and modern, confirms that the 'clearest and most striking cases of terrorism are those of state terrorism', and also Michael Stohl, in 'Old Myths', at 6, confirming that the 'number of victims produced by state terror is on a scale exponentially larger than that of insurgent terrorists', and also K. Booth, 'The Human Faces of Terror: Reflections in a Cracked Looking-glass', *Critical Studies on Terrorism*, 1 (2008), 76.

[133] Described by Richard Holmes as the 'greatest poem of political protest ever written in English'. See R. Holmes, *Shelley: The Pursuit* (HarperCollins, 1994), 532.

equality and the rule of law, and free democracy. Such an equality and such a democracy, he confirmed, can 'found sympathy / In human hearts', ensuring that 'those / Who grow together cannot choose but love'.[134] The echoes of Wordsworth's 'warmer love' are immediate. It was, of course, Shelley who famously declared the poet to be the 'priest of an unapprehended imagination', one of 'the unacknowledged legislators of the world'.[135] Shelley had little doubt regarding the value of poethics as a strategy for the pursuit of justice.[136] But it is not just a matter of finding 'sympathy'. It is also, he came to realise, albeit reluctantly, something that must be fought for. Shelley fully appreciated the paradoxes of terrorism and political violence, not just that freedom, like terror, finds its root in the faculty of the sublime, but that it also comes, as it always has, at a price.[137] 'Angry Jove' haunted Shelley, just as he haunted Wordsworth and Burke.

Two centuries on, the aesthetic 'sublime' does not figure much in contemporary counter-terrorist discourse. Our political leaders today prefer 'ass-kicking' to musing on the metaphysics, or indeed poetics, of existence.[138] Little time is spent worrying about the sense sublime. As we shall see in the next chapter, given the theological strain which pervades so much terrorism, including very obviously militant Islamic terrorism, this is a mistake. The fact that Osama bin Laden's most inspiring intellectual mentors, Abbas Mahmoud al-Aqqad and Sayyid Qutb, were both devotees of English romanticism, is not a matter of mere whimsy.[139] It suggests something altogether more important. The radical *jihadist*, like the Enlightenment romantic, is given to dreaming. For them, the sense sublime matters. It is what makes terrorism such a potent political strategy.[140]

---

[134] Shelley, *The Revolt of Islam*, ll.2686–7, 3541–2, in *Poetical Works*, 103, 124.

[135] Quoted in Holmes, *Shelley*, 585.

[136] For a recent commentary on the immanent relation of the aesthetic and the political in Shelley's poetry, see Duffy, *Shelley*, particularly 2–6.

[137] See Eagleton, *Holy Terror*, 68, and also 79, observing that absolute freedom is 'sublimely beyond the reach of representation'. See also Duffy, *Shelley*, 10–11, 27–30, 50–3 discussing the necessary tension at the heart of Shelley's political aesthetic, between an adherence to Godwinian ideas of gradualism and an alternative, if reluctant, belief that radical reform must be forced, and also 138–42 and 148, exploring the presence of this paradox at the heart of *The Revolt of Islam*. It was, Duffy observes, the defining 'anxiety at the heart' of the poem, the supposition that, in the cause of liberty, 'political violence may be inevitable'. It was not, of course, a tension peculiar to Shelley. For a broader consideration of perceptions of anger and violence in the political aesthetic of the romantics, see Stauffer, *Anger*, particularly 2–11, 111–32, focusing on Shelley, and also 167–74.

[138] For Bush's famous reference to ass-kicking, which is discussed further below, see D. Hare, *Stuff Happens* (Faber and Faber, 2004), 101.

[139] This striking affinity is noted by Malise Ruthven, in *Fury*, at 75, and also 82–3, likening Qutb's aesthetics more immediately to Nietzsche, and 91–4, exploring particular resonances between Qutb's writings and Jacobin expressions of anarchist philosophy.

[140] See Burke, *Al-Qaeda*, 83, Ruthven, *Fury*, 244–6, 274, 281, and also Eagleton, *Holy Terror*, at 25 confirming that the 'line between gods and demons is notoriously hard to draw'.

Plastic moments

In his recent play *Stuff Happens*, David Hare castigates the 'war on terror' as a thin mask for US imperialism.[141] The title of the play alludes to Donald Rumsfeld's notorious response, when challenged regarding the collateral damage caused by US military action in Iraq, that 'stuff happens'; the sentiment betrays, as Mailer confirms, a peculiar arrogance, as well as a troubling degree of self-delusion.[142] So consuming has the rhetoric become, so pervasive the strategy of dissimulation, that Hare's protagonists find it increasingly difficult to distinguish fact from fantasy. The attraction of a 'war on terror' lies precisely in its rhetorical vagueness, its first articulation in the 2002 State of the Union address presented as a 'plastic, teachable moment'.[143] Hare's President Bush acknowledges that his primary responsibility is to 'rack up the rhetoric', whilst his Vice-President is positively Orwellian in his lauding the art of 'misspeak'.[144]

A distinct discourse of 'Islamic terrorism' is created.[145] The Truth is revealed, the dissimulations of Islamic fundamentalists, and liberal jurists, laid bare for all to see.[146] We shall explore the more obviously theological implications of this particular revelation in the next chapter. Law, meanwhile, as we realised in the last chapter, is deemed useless, its principles dismissed as quaint, obsolete. The UN is a 'facility', one that is deemed incapable of effecting biblical justice; an aspiration which itself translates into nothing more inspiring than 'kicking ass'.[147] The alleged end of international law is presented, not as a muse on the crisis of jurisprudence in the contemporary world, but as an exemplar of just how apocalyptic things have got, and just how vital it is that our leaders are allowed to go hunting asses to kick. Just as the Enlightenment mind agonised

---

[141] See Hare, *Stuff Happens*, 3–4. Hare is an unremitting critic of contemporary US foreign policy, especially its 'war on terror' and the Iraq war. It describes, he alleges, a 'lethal unreason and opportunism'. See D. Hare, *Obedience, Struggle and Revolt* (Faber and Faber, 2005), 193–7.

[142] Mailer, *War*, 15, suggesting that it betrays an America that is 'growing more arrogant, more vain'. According to one of Hare's characters, Rumsfeld's response also carries a further charge, perhaps 'the most racist remark I ever heard', in *Stuff Happens*, at 120. An intriguing echo can be found in Harold Pinter's recent Nobel Lecture, in which he recalls attending a US embassy meeting in the late 1980s, on the subject of Nicaragua. When a parish priest complained to the then US ambassador, Raymond Seitz, that his village had been destroyed by US-backed Contras, and countless villagers killed, tortured and raped, Seitz replied that it was indeed a shame, but that 'In war, innocent people always suffer'. See Pinter's Lecture published in *The Guardian*, 8 December 2005, G2, comments recorded at 11.

[143] Hare, *Stuff Happens*, 24, 32.   [144] Hare, *Stuff Happens*, 32, 117.

[145] See R. Jackson, 'Constructing Enemies: Islamic Terrorism in Political and Academic Discourse', *Government and Opposition*, 42 (2007), 394–426.

[146] Gray, *Black Mass*, 103–5.

[147] Hare, *Stuff Happens*, 101, and also 110, for Rumsfeld's brutal dismissal of any attempt to secure UN resolutions in support of military action in Iraq. See also P. Sands, *Lawless World: America and the Making and Breaking of Global Rules* (Penguin, 2005), 174, 180. According to Judith Butler such a rhetorical strategy is intended to resonate with a 'cowboy tradition of vigilante justice', a tradition with which Bush feels comfortable, and which is also intended to chime with the mid-American mindset. See Butler, *Precarious Life*, 85.

over the unsettling conjunction of the Great Terror and the aesthetics of the
sublime, so too the early twenty-first-century mind is assailed with the experiences of hyper-terrorism along with the intellectual affronts of postmodernism. This is, after all, the age, not just of apocalyptic terror, but of
'transcendental nihilism' too.[148] Paul Crowther has chronicled the extent to
which the present 'sensibility of shock', of which hyper-terrorism is a primary
example, represents a mutant variety of the Burkean 'existential sublime'.[149]

The fate of law is entrapped within this intellectual mutation, whilst the
particular relation of law and terrorism represents a still more virulent and
unpredictable strain.[150] As we have already seen, absent any definitional
'magic', terrorism and the law have never enjoyed a particularly comfortable
relation.[151] It is for this reason that we are urged to abandon any hunt for an
explicit relation between the two.[152] Perhaps we have indeed entered an age
where 'there are no rules'.[153] Perhaps we have entered an exceptional age, one
which might be explained in the notorious terms projected by the German jurist
Carl Schmitt as a defence of executive despotism in the sovereign 'moment' of
crisis; a thesis to which we shall return in rather greater depth in Chapter 6.[154]
Except that the idea of an indefinite 'war against terror' militates against the
idea of an exceptional moment.

As we shall see in later chapters, the Schmittian exception has been deployed
to lend some kind of quasi-jurisprudential justification for the detention of
'unlawful combatants' at Guantanamo Bay. It might equally be thought to lend
a measure of intellectual legitimacy to some of the more controversial measures
found in the USA Patriot Act or the British Terrorism Act 2006. Section 1 of the
latter enactment, which struggled its way through the British Parliament for
much of 2005 and early 2006 is entitled the 'Encouragement of Terrorism' and
is intended to criminalise any supposed 'glorification' of terrorism.[155] Sub-
section 3 states:

> For the purposes of this section the statements that are likely to be understood by
> members of the public as indirectly encouraging the commission or preparation
> of acts of terrorism or Convention offences include every statement which –

---

[148] Megret, 'Justice', 330.

[149] See Crowther, *Postmodernism*, 17, 115–16, 128–9, and also *Kantian Sublime*, 165, tracing a
similar genealogy from the Kantian sublime.

[150] For a commentary on Crowther's idea of the existential sublime and its jurisprudential
implications, see I. Ward, 'A Kantian (Re)turn: Aesthetics, Postmodernism and Law', *Law and
Critique*, 6 (1995), 257–71.

[151] Lacqueur, *War*, 139, *New Terrorism*, 46, and also Kapitan, 'Terrorism', 48.

[152] R. Higgins, 'The General International Law of Terrorism' in Higgins and Flory, *Terrorism and
International Law*, 20, particularly 13–14, 28.

[153] In McGoldrick, *From 9–11*, 87.

[154] For a commentary on, and rebuttal of, the Schmittian position, see Butler, *Precarious Life*, 60–2,
67, 80, 86.

[155] For a critical overview of the legislation, see A. Hunt, 'Criminal Prohibitions on Direct and
Indirect Encouragement of Terrorism', *Criminal Law Review* 2007, 441–58.

    a. glorifies the commission or preparation (whether in the past, in the future or generally) of such acts or offences: and

    b. is a statement from which those members of the public could reasonably be expected to infer that what is being glorified is being glorified as conduct that should be emulated by them in existing circumstances.

A similar passage can be found at Section 2 sub-section 4, which relates to the dissemination of such materials. The defences given in Section 1 sub-section 6 and Section 2 sub-section 9 suggest that views that are not personally endorsed would not be prosecuted. For this reason, the British government suggested that ordinary comments on past instances of terrorism and political violence, particularly those in the distant past, might not, in practice, fall foul of the purported legislation. Praise for Burke, even for Shelley, would probably be excused today.

    But it was not so readily excused then. Burke abjured loudly. Shelley did not, and was haunted by the constant threat of legal proceedings for sedition. He was not alone. In his notorious *Discourse*, published in 1790, the dissenting minister Richard Price welcomed the 'ardor of liberty catching and spreading', and embraced the moment when the 'dominion of priests' should give way 'to the dominion of reason and conscience'.[156] He was prosecuted for sedition, for applauding what counted then for terrorism. For centuries, governments have sought to silence dissent, to pursue those who might be thought to glorify something that would they prefer to see abhorred. The dislocation of the law in order to furnish such rhetorical strategies with a veneer of legality is wrong, and must be condemned. There are few more obvious examples of the kind of 'intellectual intimidation' which counter-terrorist discourse presses than Section 1.3.[157]

    It is hard to imagine how such a piece of legislation is intended to help counter any serious terrorism, or any serious terrorist. The fact that it was not deployed in the prosecution of the so-called 'Lyrical Terrorist', Samina Malik, who had posted various pieces of dodgy verse in praise of Islamikaze martyrs, in the hope of seeming 'cool' and perhaps attracting a boyfriend, is perhaps suggestive.[158] In time, Section 1.3 is likely to go the same way as the Dangerous

---

[156] R. Price, *Political Writings* (Cambridge University Press, 1991), 195.

[157] For the reference to 'intellectual intimidation', see Achcar, *Barbarisms*, 23. For a more general, and caustic, denunciation of Section 1.3, see A. Lester, 'Redefining Terror', *Index on Censorship* 02, (2007), 103–7, concluding that 'The evil scourge of terrorism does not justify undermining the political and legal principles anchored not only in international human rights law, but in our common law and political tradition in this country'. Arthur Chaskalson has expressed similar reservations regarding the 'chilling effect' which the legislation is clearly intended to have on the ordinary processes of democratic discourse. See his 'Counter-Terrorism', 76–7.

[158] In the event Malik was prosecuted under Sections 57 and 58 of the 2000 Terrorist Act for the collection and possession of 'material likely to be of use to terrorists'. The idea of deploying the new provisions found in Section 1 of the 2006 act was eschewed. Alongside her poetic musings, Malik also regurgitated some hints, readily available on the internet, on how to make explosive devices and decapitate people. It was not a pleasant hobby. But neither was Malik a terribly serious, still less particularly dangerous, terrorist. She was, however, a bit confused and rather

Dogs Act and other similarly notorious pieces of hasty ill-conceived legislation. But for now at least it remains on the statute book, an iconic testament to our collective gullibility. And there is, of course, nothing to be gained by making the law seem ridiculous. As Hare's Secretary of State Powell observes, experiencing a terrorist attack 'doesn't license us to behave like idiots'.[159] It is, as ever, the hard case that tests the integrity of law. It is one thing to bring the full force of the state to bear on love-lorn teenagers such as Samina Malik, but what of Hirst and Stockhausen, who likened 9/11 to a 'work of art', or the US evangelists Pat Robertson or Jerry Falwell, the latter of whom suggested that the event represented the work of God, a divine response to the insults of the Supreme Court, and 'the pagans, and the abortionists, and the feminists, and the gays and the lesbians'?[160] Once again, it becomes immediately apparent that in cases such as these, hypothetical or not, legislative enactments such as Section 1.3 are of little value.

And what of Sartre's notorious observations, in his Preface to Fanon's *Wretched of the Earth*, his lauding of the terrorist as a man of 'unbelievable courage', his violence a mode of liberating self-affirmation? To 'shoot down the European', Sartre observed, is to 'destroy an oppressor'. 'We have sown the wind', Sartre continued, and the terrorist 'is the whirlwind', the 'child of violence, at every moment he draws from it his humanity.[161] It is difficult to read this as anything other than glorification; the kind of encomium that is echoed in countless videos of putative suicide-bombers. The same is just as true of Fanon's own applause for terrorism as a means of reinvesting human 'dignity'.[162] Today Fanon's rebel would be readily honoured as a freedom fighter. But he was not in 1961. Likewise, writing in 1943, future Israeli Prime Minister Yitzhak Shamir declared 'First and foremost, terror is for us a part of the political war appropriate for the circumstances of today'. He had, he affirmed, no 'moral hesitations' in justifying the murder and maiming of British soldiers and citizens, and their sympathisers.[163] The British government denounced Shamir as a terrorist. In time, he would be feted in Downing Street, his undoubted encouragement of terrorist violence politely ignored.[164]

---

lonely at home. Writing poetry, she had hoped, would make her 'cool', and might even attract a boyfriend. The presiding judge at her trial, who presumably had never come across a love-lorn, truculent teenager before, confessed to finding Malik something of an 'enigma'. Malik's conviction was later quashed by the Court of Appeal.

[159] Hare, *Stuff Happens*, 53, and also 93 for a similar observation. The strategy of using an anonymous, ordinary character to voice those concerns which particularly trouble the dramatist and, so he or she presumes, ordinary members of the audience, is, of course, familiar. It is, perhaps, most obviously familiar in Shakespeare. For a similar allusion, see T. Honderich, in *After the Terror* (Edinburgh University Press, 2002), at 147–8, regretting the 'stupidity' evidenced in our delusive 'war against terror'.

[160] See Ruthven, *Fury*, 31 and Faludi, *Dream*, 22.

[161] J.-P. Sartre, 'Preface', to F. Fanon, *The Wretched of the Earth* (Penguin, 2001), 18–20.

[162] Fanon, *Wretched*, 68, 70, 73, 165.   [163] In Rees, *Terrorists*, 14.

[164] For a comment on the relevance of the old adage, of one man's terrorist being another's freedom fighter, in the context of Section 1.3, see Lester, 'Redefining Terror', 105.

The problem again is definitional. If terrorism evades definition, so does any imagined encouragement or glorification of it; either historical or contemporary.[165] Or poetic, of course. As Burke readily appreciated, poetry is far and away the most effective means of glorifying any kind of violence. In this context, what are we supposed to make of the uncompromising, and very contemporary, verse of the Syrian poet Nizar Qabbani:

> I am with terrorism
> if it is able to free a people
> from tyrants and tyranny...[166]

Such lines do not enjoy the benefit of historical framing. They speak to the kind of terrorism against which we are supposed now to be at war. Should we feel threatened by such verse? Should we seek to proscribe it? Would we be safer?

Legislation to proscribe the glorification of terrorism will do nothing to address the sentiment which lies behind Qabbani's lines; though it might do much to exacerbate it. There are some things that law simply cannot do. The suppression of deeply held feelings is one of these.[167] The terrain of terrorism, a terrain of mythology and enchantment, of the aesthetic sublime, is not one in which the law should seek to tread heavily. It is not just that any such attempt might be futile, or counter-productive; though it more than likely will be. The greater danger has been recently articulated by Judith Butler. Writing to the subject of counter-terrorism, she suggests that to 'charge those who voice critical views' with treason or any other criminal offence, 'is to seek to destroy the credibility not of the views that are held, but of the persons who hold them'.[168] The greatest danger which we presently face is not the occasional terrorist atrocity. It is legislation such as Section 1 of the Terrorism Act. We shall, sadly, encounter more examples of such legislation in due course.[169]

---

[165] A fact noted by the Parliamentary Joint Committee on Human Rights, which observed that 'terms such as glorification, praise and celebration are too vague to form part of a criminal offence which can be committed by speaking'. Quoted in Hunt, 'Criminal Prohibitions', 449–50.

[166] In Tariq Ali, *Bush in Babylon: The Recolonisation of Iraq* (Verso, 2003), 12–13.

[167] For a similar insinuation, see Eagleton, *Holy Terror*, 140, concluding that 'the terrorist is not the *pharmakos*; but he is created by it, and can only be defeated when justice is done to it'.

[168] Butler, *Precarious Life*, xviii, further commenting, at 1, that since 9/11 'we have seen both a rise of anti-intellectualism and a growing acceptance of censorship within the media'.

[169] Most obviously in Chapter 6, the primary subject of which is legal, or more accurately, extra-legal, responses to 9/11.

2

Angry Jove

On the Feast of the Invention, 3 May 1606, Father Henry Garnet was strapped to a hurdle and dragged to his place of execution. According to Protestant accounts he looked guilty and terrified. According to Catholic accounts, he looked innocent and serene. Rather irritatingly, at least for the assembled dignitaries, he refused to confess his treason, and further denied that he was merely equivocating. Then, rejoicing in the fact that he had 'found my cross' he embraced the opportunity to die a martyr's death. It was all rather unsatisfactory, and the fact that a group of suspected Catholic sympathisers ran up and pulled on his legs to make sure that he died whilst being hanged, and so did not suffer the peculiar agonies of being drawn, really quite ruined the day. By the time his heart was being torn out, and his body quartered, the crowds were drifting home, and those left were reported to have been murmuring rather ominously.[1] Traitors, particularly Jesuit ones, were supposed to suffer rather more, their spectacular demise a matter of altogether greater celebration. And Garnet was no ordinary Jesuit. He was the Superior of the order of Jesuits in England.

God's 'chosen people', of whom Garnet was most definitely not one, imagined themselves living in an 'age of terror'; terrorised primarily by men like Garnet, the imagined puppet-master of a vast, if shadowy network, of Jesuit insurgents dedicated to destroying Albion and all its hard-earned freedoms.[2]

---

[1] The form of the execution, of course, was invested with its own immediate symbolism. The gory details were presented by the Attorney-General, Sir Edward Coke, in his prosecution of the Gunpowder Plotters, and are cited in J. Sharpe, *Remember, Remember the Fifth of November: Guy Fawkes and the Gunpowder Plot* (Profile, 2005), at 76. The guilty, Coke advised, should be 'strangled, being hanged up by the neck between heaven and earth, as deemed unworthy of both or either; as likewise, that the eyes of men many behold, and their hearts condemn them. Then to be cut down alive, and to have his privy parts cut off and burnt before his face as being unworthily begotten, and unfit to leave any generation after him. His bowels and inlaid parts taken out and burnt, who inwardly had conceived and harboured in his heart such horrible treason. After, to have his head cut off, which had imagined the mischief. And lastly his body to be quartered, and the quarters set up in some high and eminent place, to the view and detestation of men, and to become a prey for the fowls of the air'. For a particular account of Garnet's execution, see A. Fraser, *The Gunpowder Plot* (Phoenix, 2002), 319–23.

[2] For the assertion that contemporaries regarded themselves as living in an 'age of terror', see R. Wilson, *Secret Shakespeare: Studies in Theatre, Religion and Resistance* (Manchester University

Garnet was, in simple terms, the Osama bin Laden of early seventeenth-century England; more guilty, as Sir Edward Coke affirmed at his trial, as 'author' of the infamous Plot than 'all the actors'.[3] Garnet had been found hiding, not in a cave in the Hindu Kush, but in a closet in Hindlip House near Worcester. But the parallel is again immediate. Terrorists skulk, and Garnet had spent his life skulking. Skulking was reason enough for his vilification, his office as Superior reason more.[4] But Garnet's guilt was greater still, for he was implicated, however remotely, in one the most spectacular, if ultimately abortive, terrorist acts in British history, the Gunpowder Plot of November 1605. Whilst Garnet was not directly embroiled in the Plot, he was widely held responsible for failing to caution young Catholics against such plotting. He was, as the popular rhyme suggested, 'accessory to this damned intent'.[5]

The Powder Plot, as it was known by contemporaries, was intended to blow up Parliament and with it the new King James I and his family. It was, very definitely, a terrorist plot; a spectacular act of extreme political violence intended to disrupt the English state and terrify its people.[6] Although it failed, so spectacular was the intent, and the possible consequence, that it has retained a unique place in the English political consciousness.[7] In time, the celebration of apocalypse narrowly averted has given way to the fun of Bonfire night, to children munching toffee-apples, whilst watching firework displays and the ritual burning of effigies of Guy Fawkes. But the political and theological charge still lurks beneath, not least in the habit, which continues to this day in certain English towns, of providing the 'Guy' with companions; amongst which, in recent years, and with an appropriateness that is as acute as it is quixotic, may be included incinerated images of Osama bin Laden, Tony Blair and George Bush.[8]

'Remember, Remember, the Fifth of November', the rhyme reminds us. Cultural memories of 'the Fifth', as James Sharpe has recently argued, should, in the present context of 9/11 and its associated 'war on terror', help us to 'understand our current predicaments' that little bit better.[9] It should, certainly;

Press, 2004), 2. For the allusion to the Jesuit missionaries as 'pious terrorists', see J. Bossy, *Under the Molehill: An Elizabethan Spy Story* (Yale University Press, 2001), 31.

[3] In Wilson, *Shakespeare*, 196.

[4] The dramatic image of the terrorist as a lurking closet-dweller is an old one. See Wilson, *Shakespeare* 28 citing, amongst many, examples in Shakespeare's *Merry Wives of Windsor*.

[5] The extent of Garnet's involvement in the Plot remains uncertain. He is thought to have known about the existence of such a plot, at least in vague outline, by July 1605.

[6] See Sharpe, *Remember*, 3 and 67, describing it as a 'failed act of terrorism', and also Fraser, *Plot*, xv–vi and 359, suggesting that the Plot was intended to be a 'terrorist' act, and its 'conspirators were what we would now term terrorists'.

[7] See Fraser, *Plot*, 339.   [8] See Sharpe, *Remember*, 174–5, 177.

[9] Sharpe, *Remember*, 8 and also 195–7, emphasising that whilst historians 'should avoid facile comparisons', conversely the 'parallels' between anti-Islamic hysteria in Britain today and anti-Catholic hysteria in England four centuries ago is too acute to be ignored. Most importantly, there is the shared 'fear of an alien ideology which most people, at best, only half understand', and an equally common 'fear that this ideology has at its command forces dedicated to the destruction of our political system'.

whether or not it does is a different matter. The terrorised, as we have already noted, tend to be susceptible to the suggestion that the particular terror they perceive is so much more terrifying than any previous terror. And it is, of course, the purpose of any counter-terrorist strategy to make sure that this is the governing perception.

Aside from providing a broader historical context, memories of 'the Fifth' also serve to underline one marked characteristic of an overriding majority of terrorist events and experiences; and this is the particular and pervasive relation of terrorism and religion. The 'connection between terror and injustice in divine matters', as Terry Eagleton has recently affirmed, is present in 'every age'.[10] Martin Amis agrees. In the matter of inflicting terroristic violence, history reveals the responsibility of religion to be a 'dreadful' one.[11] We shall encounter various expressions of theologically driven terrorism in subsequent chapters; the ethnic cleansing of the Balkans, the 'black widows' of Chechnya and so on. The victims of terrorism, all too often, are chosen because they are thought to believe in the wrong god or gods or in no gods at all. Father Garnet was one such victim. Those who died in the Twin Towers on 9/11 were too. And so it might be surmised are those who continue to die in Afghanistan and Iraq, and in so many other corners of the globe. Their aligned fates are a testament to the enduring, generally malignant, power of faith.[12] Twenty-one centuries ago, so the New Testament tries to persuade us, the son of God was sent to save humanity. Sometimes it is hard to believe that it really wants to be saved at all.

The sword erect

Early modern England was saturated by theology.[13] The English were, of course, a 'chosen people', blessed, as Bishop Aylmer famously confirmed,

---

[10] T. Eagleton, *Holy Terror* (Oxford University Press, 2005), 2, 27–41. An echo can be found in Mark Juergensmeyer's observation that most violence has a religious root quite simply because most religions are necessarily militant. It is, he further adds, an intensely symbolic kind of militancy. 'The fact is', he argues, 'that the symbols and mythology of most religious traditions are filled with violent images, and their histories leave trails of blood'. See his 'The Logic of Religious Violence', *Journal of Strategic Studies*, 10 (1987), 179, and also 180–1. It has also found a strident recent affirmation in John Gray's *Black Mass: Apocalyptic Religion and the Death of Utopia* (Penguin, 2007), particularly at 1–3 and 210.

[11] M. Amis, *The Second Plane* (Jonathan Cape, 2008), 14. The fact of their agreement is, of course, intriguing, given the bitterness of the dispute between the two following the publication of Amis's *Second Plane*. The uncompromising nature of Amis's denunciation of militant Islam, which he condemned as being 'misogynist' and anti-rational, was strongly criticised by Eagleton in a manner which barely stopped short of accusing its author of cultural racism. For Amis's denunciation of militant Islam, see *Plane*, 19, 49–71.

[12] See Gray, *Black Mass*, 31, and also at 190, noting the immediate and debilitating paradox; for 'Like repressed sexual desire, faith returns, often in grotesque forms, to govern the lives of those who deny it'.

[13] Catherine McEachern has recently affirmed 'the massive centrality of religion to this period's cultural imagination and production'. See her 'Introduction', to C. McEachern and D. Shuger (eds.), *Religion and Culture in Renaissance England* (Cambridge University Press, 1997), 10.

because God Himself 'is English'.[14] But they were also a tortured and terrified people; terrified, above all, by the fear that God would forsake them if they fell back into the temptations of popery, their terrors graphically confirmed by all the tortures depicted in Foxe's *Book of Martyrs* and similar canons of militant Protestantism.[15] The great statutes of the reformation, the Acts of Supremacy and Uniformity, existed as much to confirm the expulsion of popery as they did the establishment of an Anglican Church, whilst collateral edicts, such as the 1569 *Homily against disobedience and willful rebellion*, provided a legislative complement to the horrors depicted in Foxe's *Book*. Either the 'chosen people' obeyed the edicts of their anointed monarch, or they lived in a state of 'Babilonical confusion', with the concomitant certainty of their 'utter destruction, bothe of soules, bodies, goodes and common wealthes'.[16]

The militant strain was endemic. In his final play, *Henry VIII*, Shakespeare has his Archbishop predict that the future Elizabeth will rule by a mixture of 'Peace, plenty, love' and a just measure of 'terror'.[17] Terror, particularly popish terror, must be met by terror. It was only to be expected. A generation later, England would, as Sir Thomas Digby rued in 1642, 'fly into the wilderness for religion'.[18] Marvell's Oliver Cromwell carried the 'sword erect', a true crusader of the English reformation, 'God's Englishman' indeed.[19] The English civil wars were, in every sense 'wars of religion', and they were also very definitely wars 'on terror'.[20] Marvell also presented Cromwell as the 'force of Heaven's angry flame.'.[21] Milton depicted an 'angry Jove' raging at an awed people.[22] John

---

[14] See P. Collinson, *The Birthpangs of Protestant England: Religious and Cultural Change in the Sixteenth and Seventeenth Century* (Macmillan, 1988), 7, and also 10, commenting that the 'chosen people' felt that they were 'living, in a sense, in the pages of the Bible'.

[15] Foxe's *Book* was, according to Collinson, a 'monumental influence' on the collective mind of the 'chosen people'. See his *Birthpangs*, 12, and also 17–18, 25–7. For further discussion of this mindset, see D. Shuger, *Habits of Thought in the English Renaissance: Religion, Politics, and the Dominant Culture* (California University Press, 1990), 70, commenting on the pervasive 'terror' of abandonment which possessed the 'chosen people', and also G. Wills, *Witches and Jesuits* (Oxford University Press, 1995), 16–17, and Sharpe, *Remember*, 8–10, confirming that the English protestant identity was, more than anything, 'constructed against a background of tales of popish oppression and popish atrocities.

[16] See I. Ward, *A State of Mind? The English Constitution and the Popular Imagination* (Sutton, 2000), 38 and Sharpe, *Remember*, 3–6. The idea that civil disobedience might be justified in certain circumstances, articulated across the theological spectrum from Cardinal Allen to John Knox, caused considerable consternation to sovereigns across Europe. For a commentary, see A. Hadfield, *Shakespeare and Renaissance Politics* (Routledge, 2004) 3–6.

[17] W. Shakespeare, *Henry VIII*, (Arden, 1968), 5.4.47.

[18] Clarendon, *Selections from Clarendon* (Oxford University Press, 1978), 249.

[19] A. Marvell, 'An Horatian Ode upon Cromwell's Return from Ireland', line 116, in *The Poems and Letters of Andrew Marvell* (Oxford University Press, 1970).

[20] For the definitive categorisation of England's civil wars as 'wars of religion', see J. Morrill, *The Nature of the English Revolution* (Longman, 1993), 38–9, and 45–68, concluding at 68, that the wars did not represent the 'first European revolution', but rather the 'last of the Wars of Religion'.

[21] Marvell, 'Horatian Ode', line 26.

[22] See T. Paulin, *Crusoe's Secret: The Aesthetics of Dissent* (Faber and Faber, 2005), 22–3, 31–2, 41.

Bunyan readily admitted to being 'tossed' into a state of near-perpetual 'despair' by his fear of God.[23] They were, like St. Augustine, forever filled 'with terror'.[24]

Perceptions of Jove's anger, and its focus, were various. It encompassed, certainly, the avowed papist, and most especially that 'generation of vipers' as Lord Burghley termed them, the Jesuits.[25] His 'chosen people' had taken the trouble to enact plenty of legislation to flush out the popish sympathiser; enforcing attendance at Anglican churches on pain of fine or even confiscation of property, banning Catholic rituals and restricting the movement of suspected recusants.[26] Jove's anger was also directed towards the over-zealous counter-terrorist, such as the Earl of Essex, who, in the wake of his failed coup in 1601, claimed that he had only sought to deliver his Queen and 'all Christendom from the fearful usurpation' of Rome.[27] As successive Homilies had confirmed, if there was a problem, in Albion, or with its anointed sovereign, God would sort it out. Similarly, nothing would make Jove angrier, as George Herbert implied, than the 'chosen people' allowing themselves, and their reformation, to be devoured by the 'worm' of 'schism'.[28] Richard Hooker's *Laws of Ecclesiastical Polity* was fervent in its defence of the 'golden mediocrity' in church governance.[29] The ever-anxious, ever-terrified, John Donne likewise urged a balance, of 'reason' in the 'soul's left hand' and 'faith' in 'her right'.[30]

Equally, however, many feared that Jove was angry with His people for their complacency. The fifth book of Edmund Spenser's *Faerie Queene* closes with the 'blatant Beast' of 'ugly Barbarisme' and 'brutish Ignorance' ravaging the 'new Hieru-salem that God has built'.[31] The Beast is nurtured by indifference, by a misplaced tolerance; by a willingness to countenance 'church papists', closet papists trundling to Church every Sunday, closing their ears to the godly Word and then scurrying back to their various homesteads and taking Mass.[32] The rise of Arminianism, an 'old condemned heresy raised up from hell of late by some Jesuits', as William Prynne termed it, only seemed to confirm everyone's worst fears.[33] There was always something, or so it seemed to men like Prynne, half-hearted about the Elizabethan reformation; which is why there needed to be another one. Whilst Sir John Harrington famously compared life in

---

[23] J. Bunyan, *Grace Abounding to the Chief of Sinners* (Penguin, 1987), 48.

[24] See Eagleton, *Holy Terror*, 27, 40–1, suggesting that such a theology makes its God a 'terrorist'.

[25] In Fraser, *Plot*, 46.   [26] Much collected in the 1593 Act against Popish Recusants.

[27] See W. MacCaffrey, *Elizabeth I*, (Edward Arnold, 1993), 277 and C. Hibbert, *The Virgin Queen: A Personal History of Elizabeth I*, (Penguin, 1992), 231.

[28] G. Herbert 'A Priest to the Temple', lines 9–11, 19, 50–1, 95, 101–2, 131–2, 179–86, in *The Complete English Poems* (Penguin 1991), and also D. Levarg, 'George Herbert's "The Church Militant" and the Chances of History', *Philological Quarterly*, 36 (1957), 265–8.

[29] R. Hooker, *Of the Laws of Ecclesiastical Polity* (Cambridge University Press, 1989), 79–80, 145–51.

[30] J. Donne, 'To the Countess of Bedford', line.1, in *The Complete English Poems* (Penguin, 1996).

[31] E. Spenser, 'The Faerie Queene', 1.10.57 and 5.12.41–3, in *Complete Poetical Works* (Oxford University Press, 1980).

[32] 'Church' or appellant Catholics formally defined themselves by a willingness to 'appeal' their political loyalty to Elizabeth I. See Fraser, *Plot*, 26–7, 31, 46–52, and Sharpe, *Remember*, 21–4.

[33] In K. Sharpe, *The Personal Rule of Charles 1*, (Yale University Press, 1992), 295.

Elizabethan England to a 'kind of Romanze', he also, later, compared Gloriana to an indolent scullery-maid who brushed the dirt under the kitchen mat.[34]

For the Elizabethan, of course, the 'Romanze' was everything. 'We princes', as Elizabeth had famously admitted, 'are set on stages in the sight and view of all the world duly observed'.[35] Moreover, Gloriana and her Church were inseparable in the political imagination. 'I have no dealing with the Queen', the MP Thomas Norton advised his son, 'but as with the image of God'.[36] The Protestant poetic, found in texts such as Puttenham's *The Arte of English Poesie* and Sidney's *Defense of Poesy*, was composed to confirm precisely this.[37] The papal anti-Christ would be repelled, not just by the 'sword erect', but by lyric and verse. As Sidney affirmed in his *Defense*, the poet 'doth not only show the way, but giveth so sweet a prospect into the way, as will entice any man to enter it'.[38]

The idea that the rhetoric of terror and terrorism must be met by a counter-rhetoric of counter-terrorism is not, as we have already seen, new. In the Protestant poetic it found expression in Spenser's invocation of 'savage justice' against the Papists of Ireland, or anywhere else, in Sidney's similar urgings against the 'sorceries' of Rome wherever they may be found, and, in equally brutal form, in Milton's *Eikonoclastes*, which defended the execution of Charles I, not just as cruel necessity, but as a duty demanded by the 'special mark' of God's 'favor'.[39]

And the same anti-Catholic tone can be readily found in the final book of Thomas Hobbes's *Leviathan*; against its 'Confederacy' of priestly 'Deceivers', its 'Ghostly incantations', its myriad sacramental 'Illusions', and its 'vaine and impious Conjurations'.[40] But Hobbes was not part of the Protestant poetic. Indeed, he was enormously suspicious of any poetic; a suspicion which, as would be the case with Burke and his *Reflections*, inheres its own particular ironies. Any theology, Hobbes implies, seeks to govern imaginations by nurturing 'Phantasms of the braine', by projecting a 'kingdome of darknesse' and terror into which perceived heretics must fall. Popery is merely the most

[34] See S. Greenblatt, *Renaissance Self-Fashioning* (Chicago University Press, 1980), 168–9.

[35] See Greenblatt, *Self-Fashioning*, 167. Her successor thought precisely the same, in his *Basilicon Doron* saying that God placed kings on 'public stage', so that they can 'glister and shine before their people'. See King James, *Political Writings* (Cambridge University Press, 1994), 4, 13.

[36] See Greenblatt, *Self-Fashioning*, 168 and P. Collinson, 'The Monarchical Republic of Queen Elizabeth I', 69 *Bulletin of the John Rylands Library* 1987, 409. For an instance of a similar invocation of personal divinity in King James, in a sermon by Lancelot Andrewes in 1621, see L. Ferrell, 'Kneeling and the Body Politic' in D. Hamilton and R. Strier (eds.), *Religion, Literature and Politics in Post-Reformation England 154–1688*, (Cambridge University Press, 1996), 84.

[37] See B. Worden , *The Sound of Virtue: Phillip Sidney Arcadia and Elizabethan Politics* (Yale University Press, 1996), 254, and R. White, *Natural Law in English Renaissance Literature* (Cambridge University Press, 1996), 73–86.

[38] In P. Sidney, *A Critical Edition of the Major Works* (Oxford University Press, 1989), 220–3, 226–31, and also Worden, *Virtue*, 227–39.

[39] Sidney, *Works*, at 42, 101, 110–11, 132, J. Milton, *Complete Prose Works* (Yale University Press, 1953–62), 3.342–3, 348, and also A. Hadfield, 'The "Sacred Hunger of Ambitious Minds": Spenser's Savage Religion' in Hamilton and Strier, *Religion*, 27–45.

[40] T. Hobbes, *Leviathan* (Penguin, 1985), 627–9, 633–6.

distasteful of such theologies. His later history of the English civil wars, *Behemoth*, depicts a people that did indeed fly into a war against terror precisely because they were terrified by the incantations of rival clerics. Terror and religion, Hobbes well knew, are the cosiest of bedfellows.[41]

Within the context of this fiercely anti-Popish temper, the arrival of James I from Scotland had been met with much enthusiasm by beleaguered English Catholics. Henry Garnet anticipated a 'golden time' with 'great hope' of 'toleration'.[42] For much of the previous decades Jesuit tracts had circulated pleading the cause of alternative successors, such as the Spanish Infanta. But James was the realistic expectation, and his rule in Scotland, quite apart from the notoriety of his mother as a Catholic martyr, gave Garnet every reason to hope.[43] Sadly, as tended to become characteristic of the new king, in time he began to disappoint. The future, it became apparent, was going to be like the past; with pale-faced priests emerging in the quieter hours from cramped little closets, giving hasty Masses, and then retreating back into the shadows.

Whilst the likes of Garnet were more inclined to sigh a little deeper and reconcile themselves to their disappointment, a younger generation proved to be rather less amenable, and chose, instead, the path of active resistance. The Powder Plot, the origins of which could be traced to spring 1604, was a young man's plot, an expression of visceral and discontented youth.[44] Their leader was the charismatic Robert Catesby. Guy Fawkes was the hired hand. In time, they would secure Garnet's tacit assent. But their role bears a far more ready resemblance to that of an autonomous terrorist cell existing only very loosely within a wider diaspora of disaffected Catholics.

Having blown up King and Parliament, the aim of the plotters was to install a Protectorate under the prominent Catholic Earl of Northumberland, with the young Princess Elizabeth as queen.[45] Famously, they failed. Albion was saved once more. As the King advised his Parliament, they had been delivered from a 'roaring, nay a thundering sin of fire and brimstone'.[46] The formal institutions of law swung quickly into action. So did the propaganda. Although James

---

[41] T. Hobbes, *Behemoth* (Chicago University Press, 1990), 2–3, 15–16. For similar expressions of doubt regarding the respective zeal of Jesuit and puritan, see *Leviathan*, 706, 711. Clarendon would later accuse Hobbes of atheism, having 'traduced the whole scheme of Christianity into Burlesque'. See C. Hill, *The English Bible and the Seventeenth-Century Revolution* (Penguin, 1994), 421–3, and also Gray, *Black Mass*, 185, invoking Hobbes once again in the contemporary context, as a caution against any kind of theological zeal.

[42] In Fraser, *Plot*, xxxvii.

[43] James's mother was, of course, Mary Queen of Scots, whilst his wife, Anne of Denmark, had openly converted to Catholicism as a young woman, and whilst careful not to make her practice too blatant, was, equally, disinclined to hide it. For a commentary on the initial hopes of greater toleration, see Fraser, *Plot*, 46–52.

[44] Antonia Fraser emphasises the 'feeling of family which pervaded the whole Plot'. See her *Plot*, 136 and also Sharpe, *Remember*, 29–32. The Powder Plot was preceded by the rather less notorious Bye and Main Plots. Both were condemned by Garnet, who actually informed the Privy Council of the existence of the former.

[45] Sharpe, *Remember*, 54.   [46] In Fraser, *Plot*, 231.

cautioned against assuming 'that all professing the Romish religion were guilty of the same', his counsellors thought different. Legislation designed to counter the pressing 'Danger of Papistical Practices', was rushed through Parliament. A judicial inquiry, established by Lord Salisbury with the specific remit to contemplate the necessity of a rather wider war designed to 'exterminate' the Jesuit terror, was in place within days.[47] A show-trial of captured plotters opened to audiences in January 1606.[48]

The chief protagonist, in both the inquiry and the subsequent trials, was the Attorney-General, Sir Edward Coke. He too pressed the fact that the failure of the plotters had been 'divinely illuminated' by God.[49] And the 'principle offenders' in the 'Powder Plot', he was happy to confirm, were indeed 'the seducing Jesuits; men that used the reverence of religion, yea, even the most sacred and blessed name of Jesus, as a mantle to cover their impiety, blasphemy, treason and rebellion, all manner of wickedness'.[50] Extracted confessions read out in court were obliging, confirming the thrilling picture of a vast Jesuit plot to destroy the 'chosen people'.[51]

Whilst the intended destruction of Parliament and its members was startling enough, it was the anticipated murder of the King which was so shocking. Regicide was widely regarded, not just as a crime against nature, and God, but also against the commonwealth itself. It was an act of self-immolation. Later, Milton would argue that kings who proved to be 'suttle' dissimulators deserved to be decapitated.[52] But in early 1606, and with little fear of contradiction, Coke could proclaim that the regicide countenanced by the Powder plotters was amongst the 'the greatest treasons that ever were plotted in England, and concern the greatest King that ever was of England'.[53] Good counter-terrorist rhetoric is rarely undersold.

In short order Parliament passed an Act for a Public Thanksgiving to Almighty God every Year on the Fifth Day of November'.[54] The day, it was later to prove, was peculiarly blessed. Eighty-three years later, on the fifth of November 1688, Prince William of Orange landed at Torbay, at the behest of the English Parliament, in order to sweep away the resurrected spectre of a popish king.[55] Over a century later, Samuel Baker, preaching at York in 1745,

---

[47] See Fraser, *Plot*, 305.
[48] See Fraser, *Plot*, 230, for James's initial sanguinity, 236–41, 255 and 263 for evidence of the subsequent repression of Catholics through the winter of 1605–6, including the January declaration against 'Papistical Practices'. See also Sharpe, *Remember*, at 65–6, 70, 80–2.
[49] Wills, *Witches*, 14–16, 20–3.
[50] For a commentary on Coke's strategy and rhetoric, see Sharpe, *Remember*, 70–2, and also Fraser, *Plot*, 242–6.
[51] Fraser, *Plot*, 268–70.   [52] Milton, *Prose*, 3.350–62.   [53] In Sharpe, *Remember*, 72.
[54] Thus sanctifying the failure in the still nascent Protestant calendar. See Sharpe, *Remember*, 79, 83, and also 193, noting Martin Kettle's recent comment that Bonfire Night can be identified as the one real 'Festival of Britain', the 'one surviving national celebration which is truly popular, in the sense of belonging to the people'; an observation that can only attest to the enduring power of the original statute passed by Parliament four centuries ago.
[55] Sharpe, *Remember*, 102.

and in anticipation of a Stuart incursion into northern England, invoked memories of 'the Fifth'. It was, he declaimed, an act of 'gloomy bigotry' and 'relentless popery', and presented to his audience a virtual history of the catastrophe, of the 'severed heads, mangled limbs, the torn bodies tossed and scattered in the air', of the 'distressed mother, the tender wife, pale and trembling, seeking for the sad remains of son and husband'.[56]

Back in the winter of 1605, unsurprisingly, the popular mood was peculiarly susceptible to any amount of rhetorical fantasy. A poem of the time, 'The Devil of the Vault', widely circulated, expressed the pervasive sense of apocalyptic terror which the authorities were so keen to nurture:

> So, dreadful, foul, chimera-like
> My subject must appear:
> The Heaven amaz'd and hell disturbed
> The earth shall quake with fear.[57]

Horror, horror, horror

There was certainly much quaking, and much disturbance of heaven and hell, in what was perhaps the most famous literary commentary on the Gunpowder Plot, William Shakespeare's *Macbeth*.[58] Over the following century or more, performances of *Macbeth* on 'the Fifth' provided a theatrical complement to the more formal thanksgiving prescribed by Parliamentary statute. Pepys recorded attending one such performance in 1664.[59] Whilst the more popular understanding of the term, as it was to be articulated by Burke and contemporaries, may have lain a century or more away, successive audiences in early modern England comprehended *Macbeth* to be a play precisely about terrorism, about the terror which religious bigotry could breed.

Macbeth was the first play Shakespeare completed in the months following the abortive Plot.[60] The relation between the two is well-established in Shakespearean studies; as is the dominant theme of religiosity.[61] The subject of Shakespeare's own religious affinities remains a matter of controversy. On a personal level, he was certainly brought up in a town renowned for the virulence of its religious dissension.[62] Classical Shakespearean scholars have tended to present 'the Bard' as an avowed champion of the English protestant poetic.

---

[56] In Sharpe, *Remember*, 6–7.   [57] In Fraser, *Plot*, 254.

[58] See Alan Sinfield, '*Macbeth*: History, Ideology and Intellectuals', 28 *Critical Quarterly* 1986, 66–7, observing that the peculiar eruption of chaos in *Macbeth* suggests that it is the most terrifying in the Shakespearean canon.

[59] It was, he noted, a 'pretty good play'. See Sharpe, *Remember*, 94.

[60] The composition was clearly, to quote Antonia Fraser, 'darkened by the shadow' of the Plot. See her *Plot*, xiii.

[61] Some critics argue that the Scottish setting was also intended to awaken memories of the earlier Gowrie Plot in 1600. See, A. Clark, *Murder Under Trust: The Topical Macbeth* (Scottish Academic Press, 1981), particularly 12, and 109–12, and also Wills, *Witches*, particularly 27–9.

[62] A 'little Geneva', according to Collinson, *Birthpangs*, at 55.

Henry V is a paean to a 'chosen people' on crusade, a people whose very existence is defined by its preparedness to cross the Channel and slaughter lots of Catholics.[63] *Richard III* famously closes with an appeal to a distinctively Anglican God, one that will 'Smile' again upon 'God's fair ordinance'.[64] So does the play that is more commonly cited as Shakespeare's last, *Henry VIII*.[65] The 'radical Christian' Shakespeare, increasingly concerned with the doctrine of suffering, is a variant on the classical crusading Shakespeare.[66]

A second, rather different Shakespeare, is the recusant Shakespeare; the Shakespeare who, using a popular anti-recusant metaphor, was famously dismissed by Henry Chettle in 1592, as an 'upstart crow'.[67] This is the Shakespeare described by Ted Hughes as the 'shaman' of 'old Catholicism', whose recusant father is known to have received a copy of Cardinal Borromeo's notorious *Spiritual Testament* from Edmund Campion at the Catesby family's Lapworth House, and whose mother hailed from the equally recusant Arden family.[68] It is the Shakespeare who is rumoured to have spent some of his youth with the recusant Hoghton family in Lancashire, and then, on moving to London, is known to have oscillated towards the Mermaid Tavern, an established haven for recusants with artistic pretensions, the Shakespeare whose first patron, Lord Southampton, was himself an acknowledged recusant.[69] The evidence is, however, strikingly circumstantial, and it is reasonable to suppose that if Shakespeare did retain papist sympathies they were of the conformable kind.[70]

And then there are the post-modern Shakespeares, those that insinuate a fatal ambiguity that cuts across the entire corpus. This is the Shakespeare who

---

[63] It was *Henry V* that Laurence Olivier chose to film in 1944, hoping that, of all Shakespeare's plays, it would most readily resonate with the contemporary image of a nation again on a crusade to save Europe.

[64] W. Shakespeare, *Richard III*, (Arden, 1981) 5.5.29–34. Resonances between the two plays were drawn by Margaret Hotine, in '*Richard III* and *Macbeth* – Studies in Tudor Tyranny?' *Notes and Queries*, 236 (1991), 480–6, noting in particular their shared interest, not just in the providential intercession of a protestant God, but in the destructive capacity of dissimulation and equivocation.

[65] W. Shakespeare, *Henry VIII*, (Arden, 1968), 5.4.17–20, 45–6

[66] See D. Shuger, 'Shakespeare and Christianity' in Hamilton and Strier, *Religion*, particularly 47–9, and more broadly, T. McAlindon, 'What is a Shakespearean Tragedy?' in C. McEachern (ed.), *Cambridge Companion to Shakespeare* (Cambridge University Press, 2002), 16–20.

[67] The metaphorical affinity between Jesuits and 'massing crows' was well-understood by contemporaries. The case for a recusant Shakespeare has been most recently argued by Stephen Greenblatt in his *Hamlet in Purgatory* (Princeton University Press, 2001), particularly at 198 and 249, and more recently still by Richard Wilson, in his *Secret Shakespeare*, focusing particularly upon the crow metaphor at 11–13, and also at 295–6, concluding that Shakespeare was born into a 'suicidal Counter-Reformation milieu'.

[68] T. Hughes, *Shakespeare and the Goddess of Complete Being* (Faber and Faber, 1992), 86, 90. See also Wilson, *Shakespeare*, 15–16, 34, and also 112 suggesting that attesting to Borromeo's *Testament* was the 'equivalent of joining the Taliban'.

[69] See Wilson, *Shakespeare*, 21–2, 44–8, 56 and also 117, referring in this context to Shakespeare's 'Catholic terrorist affiliations'.

[70] See Wilson, *Shakespeare*, ix, 4 and also 297 concluding that he was, most probably, a putative Arminian.

fully appreciated, even embraced, the innate capacity of language to nurture dissimulation, who recognised that any textual politics is a necessarily ironic politics.[71] It is this Shakespeare who has his Archbishop in *Henry V* praise the young king precisely because he can 'steal his sweet and honey'd sentences; / So that the art and practic of life / Must be mistress to this rhetoric'.[72] All Shakespeare's princes, particularly the successful ones, are first and foremost consummate actors.[73] The dissimulating Shakespeare might be readily aligned with the recusant Shakespeare; as the embittered puritan John Speed insinuated as early as 1611, in his passing dismissal of Shakespeare, 'This papist and this poet, of like conscience for lies, the one ever feigning and the other ever falsifying the truth'.[74] There again, of course, he might not. Any dramatist dissimulates to some degree; as any good post-modernist will urge.

Shakespeare is famously evasive, and so are his plays. In one sense, the terror in *Macbeth* is overt, and so is the terrorist. Macbeth is Shakespeare's Catesby.[75] Macduff's distress at his discovery of the body of the murdered king would certainly have resonated:

> O horror! horror! horror!
> Tongue nor heart cannot conceive, nor name thee![76]

Regicide, a breach of 'absolute trust', a most 'sacrilegious Murther', is a crime that almost defies description.[77] But nothing in the rhyme and rhetoric of terror and counter-terror is ever truly beyond description. In *Macbeth* regicide leads, inexorably, to the immediate dissolution of the body politic, as well as the mental disintegration, and finally physical destruction, of the guilty. As Macbeth attests, the 'infliction of these terrible dreams, / That shake us nightly' are as one with the greater 'frame of things disjoint'.[78] Shakespeare's audience would have expected no less.[79]

---

[71] See J. Bate, *The Genius of Shakespeare* (Picador, 1997), 7–8.

[72] W. Shakespeare, *Henry V*, (Arden, 1954) 1.1.50–2.

[73] See Hadfield, *Shakespeare*, 59–61, and I. Ward, 'A Kingdom for a Stage, Princes to Act: Shakespeare and the Art of Government', *Law and Critique*, 8 (1997), 141–65.

[74] Speed's insinuation should be placed within the context of the broader puritan antipathy towards the theatre. See Wilson, *Shakespeare*, 5, and also 148–9, and also J. Knapp, *Shakespeare's Tribe: Church, Nation, and Theater in Renaissance England* (Chicago University Press, 2002), 53, 169.

[75] For an original suggestion of this affinity, see L. Hotson, *I, William Shakespeare* (Jonathan Cape, 1937), 197–8.

[76] W. Shakespeare, *Macbeth* (Arden, 1964), 2.3.62–3.

[77] 1.4.13–14, 2.3.66. Macbeth acknowledges precisely this. The king is sleeping under his roof 'in double trust', Macbeth being his 'kinsman and his subject', and 'his host' (1.7.12–14). For a discussion of 'trust' in the play, see Hadfield, *Shakespeare*, 78.

[78] 3.2.16, 18–19.

[79] It is quite likely that amongst the audience for the first performance would have been King James himself. Shakespeare's King's Men performed at Whitehall on 26 December 1605. Custom, as Alvin Kernan has argued, would suggest that they play their principle playwright's most recent work, which would have been *Macbeth*. The first verified performance, however, was August 1606, on the occasion of the visit of the king's brother-in-law, Christian of Denmark. See A. Kernan, *Shakespeare, the King's Playwright: Theater in the Stuart Court 1603–1613*, (Yale University Press, 1995), 71–2.

In another sense, however, the terror is indeed evasive; an expression of a fatal textual ambiguity.[80] Here, the porter's speech just prior to the discovery of Duncan's body, is justly renowned. Taking exception at such an urgent 'knocking' on his door, the porter exclaims:

> Here's a farmer, that hang'd himself on th'expectation of plenty: come in, time-pleaser; have napkins enow about you; here you'll sweat for it. Knock, knock. Who's there, i'th'other devil's name – Faith, here's an equivocator, that could swear in both the scales against either scale; who committed treason enough for God's sake, yet could not equivocate to heaven: O! come in equivocator.[81]

The speech is notoriously opaque. But allusions to Henry Garnet are unmistakable. The Jesuit Superior, who used the alias Farmer, is welcomed fresh from the scaffold, carrying his 'napkins'; items that he will certainly need as he sweats in hell, but which carried a very different consonance in Catholic martyrology, so often the bloodied relics of butchered priests.[82] The subject of equivocation was equally, and indelibly, associated with Garnet. The allusion to the Farmer who 'could not equivocate to heaven', carried a particular, and grim, resonance; at least Garnet, it was joked at the time, would be 'hanged without equivocation'.[83]

In his report on the 'Powder Plot', Coke spoke of the 'perfidious and perjurious equivocating' of the conspirators; a practice encouraged in 'certain heretical, treasonable and damnable books' including Garnet's own treatise *On Equivocation*.[84] For priests like Garnet, equivocation was justified by the unbreakable sanctity of the confessional.[85] As far as Coke was concerned, however, when it came to dealing with papists, a failure to tell the whole truth was tantamount to 'open and broad lying and forswearing', and should be treated as such. A priest who knew, but declined to confess his knowledge, like Garnet, was just as guilty as those who were found lurking in the cellars of Westminster. Coke spent much time at Garnet's trial painting a lurid picture of equivocating priests. Equivocation and dissimulation, he suggested, were the 'bastard children' of popery.[86]

---

[80] R. McDonald, 'The Language of Tragedy' in McEachern, *Companion*, 46–7.   [81] 2.3.4–13.

[82] See Wills, *Witches*, 96–101 and Wilson, *Shakespeare*, 171, 172–4, both further emphasising the place of such napkins in Catholic martyrology.

[83] Comment attributed originally to Dudley Carleton, and cited in Fraser, *Plot*, 315.

[84] A text which, on its discovery, was ascribed by the Royal Chaplain, to a 'priest of Satan'. See Wills, *Witches*, 93 and Fraser, *Plot*, 268.

[85] Garnet wrote his treatise as a defence to the captured Jesuit, Robert Southwell, who had, it was attested, given instruction on how to lie in 'good conscience'. In quoting authorities such as St. Gregory, who had held that 'Men judge a man's heart by his words. God judges words by the heart', he was following an established theological track. Edmund Campion had consistently sought to distinguish equivocation from simple lying. For a discussion of the strategy of equivocation in early modern recusancy, see P. Zagorin, *Ways of Lying: Dissimulation, Persecution and Conformity in Early Modern Europe* (Harvard University Press, 1990), 14, and also Wilson, *Shakespeare*, 54–5 and Wills, *Witches*, 93–6.

[86] Fraser, *Plot*, 311–13.

Equivocation has seduced Macbeth.[87] First, in the person of his wife who propels her husband to commit the most heinous of acts, and to do so by adopting strategies of dissimulation:

> Your face, my Thane, is as a book, where men
> May read strange matters. To beguile the time,
> Look like the time; bear welcome in your eye,
> Your hand, your tongue: look like th'innocent flower,
> But be the serpent under't.[88]

And second, in the form of the witches. The temptation to identify the 'juggling fiends' which Macbeth encounters upon the heath with contemporary Jesuit caricatures is itself seductive.[89] The witches 'fight against the / Churches', they treasure icons such as the 'pilot's thumb', a clear allusion to the notorious thumb of the martyred Campion, and indulge in satanic rituals, of the kind which, in the febrile imagination of the time, were barely distinguished from the shadowy Masses conducted by closeted priests in country houses up and down the country.[90]

And they play with language. Their sorcery is written in riddles. It is, as Hecate affirms in her 'angerly' confrontation with the three witches in Act 3 Scene 5, her 'art':

> How did you dare
> To trade and traffic with Macbeth,
> In riddles, and affairs of death;
> And I, the mistress of your charms,
> The close contriver of all harms,
> Was never call'd to bear my part,
> Or show the glory of our art?[91]

It is her 'magic sleights' which, 'Shall raise such artificial sprites, / As, by the strength of the illusion' shall draw Macbeth to his ultimate demise.[92] As

---

[87] See Wilson, *Shakespeare*, 195, and also J. Stachniewski, 'Calvinist Psychology in *Macbeth*', *Shakespeare Studies*, 20 (1988), 172–3, 182 exploring the extent to which Macbeth's seduction is symptomatic of a fatalist mindset that is peculiarly Calvinist. See also C. Belsay 'Gender and Family' in McEachern, *Companion*, 133–5, and D. Norbrook, '*Macbeth* and the Politics of Historiography' in K. Sharpe and S. Zwicker (eds.), *Politics of Discourse: The Literature and History of Seventeenth Century England* (California University Press, 1987), 104–5, both suggesting that the same fatalism could be interpreted as representing a failing of gender, a critical emasculation of the protagonist.

[88] 1.5.62–6. For the assertion that Lady Macbeth is depicted as a fourth witch, see Wills, *Witches*, 80.

[89] 5.10.19. See also Wilson, *Shakespeare*, 193–9, and Wills, *Witches*, 35–7, 43–8.

[90] 4.1.52–3. Campion's thumb has a suitably odd and grisly history. It was hacked from a quartered limb in the minutes following his final demise. It was the only relic that the hangman permitted, and for a while seemed to disappear. In time it appeared in two pieces, a bit in Roehampton and a bit in Rome. Harsnett chronicled that it was used by exorcists in 'diabolical service', to seek out the devil in places where, it was thought, he might reside, most commonly the private parts of suspected witches. See Wilson, *Shakespeare*, 188–93.

[91] 3.5.3–9.   [92] 3.5.26–8.

Macbeth begins to sense his own fate, he appreciates the irony of his seduction; his own dissimulation founded on the impenetrable riddles of the witches. 'I pull in resolution', he reflects, as Birnam wood does indeed appear to 'come to Dunsinane', and 'begin / To doubt the equivocation of the fiend. / That lies like truth'.[93] But it is too late to eschew dissimulation; at least it is for Macbeth.

But not for Scotland, or by implication for Albion. The 'special providence' which will pervade Hamlet's Denmark in Shakespeare's next great tragedy is visited upon Scotland in the closing scenes.[94] Macduff recognises the 'holy' relation of the English Crown and 'Him above' when he flees across the border.[95] Malcolm too puts his faith in the 'Angels', leaving to God the question of a proper succession, and trusting in the 'Powers above' to wreak a biblical vengeance upon the 'Devilish Macbeth'.[96] Scotland will be saved 'by the Grace of God', and by England.[97] And it is in 'the great hand of God' that Banquo places himself.[98] Of course, Banquo's faith proves to be a little misplaced, at least in the short run; an intimation of the chaos that might befall a people that God forsakes.[99] But in the end, it is God who saves Scotland, and Shakespeare would have his audience surmise, Albion too. It is from Banquo's line that King James was said to trace his succession; a fantasy that James was, by all accounts, more than happy to sustain.[100]

On crusade

The impact of 'the Fifth' upon the political imagination of early Jacobean England was just as great as the impact of 9/11 on the political imagination of early twenty-first-century America. The similarities between the anti-Jesuit hysteria of early seventeenth-century England and our present responses to the perceived threats of militant Islam are acute.[101] As a 'hybrid of apocalyptic myth and utopian hope', there is anyway much in militant Islam that should be

---

[93] 5.5.42–4.

[94] 5.2.210. For a discussion of this providence, arguing its Calvinist credentials, particularly in *Hamlet*, see A. Sinfield, 'Hamlet's Special Providence', *Shakespeare Survey*, 33 (1980), 33–89–97. A similar argument is presented, again aligning the two tragedies, in Stachniewski, 'Calvinist Psychology', 169–89.

[95] 3.6.30, 32.   [96] 4.3.22, 117, 120–1, 238–9.   [97] 5.9.29–30, 38.   [98] 2.3.128.

[99] For a critical discussion of providence in the play, noting its various ambiguities, see J. O'Rourke, 'The Subversive Metaphysics of *Macbeth*', *Shakespeare Studies*, 21 (1993), 213–27, and also H. Diehl, 'Religion and Shakespearean Tragedy' in McEachern, *Companion*, 92–5.

[100] Shakespeare alludes to this claim in Act 4 Scene 1, where the witches raise the spectre of a train of kings, at the end of which is the ghost of Banquo. It depicts, as Macbeth comes to realise, the succession from Banquo; something confirmed by the final king carrying 'two-fold balls and treble sceptres', representing the combined regalia of English and Scottish coronations. For Macbeth, it is, of course, a 'horrible sight' (4.1.121–2). The veracity of the succession of Scottish kings through Banquo's line was confirmed in Holinshed's *Chronicles of Scotland*. For a commentary, see Kernan, *Playwright*, 77

[101] See Wilson, *Shakespeare*, 7, sketching the obvious parallel.

familiar to the Christian or Enlightenment political philosopher; the intellectual, and theological, root is shared.[102]

One thing is deniable; terror and faith go hand in hand, half a step behind dogma and paranoia.[103] One side in the present 'war on terror' certainly seems to think so. According to bin Laden's deputy, Ayman al-Zawahiri, the 'love of death' which drives the Islamic 'warrior' is a 'testament' to the 'fury for God' which defines *jihad*.[104] In the words of one of the fathers of modern *jihad*, Abdullah Azzam, militant Islam is 'solely dependent on the ink of its scholars and the blood of its martyrs', such that 'the map of Islamic history becomes coloured with two lines: one of them black, with the ink of scholar's pen; the other one red with the martyr's blood'.[105]

The other side, it might be hoped, would be rather more circumspect. Not so. The immediate response to 9/11, particularly amongst members of the Bush administration, was to confirm their engagement in a latter-day war of religion; just as bin Laden and al-Zawahiri had hoped. The rhetoric was both prophetic and visceral. The 'war on terror', President Bush announced, would be a 'crusade', and it 'was going to take a while'.[106] Speech after speech closed with an injunction for prayer. A messianic culture of 'suffering' was invested, a rhetoric of 'apocalyptic fundamentalism' invoked.[107] The spirit of Herman Melville walked again in the American consciousness. 'We Americans', Melville had held a century before, 'are the chosen people – the Israel of our time; we bear the ark of the

---

[102] Gray, *Black Mass*, 72–3.

[103] For a comment on the complexities of these alignments, see R. Israel, 'Islamikaze and their Significance', *Terrorism and Political Violence*, 9 (1997), particularly 107–15, and also Amis, *Plane*, 90–2.

[104] The literature on the place of a 'cult of death' within strains of Islamic political theology is considerable. See P. Rees, *Dining with Terrorists* (Macmillan, 2005), 247–8; J. Burke, *Al-Qaeda: The True Story of Radical Islam* (Penguin, 2004) 32–5; and also M. Ignatieff, *The Lesser Evil: Political Ethics in an Age of Terror* (Edinburgh University Press, 2005), 150; S. Zizek, *Welcome to the Desert of the Real* (Verso, 2002), 141–2; W. Lacqueur, *No End to War: Terrorism in the Twenty-First Century* (Continuum, 2004), 71–3, 85–7; and W. Sofsky, *Violence: Terrorism, Genocide, War* (Granta, 2003), 95. Suicide-bombing remains a matter of scriptural controversy in Islam. It is forbidden in the Koran. But the 'cult of the martyr' is not. The crucial texts are verses 2. 216: 'Prescribed for you is fighting though it be hateful to you', and 9.5, the so-called 'sword-verse', 'And when the sacred months are over, kill the polytheists wherever you find them, and take them captive, and besiege them, and lie in wait for them in every strategem'. For a commentary on the ambiguous nature of Koranic texts in the matter of warfare and martyrdom, see M. Ruthven, *A Fury for God: The Islamist Attack on America* (Penguin, 2002), 48–52, 58–9.

[105] Quoted in Ruthven, *Fury*, 203–4, who also confirms, at 208–9, the extent to which bin Laden sees himself as a protégé of Azzam.

[106] Speaking seven days after the attack on the Twin Towers. In R. Blackburn, 'The Imperial Presidency, the War on Terrorism, and the Revolutions of Modernity', *Constellations*, 9 (2002), at 7.

[107] See R. Jackson, *Writing the War on Terrorism* (Manchester University Press, 2005), 33–5, 103, 142–3; E. Hobsbawn, *Globalisation, Democracy and Terrorism* (Little Brown, 2007), 60–1, 128–9; Gray, *Black Mass*, 1–3; and Ruthven, *Fury*, 32–3.

liberties of the world'.[108] The particular enchantment that 9/11 had cast was to be of a peculiarly theological, intensely messianic and puritan kind.[109]

The particular invocation of 'crusade' was recanted, the term banished from the lexicon of Presidential counter-terrorist rhetoric. It seemed just too obvious and too incendiary. But the sentiment remained. The rhetoric of post-9/11 counter-terrorism was as militant and fundamentalist as the terrorism which it promised to destroy. The experience of terrorism inflicted on New York in September 2001, like the counter-terrorism inflicted upon the peoples of Afghanistan and Iraq in the proclaimed 'war' that followed, was an expression of theological fundamentalism.[110] In this, as in so much, the elusive clerics of the Hindu Kush got to set the rules, and thereby control the players and the game.[111]

America, accordingly, went to 'war on terror' emboldened by the iconography of militant Christianity.[112] Much was made of a people being crucified, 'suffering' at the hands of evil. The Blatant Beast was abroad again. False prophets were everywhere. There were lots in Afghanistan, and it transpired, rather conveniently, in Iraq too. Needless to say, they were also 'at home', as Attorney-General Ashcroft repeatedly advised, swarming across God's own country and insinuating themselves in the homesteads of middle America.[113] Secretary of State Powell noted that, unlike the 'chosen people', these prophets, and their followers, had no real 'faith', and neither, by implication, did their followers. He, however, believed in the right God, and so, he presumed, did his compatriots, or at least most of them.[114]

General William Boykin, the man specifically tasked to capture bin Laden, was just as sure, reassuring fellow supplicants at his Oregon church that theirs was a 'real God', and a 'bigger' one too. The enemy, he advised, was not just bin Laden, but a 'guy called Satan'.[115] Boykin, it seems reasonable to assume, rather fancied himself as 'Heaven's angry flame', venturing into southern Afghanistan with his 'sword erect' and his gun-ships whirring. Whether Marvell would have been impressed by the juvenile rhetoric which he visited upon his Oregon congregation is rather more doubtful.

---

[108] In Ruthven, *Fury*, 33. For the similar invocation of Melville's spirit, see B. Barber, *Fear's Empire: War, Terrorism and Democracy* (Norton, 2004), 67–70. For invocations of America's 'foundational myth' in post-9/11 rhetoric, see Jackson, *Writing*, 48–9.

[109] For the puritan analogy, see Blackburn, 'Imperial Presidency', 16–17, and Gray, *Black Mass*, 107–8.

[110] See S. Buck-Morss, *Thinking Past Terror* (Verso, 2003), xii.

[111] See S. Faludi, *The Terror Dream: Fear and Fantasy in Post-9/11 America* (Metropolitan Books, 2007), 294–5.

[112] See G. Achcar, *The Clash of Barbarisms: The Making of the New World Disorder* (Saqi, 2006), 28–9.

[113] Jackson, *Writing*, 112–13.   [114] Jackson, *Writing*, 68.

[115] In D. Rose, *Guantanamo: America's War on Human Rights* (Faber and Faber, 2004), 138–9, and also Gray, *Black Mass*, 115.

The insinuation – and depictions of Islam have always, as Edward Said confirms, been matters of 'insinuation' – was clear.[116] Where God-fearing Christians went to church, the false prophets of militant Islam were depicted scurrying about from cave to cave indulging in all kinds of cultish rituals; just, indeed, as Garnet's Jesuits were portrayed as flitting from priest-hole to priest-hole, only occasionally venturing into the light to administer all the horrors of the popish Mass. God, as President Bush reassured his people, is not 'neutral'.[117] It was his 'strong belief' that the cause for which America fought, the cause of freedom, was the 'Almighty's gift'.[118] The messianic rhetoric reached something of an apogee in the President's address at the National Cathedral in Washington five days after 9/11. 'God's signs', he declared, 'are not always the ones we look for'. But 9/11 was such a 'sign', a confirmation that America had a 'responsibility to history' to 'answer these attacks and rid the world of evil'. It was a divine 'calling'.[119]

The messianic tone is given centre-stage in David Hare's *Stuff Happens*; a play which we have already encountered and which, moreover, or so its author claims, is akin to a 'Shakespearean tragedy' precisely because it is about the ultimately fatal consequences of profound political dishonesty.[120] Hare's Bush sees himself as God's messenger, a latter-day crusader, or at least one inclined to wave enthusiastically as he sends others off to war on his behalf.[121] The central character in *Stuff Happens* never speaks; except, it appears, to George Bush. God, Bush claims, 'wants me to do it'. The play closes with the President's notorious declaration, made to an astonished, and it is reasonable to assume appalled, Lebanese premier, Mahmoud Abbas, 'God told me to strike Al-Qaeda and I struck them, and then he instructed me to strike at Saddam, which I did'.[122] Bush's collateral contempt for the law is rooted in a defining belief; that, as a latter-day prophet, he has the authority of a greater testament. The common recourse to rhetorical dissimulation, shared by both Bush and Blair, can be similarly attributed.[123] The messianic tone provides simplicity; the simplest expression of the pervasive delusion, the simplest, and most troubling, justification for the abrogation of legal principle.

Hare closes his play with an Iraqi voice contemplating the 'uncounted' dead, and lamenting a country that has been 'crucified'.[124] The irony is immediate. It finds an apparently unwitting, but no less tragic, echo in Ashcroft's declaration, again in the months immediately following 9/11, that 'Islam is a religion in

[116] E. Said, *Orientalism* (Penguin, 2003), 320   [117] Jackson, *Writing*, 144, and also 146.

[118] In Rees, *Terrorists*, 368–9.   [119] Jackson, *Writing*, 143 and 145.

[120] See his comments in the *Guardian*, 30 May 2006, at 10, that the mark of political tragedy lies in the 'conflict between the politicians' true intentions and their purported intentions'. Shakespeare, he concludes, 'tells us in plays like *Macbeth* that this scenario can never improve'.

[121] D. Hare, *Stuff Happens* (Faber and Faber, 2004), 17, 19.

[122] Hare, *Stuff Happens*, 9–10, 15, 119, and also Gray, *Black Mass*, 115.

[123] See Gray, *Black Mass*, 103–5, commenting on their construction of a convenient rhetorical 'pseudo-reality', justified in terms of their assumed providential responsibilities.

[124] Hare, *Stuff Happens*, 120.

which God requires you to send your son to die for him. Christianity is a faith in which God sends his son to die for you'.[125] The true depth of the irony can perhaps only be appreciated by the parents of those thousands who have since died in pursuit of the 'war on terror' in Afghanistan and Iraq.

This rhetoric, of testament and crusade, is as reckless as it is ignorant and perverse. Slavoj Zizek warns against 'our warriors on terror' seemingly 'ready to wreck their own democratic world' out of a visceral 'hatred for the Muslim other'.[126] He is right. There is little to be gained by situating Islam as an enemy, just as there is little to be gained by constructing fantastical bogey-men.[127] But we continue to do so all the same. Islamophobia has become a hallmark of modern western popular culture, the image of the devious, rapacious, endemically violent Islamic terrorist a staple of our cinematic and literary diet. Where the 'chosen people' were once terrified by the dreaded papist, they are now terrified by the dreaded Islamic. It is a fear, as Edward Said suggests, that has, over the centuries, become 'woven into the fabric' of western cultural 'life'.[128] Here again, our craving for terror, and to be terrified, seems to be unquenchable.[129] We live in an 'empire of fear', possessed of a terror that we have essentially 'conjured' for ourselves.[130]

The mythology of al-Qaeda, and all its constituent mythologies, of suicide-bombers and insurgents, fundamentalists and *jihadists*, is all-consuming.[131] Set within the broader heritage of orientalist fetish and prejudice, it raises ghostly networks of highly trained Islamic terrorists, roaming, as President Bush was so keen to advise us, the streets of London and New York.[132] The reality, of course, is rather different. On closer inspection, it is apparent that there are myriad essentially autonomous Islamic terrorist groups, each grounded in particular geopolitical

---

[125] In T. Seto, 'The Morality of Terrorism', *Loyola of Los Angeles Law Review*, 35 (2002), 1261.

[126] Zizek, *Desert*, 84.

[127] See Ahdaf Soueif, *Mezzaterra: Fragments from the Common Ground* (Anchor, 2004), 19.

[128] See Said, *Orientalism*, 48–9, 59, 60–3, 94–5, 232–3, emphasising the extent to which Islam has been deployed as the 'natural' other in western culture. The critical literature here is vast. Aside from Said, see also Ruthven, *Fury*, 16–18, and P. Fitzpatrick, *The Mythology of Modern Law* (Routledge, 1992), ix, 30–2 and 45–63 suggesting that the mythology of the heathen 'other' defines Christian theology.

[129] See Ruthven, *Fury*, 34–5, commenting on the 'peculiarly vulnerable' nature of our political and theological imagination, and its craving for the seemingly 'apocalyptic'.

[130] See B. Barber, *Fear's Empire: War, Terrorism and Democracy* (Norton, 2003), 18, 33. For a devastating critique of the British government's attempt to cultivate an 'atmosphere of near hysteria', see the comments of the former head of the UK's Joint Intelligence Committee, Sir Rodric Braithwaite, quoted in Tariq Ali, *Bush in Babylon* (Verso, 2003), 150–1, noting that 'fishmongers sell fish, warmongers sell war', and concluding wryly that Prime Minister Blair has proved to be a consummate salesman.

[131] For a critique of the implicit racism that these taboos tend to carry, see Said's observations in J. Pilger (ed.), *Tell Me No Lies: Investigative Journalism and its Triumphs* (Vintage, 2005), 586–7 and 591, suggesting that they constitute a more general 'discourse of Islamic peril'.

[132] For a compelling critique of this illusion, consciously nurtured by western political leaders, see Burke, *Al-Qaeda*, xxv.

contexts, each pursuing often radically different theological agendas.[133] What passes for 'Al-Qaeda' is merely one loosely defined variant of political Islamism, its projected leader, Osama bin Laden, one former mujahideen warlord who, partly through his own strategic acumen, and partly through the naivety of his pursuers, has acquired for himself an iconic status.[134] Ultimately, the Al-Qaeda so cherished by our political leaders, and so much of our media, is essentially a fantasy, a 'mode of thinking', a 'discourse'; one that is sufficiently vague and 'messy' that it can be readily used and misused to suit.[135]

Of course, the iconic, fantastical image matters, hugely. In the manner of a self-fulfilling prophesy, it lends a coherence to Islamist terrorism which would not otherwise be readily discernible, whilst also nurturing the discourse of fear so vital to the myriad wars which are currently engaged against terrorism, against Taliban 'mullahs', Chechen 'rebels', Iraqi 'insurgents', and so on. It is a fundamental, if historically familiar, deceit. And it should trouble us. First, because the raising of spectres does indeed fulfil prophesies. With each passing 'war', the Islamic world becomes ever more radicalised, its youth ever more intent upon embracing the 'fury for God'.[136]

And second, because the constant weaving of counter-terrorist mythology actually serves to detract from the need to address the real threat that exists. If we pretend that there is an identifiable enemy, one that might be defeated in a 'war on terror', our strategies to counter the terrorism which we actually experience, at the hands of various disenchanted and largely dislocated individuals and groups, will remain ineffective.[137] 'Democracies', as Seyla Benhabib has recently put it, 'cannot fight holy wars', and nor should they want to. The weapons of modern liberal democracy are 'reason, compassion, respect for the dignity of human life, the search for justice, and the desire for reconciliation'.[138]

---

[133] Burke, *Al-Qaeda*, 10–11, 24, suggesting that for geopolitical reasons in particular, there is no sense in trying to define something as putatively concrete as an 'Islamic terrorist'.

[134] Burke uncompromisingly rejects the notion that Al-Qaeda might represent anything that passes for a coherent terrorist group or organisation, and similarly doubts the extent to which it might even be thought of as a determinate network. See Burke, *Al-Qaeda*, 231–3, and also 79–83, discussing bin Laden's more particular image as a successful mujahideen warlord, and the doubts that surround the extent of his engagement, and success, in the Afghan wars of the 1990s.

[135] The term 'Al-Qaeda' actually means base or foundation, both in the material sense and in the more metaphysical sense of rule or precept. See Burke, *Al-Qaeda*, 1–2, and also 14 suggesting that it might be best thought to represent a 'mode of thinking', and 38–40 exploring the evolution of the Al-Qaeda 'discourse'. For a critique of the mythology, see A. Curtis, 'Creating Islamist Phantoms', the *Guardian*, 30 August 2005, 18. For a review of the thesis, see P. Bergen, 'A Real Nightmare', *Prospect*, August 2005, 26–31.

[136] See Burke, *Al-Qaeda*, 274–6, and 284, confirming that 'modern Islamic terrorists are made not born', and also Barber, *Fear's Empire*, 26, referring to the 'toxic combination of powerlessness, resentment and humiliation' which US foreign policy in the Middle East has nurtured amongst a generation of disaffected Islamic youth.

[137] See Burke, *Al-Qaeda*, 15–16, and 291, confirming that the 'battle for hearts and minds' in the wider Islamic diaspora is being lost.

[138] S. Benhabib, 'Unholy Wars', *Constellations*, 9 (2002), 44.

As we have already noted, the overt rhetoric of crusade was rapidly recanted. It has been more recently overlaid by a more prosaic rhetoric of pre-emptive self-defence and weapons of mass destruction. But its presence, and certainly its spirit, cannot be so easily erased. Where terror is, theology of one form or another is never far away.[139] Down the centuries, the struggle between terrorism and counter-terrorism has always represented the violent expression of an original struggle between antagonistic fundamentalisms, between dogma and counter-dogma.[140] The fact that the present strain of terrorism associated with Al-Qaeda has a more overtly theological tone is simply a matter of degree, not essence. Sometimes the drivers are more obviously ideological, sometimes more obviously theological. More often than not, sharing an equivalent eschatological zeal, there is no clear distinction between the two; we shall encounter a recent example of this elision in the next chapter, the subject of which is the terrorist wars that convulsed the Balkans during the 1990s.[141] Sometimes the political theology is overt, sometimes it lurks, sometimes it is preached by supposedly rogue imams, or generals in Oregon, sometimes by states and established churches, presidents and popes. In whatever form it appears, the presumed necessity of violence and terror is never far from the accompanying rhetoric.[142] Fundamentalists like to kick ass.

Sometimes, of course, it seems rather more benign. In this form, it can find an insidious expression in the mouths of politicians who choose to pontificate on the threat facing 'our values' or our 'ways of life'.[143] Hare's Prime Minister Blair in *Stuff Happens* ruminates much upon this subject, constantly striving to locate a moral justification for war, whilst remaining wary that a more blatant invocation of divine injunction, of the kind declaimed by his American counterpart, is likely to be received with derision by his own compatriots. Instead, he prefers to recast the 'war against terror' as a war in defence of the 'free and democratic world' and, as such, a 'moral duty'.[144] In this form, his rhetoric seeks to mask its fundamentalist impulses.[145] The dissimulating insidious fundamentalist is just as dangerous as the pulpit-bashing zealot; as Coke and Shakespeare knew only too well.

The problem with invoking such a fundamentalist morality is obvious. It can very easily transmute into talk about cultures and civilisations, and their presumed merits and demerits, and their supposed clashes. Makua Matua argues that the 'war on terrorism' is a thin mask for a war on 'Islamic traditions

---

[139] Benhabib, 'Unholy Wars', 42–3.

[140] See A. Heller, '9/11, or Modernity and Terror', *Constellations*, 9 (2002), 57–9, and also Gray, *Black Mass*, 17–19, 38.

[141] See Gray, *Black Mass*, 4–12, 17–19.   [142] Heller, '9/11', 59–61

[143] See R. Johnson, 'Defending Ways of Life: The (Anti-)Terrorist Rhetorics of Bush and Blair' *Theory, Culture and Society*, 19 (2002), 212–21, and also F. Halliday, *Two Hours that Shook the World: September 11th 2001*, (Saqi Books, 2002), 51–68.

[144] Hare, *Stuff Happens*, 18.

[145] Johnson, 'Ways of Life', 226. For a damning commentary on the dissimulation with which Blair sought to mask his crusading impulses, see Gray, *Black Mass*, 97, 103–6.

and political projects', the realisation of the 'them-and-us dialectic' which underpins the project of modernity.[146] Tariq Ali likewise identifies the war as a simple expression of neo-liberal 'imperialism'.[147] The argument, which finds an original expression in the writing of Edward Said, is only too familiar.[148] It finds contemporary sustenance in Samuel Huntington's notorious 'clash of civilizations' thesis.[149] Gilbert Achcar's derivative 'clash of barbarisms' thesis is rooted in the same intellectual subsoil.[150] If there is a cultural 'fault-line' between the 'west' and Islam, it is one which we are in acute danger of wishing into a more vital existence.[151]

The dilemma, obvious and immediate, has been recently explored in Orhan Pamuk's critically acclaimed novel, set in his native Turkey, *Snow*; at the heart of which is a dramatic reinterpretation, by an avowedly secular theatrical company, of Thomas Kyd's fiercely anti-Catholic play, *The Spanish Tragedy*, first published in 1592.[152] The ridicule of theology, particularly the theology of the 'other', is a peculiarly incendiary strategy, one that backfires spectacularly upon the performers in Pamuk's novel.[153] It is an age-old error, the product of an equally timeless tendency to bigotry and prejudice. And it is this kind of bigotry, Pamuk suggests, which continues to afflict his compatriots, just as it afflicted early seventeenth-century England, and just as it continues to drive the current 'war on terror'. There is nothing to be gained by persecuting those who subscribe to a different faith, less still in ridiculing them. We shall revisit Pamuk's novel in due course.

At the end of the day, the presumed, or contested, acuity of the 'clash of civilizations' thesis is less important than the insinuation. There may be no necessary association between militant *jihad* and the philosophy or jurisprudence of Islam.[154] It may well be the mutant figment of an orientalist, even racist, political and cultural imagination. But it does not need to be accurate or apposite. What matters, sadly, is that so many are deluded by the supposition. Again, the prophecy fulfils itself.

---

[146] M. Mutua, 'Terrorism and Human Rights: Power, Culture and Subordination', *Buffalo Human Rights Law Review*, 8 (2002), 2.

[147] Tariq Ali, *Babylon*, 3, 143, 155. The same conclusion is reached by Eric Hobsbawn, in his *Globalisation*, at 54–71 in particular.

[148] See Said, *Orientalism*, particularly xiii, 1–3, 12, 43, 52, 201–4, 319–20, and also *Power, Politics and Culture* (Bloomsbury, 2005), 242–3 and 388–92.

[149] See, for example, Ahdaf Soueif, *Mezzaterra*, 65, 78–9 rightly suggesting that acceptance of Huntington's thesis nurtures an ultimately self-destructive siege mentality. For Said's dismissal of Huntington's 'preposterous' thesis, see *Orientalism*, 348. For Huntington's original statement, see his *The Clash of Civilizations and the Remaking of World Order* (Simon & Schuster, 1997), 129–1, 28, 248–52.

[150] Achcar, *Barbarisms*, 84.

[151] Ruthven, *Fury*, 240–3. For Huntington's deployment of the metaphor, see *Clash*, 252–4, 281–91.

[152] For a commentary on Kyd's play and its anti-Catholic notoriety, see Hadfield, *Shakespeare*, 19.

[153] O. Pamuk, *Snow* (Faber and Faber, 2004), 341, 399–413.

[154] N. Feldman, *After Jihad: America and the Struggle for Islamic Democracy* (Farrar, Straus & Giroux, 2003), 6–7, 20–1, 62–3, 75–6, 232–4. See also Ruthven, *Fury*, 48, and Barber, *Empire*, 202–3.

On the one hand, there are plenty of disenchanted and dispossessed young Muslims who are all too easily persuaded into thinking that theology justifies terror. To them, bin Laden's rhetoric 'makes sense', in the same way as Borromeo's *Testament* impelled young Catholics such as Robert and Thomas Catesby to risk their lives four hundred years ago.[155] On the other, there is a 'western' populace that appears to be all too ready to embrace the rhetoric of the apocalypse, to suppose that the 'blatant Beast' is abroad once more, to believe that America and its allies have a moral duty, a divine calling even, one which justifies the presence of their crusaders across vast tracts of the Middle East, from Qom to Kabul. The alternative fantasies, as is so often the case, are mutually sustaining. They nurture the terror, and the tragedy.

On 5 November 1753, another Garnett, no relation of the unfortunate Henry, John Garnett, Bishop of Ferns and Leighlin, preached a sermon at Christ Church Dublin. It was, of course, in commemoration of the peculiarly wedded 'anniversary of the Gunpowder Plot and of the happy arrival of King William III'. Anticipating the emergence of a nascent Enlightenment, and embracing 'the cultivation of the liberal arts and sciences', he concluded with the impassioned hope that 'the Christian world at length will be right rid of crusades and pilgrimages, those quixoticisms in religious chivalry', and, with them, the 'pious solecism in holy-church politiks' which, for so long, had nurtured the associated mythologies of holy war. Such infantile rhetoric, and infantile theology, must, he predicted, 'be now no more'.[156] Sadly, it seems, not quite yet.[157]

---

[155] See Rees, *Terrorism*, 338–43 and 370–1, and also Barber, *Empire*, 24, and Wilson, *Shakespeare*, 136.

[156] In Sharpe, *Remember*, 112.

[157] Though some, such as Martin Amis, increasingly sense a hardening of attitudes borne of a growing realisation, by many, that the affinity of religion and violence is endemic. See his comments in *Plane*, at 92, that 'the time has come for a measure of impatience in our dealing with those' who present faith as an excuse for violence. 'Opposition to religion', he confirms, 'already occupies the high ground intellectually and morally. People of independent mind should now start to claim the spiritual high ground too'.

3

Voices of the terrified

Criminal proceedings tend to be surprisingly dull. There again, dullness is supposed to be a requisite of impartial justice; so perhaps it is not so surprising. The problem, of course, is that this can very easily lead to what has been termed 'emotional disconnect'.[1] In her account of proceedings at the *Zigic* trial at the International Criminal Tribunal for Yugoslavia (ICTY) at The Hague, the Serbian journalist and writer Slavenka Drakulic testified to the sheer boredom of events, as well as the experience of emotional disconnect. The courtroom, she reported, looked 'more like a hospital waiting room'; the epitome of 'aseptic' décor. Boredom rapidly set in. She was bored. The defendant looked bored. The judge looked particularly bored. It was 'not a show for an audience'.[2] Of course, the idea that law, like the evil which it is so often supposed to address, might be surprisingly banal is not new.[3]

But suddenly, whilst listening to the distant account of a particular room in the concentration camp at Keraterm, Drakulic was aroused from her dozing:

> Suddenly I see that picture in front of my eyes, and I realise what the judge is talking about. The death of 120 prisoners is no longer abstract, no longer mere words. Now the tedious, precise interrogation takes on a new meaning. Now I realise how much we are all poisoned by the trials depicted in television shows and Hollywood movies, with their rapid exchange of arguments between good-looking lawyers in expensive suits. In The Hague there is no such false drama. The drama here is that everything really happened: there were real deaths, real

---

[1] E. Neuffer, *The Key to My Neighbour's House: Seeking Justice in Bosnia and Rwanda* (Picador, 2001), 181.

[2] S. Drakulic, *They Would Never Hurt a Fly: War Criminals on Trial in The Hague* (Abacus, 2004), 19–21.

[3] See H. Arendt, *Eichmann in Jerusalem: A Report on the Banality of Evil* (Penguin, 1963), particularly 253–79. For a thoughtful recent assessment of Arendt's work, in the context of ICTY and the Rwanda Tribunal, see M. Osiel, 'Why Prosecute? Critics of Punishment for Mass Atrocity', *Human Rights Quarterly*, 22 (2000), 118–47. For a broader discussion of Arendt and the Eichmann trial and the nature of legal judgement as a form of dramatic event, see L. Bilsky , 'In a Different Voice: Nathan Alterman and Hannah Arendt on the Kastner and Eichmann Trials', *Theoretical Inquiries in Law*, 1 (2000), 509–39. In his account of the Truth and Reconciliation Commission for Sierra Leone, Tim Kelsall similarly confesses himself to be 'faintly disappointed' at the lack of 'dramatic' outpourings. See his 'Truth, Lies, Ritual: Preliminary Reflections on the Truth and Reconciliation Commission in Sierra Leone', *Human Rights Quarterly*, 27 (2005), 369.

victims and real murderers. Real blood. The drama is that there can be no escape from that reality. When at the end of that day in the court I take a long look at the defendants, they suddenly seem different to me. I see what I did not see before – not their dull faces, but a room with its walls splashed with blood.[4]

Suddenly the trial mattered; not just because it might or might not lead to a conviction against those, including Zigic, who were accused of perpetrating the various crimes at Keraterm, but because a real horror had been brought into open view. Injustice had been chronicled, and this, as Drakulic realised, mattered more than anything. The 'struggle of men against power', as Milan Kundera famously put it, 'is the struggle of memory against forgetting'. The presence of a vital 'testimonial culture' is essential to the health of a free society.[5]

For this reason, in moments of acute 'traumatic disruption', it is the capacity of an afflicted community to memorialise, and then to come to terms with loss and suffering which matters, its ability to forge chronicles of suffering that can unite those who suffered loss, and promote their reconciliation, not just with others, but with themselves.[6] It is this appreciation, of the need to memorialise, which underpins various Truth and Reconciliation Commissions (TRCs).[7] Controversy regarding the efficacy of such bodies remains. But, for advocates, such as Arthur Chaskalson, the first president of the post-apartheid Constitutional Court in South Africa, their capacity as supplements, even alternatives, to the 'impoverished' jurisprudence of legal positivism remains unarguable.[8] It is a conclusion which has been forcefully echoed by Martha Minow who concludes that whilst ordinary trials tend to steer 'clear of forgiveness', Commissions furnish the terrorised and traumatised with a vital opportunity to show the world their 'tears'.[9]

A jurisprudence of memorialisation is an inherently narrative jurisprudence. It speaks to the particular aspiration ventured earlier, to provide spaces for testamentary supplements and chronicles; testaments which, in turn, can then better approach some of the deeper ethical and poethical issues which an

---

[4] Drakulic, *Fly*, 22.

[5] J. Edkins, *Trauma and the Memory of Politics* (Cambridge University Press, 2003), xiii, 18, 119, and also 228 and 232–3, emphasising the extent to which an aggressive counter to any experience of cataclysmic violence, a strategy so commonly preferred by states that wish to reassert their control over processes of mourning, can actually enhance the trauma of original victims, rather than diminish it, whilst also, and rather obviously, inhibiting the prospects of reconciliation which such victims need.

[6] Edkins, *Trauma*, 33, 54 and also 224–7 emphasising the extent to which the traumatic depth of 9/11 momentarily silenced all public or political commentary. For days, television stations just replayed pictures in silence, as if unable, or unwilling, to venture commentary.

[7] For the idea that the invocation of such Commissions represents a significant moment in the evolution of modern legal thought and 'poetics', see A. Gearey, '"Tell the Truth, but Tell it Slant": A Poetics of Truth and Reconciliation', *Journal of Law and Society*, 31 (2004), 44–5.

[8] In D. Dyzenhaus, *Judging the Judges, Judging Ourselves: Truth, Reconciliation and the Apartheid Legal Order* (Hart, 1998), 81.

[9] M. Minow, *Between Vengeance and Forgiveness: Facing History After Genocide and Mass Violence* (Beacon Press, 1998), 26, 67–73.

inquiry into justice and law must address. The testaments presented to the TRC, and given before ICTY do this. It is the primary and supplementary jurisprudence of the latter institution that is the main subject of this chapter; something which leads us to a second critical strategy in our more precise investigation into contemporary discourses about law and terrorism.

The idea that terrorism is something exclusively inflicted upon states is one of the most cherished of the constituent myths of this discourse; one that is, unsurprisingly, cherished most dearly by these states, and presented so robustly in their counter-rhetorical strategies. It is, of course, nonsense. What was the point of dropping atomic bombs on Hiroshima and Nagasaki if it was not wreak terror in order to secure a strategic aspiration?[10] If we look beyond the momentarily blinding events of 9/11, we can discern terrorism in all kinds of guises.[11] We have already investigated the terrorism denounced by Hobbes and Burke and Shelley in earlier chapters. Whilst the objects of their denunciation might have been very different, and their motivations too, each presumed that terror is something not inflicted on states, but inflicted by states upon their citizens and subjects. Modern states have inflicted far more terror, than they have ever suffered at the hands of external assailants.[12] We should not therefore be surprised that states at war, either with others or with themselves, should commonly adopt terrorist tactics, not just as a last, but very often as a first resort.[13] Events in the Balkans in 1990, and their subsequent revelation in juristic and non-juristic testaments, merely provide one of the most compelling of recent examples of this sorry truth.

The law of bitter little wars

The Balkan wars provided a searing conclusion to the twentieth century, one which cast into ridicule the assumption that the end of the Cold War had finally

---

[10] See Anthony Burke, 'The End of Terrorism Studies', *Critical Studies on Terrorism*, 1 (2008), 41, posing precisely this question.

[11] See Virginia Held's opening injunction, 'A serious mistake to be avoided, in current discussions about terrorism, is to suppose that all terrorism is alike. There are different kinds of terrorism as there are of war'. In her 'Terrorism and War', *Journal of Ethics*, 8 (2004), 59. For a similar observation, see K. Booth, 'The Human Faces of Terror: Reflections in a Cracked Looking-glass', *Critical Studies on Terrorism*, 1 (2008), 75.

[12] See A. Dorfman, *Some Write to the Future: Essays on Contemporary Latin American Fiction* (Duke University Press, 1991), 140 and also *Other Septembers, Many Americas: Selected Provocations 1980–2004*, (Pluto, 2004), xii–xvi, stressing the irony of the USA experiencing such deep post-9/11 trauma, given the centrality of its role in inflicting terrorist trauma across so much of Latin America during the last three decades. The same view is iterated in Booth, 'Human Faces', at 76.

[13] See W. Sofsky, *Violence: Terrorism, Genocide, War* (Granta, 2003), 76, and also R. Blackburn, 'The Imperial Presidency, the War on Terrorism, and the Revolutions of Modernity', *Constellations*, 9 (2002), 28–30, and H. Muenkler, 'The Brutal Logic of Terror: The Privatization of War in Modernity', *Constellations*, 9 (2002), 68–70.

secured for Europe a state of 'perpetual peace'.[14] It ended with Serb militia murdering and raping its way across Kosovo, just as it and various Croat and Bosnian militia had murdered and raped their way across much of the Balkans for the previous eight years. Alain Finkielraut has memorably cast contemporary international relations in terms of a 'sickness of geography', the reduction of superpower confrontation to 'bitter little wars, to disagreements over borders, to a ridiculous and bloody hotch-potch of squabbles, to the tautology of identity politics'.[15] The Balkan wars, brought to a devastating end by NATO's saturation bombing of Belgrade in 1999, were just such wars.[16] They described the kind of threat with which the modern world would, with increasing frequency, have to come to terms in the new century; of a new kind of asymmetrical warfare, between fragmentary, elusive, terroristic organisations, and an international political and legal order which is clearly, in its present form, unable to provide any kind of coherent or convincing response.[17]

There was, of course, a particular history; one that the International Criminal Tribunal for Yugoslavia (ICTY) would strive mightily to comprehend.[18] Even so, the conduct of those who appeared before the Tribunal, and those countless thousands who did not, was peculiar in its brutality. The Balkan wars were wars

[14] The phrase 'perpetual peace' is, of course, Immanuel Kant's, most famously articulated in his essay of that name.

[15] See A. Finkielraut, *In the Name of Humanity: Reflections on the Twentieth Century* (Pimlico, 2001), 97, and also, taking a similar line, J. Schell, *The Unconquerable World: Power, Nonviolence and the Will of the People* (Penguin, 2003), 306–9, suggesting that such localised, peculiarly brutal, squabbles are characteristic of the post-Cold War world.

[16] A campaign which itself is generally thought to have been of questionable legality in terms of international jurisprudence. The literature on this particular issue is, unsurprisingly, considerable. For a sample, see M. O'Connell, 'The UN, NATO, and International Law after Kosovo', *Human Rights Quarterly*, 22 (2000), 57–89; D. Kritsiotis, 'The Kosovo Crisis and NATO's Application of Armed Force against the Federal Republic of Yugoslavia', *International and Comparative Law Quarterly* 49, 330–59; and C. Chinkin, 'The Legality of NATO's Action in the Former Republic of Yugoslavia under International Law', *International and Comparative Law Quarterly*, 49 (2000), 210–25.

[17] See E. Hobsbawn, *Globalisation, Democracy and Terrorism* (Little Brown, 2007), 9–10, 33–7, 83–5, and also Held, 'War', 68, confirming that the distinction between what is commonly termed terrorism and 'smaller' wars, particularly between sub-state groupings, is virtually indiscernible.

[18] Famously, the first sixty-six pages of the Tribunal's very first judgement, in *Tadic*, were devoted to explicating this history and contextual background. The Tribunal entertained expert witness evidence that sought to root inter-ethnic hostilities in the fourth century. This contextual strategy was deployed by the prosecutors in order to persuade the Tribunal that the Bosnian wars were 'international' as opposed to purely civil or domestic, and thus could be set within the ambit of international laws of war. Whilst the tribunal accepted Tadic's defence, that the wars were in fact 'internal', and thus outwith the ambit of the Geneva Conventions, it also held that this did not preclude the application of customary humanitarian law. For a discussion of this issue, see M. Scharf and W. Schabas, *Slobodan Milosevic on Trial* (Continuum, 2002), 14–15; T. Meron, *War Crimes Law Comes of Age* (Oxford University Press, 1998), 262–77 and 286–95; and also Neuffer, *Key*, 181–2. For a slightly more sceptical commentary of the justification for such a contextual approach, see L. May, *Crimes Against Humanity* (Cambridge University Press, 2005), 4, 133. For a general commentary on the Tribunal in *Tadic*, see P. Akhaven, 'Justice in The Hague, Peace in Former Yugoslavia? A Commentary on the United Nations War Crimes Tribunal', *Human Rights Quarterly*, 20 (1998), 786–9.

of annihilation and extermination, where success was measured in terms of terrified populations, ethnically cleansed villages, exterminated peoples, and brutalised children. In the place of the heroic 'warrior' could be found the marauding rapist and butcher; the man, or occasionally woman, who actually lives for the satisfaction and pleasure of the slaughter.[19] In juristic terms, the Balkan wars appeared to be wars of 'criminal anarchy'; terrorist wars in which strategies of terror lay at the heart of the enterprise, rather than the periphery.[20] Most importantly, for the citizens of towns and cities such as Sarajevo or Srebrenica, the wars were experienced as a 'series of systematic terrorist attacks'.[21]

We have already noted the extent to which the classic tenets of international law, international humanitarian and criminal law included, have come under increasing pressure during the last two decades. And we have also noted the extent to which the contemporary experience of terrorism has contributed to this pressure. The same is true of 'bitter little wars' such as those inflicted upon the Balkans during the 1990s. The idea that these were not, in the absence of a formal declaration, wars which could fall within the ambit of international jurisprudence, has been rightly rejected as ridiculous.[22] If international law cannot deal with these kinds of events, it needs to be amended; just, indeed, as it must be if it cannot recognise and then address the fact that such wars were wars in which terrorism was a vital strategy deployed by both state and non-state actors.

The establishment of ICTY went some way to acknowledging the veracity of both suppositions. It was called into existence by UN Resolutions 808 and 827, and tasked 'for the prosecution of persons responsible for serious violations of international humanitarian law committed in the former Yugoslavia since 1991'.[23] It is a peculiar institution, the first of its kind since the Nuremberg Tribunal half a century earlier. Its history and its jurisprudence are no less peculiar, hurriedly established, as much out of shame according to many as pride, cripplingly under-funded, and perhaps most importantly, at least for jurists, left to work out an appropriate procedure, even an appropriate humanitarian law, for itself.[24]

---

[19] Sofsky, *Violence*, 82–4, 122, 154–6, 173–5.

[20] For a strong affirmation that the Balkan wars were terrorist wars, see P. Rees, *Dining With Terrorists* (Macmillan, 2005), 137–9; X. Raufer, 'New World Disorder, New Terrorisms: New Threats for Europe and the Western World', *Terrorism and Political Violence*, 11 (1999), 39, 42, 47; and also W. Lacqueur, *No End to War* (Continuum, 2004), 202 and 225 commenting on the 'new realities' of war at the dawn of the new century.

[21] For this observation, see M. Taylor and J. Horgan, 'Future Developments of Political Terrorism in Europe', *Terrorism and Political Violence*, 11 (1999), 87, and also 88.

[22] See D. Held, 'Violence, Law and Justice in a Global Age', *Constellations*, 9 (2002), 76–7.

[23] A similar institution, tasked with a comparable responsibility in the wake of the Rwandan wars, was established at Arusha in Tanzania.

[24] For an intriguing account of the difficulties encountered by the Tribunal, particularly in its early years, see R. Goldstone, *For Humanity: Reflections of a War Crimes Investigator* (Yale University

As we have also already noted, the experience of modern terrorism poses a number of challenges for legal regimes, both domestic and international, many of which can be traced back to definitional anxieties. In this context, the idea that *ad hoc* tribunals tasked with reinvesting justice in particular circumstances might be the best strategy for dealing with acts of acute political violence has attracted support.[25] The newly established International Criminal Court (ICC) offers a similar facility, even if it should be remembered that the US has supported ICTY precisely as an alternative to an International Court.[26] The more optimistic argue that the presence of these two institutions evidences a renewed resolve for the prosecution of humanitarian justice.[27]

Of course, as could reasonably be expected of an evolving jurisprudence, there is much that remains uncertain in the discipline of international criminal law.[28] The present condition of human rights and humanitarian law has been described as a 'tangled meshing', redeemed only by the fact that it aspires to reinvest a universal 'principle of humanity'.[29] This entanglement is even more

Press, 2000), 75–109. See also Neuffer's condemnation of the provision made by the international community for the functioning of the Tribunal, in *Key*, 173–80, and Gary Bass's similar observations regarding a Tribunal that was 'built to flounder', in his *Stay the Hand of Vengeance: The Politics of War Crimes Tribunals* (Princeton University Press, 2000), at 207, and also 243–4.

[25] R. Higgins, 'The General International Law of Terrorism' in R. Higgins and M. Flory (eds.), *Terrorism and International Law* (Routledge, 1997), 28, adding that the term has simply become a 'convenient way of alluding to activities, whether of States or of individuals, widely disapproved of and in which either the methods used are unlawful, or the targets protected, or both'.

[26] The ICC was established in 2002, following the required ratification of 60 states. The US was not one of them. The US prefers a system of bilateral agreements with signatories to the Statute; agreements which invariably provide assurances that signatories would not proceed with any action against the US or its citizens. See P. Sands, *Lawless World: America and the Making and Breaking of Global Rules* (Penguin, 2005), 50–1, 60–3. For a critique of the US position here, see H. Koh, 'On American Exceptionalism', *Stanford Law Review*, 55 (2003), 1507. For a wider critique of the idea of an International Criminal Court, focusing particularly upon anxieties about the infringement of state sovereignty, see L. May, *Crimes Against Humanity: A Normative Account* (Cambridge University Press, 2005), 8.

[27] See M. de Guzman, 'The Road from Rome: The Developing Law of Crimes against Humanity' *Human Rights Quarterly*, 22 (2000), 336, and also 343, and also Meron, *War Crimes*, 282–4, 297–301, and Goldstone, *Humanity*, 125–6. Others are not so sure. For a more sceptical commentary, see J. Fitzpatrick, 'Speaking Law to Power: The War Against Terrorism and Human Rights', *European Journal of International Law*, 14 (2003), 242.

[28] See T. Meron 'International Criminalization of Internal Atrocities', *American Journal of International Law*, 89 (1995), 554, arguing that the horrific events in the Balkans necessitated a degree of jurisprudential innovation. For understandable reasons, such events 'shocked the conscience of people everywhere, triggering, within a short span of time, several major legal developments' in international criminal law. Any residual uncertainties are, therefore, equally understandable.

[29] Meron, 'Criminalization', 557, and also 'The Humanization of Humanitarian Law', *American Journal of International Law*, 94 (2000), 245, 265–6. For the similar argument that a broader idea of crimes against humanity might encompass existing humanitarian law, see W. Fenrick, 'Should Crimes Against Humanity Replace War Crimes?', *Columbia Journal of Transnational Law*, 37 (1999), 767–85. This latter supposition finds support in de Guzman, 'Road from Rome', particularly at 342–3, 402–3.

apparent at the uncertain margins of terrorism and criminal responsibility.[30] Arguments continue to oscillate around the suggestion that the Rome Statute should include a specific crime of terrorism, or at least enumerate terrorism within existing crimes against humanity.[31] Alongside recognised categories of international crime, including crimes against humanity and war crimes, the Statute adds crimes of 'aggression', which might, or might not, be deployed in the future to address instances of international terrorism committed within the context of illegal warfare.[32]

The inability of classical laws of war to properly address the challenges of 'criminal terror violence' has been acknowledged by ICTY. In the *Delalic* case, the Tribunal recognised that the kind of conflict which characterised the wars reflected a 'complexity' that was not envisaged half a century earlier.[33] In the *Tadic* case, the Tribunal accepted that terrorism lay at the heart of modern strategies of war, or at least those strategies in evidence in south-east Europe during the 1990s. It identified, as 'aggravating factors', the 'terrorizing of victims, sadism, cruelty and humiliation, espousal of ethnic and religious discrimination, and the number of victims'.[34] Further, in the *Furundzija* case, the Tribunal further commented that when faced with crimes of terrorist violence, there is a strong argument for recasting the classical idea of human rights in terms of human 'dignity', and its infringement.[35] Notably, as we shall see, the South African TRC identified the 'restoration of the dignity of victims' as its primary aspiration.[36]

Interestingly, such a conclusion tends to resonate with those who advocate a distinctive post-modern idea of human rights. Drucilla Cornell, for example, has urged the need to reinvest a sense of 'fundamental humanity' in human rights jurisprudence.[37] Similarly Costas Douzinas has argued that post-modern human rights, as an expression of 'philosophical anti-humanism', should seek to renew its essential mission in 'defence of the human'. It should, accordingly, focus on human dignity, and the essential 'integrity of unique beings in their

---

[30] C. Blakesley, 'Ruminations on Terrorism and Anti-Terrorism Law and Literature', *University of Miami Law Review*, 57 (2003), 1075, and 1101 concluding that, whilst there may be a case, for jurists at least, in maintaining technical distinctions between war crimes, crimes against humanity and notional terrorist 'crimes', the effect on those who suffer such forms of political violence is pretty much the same.

[31] The idea of a crime of terrorism has been proposed by Algeria, India, Sri Lanka and Turkey. See Blakesley, 'Ruminations', 1080–1.

[32] See Sands, *World*, 56–9, discussing the idea of a crime of aggression. Of course, the ICC retains a secondary jurisdiction, deferring where possible to credible domestic criminal proceedings against any alleged war criminals or terrorists. See T. McCormack, 'Their Atrocities and Our Misdemeanours: The Reticence of States to Try Their "Own Nationals" for International Crimes' in M. Lattimer and P. Sands (eds.), *Justice for Crimes Against Humanity* (Hart, 2003), 107–42.

[33] In Meron, 'Criminalization', 258.   [34] In May, *Humanity*, 215.

[35] See Meron, 'Criminalization', 266–7.

[36] Quoted in F. du Bois, 'Nothing but the Truth: the South African Alternative to Corrective Justice in Transitions to Democracy' in E. Christodoulidis and S. Veitch (eds.), *Lethe's Law: Justice, Law and Ethics in Reconciliation* (Hart, 2001), 98.

[37] D. Cornell, *The Philosophy of the Limit* (Routledge, 1992), 115–16.

existential otherness, by promoting the dynamic realisation of freedom with others'. Perhaps most significantly, for Douzinas such a human rights jurisprudence will be narrative and imaginary, as well as ethical and human, one that also promotes a jurisprudence of 'passion', a jurisprudence that is constructed from the 'imaginary', from 'memories of fear, tales of pain and suffering and the experience of oppression'.[38] Such conceptualisations further resonate with those articulated by the likes of Martha Nussbaum, or Richard Rorty, the latter of whom has argued the case for a revitalised idea of human rights founded upon a philosophy of 'sensitivity' and 'sympathy', on an original concern with 'humanity as such'.[39]

Of course, the extent to which ICTY or the ICC might be thought to be an expression of this revitalised idea of human rights and dignity is a matter of controversy. Taken broadly, Madam Justice Arbour of the Canadian Supreme Court has suggested that the very presence of such institutions necessarily nurtures a 'global' culture of human rights, as well as a new 'sense of entitlement'.[40] David Hirsch likewise argues that they represent an emergent postmodern cosmopolitan legal order.[41] Others are inclined to proffer more prosaic justifications for the institutions. There is, Theodore Meron urged, a 'moral imperative' to prosecute 'those who commit crimes against humanity'.[42] For those who commit such crimes, the world should be made a 'smaller, more uncomfortable place'.[43] Moreover, in instances such as the Balkan wars, there is no obvious alternative, given the inherent unreliability of domestic Serbian, Croatian and Bosnian legal systems.[44]

The various justifications found expression the words of Secretary of State Madeleine Albright in 1997, when she applauded the establishment of ICTY;

---

[38] C. Douzinas, *The End of Human Rights: Critical Legal Thought at the Turn of the Century* (Hart, 2000), 1–4, 17–19, 121–31, 253, 259, 341.

[39] The lecture is reproduced in R. Rorty, *Truth and Progress* (Cambridge University Press, 1998), Chapter 9. For similar comments, see his *Contingency, Irony, and Solidarity* (Cambridge University Press, 1989), 189. For a discussion of Rorty's writings on human rights, see I. Ward, 'Bricolage and Low Cunning: Rorty on Pragmatism, Politics and Poetic Justice', *Legal Studies*, 28 (2008), 295–6. We shall revisit Rorty in the concluding chapter.

[40] Madam Justice Arbour, 'Is the Growth of International Criminal Law a Threat to State Sovereignty', the Irving Segal Lecture at the University of Pennsylvania, 24 September 2003, quoted in J. Steyn, 'Guantanamo Bay: The Legal Black Hole', *International and Comparative Law Quarterly*, 53 (2004), 6.

[41] A point strongly argued by David Hirsch. See his *Law Against Genocide: Cosmopolitan Trials* (Glasshouse, 2003), xii, 5–6, 152–3.

[42] Meron, *War Crimes*, 187.

[43] Neuffer, *Key*, 310. See also P. Akhavan, 'Beyond Impunity: Can International Criminal Justice Prevent Future Atrocities?' *American Journal of International Law*, 95 (2001), at 9, referring to the spread of 'an unmistakable contagion of accountability' across the world, and at 13, hoping that, as a result, a 'new reality of habitual lawfulness may take root and develop'. See also J. Mendez, 'National Reconciliation, Transnational Justice, and the International Criminal Court', *Ethics and International Affairs*, 15 (2001), 25.

[44] For an account of the limitations of domestic legal proceedings against alleged Balkan war criminals, see McCormack, 'Atrocities', 127–34.

albeit as a pointed alternative to the International Court of Justice. When the trauma of terrorist war was so deeply embedded, she declared, 'Justice is essential to strengthen the rule of law, soften the bitterness of victims' families, and remove an obstacle to cooperation among the parties'. To this end, the Tribunal would 'establish a model for resolving ethnic differences by the force of law rather than the law of force', whilst also providing a deterrent, as well as focusing attention on individual, as well as collective, responsibility.[45] More than this, ICTY would invigorate 'our collective memory'.[46] From the very beginning, memorialisation and narrativity were writ large in the genetic code of the International Criminal Tribunal for Yugoslavia.

Fuck their mothers

It has often been observed that popular perceptions of, and reactions to, events in the Balkans were framed by narrative and pictorial accounts provided by journalists and media. The same is true, as we have already noted, of reaction to the destruction of the Twin Towers. Lawrence Freedman terms it the 'CNN effect', and cites former British Foreign Secretary Douglas Hurd observing that the novelty of narrativity in the Balkan wars lay not in 'mass rape, the shooting of civilians, in war crimes, in ethnic cleansing, in the burning of towns and villages', but in the fact that 'a selection of these tragedies is now visible within hours to people around the world'. 'People', he affirmed, 'reject and resent what is going on because they know it more visibly than before'.[47]

The written word, too, can provide a powerful chronicle; not just that recorded in courts of law, but that which is intended to supplement it. Two such texts, both of which were intended to provide a narrative supplement to the jurisprudence of the International Criminal Tribunal for Yugoslavia, are Slavenka Drakulic's *They Would Never Hurt a Fly*, and Elizabeth Neuffer's *The Key to My Neighbour's House*. The vitality of such texts lies in their determination to raise voices, most immediately the voices of the terrorised, those who are otherwise silenced by the very trauma of their suffering.[48] Trauma is healed,

[45] See Bass, *Vengeance*, 284, and also 290 and 297.

[46] In Neuffer, *Key*, 63. Albright was, as Gary Bass also emphasises, one of the few 'true believers' in the idea of international tribunals. See Bass, *Vengeance*, 262. An echo of her sentiments can be found in Wolfgang Sofsky's observation, 'when the gods of retribution sleep, the benign goddess of memory reigns'. See his *Violence*, 208.

[47] In L. Freedman, 'Victims and Victors: Reflections on the Kosovo War', *Review of International Studies*, 26 (2000), 338. For a similar commentary on the power of televisual images, in the particular context of the Kosovo refugee crisis, see Edkins, *Trauma*, 200–2.

[48] As Sarah Kofman writes, speaking to the particular experience of Holocaust victims, whilst the depth of the trauma so often seems to disarticulate the victim this merely makes the 'duty to speak', at least insofar as it is incumbent upon others, so pressing, 'to speak endlessly for those who could not speak because to the very end they wanted to guard true speech from betrayal', see S. Kofman, *Smothered Words* (Northwestern University Press, 1998), 36. The same sentiment is strongly presented in D. Laub, 'Truth and Testimony', in C. Caruth (ed.), *Trauma: Explorations in Memory* (Johns Hopkins University Press, 1995), 62–5.

so far as is ever possible, by translating the extraordinary experience of terror into those 'narratives' which seem to be, in contrast, 'everyday'. It is for this reason that chronicle is so vital to processes of reconciliation.[49] At the same time, such texts also address the wider audience, engendering, it can be hoped, the kind of empathetic responses which such processes also need.[50]

Of the many horrific images which emerged from the Balkan wars, three gained a peculiar notoriety; the shelled market-place in Sarajevo, chained UN peacekeepers at Srebrenica, and emaciated inmates peering lifelessly out of the mesh-fencing at the Omarska concentration camp.[51] Each is chronicled further by Drakulic and Neuffer. Images of the former, the shelling of the market-place at Sarajevo, had a stunning effect on public opinion across much of the world. But it is important that the horrific events that took place on that February lunchtime are chronicled in full. A 120 millimetre shell killed 66 and wounded over 140, including 3 children under the age of fifteen. Subsequent criminal indictments included the statistics. But the chronicle needs more. The narrative is important; of shattered market-stalls, of limbs lying in pools of blood, of a piece of head 'impaled on a metal post', of 'bloodstained rags draped over unidentified body parts', of men 'wailing and crying' who 'hefted bodies into cars doubling as ambulances'. It makes the indictment real. As Neuffer, who was present at the shelling concludes, 'It looked like a war crime to me'.[52]

Alongside Sarajevo must be placed a still more grotesque tragedy; that of Srebrenica. Between 13 and 19 July 1995, more than 7,000 Bosnian Muslims were massacred in the environs of Srebrenica, a supposed 'safe-haven' under the nominal protection of the UN. The massacre followed the effective surrender of the UN force, and involved its possible complicity, even if unknowing, in the slaughter that followed.[53] Srebrenica represents one of those watersheds that occasionally define, not just a war, but the fate of an ideal; a peculiar tragedy, even within the context of a war of barely comprehensible cruelty and atrocity.[54] And it is for this reason that it provides such a stunning narrative of injustice. As David Campbell notes, to 'think about the events that took place at Srebrenica in July 1995 is to confront the impossibility of escaping narrativity'.[55]

It is Drakulic who describes Bosnian Serb General Ratko Mladic striding around Srebrenica following the capitulation of the UN 'peacekeepers', and

---

[49] For a discussion of this tendency, see Edkins, *Trauma*, 8, and 15, concluding that the rein-scription of trauma takes the form of 'practices of remembrance, memorialisation and witnessing', and also 40–1.

[50] See Edkins, *Trauma*, 156–7, citing the particular impact of the US Holocaust Memorial Museum.

[51] For an insightful discussion of the impact of photographic evidence of terrorism, see Dorfman, *Other Septembers*, 4–7, suggesting that it very often represents the 'only vocabulary left to the dead'.

[52] Neuffer, *Key*, 62.　　[53] Neuffer, *Key*, 154–6. See also Hirsch, *Genocide*, 62.

[54] According to Richard Holbrooke, it was the lowest point in the history of the UN. See A. Neier, *War Crimes: Brutality, Genocide, Terror and the Struggle for Justice* (Random House, 1998), 133.

[55] D. Campbell, *National Deconstruction: Violence, Identity and Justice in Bosnia* (Minnesota University Press, 1998), 40.

chattering excitedly to journalists about avenging 'the Turks' and 'Muslims', thousands of which were about to be driven in trucks to neighbouring fields and shot.[56] Mladic, though indicted on counts relating to both the Sarajevo shelling and the Srebrenica massacre, has never appeared before ICTY. Drakulic's chronicle, like Neuffer's, provides a measure of compensation; arraigning them before the court of world opinion, and helping to shatter, in the process, the associated 'fairy tale' mythologies of the Bosnian Serb 'nation' and the collateral, if grotesque, logic of 'ethnic cleansing'.[57] And the arraignment is wider. For the crime of complicity must be chronicled too. As Neuffer confirms, the Srebrenica massacre was 'a tragedy spawned by military incompetence, the UN's trepidation, and the international community's cowardice'.[58] The evidence that the Dutch peacekeeping force actually assisted the Bosnian Serb army in the preliminaries for the subsequent massacre, most readily it appears in the listing and distinguishing of men from women, is compelling. The fact that they witnessed the initial stages of the slaughter, moreover, is shaming; for all of us. The enactment of a shiny new Union was supposed to mean that such medieval barbarism would never again be inflicted upon the continent of Europe. As yet, no UN commander or soldier has been indicted by ICTY, and none is likely to be.[59] But the responsibility, again, is one we must all share. We might like to forget. But we should never be allowed to do so.

A full narrative of the Srebrenica massacre needs this perspective. It confirms our responsibility, bringing home the true horror of what happened, providing a contextual complement to the bare statistics that were provided to the tribunal, of the 7,000 who disappeared, the 120 UN troops who froze in horror and surrendered. It can, for example, describe the 'stinking stew of rotted clothes and outflung hands and hunks of flesh' that faced those who excavated the Cerska graves, and those in surrounding fields. As Neuffer concludes, the most striking effect of viewing these graves was to impress their humanity. At Cerska, she observed, 'there was no avoiding the fact that these were not just skeletons'. Rather they 'were remains of human beings: someone's son, lover, brother, husband'.[60] ICTY, as she further observed, would see plenty of photographs, of Srebrenica and similar atrocities elsewhere.[61] But it would never experience the full horror. If we are to get a better understanding of what happened in Srebrenica, and what it means today, there is a whole lot more that

---

[56] Drakulic, Fly, 147–8, and Neuffer, Key, 149.

[57] Neuffer, Key, 12, 19–21. See also Neier, War Crimes, 157–8.   [58] Neuffer, Key, 148.

[59] Though the Dutch government itself, pressed by the horror of its citizens, was persuaded to hold an inquiry, and in time both the Prime Minister and the head of the Dutch armed forces resigned. See Neuffer, Key, 148–59.

[60] Neuffer, Key, 215–17, and also 236–8.

[61] Video evidence of some of the associated atrocities has subsequently been released to the press, and images duly beamed around the world. See The Observer, 5 June 2005.

we 'need to know'. We need to know, for example, 'that the poppies that sprouted from a particular spot by the side of the road were growing out of the earth piled on top of clothing stripped from Srebrenica men'.[62]

Two of the most notorious cases to come before ICTY related to the Srebrenica massacre; those of Drazen Erdemovic and General Radislav Krstic. Erdemovic was an executioner in the Bosnian Serb army. He lost count of how many he killed. But he was profusely, and famously, sorry; famously, in the sense that the tribunal took the important step, as a precedent, of accepting his sorrow in mitigation. Erdemovic also testified against Krstic. For hour after hour, Erdemovic had stood in the hot sun shooting unarmed prisoners in a field. His evidence was devastating, an indictment not just of himself, but of humanity. And it was also a narrative, a horror story of ritualised, systematic murder. It is not merely the description of line after line of prisoners shot which catches the attention, it is again the small details; the prisoners that stained their own trousers in terror, the pouring of a glass of orange juice for an old man about to be shot, the sustenance of brandy as exhaustion set in and trigger fingers numbed, the boy who knelt down in front of him and whispered 'Mother'.[63] This again we need to know.

Erdemovic was not a career soldier, and ICTY accepted that his options that day were strictly limited; either shoot or be shot. There were no such mitigating circumstances for Krstic, the commander of the infamous Drina corps which conducted most of the Srebrenica massacre. There was no evidence that Krstic shot anyone, even fired a gun in anger. But the responsibility for what followed, as ICTY determined, was very much his.[64] Drakulic records the testimony of one teenage survivor of the massacre:

> Some people shouted 'Give us some water first, then kill us'. I was really sorry that I would die thirsty and I was trying to hide amongst the people as long as I could, like everybody else. I just wanted to live for another second or two… I saw rows of killed people. It looked like they had been lined up, one row after the other. And then I thought that I would die very fast, that I would not suffer. And I just thought that my mother would never know where I had ended up.[65]

Whilst he admitted being the commanding officer of the Drina corps which instituted the massacres, Krstic simply denied that it was anything to do with him. He had never shot anyone. It was not his fault. When an audio-tape was played which proved his complicity, he just buried his face in his hands. 'Fuck their mothers!' the Tribunal heard him say, 'Don't leave a single one alive!'[66]

---

[62] See Neuffer, *Key*, 368. Perhaps more troubling still we need to know that children who witnessed the Muslim women visiting the graves 'were not waving, but giving a defiant, three-fingered salute'.
[63] Drakulic, *Fly*, 100–3.   [64] Drakulic, *Fly*, 84–6.   [65] Drakulic, *Fly*, 87.
[66] Drakulic, *Fly*, 87–93 and Neuffer, *Key*, 3–4.

A third instance of peculiar inhumanity was again captured in visual images, this time of the emaciated, brutalised inmates of Omarska prison camp. It was these images, so obviously resonant of images of Nazi concentration camps, that led the German Foreign Minister, Klaus Kinkel, to demand the establishment of an international criminal tribunal.[67] In due course, the first indictee to appear before this tribunal would be a former Omarska guard, Dusko Tadic. His association with Omarska was oddly, even perversely, propitious; at least in the sense that the camp represented a 'crime' that everyone had read about or seen pictures of.[68] It is often argued that the *Tadic* trial symbolises a notable weakness in ICTY's proceedings; that it generally focuses on the 'smaller fish'. This might be true. At the same time, the crimes that Tadic was accused of committing, and for which he was convicted, are as serious as any that might be levelled in criminal or humanitarian law; torture, sexual abuse, murder, all fall readily into the ambit of 'crimes against humanity'. And it is hard to imagine more grotesque particulars, systematic rape and sodomy, most notoriously, perhaps, his forcing one prisoner to bite off the testicles of another.[69] All the 'bestial passions' of terroristic warfare were encapsulated in the horror of Omarska.[70]

One of the most bestial of all is rape.[71] The idea that rape is a necessary expression of a fundamental power disparity in gender relations is familiar. Catherine MacKinnon has made much of this supposition, emphasising in the process the ritualistic nature, as well as the sheer number of rapes in camps such as Omarska.[72] Rape, it became very obviously apparent from various victim testimonies, was performative, a strategy of war that was intended to demoralise the enemy whilst also entertaining, even inspiring, colleagues in arms.[73] The prosecution of Tadic focused on allegations of rape, and the judgement of the Tribunal in this case, and in *Furundzija*, represents, in its acceptance of rape as a crime against humanity, a justly famous advance in the ambition of international criminal jurisprudence.[74]

---

[67] Neuffer, *Key*, 47–8.   [68] Neier, *War Crimes*, 143.

[69] Neuffer *Key*, 42. For a discussion of the *Tadic* case, and the evidence that was brought before the tribunal, see Hirsch, *Genocide*, 84–93.

[70] Neuffer, *Key*, 40.   [71] Neuffer, *Key*, 41, 47.

[72] See C. MacKinnon,. 'Turning Rape into Pornography: Post-modern Genocide', and 'Rape, Genocide, and Women's Human Rights' in A. Stiglmayer (ed.), *Mass Rape: the War Against Women in Bosnia-Herzegovina* (Nebraska University Press, 1994), at 83–81 and 193–229 respectively.

[73] For a commentary on rape, as both an aesthetic and 'legal' phenomenon, in the context of ICTY and the Balkan wars, see C. Niarchos, 'Women, War and Rape: Challenges Facing the International Tribunal for the Former Yugoslavia', *Human Rights Quarterly*, 17 (1995), 649–90 and T. Salzman, 'Rape Camps as a Means of Ethnic Cleansing: Religious, Cultural and Ethical Responses to Rape Victims in the Former Yugoslavia', *Human Rights Quarterly*, 20 (1998), 348–78.

[74] For a commentary, see May, *Humanity*, 100–2, Meron, *War Crimes*, 194–5, and 205–9, and also C. Booth, 'Prospects and Issues for the International Criminal Court: Lessons from Yugoslavia and Rwanda' in P. Sands (ed.), *From Nuremberg to The Hague: The Future of International Criminal Justice* (Cambridge University Press, 2003), 172–5.

Various statistics have been churned out in an attempt to quantify instances of rape during the Balkan wars. All are, ultimately, guesses, subject to various multipliers based on supposed numbers of abortions, births and so on. Aside from the simple fact that the rape of one person is as heinous, in terms of its simple violence and injustice, as the rape of many, the slide-rule of the statistician can never convey the true horror of the suffering, the true extent of the terror inflicted.[75] Only testament can do this. Depositions before courts and tribunals can to a degree, and the extent to which the Tribunal responded to such testamentary accounts has attracted critical approval.[76] But the need for supplement is compelling, particularly in a situation where the trauma of the experience so commonly inspires silence.[77]

The official court transcript, moreover, simply records what is said. It does not record what is not said, or what is felt, the sheer agony of recollection and articulation. Describing one such instance, Drakulic noted how one victim of rape could do little more than 'utter' a 'tiny sound' in court, that her sobbing, on being shown a picture of her daughter who was also raped and subsequently disappeared, 'sounded as if there was a microphone in her belly'. She also noted that one of the defendants had a daughter of precisely the same age, and that like so many who appeared so eager to commit such horrific crimes, he seemed so ordinary, so unthreatening in the flesh.[78] This juxtaposition, of the ordinary and extraordinary, emerges as a central motif in the narrative and dramatic discourses of terror and terrorism. We shall encounter it again on a number of occasions in subsequent chapters.

Narrating one particular meeting with a rape victim, Drakulic reinforces one of the most familiar aspects of contemporary rape critique; that rape is not, as the legal process would have it, an event, but an experience:

> In her quick glances I recognised fear. She held her head bent slightly forward, as if expecting a blow at any moment. She knew some of her rapists in the camp by name – they were from her neighbouring village – but this did not help her. She described the feeling of humiliation, of utter helplessness, of a kind of absence from her own body; she told of her desire to disappear, to die instantly. The rape had left her feeling dirty, she said, as though she had been wrapped up in a layer of filth, almost like a blanket.[79]

We shall revisit the particular terror and trauma of the female victim of political violence, of which rape is an all too familiar expression, in the next chapter.

---

[75] The European Commission suggested in a 1993 report that the figure in Bosnia was likely to be around 20,000 instances of rape. The Bosnian government preferred 50,000. For a cautionary comment on slide-rule rape statistics, see Neier, *War Crimes*, 175–91.

[76] Minow, *Vengeance and Forgiveness*, 6–7.

[77] For a comment on the particular nature of female trauma in the event of rape, see Edkins, *Trauma*, 2–3, and also L. Brown, 'Not Outside the Range: One Feminist Perspective on Psychic Trauma' in Caruth, *Trauma*, 100–3.

[78] Drakulic, *Fly*, 47.   [79] Drakulic, *Fly*, 54.

Justice and memory

Omarska is an epitome of evil; as are Sarajevo and Srebrenica. And it is right that those responsible should be indicted, and where possible arraigned, before a criminal tribunal. As Sir Hartley Shawcross observed at Nuremberg, 'this Tribunal will provide a contemporary touchstone and an authoritative and impartial record to which future historians may turn for truth and future politicians for warning'.[80] The same sentiment can be found in Secretary of State Albright's prophesy, that ICTY would, as a chronicle of injustice, take hold and invigorate 'our collective memory'.[81] It is also echoed in David Campbell's observation that 'the greatest contribution of the war crimes trials may come from the construction of an archive and the furtherance of historical memory they aid'.[82]

But legal proceedings are not, to repeat, enough. Law, it has been rightly suggested, 'does not exhaust the question' of justice, particularly if the injustice was terrorist in conception and traumatic in effect.[83] The kind of supplements provided by Drakulic and Neuffer can bridge the jurisprudential chasm, infusing the potentially staid chronicle presented before a tiny audience in a tribunal with a compelling, even poetic, invariably tragic, narrative that will be considered by a vastly greater jury.[84] They transmit what Charles Webel has succinctly termed 'the voices of the terrified'.[85] The narrative supplement humanises, and in an age of terror, of terrorist atrocities and terroristic wars, rarely has this quality been more valuable.[86] As Richard Goldstone acknowledged, 'people don't relate to statistics, to generalizations'. They can only 'relate and feel when they hear somebody that they can identify with telling what happened to them'.[87]

Any judicial institution has the potential to narrate. But the potential of international tribunals, driven as they are by a particular humanitarian impulse, is striking. The same, as we have already noted, is true of Truth and Reconciliation Commissions. The proceedings of the South African TRC have attracted much critical comment.[88] Whether or not it is a suitable body for effecting justice for individual crimes, there can be little doubting its capacity to

---

[80] In Minow, *Vengeance and Forgiveness*, 47.   [81] In Neuffer, *Key*, 63.

[82] Campbell, *National Deconstruction*, 234.   [83] Edkins, *Trauma*, 205.

[84] For the same use of the metaphor of a 'bridge' to memory, see Dorfman, *Future*, 144. It has been suggested that narrative form is the only effective medium with which to transmit deep trauma to the wider audience of non-victims. See K. Newmark, 'Traumatic Poetry: Charles Baudelaire and the Shock of Laughter' in Caruth, *Trauma*, 239. 253–4.

[85] C. Webel, *Terror, Terrorism and the Human Condition* (Palgrave, 2004), 45.

[86] Lacqueur, *War*, 7, 9.   [87] In Scharf and Schabas, *Milosevic*, 53.

[88] The aspiration to promote reconciliation was originally stated in Act n.200 of 1993, and then reaffirmed in the Promotion of National Unity and Reconciliation Act. For a discussion of the circumstances of its institution, see B. Sarkin, 'The Development of a Human Rights Culture in South Africa', *Human Rights Quarterly* 20 1998, 628–65.

memorialise.[89] Between 1996 and 1999, its three constituent committees received 20,000 statements and conducted 2,000 public hearings.[90] It was tasked with investigating 'gross violations' of human rights, as well as promoting the 'reconciliation between the people of South Africa and the reconstruction of society'. Such an aspiration presumed that 'the future could not be faced without memory', that it depended upon bringing some sort of closure to the past. The 'moral and therapeutic' aspiration was central.[91] Truth was sought; but as a means.[92] The end was Reconciliation.[93] In terms more familiar to the jurist, the TRC aspired to the idea of 'restorative' justice.[94]

The postscript to the 1993 Act which enabled the TRC spoke to a jurisprudence based on the 'need for understanding not vengeance; on reparation, not retaliation; a need for *ubuntu*, not victimisation'.[95] According to Archbishop Desmond Tutu, who chaired the TRC hearings, the idea of *ubuntu* in African jurisprudence seeks the 'healing of breaches, the redressing of imbalances, the restoration of broken relationships'. It 'speaks of the very essence of being

---

[89] For discussions of the narrower juristic merits and demerits of the South African TRC, see H. Corder, 'The Law and Struggle: the Same, but Different', and N. Biko, 'Amnesty and Denial', both in C. Villa-Vicencio and W. Verwoerd (eds.), *Looking Back, Reaching Forward: Reflections on the Truth and Reconciliation Commission of South Africa* (Cape Town University Press, 2000), at 99–106 and 193–98 respectively, and also A. Gutmann and D. Thompson, 'The Moral Foundations of Truth Commissions' in R. Rotberg and D. Thompson (eds.), *Truth v Justice: The Morality of Truth Commissions* (Princeton University Press, 2000), 22–44, and K. Guenther, 'The Criminal Law of Guilt as Subject of a Politics of Remembrance', and B. Schaefer, 'Sometimes You Must be Kind to be Cruel', both in Christodoulidis and Veitch, *Lethe's Law*, at 11–12 and 18–19 respectively. For a more stridently critical commentary, see du Bois, 'Alternative', 112–14.

[90] Richard Goldstone attests to the efficacy of the process, commenting that 'If it were not for the Truth and Reconciliation Commission people who today are saying that they did not know about apartheid would be saying that it didn't happen. This is a fact, and it cannot be underestimated.' Quoted in J. Balint, 'Law's Constitutive Possibilities: Reconstruction and Reconciliation in the Wake of Genocide and State Crime' in Christodoulidis and Veitch, *Lethe's Law*, at 135.

[91] See Gearey, 'Poetics', 50, and S. Veitch, 'The Legal Politics of Amnesty' in Christodoulidis and Veitch, *Lethe's Law*, 44, and more generally on the issue of 'collective memory' as a constituent of 'living history', see A. Czarnota, 'Law as Mnemosyne and as Lethe: Quasi-Judicial Institutions and Collective Memories', and E. Christodoulidis, 'Law's Immemorial', both also in Christodoulidis and Veitch, *Lethe's Law*, at 115–28 and 208–27 respectively. See also Dorfman, *Future*, at 136, commending precisely this 'cathartic, almost therapeutic and confessional' aspiration.

[92] The TRC actually defined four kinds of 'truth', factual truth, personal or narrative truth, social or 'dialogue' truth, and restorative truth. As commentators have noted, each was narrative to some degree. See Gearey, 'Poetics' 52–4.

[93] For a judicious discussion of the immanent relation between the two aspirations, see Mendez, 'National Reconciliation', particularly 27–9. A similar approach is emphasised, again from within the particular South American context, by Fernando Atria, in 'The Time of Law: Human Rights Between Law and Politics', *Law and Critique*, 16 (2005), 140.

[94] Mendez is rightly at pains to distinguish restorative justice and reconciliation from a simplistic, and mechanical, process of 'official forgiveness'. See his 'National Reconciliation', 33.

[95] For discussions, see J. de Lange, 'The Historical Context, Legal Origins and Philosophical Foundation of the South African Truth and Reconciliation Commission', and C. Villa-Vicencio, 'Restorative Justice: Dealing with the Past Differently', both in Villa-Vicencio and Verwoerd, *Looking Back*, at 14–31 and 68–76 respectively, and also R. Rotberg, 'Truth Commissions and the Provision of Truth, Justice and Reconciliation' in Rotberg and Thompson, *Truth v Justice*, 3–21.

human'.[96] The very first hearing of the TRC opened with the Xhosa hymn 'The forgiveness of sins makes a person whole'.[97] When asked to explore further his understanding of this essence, Tutu added, 'the most forgiving people I have ever come across are people who have suffered – it is as if suffering has ripped them open in empathy'. Such people, he added, are 'wounded healers'.[98] At the very heart of *ubuntu*, of reconciliation, are the qualities of forgiveness and empathy, and of confession.[99]

So is the presumption of narrative. Reconciliation depends not just on hearing the stories of those who suffered, but on hearing the stories of those who caused their suffering. Narrative nurtures empathy, the appreciation of the suffering of others that is so vital for reconciliation.[100] In his opening 'welcome' to the Commission, Tutu emphasised that the 'healing of a traumatised and wounded people' could only be facilitated by the readiness of everyone to listen to 'stories'.[101] Speaking in the context of the comparable Rettig Commission in Chile, Ariel Dorfman likewise stresses the importance of a terrorised people retrieving its sense of 'narrative' voice, and thus a sense of its own 'destiny'.[102] Martha Minow has emphasised the extent to which such Commissions are able to reinvest communal 'sensibilities' precisely because they concentrate on 'the voices and lives of real people'.[103] In this way, justice becomes more than a matter of judging guilt or innocence. It becomes a matter of entering into the dramatic life of a wounded community.[104]

The impact can be harrowing. 'Week after week; voice after voice; account after account', observed Antije Krog, in her renowned chronicle of the South African TRC. 'It is like travelling on a rainy night behind a huge truck – images of devastation breaking in sheets on the windscreen'.[105] But it is precisely for this reason that such testamentary forms of justice are, again, so vital. It is here

---

[96] D. Tutu, *No Future Without Forgiveness* (Ebury Press, 1999), 34–5, 51–2, and also Gearey, 'Poetics', 58.

[97] A. Krog, *Country of My Skull* (Vintage, 1999), 38–9.   [98] Krog, *Skull*, 24.

[99] See Tutu, *Future*, 74–5, Krog, *Skull*, 165–9 and E. Moosa, 'Truth and Reconciliation as Performance: Spectres of Eucharistic Redemption' in Villa-Vicencio and Verwoerd, *Looking Back*, 113–22.

[100] A strident defence of this function can be found in K. van Marle, 'The Literary Imagination, Recollective Imagination and Justice', *South African Public Law*, 15 (2000), at 143–4, affirming that the 'stories told' to Commissions such as the South African TRC 'showed us how confrontation with concrete humans and their stories can contribute to a more reflective, sympathetic and ethical response'. See also M. Nussbaum, 'Compassion and Terror' in J. Sterba (ed.), *Terrorism and International Justice* (Oxford University Press, 2003), 231, 244–5, 249–51, for a similar comment.

[101] Tutu, *Future*, 86–7.   [102] Dorfman, *Future*, 136.

[103] M. Minow, 'The Hope for Healing: What Can Truth Commissions Do?' in Rotberg and Thompson, *Truth v Justice*, 238–45, 254.

[104] It is for this reason that Drakulic comes to characterise ICTY as a 'theatrical performance', albeit a 'deadly serious' one. See Drakulic, *Fly*, 75. The same metaphor is actively deployed by Scharf and Schabas, in their particular account of the Milosevic trial *Slobodan Milosevic on Trial*. It is, they repeatedly aver, a drama replete with dramatis personae. See, for example, 74–85.

[105] Krog, *Skull*, 48.

that the limits of formal law are reached, where the trauma of terror defies reason, where the striving for 'understanding is pure madness'.[106] As Drakulic concludes in her chronicle, when faced with the kind of testimonies that were given at The Hague, our 'thin layer of rationality easily falls away under the pressure of emotions'.[107] Sensibility is all that is left.[108]

It has been suggested, most notably by ICTY prosecutor Carla Del Ponte, that such a Commission might be appropriate as a means to reconciliation in the Balkans; a desirable supplementary stage in the process of healing the various dislocated communities in the region.[109] But the context must be right.[110] There must, in simple terms, be a greater common desire to forgive than to seek vengeance. And there must be a genuine desire to confess too.[111] It is debatable whether such conditions presently exist in the Balkans, and until this is so an international tribunal is the more credible alternative.[112] At the same time, whilst their institutional structures, and their juridical aspirations, might be very different, what aligns ICTY with the South African and other TRCs is a shared appreciation of the vitality of the narrative supplement. As David Campbell argues, the revitalisation of an 'ethic' of reconciliation is dependent upon the presentation of various 'micronarratives' of subjective experience alongside the 'macronarratives' of international judicial tribunals.[113] Remarkable here, perhaps, is ICTY's preparedness, in *Erdemovic*, to accept remorse as a 'mitigating circumstance'.[114]

---

[106] See Osiel, 'Why Prosecute?' 145, and also C. Lanzmann, 'The Obscenity of Understanding: An Evening with Claude Lanzmann' in Caruth, *Trauma*, commenting at 211 on the particular problems of 'transmission' in depictions of cataclysmic devastation. Hannah Arendt likewise suggested that the nature of the 'guilt' explored at Nuremberg overstepped 'any and all legal systems', cited in Bass, *Vengeance*, at 13, commenting in addition that there is, very probably, 'no such thing as appropriate punishment for the massacres at Srebrenica or Djakovica; only the depth of our legalist ideology makes it seem so'.

[107] Drakulic, *Fly*, 13.

[108] See Scott Veitch's observations, writing in the particular context of the Amnesty Committee of the South African TRC, that only by chronicling atrocities in 'narrative' form could some kind of 'coherence' be realised. See his 'Amnesty', 37.

[109] Minow, *Vengeance*, 4–5, and Neuffer, *Key*, 396

[110] For the importance of context, see B. van Roermund, 'Rubbing Off and Rubbing On: The Grammar of Reconciliation' in Christodoulidis and Veitch, *Lethe's Law*, 175–6. For a commentary on the limitations of truth commissions, with a specific focus on problems encountered by the Argentinian 'commission' and its report, see Osiel, 'Why Prosecute?', 135–7. For a similar analysis in the Chilean context, see Atria, 'Human Rights', particularly 150–9.

[111] See Dyzenhaus, *Judging*, particularly 136–83, suggesting that many supposed confessions have been decidedly half-hearted.

[112] See Goldstone, *Humanity*, 65. Interestingly Goldstone also hazards the thought, at 72–3, that a truth commission might, in time, serve a purpose in the Balkans; but not yet. The same view is hazarded by Neuffer, in *Key*, 390.

[113] See Campbell, *National Deconstruction*, discussing the deeper ethical aspirations of his work, at 3–5, 34–43, and also 110–11 and 234.

[114] Under Rule 101 of the Statute and Rules of Procedure and Evidence. A degree of ambiguity was leant to Erdemovic's remorse by his supplementary plea of duress. But the Tribunal's willingness to accept his remorse as 'genuine' has set a remarkable trend, one that has been followed, perhaps most notably, in the proceedings against Biljana Plavsic, the former President of Republika Srpska. At the same time in *Blaskic*, the Tribunal was quick to reject any expression of

At the same time, of course, the allusion to a democratic 'ethic' adds a further dimension to the nature of political reconciliation.[115] It also spreads responsibility; not just for the revitalisation of democracy itself, but for the horrors that make the reconciliation so vital.[116] In an earlier collection of essays, Drakulic concluded with the primal acknowledgement that those who lived in the Balkans, and who experienced the wars, are, ultimately, responsible for them, 'There is only us – and yes, we are responsible for each other'.[117] The 'other', and the fear of it, is pervasive; as the UN commander in the Balkans, General Morillon, observed, with a conspicuously post-modern flourish, Bosnia is 'afflicted by a human illness', a 'fear of others, a fear of the other'.[118] In the context of terrorism and counter-terrorism, as we have already seen, the greatest danger is resignation to fear. However strong the temptation, it must be resisted.[119]

This emphasis on the human invites a collateral issue which we encountered at the very outset of this chapter; the issue of banality which so famously haunted Hannah Arendt's account of the Eichmann trial.[120] Banality pervades the chronicles of Drakulic and Neuffer, as it does so many of the testaments which have come before ICTY. What can we make of Goran Jelisec, who murdered prisoners at Brcko police station and Luka camp, and who, it was alleged, so obviously enjoyed it, but who also possessed such a 'reassuring grin'? Of all people, it was said, by so many, Goran 'would never hurt a fly'; at least not ordinarily.[121] Is Jelisec simply evil, or is he an ordinary person thrust into extraordinary circumstances who momentarily neglected the demands of his

remorse which seemed to be less than genuine. See May, *Humanity*, 198–9, and also Minow, *Vengeance*, 112–17; A. Tieger, 'Remorse and Mitigation in the International Criminal Tribunal for the Former Yugoslavia', *Leiden Journal of International Law*, 16 (2003), 785–6; and also B. Orend, 'Justice after War', *Ethics and International Affairs*, 16 (2002), 51–2.

[115] For a broad discussion of the relation between democracy and human rights, see J. Donnelly, 'Human Rights, Democracy, and Development', *Human Rights Quarterly* 21 1999, 608–32. See also Mendez, 'Reconciliation', 32–3.

[116] 'In the Bosnian war', Campbell asserts, 'the call of the other has rung out loud and clear'. At the heart of Campbell's overtly post-modern chronicle is the same call to an 'ethic' of responsibility that he locates in Heideggerian conceptions of *Ruf*. See Campbell, *National Deconstruction*, 23, 166, 171–81.

[117] S. Drakulic *Balkan Express* (Norton, 1993), 146. Strikingly David Campbell expressly cites the work of Drakulic and other writers in presenting narratives which demand such ethical engagement. See his *National Deconstruction*, 10–11.

[118] In Campbell, *National Deconstruction*, ix.

[119] According to Francesca Klug, NATO's intervention in the Kosovo war was remarkable, precisely because it represented the 'first war initiated in the name of human rights', the first war compelled by a concern for the fate of 'others' in the abstract. See F. Klug, *Values for a Godless Age* (Penguin, 2000), 2–3.

[120] Slobodan Milosevic, for example, just seemed 'too small, too ordinary', to be deemed responsible for the various atrocities listed by prosecuting counsel. So, too, Biljana Plavsic, who succeeded Radovan Karadzic, as President of Republic Srpska. See Drakulic, *Fly*, 113–14, 119–20, 157. Gary Bass is also struck by the sheer ordinariness of defendants such as Dusko Tadic. See Bass, *Vengeance*, 206, and also Michael Sharf and William Schabas, commenting on the ordinariness of Milosevic in *Milosevic*, 4–5.

[121] Drakulic, *Fly*, 58, 64, 68–73.

own humanity?[122] The same question can, of course, be asked of others. Judge McDonald pointedly asked it of Dusko Tadic. Tadic had no answer. No explanation, justificatory or not, was forthcoming. Perhaps there was no answer to be had.[123]

This leads inexorably to a series of further, no less haunting questions. What makes instances of terrorism or acute political violence, in war or at any other time, really so extraordinary?[124] What do the events in the Balkans in the 1990s and in The Hague tell us about ourselves? Would we have done any different if we had been in Erdemovic's position, or even Tadic's? Drakulic follows Arendt. To dismiss such men as intrinsically evil, and such events as necessarily extraordinary, is to evade our own responsibility as human beings. We may not be guilty of their particular crimes, but we must accept our share of responsibility.[125]

Investigating the ordinary requires a far more subtle inquisition than that which is demanded by the extraordinary. The extraordinary can be consigned to mythology. The ordinary is far more troubling. It is men such as Jelisec and Tadic who should terrify us, not pompous buffoons such as Mladic or Milosevic. Indeed, it is the very fact that we are terrorised by ordinary people that makes the terror so terrifying. If we are entertained, even thrilled, by the mythic and the preposterous, we are paralysed by the ordinary.[126] For this very reason, it is the minds of Jelisec and Tadic that we need to get into; not just if we are to comprehend the extent of their guilt, and their motivation, but if we are to somehow chart the prospects of reconciliation in the communities they sought to devastate.

We need to be startled by events at camps such as Omarska and Keraterm, just as we need to be troubled by the behaviour of Goran Jelisec, and numbed by accounts of the massacres of Srebrenica. The ability of Tribunals such as that established at The Hague to do this furnishes a validity that is immune from any criticisms regarding its capacity to arraign alleged war criminals.[127] They can present chronicles that test our moral reflexes by means of engaging the most acute of our aesthetic and emotional sensitivities.[128] In presenting 'new historical narratives', it has been argued that ICTY and the chronicles which oscillate

---

[122] Drakulic, *Fly*, 7–8.   [123] Neuffer, *Key*, 307–8.

[124] The question haunts Charles Webel's chronicle of the various accounts of victims of terror, ranging from the Holocaust to 9/11. The 'border between normality and abnormality in life and war', as one of his victims comments, 'is very thin'. See Webel, *Terror*, 67.

[125] Drakulic, *Fly*, 164–72. Charles Webel poses precisely this question, in his *Terror*, 96. Are terrorists intrinsically evil or simply 'the shadow side of civilized peoples, the unleashed and unrepressed violence lurking in virtually all of us?'

[126] Webel, *Terror*, 82, 86–7.

[127] For an intriguing prospective regarding the effectiveness of ICTY, written in 1995 and 1998, see P. Akhavan, 'The Yugoslav Tribunal at a Crossroads: The Dayton Peace Agreement and Beyond', *Human Rights Quarterly*, 18 (1996), 259–85.

[128] Neuffer fears that, in strictly legalistic terms, ICTY will serve up the kind of 'justice more aimed at international lawyers than genocide survivors'. See Neuffer, *Key*, 391.

around it provide the foundations with which damaged communities can begin to 'build bridges between past and present', whilst also establishing and 'maintaining a moral stance' against the recurring temptations of 'genocide and collective violence'.[129]

They invoke what Georges Bataille termed 'sovereign sensibility'; a sensibility that does not concede all to visceral emotion, but which recognises that the reconciliation of any devastated civil society depends upon the progress of empathy and compassion.[130] It is this hope to which Rudy Giuliani gestured in the days following 9/11, when he suggested that the catastrophe should be remembered 'in its reality', for the sake of the 'future'.[131] It requires us to 'think more creatively' about the experience of terror and its consequences.[132] It accepts that any sophisticated idea of restorative justice must accept the implications of narrativity. It must admit that a comprehensive jurisprudence is, to quote Antije Krog, one 'quilted together from hundreds of stories'.[133] In her chronicle, Krog recounted one deponent who confirmed that the 'process' of the Commission 'allows me to remember but also to believe that we as human beings are all interdependent, that we can only exist through our common humanity'. As Krog added, people need to be given the opportunity to tell their 'stories', simply because 'there are different perceptions of the truth'.[134]

The ability to tell your story, to participate in the narrative construction of your society, is an essential expression of democracy.[135] It is also, of course, a necessary component of reconciliation, both within a community and within a self. In allowing people to voice their experiences of terror, their past, their present and their future, such stories provide a medium with which the breaches of trust, the simmering hatreds and fears, and the agonies of disarticulation can perhaps be reconciled.[136] We shall revisit this thought, in a very different circumstance, in Chapter 6, when we contemplate the difficulties experienced in presenting a narrative supplement which can address the varieties of hurt experienced in the aftermath of 9/11.

Krog also chronicled the justly renowned testimony of one young man blinded by the apartheid police. 'I feel', he declared, that 'what has been making me sick all the time is the fact that I couldn't tell my story'. But now 'it feels like

---

[129] For Minow's eloquent confirmation, see *Vengeance*, 143.
[130] G. Bataille, 'Concerning Accounts Given by Residents of Hiroshima' in Caruth, *Trauma*, 230.
[131] In Edkins, *Memory*, 226–7.   [132] May, *Humanity*, 234.   [133] Krog, *Skull*, 259.
[134] See Y. Henry, 'Where Healing Begins' in Villa-Vicencio and Verwoerd, *Looking Back*, 170, 173.
[135] For a discussion of this idea within the South African context, see D. Crocker, 'Truth Commissions, Transitional Justice, and Civil Society' in Rotberg and Thompson, *Truth v Justice*, 99–121.
[136] For a commentary on this disarticulation, and more particularly the need to address breaches of trust which underlie trauma, see K. Erikson, 'Notes on Trauma and Community' in Caruth, *Trauma*, particularly 197–8, and also Laub, 'Truth', commenting at 73, that it is 'this very commitment to truth, in a dialogic context and with an authentic listener, which allows for a reconciliation with the broken promise, and which makes the resumption of life, in spite of the failed promise, at all possible'. See also Edkins, *Trauma*, 189, concluding that testimony 'refutes' terror, tyranny and trauma.

I've got my sight back by coming here and telling you the story'.[137] Likewise, one of the most telling commentaries in Neuffer's chronicle is the account of Hamdo Kharimanovic's testimony in the *Tadic* trial, and most strikingly the attempt of the prosecutor to get his witness to resist the temptation to 'reverie'.[138] Hamdo, too, had a story to tell; of a neighbour with whom he had exchanged keys, and much else, but who had, when the opportunity arose, thought nothing of brutalising him, terrorising his family and stealing his property. At last, at The Hague, Hamdo got to tell his story.[139]

[137] See Krog, *Skull*, 45–6, Tutu, *Future*, 127–9, and E. Kiss, 'Moral Ambition Within and Beyond Political Constraints' in Rotberg and Thompson, *Truth v Justice*, 72. For an example, see G. Fourie, 'A Personal Encounter with the Perpetrators' in Villa-Vicencio and Verwoerd, *Looking Back*, 230–8.

[138] The same point is acknowledged by one of the ICTY prosecutors, Geoffrey Nice, who observes, 'The abiding impression I have, after calling so many of the witnesses, is that the process of coming to The Hague is inevitably imperfect *for them*. Under pressure of time, the advocates on both sides squeeze from them what is necessary to the case and deny them the chance to speak at length when they want to'. See G. Nice, 'Trials of Imperfection', *Leiden Journal of International Law*, 14 (2001), 392.

[139] Neuffer, *Key*, 183–6. She provides a similar account of witnesses struggling to be allowed to tell their 'stories', in the 'Celebici' case, at 297–9.

4

Where are the women?

'I pushed the button about twenty times to set off the bomb', the Chechen terrorist Zarema Muzhakhoyeva confessed, shortly after her arrest following a failed suicide mission to Moscow in summer 2003, 'but it just wasn't working'.[1] Zarema Muzhakhoyeva is an exceptional terrorist. Not because she was willing to kill and be killed. Not because she was incompetent and survived. She is exceptional because she is a woman. For this reason she has an added fascination. She is one of the Chechen 'black widows'.[2] Muzhakhoyeva broke all the usual taboos which shroud the discourse of terrorism, plus the one that assumes that women do not ordinarily commit acts of political violence. Terrorism is supposed to be a 'man's game'; much as politics is.[3]

Of course there are some women to be found. But they have a particular role to play; the essentially passive role of victim. In one sense, such a role has a quotidian and all too familiar banality, as many feminist critics often allege.[4] The grander meta-narratives of terrorism may be signified by planes crashing into New York skyscrapers. The micro-narratives of female terror, however,

---

[1] Quoted in V. Groskop, 'Chechnya's Deadly "Black Widows"', *New Statesman* 6 September 2004, 32.

[2] For a commentary on the exceptional nature of the Chechen 'black widows', an exceptionality which is, of course, more in the perception than the reality, see A. Nivat, 'The Black Widows: Chechen Women Join the Fight for Independence – and Allah', *Studies in Conflict and Terrorism*, 28 (2005), 413–19.

[3] For various expression of this supposition, see S. Greenhalgh, 'The Bomb in the Baby Carriage' in J. Orr and D. Klaic (eds.), *Terrorism and Modern Drama* (Edinburgh University Press, 1990), 161; L. Neuberger and T. Valentini, *Women and Terrorism* (Macmillan, 1996), 35, 57 and more recently B. Nacos, 'The Portrayal of Female Terrorists in the Media: Similar Framing Patterns in the News Coverage of Women in Politics and in Terrorism', *Studies in Conflict and Terrorism*, 28 (2005), 435–6.

[4] See Z. Eisenstein, 'Feminisms in the Aftermath of September 11', *Social Text 72*, 20 (2002), 79–81, and more recently Susan Faludi, in *The Terror Dream: Fear and Fantasy in Post-9/11 America* (Metropolitan Books, 2007), confirming at 81 and 90–101, that the US media was only prepared to countenance female 'victims' and 'widows', not 'heroes'; a prejudice which reached its notorious apogee in the 'cult' of Lisa Beamer, the widow of one of those who may have attempted to thwart the hijack of 'Flight 93'. The nature of the passivity can be various, and sometimes bizarre in the extreme. As Faludi notes, at 41–2, amongst all the signal absurdities of the 'war on terror', one of the oddest must surely be the State Department inspired 'Beauticians without Borders' campaign, in which various high-profile cosmetics companies, including Revlon and Clairol, were persuaded to stump up the funding for the establishment of a Beauty School attached to the Women's Ministry in Kabul.

occur behind closed doors, in murky side-streets, inside police cells. In her drama written against the Irish 'troubles' *Ourselves Alone*, Anne Devlin's Frieda relegates the distant terrorism of car-bombs and RUC raids behind the everyday terror of being gang-raped in an alley-way.[5] This, for many women, is the terrorism that dare not speak its name. In the last chapter we noted the difficulty that female victims in particular experienced in presenting personal testimonies of precisely this kind of terrorism before ICTY and the South African TRC.[6]

The female who actually engages in terrorism, moreover, appears to be rarer still; and so, accordingly, is their presence in our political or cultural imagination. The excision of women from accounts of warfare has been long noted. To this extent their absence from accounts of 9/11 and its immediate aftermath was, perhaps, less of a surprise.[7] But the question, as Hilary Charlesworth and Christine Chinkin reiterated, still needed to be asked: 'where are the women?'[8] The question is presented more starkly in the counter-factual. What if all the terrorists in September 2001 had been female? Likewise, what if all the fire-fighters who raced into the Twin Towers, and all the other rescuers in New York and Washington and outside Philadelphia had been women?[9] As it is, 9/11 has been presented as an essentially masculine event, its heroic narrative exclusively and conspicuously male.[10] The seeming absence of the woman counter-terrorist is just as striking as the absence of the woman terrorist.[11] The physical

---

[5] See A. Devlin, *Ourselves Alone* (Faber and Faber, 1990), 18, 30.

[6] See, for example, the gruesome account of a rape victim chronicled in Krog's, *Country of My Skull* (Vintage,1999), at 278–9.

[7] See C. Nordstrom, '(Gendered) War', *Studies in Conflict and Terrorism*, 28 (2005), 400.

[8] H. Charlesworth and C. Chinkin, 'Sex, Gender and September 11', *American Journal of International Law*, 96 (2002), 600. The 'failure to ask the gender question' is also challenged in C. Gentry, 'The Relationship Between New Social Movement Theory and Terrorism Studies: The Role of Leadership, Membership, Ideology and Gender', *Terrorism and Political Violence*, 16 (2004), at 278 and 288–9.

[9] A point made by Charlesworth and Chinkin, 'Sex', at 602.

[10] See Faludi, *Dream*, 46–64, describing the increasingly frenetic search for a male 'superhero' conducted by the US media in the weeks and months that followed 9/11. See also 65–6 discussing the particular myths that were written into the role of the New York fire-fighters; myths in which the truth about faulty equipment, poor leadership and unnecessary loss of life was carefully excised. See also Charlesworth and Chinkin, 'Sex', 601–2 and Eisenstein, 'Feminisms', 86–7. In Chapter 6 we shall encounter the likes of Jay McInerney seeking to deconstruct this narrative of masculine heroism in his post-9/11 novel, *The Good Life*. A similar aspiration, albeit deploying a rather more gentle satire, can be found in Ken Kalfus's *A Disorder Peculiar to the Country* (Simon & Schuster, 2006), commenting, for example at 21, on the extent to which images of fire-fighters and the like 'had taken on the graces of classical heroes'.

[11] And if a woman should accidentally find herself in the role of active counter-terrorist, such as Private Jessica Lynch, it is merely assumed that they made a mistaken career choice. Lynch was momentarily famous as the heroine of a Special Forces rescue from a Baghdad hospital following her apparent capture by Iraqi guards. It later transpired that Lynch was not being 'held' in the hospital at all, and could have walked out pretty much any time she liked. But that was not how the US media was encouraged to present the fantasy. When Lynch subsequently turned out to be less than willing to subscribe to the overarching fantasy, the media turned against her with a vengeance. For an account of her case, and that of other female soldiers in the Iraq war, see Faludi, *Dream*, 165–93.

and narrative absences must, furthermore, be placed alongside another necessarily related absence; that of voice. Once again, we noted this critical alignment
in the previous chapter.

Aside from interrogating the nature of these related absences, we will in this
chapter encounter two other characteristics of the woman terrorist. The first is
that the distinction between the woman terrorist and the woman victim is an
unstable one. We will investigate this instability more closely in the first part of
this chapter, focusing in particular on framing the maternal construct. Second,
as we progress, we will encounter much that is rather familiar; for the absence of
the female voice in the discourses of terrorism is indicative of an absence that
cuts across so many of the associated discourses of law and politics. As feminist
scholars have repeatedly alleged, the women have long been presented as 'other'
in these discourses. Women terrorists, especially terrorists such as Zarema
Muzhakhoyeva, who proclaim a militant Islamic identity, assume a radical
position along this margin of exclusion.[12]

Small wonder that their voices should be quieted. And small wonder too
perhaps that the silencing might nurture its own violence. Half a century ago,
Frantz Fanon suggested that terrorism was a justifiable weapon of sexual
liberation, the only practicable means of an emancipation that is otherwise
denied.[13] Writing in the immediate context of the Algerian war of independence, he further, and specifically, voiced his admiration for those younger
Muslim women who used the veil, the supreme symbol of patriarchal authority,
as a mask behind which they could more effectively destroy precisely that
culture.[14] Three decades ago, Freda Adler ventured the same supposition;
that the female terrorist might be better comprehended as someone who
perceives themselves to be fighting for 'sexual equality'.[15] It is a provocative
supposition, and one to which we will again return as the chapter progresses. A
search for the woman terrorist, and indeed the woman as victim of terror, takes
us right to the heart of modern debates regarding the relation between law and
gender. It also immerses us in a necessarily textual investigation, a search for

[12] Unsurprisingly, some of the most challenging work in the broader environs of law and critical
theory can be found in areas of intersection between feminist and critical race theory. See, for
example, K. Crenshaw, 'Demarginalizing the Intersection of Race and Sex: A Black Feminist
Critique of Antidiscrimination Doctrine, Feminist Theory and Antiracist Politics', *University of
Chicago Legal Forum* 1989, 139–67.

[13] An injunction which finds a contemporary echo in the words of Samia Sa'd a-Din who lauds
female Palestinian suicide-bombers for the determination to 'write the history of their liberation
with their blood'. See R. Israeli', 'Palestinian Women: The Quest for a Voice in the Public Square
Through "Islamikaze Martyrdom"', *Terrorism and Political Violence*, 16 (2004), 86, and also 66
citing Fanon.

[14] See J. Decker, 'Terrorism (Un)Veiled: Frantz Fanon and the Women of Algiers', *Cultural
Critique* 1990, 180–5, 189–93, discussing more particularly the implications of Fanon's essay
Algeria Unveiled, originally published in 1959.

[15] See F. Adler, *Sisters in Crime* (Waveland Press, 1975), 20–2. The suggestion has been revisited
more recently by Brigitte Nacos, in 'Portrayal', at 442–3, and also Caroline Nordstrom, in 'War',
at 408–9.

voices, for alternative discourses, for alternative supplements and texts; for, as Annie Leclerc puts it, 'The world is man's word. Man is the word of the world'.[16]

Weep for me

Images of the woman as victim of terror can be traced throughout the canon. Commonly they provide a chorus, often unseen, more often still unheard. In his poem *The Road*, writing in August 1916, Siegfried Sassoon wrote:

> The road is thronged with women; soldiers pass
> And halt, but never see them; yet they're here-
> A patient crowd along the sodden grass,
> Silent, worn out with waiting, sick with fear.[17]

And they can be found three centuries earlier in Shakespeare, in his proto-tragedy, *Titus Andronicus*. Here the savage rape and maiming of Lavinia, her tongue removed, 'torn from forth that pretty hollow cage', and her hands cut off, speaks very obviously to the collateral terrors of physical violence and disarticulation.[18] The 'signs' of her martyrdom carry an obvious consonance.[19] And two millennia before Shakespeare, the alignment of the victimised, silenced woman and the state of tyranny and terror was a defining theme in classical Hellenic drama. Indeed, the Rome of the fallen Andronici is presented to Shakespeare's England as 'our Troy'.[20]

This alignment finds one of its most striking expressions in Euripides' *The Women of Troy*.[21] As Troy burns, and its men are slaughtered, the women of Troy are enslaved, taken as 'plunder' and 'allotted'.[22] Their rape is imminent. They will be passed like chattels, 'forced, perhaps, into the bed of some lustful Greek'.[23] Queen Hecabe will be passed to Odysseus, one daughter, Cassandra,

---

[16] A. Leclerc, 'Woman's Word' in D. Cameron (ed.), *The Feminist Critique of Language: A Reader* (Routledge, 1990), 79.

[17] In S. Sassoon, *Collected Poems* (Faber and Faber, 1961), 32.

[18] W. Shakespeare, *Titus Andronicus* (Arden Shakespeare, 1995), 3.1.85.

[19] 3.2.36, with Marcus commenting on her 'martyred signs'. For an interesting discussion of *Titus* and its contemporary resonances, most particularly the themes of tyranny and political dislocation, see M. Pincombe, 'Titus our Contemporary?: Some Reflections on Heiner Mueller's *Anatomie Titus Fall of Rome*' in O. Kubinska and E. Nawrocka (eds.), *Playing Games with Shakespeare: The Contemporary Reception of Shakespeare in the Baltic Region* (Theatrum Gaedanense Foundation, 2004), 27–61.

[20] For the immediate alignment of the two, see *Titus Andronicus*, 5.3.86.

[21] A. Kubiak, *Stages of Terror: Terrorism, Ideology, and Coercion as Theatre History* (Indiana University Press, 1991), 5–9, and also 30–8, suggesting that Euripides' plays represent something of an epitome of this fascination with terror and terrorism in fifth-century Hellenic drama. *The Women of Troy* was the third part of a trilogy. The first two plays, *Alexandros* and *Palamedes*, are lost. For a discussion of the probable broader construction of the trilogy, see D. Conacher, *Euripidean Drama: Myth, Theme and Structure* (Toronto University Press, 1967), 127–34.

[22] Euripides, *The Women of Troy*, in *The Bacchae and Other Plays* [hereafter WT], 96–7, and also 100 for confirmation that the remaining women will be distributed 'according to the draw'.

[23] WT, 96.

will be the 'concubine' of the Greek king, Agamemnon, whilst another, Andromache, will see her son Astynax murdered, before being given to yet another Thessalonian prince.[24] All 'love', as Andromache puts it, 'we have lost'.[25] It is their fate, and their lamentation, that fascinates Euripides.[26]

Troy's fall is cataclysmic, and so is the misery of its survivors.[27] Their 'suffering has no limit, none', and neither has the extent of their lamentation.[28] It overwhelms; the cascade of raw emotions, the sense of utter despair, of cataclysmic terror. 'Weep for me, and veil my head', Hecabe beseeches of her audience, 'Hope is dead'.[29] The horror and the shrouding go together, the rape, the veiling, the removal of dignity, of face, of identity:

> I mourn for my dead world, my burning town,
> My sons, my husband, gone, all gone!
> …
> How must I deal with grief?
> …
> My heart would burst,
> My sick head beats and burns,
> Till passion pleads to ease its pain
> In restless rocking, like a boat
> That sways and turns,
> Keeping sad time to my funereal song.[30]

---

[24] WT, 98. Euripides' audience would have known the fate that would befall Agamemnon, having chosen to take Hecabe's unbalanced daughter.

[25] WT, 109. See also M. Aristodemou, *Law and Literature: Journeys from Her to Eternity* (Oxford University Press, 2000), 73–4.

[26] Euripides was one of the three great tragedians, the others being Aeschylus and Sophocles, who together were hailed by Pericles as the 'school of Hellas'. Famously, according to Aristotle, Euripides was 'the most tragic of the poets'. See Aristotle, *Poetics* (Penguin, 1996), 21–2. It was he, according to Aristophanes, in the *Frogs*, who made his characters 'speak like human beings'. The Euripides portrayed in Aristophanes' sparkling comedy rails against dramatic pretence and verbiage. The fact that his critique of pretentiousness is so pretentious is, of course, a pleasing irony. See Aristophanes, *The Frogs* (Penguin, 1964), 190–2. For general commentary on the three poets of the 'school', see P. Vellacot, 'Introduction' to *The Bacchae and Other Plays* (Penguin, 1973), 9. For a commentary on the seemingly ever-present role of 'wailing women dressed in sheets' in classical Hellenic drama, see R. Hazel, 'Women's Voices, Women's Hands' in D. Stuttard and T. Shasha (eds.), *Essays on Trojan Women* (AOD Publications, 2001), 10–29.

[27] See A. Poole, 'Total Disaster: Euripides' *The Trojan Women*', *Arion*, 3 (1976), particularly 263–5 and 271, discussing the extent to which the play excavates the nature of *eremia*, or total destruction.

[28] WT, 110. Except that suffering was supposed to be constrained by rituals of lamentation. Even here the women of Troy, in their unconstrained lament, are somehow threatening. The same was true of Sophocles' Antigone, her challenge to Creon's sovereignty rooted in a determination to follow her interpretation of the rituals of burial and lamentation. For the use of these rituals, particularly their excessive use, as a form of disobedience, see N. Croally, *Euripidean Polemic: The Trojan Women and the Function of Tragedy* (Cambridge University Press, 1994), 74–7, and also E. Hall, 'Introduction' in *Euripides: The Trojan Women and Other Plays* (Oxford University Press, 2000), xxxvii–viii.

[29] WT, 99.

[30] WT, 93. For a commentary on Hecabe's lament, the 'heart of the play', see J. Griffin, 'The *Trojan Women*' in Stuttard and Shasha, *Essays*, 66–7.

So overwhelming is the misery that the play, famously, progresses without any real sense of plot or evolution. There are no dilemmas in *The Women of Troy*, nothing to be uncovered; just a series of episodes to be experienced.[31] There is, as the Chorus confirms, merely the drama of 'weeping wives' and distraught mothers.[32]

For not only are Hecabe and Andromache widows, so too are they dispossessed mothers.[33] The murder of Andromache's son Astynax is perhaps the most horrific of the myriad horrors Euripides presents. 'Now accept this decision and be sensible', the Greek messenger advises Andromache. How, Andromache retorts, can such a 'barbaric' cruelty, a barbarism that flies in the face of nature, be reconciled with reason.[34] History will 'make Hellas blush'.[35] It is the voice of the mother, of successive mothers, 'allotted', raped, their children 'torn' from their arms, which excavates most deeply the true terror which patriarchal rule represents.[36] The peculiar relation of terror and the maternal is one which we shall encounter on more than one occasion.

The theatre of fifth-century Athens, it is commonly suggested, was a primary site of public debate, whilst the 'invention of tragedy' coincided with, and complemented, the 'invention of politics'.[37] More than anything, like his

---

[31] See G. Grube, *The Drama of Euripides* (Methuen, 1973), 282; Conacher, *Drama*, 137–9; R. Rutherford, 'The Cassandra Scene' in Stuttard and Shasha, *Essays*, 99–100; and also Croally, *Polemic*, 225–7, suggesting the extent to which this lack of narrative drive is a result of Euripides' latent sophism. Adrian Poole also explores the extent to which critical commentary on the play has been hampered by the 'torpor' produced by a sense of dissatisfaction at the absence of narrative drive. See Poole, 'Total Disaster', 257–9.

[32] WT, 126.

[33] According to Poole, the 'Euripidean body is always viewed through the eyes of a parent'. See his 'Total Disaster', 280.

[34] WT, 114–15.

[35] WT, 128. See Croally, *Polemic*, 109–10, discussing the extent to which Euripides would have sowed confusion in his audience, destabilised by the realisation that the Greeks would suddenly have seemed 'more barbarian than barbarians', and also A. Garvie, 'Euripides' *Trojan Women*: Relevance and Universality' in Stuttard and Shasha, *Essays*, 54–5.

[36] WT, 106. See Grube, *Euripides*, 290 and 295–6, and also Poole, 'Total Disaster', 262, commenting that the murder of Astynax, and the lament of his mother and grandmother, Andromache and Hecabe, 'constitutes the moment of supreme pain and recognition'.

[37] The major tragedies of Euripides and his contemporaries were performed often as part of a contest during the Great Festival of Dionysus. According to Croally, such presentations were a 'central event in civic discourse'. See Croally, *Polemic*, 1–5, and also 249–50, broadly supporting Nietzsche's famous view that Euripides actually ended classical tragedy precisely because he democratised it, entertaining the more sceptical views of the ordinary man, and just possibly woman. Martha Nussbaum argues that to attend the theatre in classical Greece was to 'acknowledge and participate in a way of life'. See her *Love's Knowledge: Essays on Philosophy and Literature* (Oxford University Press, 1990), 16. For further discussion of the relation of politics and theatre in fifth-century Athens, see O. Longo, 'The Theater of the *Polis*' in J. Winkler and F. Zeitlin (eds.), *Nothing to do with Dionysos?: Athenian Drama in its Social Context* (Princeton University Press, 1990), 15–19, and J. Ober and B. Strauss, 'Drama' also in Winkler and Zeitlin, *Dionysos*, 245–9, 270. For further commentary on the Great Festival of Dionysus, see S. Goldhill, *Love, Sex and Tragedy* (John Murray, 2005), 204, and also the debate conducted between S. Goldhill, 'The Great Dionysia and Civic Ideology', *Journal of Hellenic Studies*, 107 (1987), 58–76, and J. Griffin, 'The Social Function of Attic Tragedy', *Classical Quarterly*, 48 (1998), 39–6, and revisited in D. Carter, 'Was Attic Tragedy Democratic?', *Polis*, 21 (2004), 1–25.

contemporary, Gorgias, who suggested that only by listening to poetry might men, and women, 'experience the shudders of fear, the tears of pity, the yearnings of grief', Euripides wanted his audience to appreciate the emotional, often tragic, consequences of a politics that was driven by a fascination with violence.[38] He particularly wanted to challenge those who presumed Homeric politics to be virtuous, to be an ideal.[39] The context is, of course, prescriptive. All of Euripides' plays were produced during another rather earlier Balkan war, the Peloponnesian. Political violence is endemic, terror a pervasive experience.[40]

And the fate of Troy stalked all.[41] The Greeks had shown no compassion in victory, and in time the gods punished them accordingly. The recent and brutal treatment of the Melians at the hands of their Athenian conquerors would have been fresh in the memory of those who sat in Euripides' audience. The implication was clear, and prophetic. Athens had learnt nothing; and its time would come.[42] Brutality is not something that can be resigned to fate or divine

---

[38] The Gorgias quote, taken from his *Helen*, is cited in Griffin, 'Tragedy', at 55. In his *Life of Pelopidas*, Plutarch recorded the tyrant Alexander of Pherae fleeing a performance of *The Women of Troy*, 'because he was ashamed to have the citizens see him, who had never taken pity on any man that he had murdered, weeping over the sorrows of Hecuba and Andromache'. Quoted in Hall, 'Introduction', ix. The educative aspiration of classical tragedy was controversial. Plato was famously critical. For a discussion of this controversy, see Nussbaum, *Love's Knowledge*, 16–17; J. Redfield, 'Drama and Community: Aristophanes and Some of His Rivals' in Winkler and Zeitlin, *Dionysos*, 325–6; and also Croally, *Polemic*, 17–26, at 35–6, arguing that the very form of classical tragedy demanded a constitutive contribution of the audience, and at 43, concluding that tragedy 'is a discourse, produced by the *polis*, which allows Athens to examine itself in a Dionysiac, other-worldly and transgressive manner, with the potential of teaching the citizens about themselves and their city'. Keith Sidwell quotes a speech ascribed to Andocides, 'When you watch such things in tragedies you regard them with horror, but when you see them taking place in the *polis* you think nothing of them'. See K. Sidwell, 'Melos and the *Trojan Women*' in Stuttard and Shasha, *Essays*, 38–9.

[39] As Croally noted, the very idea of war had never really be questioned before, at least not in classical Hellenic drama. See Croally, *Polemic*, 254–8, and also Poole, 'Total Disaster', 277–9, identifying the central importance of the anti-Homeric theme. The same aspiration, to disrupt the dominance of Homeric political morality, was shared by others, most obviously perhaps Aeschylus. See Goldhill, *Love*, 229, 310–12.

[40] Croally, *Polemic*, 50–6, and also 122–34.   [41] See Hall, 'Introduction', ix.

[42] It did. Athens was eventually defeated in the Peloponnesian wars in 404BC. But it was spared total destruction. Whilst Corinth and Thebes were inclined to wreak a brutal vengeance on the 'tyrant city', Sparta vetoed the idea. The Melian tragedy was famously recorded by Thucydides in the fifth book of his *History of the Peloponnesian Wars*. During the winter of 416–415BC, a few months before the first performance of *The Women of Troy*, the Melians had put up a spirited resistance against a far greater invading Athenian army. Athens refused to treat, and on seizing Melos had put all the Melian men to death, and enslaved its women. Much of contemporary Athens, including, it is reasonable to suspect, Euripides, was appalled. It is sometimes thought that the Melian incident was an exception. It was not. Athens had treated Skione similarly five years earlier and Sparta Hysiai a year before that. For the alignment of the Melian context with the play, see Hall, 'Introduction', xvii–viii; Grube, *Euripides*, 280; K. Dover, 'Who was to Blame?' in Stuttard and Shasha, *Essays*, 8–9; and also Garvie, 'Relevance and Universality', also in Stuttard and Shasha, *Essays*, 45, 48–50. For an alternative, rather more sceptical, view of this presumed context, see Sidwell, 'Melos', 30–44.

whim. Terror is the product of human emotions, its expression a failure of human compassion.[43]

But it is not just the message that is significant. Euripides also wanted his audience to be challenged by the messenger. For what is really striking about *The Women of Troy*, and so many of Euripides' other tragedies, is the fact that the associated horrors are seen through the eyes of the victims, and these victims are, almost exclusively, women.[44] And it is not just the high-born women of Troy. Much of the reflecting is articulated by the Chorus of lesser-born women.[45] It is they who attest to the 'bitter words' of Andromache and her mother, words that 'Teach us to sound the depths of our own misery'.[46] The female voice was, of course, wholly absent from Greek politics; an exile warmly recommended by the likes of Plato.[47] Accordingly the presence of this voice in dramatic form was a challenge.[48] Moreover, the deployment of women as voices of scepticism, even protesting at the agonistic nature of Hellenic politics, intensified the challenge.[49]

The paradoxes abound.[50] There is something very obviously fascinating about dramatists displaying the female voice in a way that was impossible in contemporary political society. But there is also an immediate irony in the fact that it is a voice written by a man, and performed on stage by men. And then there is the collateral irony in the fact that Euripides uses women to articulate a politics that is sceptical, that might otherwise be silenced. In doing so, of course, he can only reinforce the critical juncture, between what is deemed to be the norm and what is thought to be sceptical and disruptive, whilst also

[43] See Hall, 'Introduction', xxvi.
[44] See Croally, *Polemic*, 210, and also Garvie, 'Relevance and Universality', 58–9.
[45] For the importance of the Chorus as a voice of the common woman, see Hazel, 'Women's Voices', 14–15, and also C. Barry, '*Trojan Women*: Sex and the City' in Stuttard and Shasha, *Essays*, 79–81.
[46] WT, 112.
[47] For a broad commentary on the position of women in Athenian society, see J. Gould, 'Law, Custom and Myth: Aspects of the Social Position of Women in Classical Athens', *Journal of Hellenstic Studies*, 100 (1980), 39–59, and also Goldhill, *Love*, 43, 52–3, 191.
[48] See Aristodemou, *Law and Literature*, 30–2, and also at 57, observing that 'Woman's origins, woman's achievements, woman's justice continue to inhabit a silent dark continent', precisely as a result of the canonical authority of Plato, Sophocles and the like.
[49] Froma Zeitlin famously suggested that the Euripidean woman represents the original 'other' in modern theatre. See her 'Playing the Other: Theater, Theatricality, and the Feminine in Greek Drama', *Representations*, 11 (1985), 66, and also 81, attesting to Euripides' peculiar sensitivity to the 'psychology of female characters'. For this reason, it has even been suggested that Euripides 'might be described as a proto-feminist playwright'. See Hazel, 'Women's Voices', 25–6, adding that whilst it would be 'anachronistic' to say that the play is a 'feminist play', given that there was no sensible conception of feminism in fifth-century Athens, nevertheless it is 'undoubtedly a play in which the voice of the victimised, the enslaved, the abused and the bereaved is heard'. For the thought that the 'most tenacious Euripides' is the 'pacifist feminist' Euripides, see Hall, 'Introduction', xiv.
[50] The presentation of paradox was, of course, a central tool in Euripidean drama, and classical Greek drama more broadly described. For a discussion, see Croally, *Polemic*, 118–19.

perpetuating stereotypes of the female voice as irrational, threatening, disruptive, even terroristic.[51]

This suspicion is reinforced by the role of women in Euripides' last play, *The Bacchae*.[52] The drama revolves around the women of Thebes who, in defiance of the usurper King Pentheus, but in obedience to the dictates of the god Dionysus, have taken to the hills, and can be seen by all 'dancing' in his honour.[53] Here the distinction between terrorist and terrorised becomes ever less clear. Where the Trojan women are supposed to inspire pity, the Theban women, a 'maniacal horde', seem to be altogether more disturbing.[54] Their 'strange and terrible doings', their 'extraordinary / Performances', are threatening precisely because they are so carnivalesque.[55] Their dances are 'frantic' with pleasure. Pentheus sees them as an 'army', one that has declared war, not just against him, but against the principle of patriarchy.[56] It is, Pentheus finally pleads in despair, 'beyond / All bearing, if we let women defy us'.[57]

Of course, there is a further series of paradoxes. Pentheus is a usurper, and so doubts remain regarding his claim to exercise sovereign authority; his refusal to admit the authority of Dionysus lending a critical sense of political disobedience to a fundamental failure of faith. The seer Teiresias puts it bluntly, 'You rely / On force, but it is not force that governs human affairs'.[58] It is legitimacy, and

---

[51] See Croally, *Polemic*, 7–8, and also 86–7, discussing the problem of using 'woman as an inferior other in male self-definition' in Euripides, and also Zeitlin, 'Other', 75, arguing that the 'same exclusion which relegates' women 'to the inside as mistresses of interior space equips them for deviousness and duplicity, gives them a talent, or at least a reputation, for weaving wiles and fabricating plots', characteristics that were readily deployed by classical dramatists.

[52] *The Bacchae* was written in exile in Macedon, and first performed in 407BC. According to Zeitlin, the play represents something of an epitome in the treatment of women in classical Hellenic drama. See Zeitlin, 'Other', 63.

[53] Euripides, *The Bacchae*, in *The Bacchae and Other Plays* [hereafter B], 198. For a recent reaffirmation of *The Bacchae* as an original statement of terrorist literature, see T. Eagleton, *Holy Terror* (Oxford University Press, 2005), 5–8.

[54] B, 232. Only Helen, of the women of Troy, is supposed to be denied our pity. Whilst not a Trojan by birth, Helen, in so eagerly embracing her life in Troy, and appearing so easily reconciled to abduction by Paris, is clearly implicated in the tragedy that befalls her adopted city. Her portrayal in *The Women of Troy*, as in countless other Hellenic plays, including Euripides' own *Helen*, is negative in the extreme. It was, of course, just as negative in Homer's *Iliad*, where Helen appears as a self-confessed 'slut' and one who revels in the ascription. See Homer, *Iliad* (Penguin, 2003), 49–50, and also 108–9. For a discussion of Helen in *The Women of Troy*, see Croally, *Polemic*, 93–7. For a broader discussion of male perceptions of women in ancient Greece, which were mostly countenanced in terms of a fear of their rapacious sexuality, see Gould, 'Law', 55–6.

[55] B, 215–16. See Zeitlin, 'Other', 65–6, 76–7, 79, discussing the alignment of chaos and the female body, and also Goldhill, *Love*, 52–3, 77. See also Croally, *Polemic*, 8–10, discussing the obvious resonances with Bakhtin's idea of rituals of misrule. For a renowned analysis of the Dionysian tradition in Greek tragedy, see F. Nietzsche, *The Birth of Tragedy* (Penguin, 1993), 28–32, 39. According to Nietzsche, the dramatic invocation of the Dionysian was always intended to destabilise, not just the pretences of reason, but also those of Homeric virtue. The Dionysian tradition appreciated the centrality of 'pain and contradiction' at the heart of the human condition, and the sheer unadulterated subjectivity of 'primal oneness'.

[56] B, 192–3, and also 200, where Pentheus confirms, in seeking to justify his intentions to bring the women to heel, that 'No good will follow from such Bacchic ceremonies'.

[57] B, 219.   [58] B, 201.

the judicious use of reason. The danger is patent. Authority seems uncertain, and nothing could be better calculated to trouble a fifth-century Athenian audience. And it is here, at this juncture, when authority is questioned, that the temptations of Dionysus are greatest. 'There', as the god exclaims in triumph, ridiculing Pentheus and his attempts to constrain him, 'I made a mockery of him. He thought he was binding me; / But he neither held nor touched me, save in his deluded mind'.[59] It is Dionysus who rules, his women who enact his misrule. It is they who tear Pentheus limb from limb when he is caught spying upon them, in the guise, significantly, of a woman. Significantly, it is Pentheus's own mother, 'foaming at the mouth', who inaugurates the 'rite of death'.[60]

The mother devours the child; a classical theme in Hellenic drama. There is much in Euripides that resonates with contemporary arguments in feminist legal theory, themes of inclusion and exclusion, of terror and tyranny, of the conflicting faculties of reason and emotions.[61] But the maternal theme, the theme of guilt and responsibility, is perhaps the most compelling of all. According to Maria Aristodemou, the very existence of the female voice in classical drama pronounces a contrast between alternative forms of genesis, between the contrived matriarchal aspirations of men who would make law, and the natural maternalism of women who make men.[62] The insinuation is patent. The vitality of the civil society depends, not on its law, but upon its women, its mothers.[63]

The theme of maternal guilt, passed down the centuries, recurs in contemporary drama. Its deployment in dramatic studies of the relation of women and terrorism is conspicuous. It recurs, for example, in Franca Rame's dramatic

---

[59] B, 212.   [60] B, 229, 232.

[61] Alex Garvie concludes that it is a play 'that could have been written at any time', noting how unsurprising it is that *The Women of Troy* should be performed so often during times of war and civil dislocation. See Garvie, 'Relevance and Universality', 60. For similar sentiments, see Griffin, 'Tragedy', 61, and also Goldhill, *Love*, at 8 noting the particular popularity of *The Bacchae* in the twentieth century, at 215 recording the particular impact in Northern Ireland of a production of Sophocles' *Electra* in the context of sectarian violence in 1990, and at 246–7 placing the insight of Hellenistic tragedy within the more immediate context of 9/11. In his 'Introduction' to a special edition of *Classical World*, on the theme of 'Destruction, Loss and Recovery in the Ancient World', in 2003, Matthew Santirocco makes an immediate, and eminently understandable, allusion to the impact of 9/11. See his 'Saving the City', *Classical World*, 97 (2003), 3–4. A jurisprudential complement to these conclusions can be found in C. Douzinas and R. Warrington, *Justice Miscarried: Ethics, Aesthetics and the Law* (Harvester Wheatsheaf, 1994), suggesting at 26 that Greek tragedy remains a defining point in modern legal and political philosophy.

[62] Aristodemou, *Law and Literature*, 58–9, and also 195.

[63] It is for this reason that Aristodemou suggests that a 'new ethics' might be found, not just in feminist jurisprudence, but in the rawest of maternal emotions, the 'mother's love for the strangest and most intimate of others'. Such an emotion constantly militates against the countervailing patriarchal and jurisprudential 'notion of the individual as separate, self-interested and uniquely self-sufficient'. See Aristodemou, *Law and Literature*, 225.

monologue, *A Mother*.[64] Rame's mother mourns for her lost, incarcerated son who has been denounced by a *pentiti* or 'repenter', a former terrorist who has sought to mitigate his own guilt by denouncing alleged accomplices.[65] She mourns as Hecabe and Andromache mourn.[66] But it is the transference of guilt that is so pivotal. At the centre of the monologue is a dream sequence, in which the mother attends her son's pending trial. It is here that the president of the court seeks to impress the extent of her maternal guilt. She was, after all, 'responsible' for breeding and nurturing a terrorist. So now she must make amends, she must persuade her son to become a 'repenter', to implicate others, and to torture their mothers likewise.[67] The fact that the sequence is dreamed merely intensifies the sense of guilt.

The guilt that Rame's mother feels is a guilt that is shared by all mothers. At least it is a guilt that so many societies would like all mothers to share. The conclusion to the monologue is peculiar in its intensity:

> Your honour, here's my boy. I caught him. I'm handing him over to you. I've done my duty as a responsible citizen who trusts our democratic institutions. Here you are, sir … Oh, I'm sorry, your honour. I've held him too tight. I've strangled him. He's dead.

There is, too, an echo of Coetzee's exploration of paternal guilt in the *Master of Petersburg*, a novel we will encounter in the next chapter. But maternal guilt has a different intensity.[68] Mothers have the greater responsibility for the emotional development of their children. The insinuation pervades Euripides, and two thousand years on, it remains. The mother is responsible for the child, and so she is responsible for the terrorist. And because she is, the deeper insinuation follows, the state is not, and neither are the rest of us.

The maternal theme also underpins Deborah Brevoort's acclaimed *The Women of Lockerbie*, a drama which its author readily places within the Euripidean tradition.[69] Brevoort's play explores the agonies of one mother,

---

[64] The theme of the destructive mother was explored by Fo and Rame in their own reinterpretation of *Medea*, as well as its progenitor monologue, *Freak Mother*. The immediate inspiration for their *Medea* is rooted in earlier Italian, as opposed to classical, sources. For an account of this genesis, see T. Mitchell, *Dario Fo: People's Court Jester* (Methuen, 1984), 81 and also D. Hirst, *Dario Fo and Franca Rame* (Macmillan, 1989), 151. For a broader commentary on their *Medea*, stressing the theme of matriarchal guilt, see M. Guensberg, *Gender and the Italian Stage: From the Renaissance to the Present Day* (Cambridge University Press, 1997), 226–7.

[65] For a commentary on the strategy of 'turning' *pentiti*, see M. Burleigh, *Blood and Rage: A Cultural History of Terrorism* (HarperCollins, 2008), 214–15.

[66] Only a mother, perhaps, could contemplate what might have happened if she had aborted her child instead of allowing it to grow up, apparently, as a terrorist. For this musing, see 'A Mother' in S. Hood (ed.), *A Woman Alone and Other Plays* (Methuen, 1991), 201. At no point does Coetzee have his Doestoevski make any comparable reflection in the *Master of Petersburg*. Similarly, it is unlikely that many fathers would, on looking at their son from behind a glass shield, recall how he looked as a baby in an incubator. For this recollection, see *Mother*, 204.

[67] *Mother*, 204–6.   [68] See Guensberg, *Gender*, 225.

[69] See her comments in the 'Author's Note' in D. Brevoort, *The Women of Lockerbie* (Dramatists Play Service, 2005), [hereafter WL], 3. See also Michael Billington's review in *The Guardian*, 5 September 2005, 19.

Madeleine, desperately seeking the remains of her son seven years after he was blown up in a Pan-Am jet in the skies above Lockerbie in south-west Scotland.[70] It is a play about grief, a grief that Madeleine 'can't put aside'.[71] She has 'been weeping for seven years', 'split down the middle' with grief.[72] Her husband Bill attests to having 'seen an ocean pour from her eyes'. It is an intense grief, because it is a maternal grief. 'There is no greater sorrow than the death of a child', as Bill tries to explain, not least to himself.[73]

As in Euripidean drama, the agonies of the central figure in *The Women of Lockerbie* are complemented by those of a Chorus. Here it is provided by the eponymous women of Lockerbie, who have set up a 'laundry project' dedicated to washing the 11,000 articles of clothing salvaged from the crashed plane. 'We want', they attest, 'to give love to those who have suffered'.[74] As Olive, one of the women observes, 'When evil comes into the world it is the job of the witness to turn it to love'.[75] The laundry project thus serves as a ritual lamentation or purification. They wash the clothes 'To make our hearts pure again'.[76] A similar ritual is performed when the women wash Madeleine after she has harmed herself in a frantic search for her son's remains.[77]

The dichotomy that Brevoort presents in *The Women of Lockerbie* is an obvious one. The women deal in emotions. They reach out, they seek empathy. The men do not, or in the case of Bill, too struck 'numb' to try, cannot.[78] Accordingly, the telling of stories is essential. 'Grief', as Olive observes, 'likes to talk'.[79] 'Talk to us. Please', she begs of Madeleine, 'Tell us your story'.[80] As the play proceeds, a defining struggle emerges between the women and a State Department official, George. Despatched to south-west Scotland, George is tasked with establishing 'procedures for dispersal and containment'.[81] He is a 'busy' man, and has no time for weeping and wailing, or rituals of lamentation.[82] He views the women of Lockerbie much as Pentheus viewed those who cavorted around the hills above Thebes. 'Goddamn those Goddamn women', he exclaims in exasperation.[83] 'Don't be fooled by the lace on their collars', he

---

[70] The controversy which surrounds the Lockerbie bombing, and the array of possible culprits, remains fierce. According to many commentators, official inquiries into the disaster were nothing more than a 'whitewash', covering a bungled CIA operation to implicate Libyan terrorists, as part of a wider foreign policy assault against the Gaddafi regime. Subsequent proceedings taken against two 'suspects' at a specially convened court in the Netherlands are deemed to be equally dubious. Paul Foot calls them a 'disgrace'. Amongst alternative putative culprits can be found the governments of Syria and Iran. It has even been suggested that the CIA itself might have operated as an *agent provocateur*. Thus far there is no convincing account of responsibility. See J. Pilger (ed.), *Tell Me No Lies: Investigative Journalism and its Triumphs* (Vintage, 2005), 215–7, 211–12, 225–6, 249–54.

[71] WL, 10.   [72] WL, 21.   [73] WL, 12.   [74] WL, 17.   [75] WL, 18.

[76] WL, 100. The play closes with the Fourth Choral Ode, in which the women silently begin the process of washing the clothes.

[77] WL, 97.   [78] WL, 50.   [79] WL, 26.   [80] WL, 28.   [81] WL, 73–4.

[82] WL, 18. To George, the destruction of the plane may have been tragic. But reason dictates that it should be treated like any other 'incident at altitude'.

[83] WL, 55.

warns Bill, 'Or the flowers on their teacups. They're not the sweet little old ladies they appear to be. They're tigers. And they're ferocious'.[84]

The women of Lockerbie, like the women of Thebes, are a threat to order. They disdain 'procedures'. 'You can always reason with a man', George observes, nearing despair.[85] Maybe. But as Olive observes, 'You can't reason with grief. It has no ears to hear you'.[86] Love, George tries to maintain, 'is not a good enough reason' for doing away with procedure. On the contrary, Olive contests, 'There is no better reason than love'.[87] Ultimately terrified by the prospect of hundreds of women storming into his warehouse, George opens up access to the 'Shelves of Sorrow'. It is not something he wanted to do. Only with reluctance does he concede that there is nothing to be gained from suppressing grief and nothing ultimately to profit from suppressing the voices of those who seek to grieve. The lines, as ever, are blurred. Woman as victim, woman as terrorist, woman as mother of terrorist; distinctions are elusive.

Howling

As we have noted before, images of the woman terrorist are rare.[88] If the male terrorist is elevated as a subject of peculiar fetish and fascination, the female terrorist is silenced, cast to the edges of the terrorist discourse. It is a cultural and historical prescription, pressed just as much by the terrorist as the counter-terrorist.[89] In its early days the Spanish terrorist organisation ETA refused female membership, on the grounds that women would be busy enough 'in the home'.[90] In time, perceptions would change, as one socially constructed prejudice was replaced by another; the housekeeper terrorist morphing into a sexualised terrorist. When leading ETA member Idoia Lopez Riano was captured in 1995, the media preferred to focus on her 'fuchsia lipstick' and 'black curls', and most particularly on the titillating thought that she had used her sexuality as a strategy to first seduce her victims.[91] The necessarily pornographic relation of violence and the sexualised female body carries an obvious resonance, and will be revisited shortly.

The more staid, if rather less exciting, image of the housekeeper terrorist, however, retains its place in the associated literary cultures of women and political violence. It reassures as much as it serves to categorise and control. Alice, the eponymous 'good terrorist' in Doris Lessing's novel, is a classic example.[92] Lessing's novel is not really about terrorism. It is rather about

---

[84] WL, 62.   [85] WL, 63.   [86] WL, 24.   [87] WL, 75.

[88] Over half of those terrorists who took part in the Moscow theatre siege were women; a subject of particular fascination to the Russia media.

[89] See Eisenstein, 'Feminisms', 85, referring to women in terrorist discourse as 'passive receptors of historical moments', and also Nordstrom, 'War', 401–2, observing in similar vein, that the 'silence' of women in accounts of war and terrorism 'is not haphazard'.

[90] See L. Weinberg and W. Eubank, 'Italian Women Terrorists', *Terrorism*, 9 (1987), 243.

[91] Nacos, 'Portrayal', 438–9.

[92] D. Lessing, *The Good Terrorist* (HarperCollins, 2003), 278 [hereafter GT]. Margaret Scanlon argues that Lessing's novel is pivotal in the evolution of modern terrorist literature, precisely

gullible young men and women, but mainly women, who become terrorists in order to make friends. It is the ordinariness that is so striking. Terrorism may be an extraordinary experience, but as we have already noted, and will again, terrorists more often than not are intensely ordinary. Alice is not a proper terrorist at all; partly because she is a woman, and partly too because it becomes ever more difficult, as the novel progresses, to distinguish Alice the terrorist from Alice the victim.[93] Alice is first and foremost a woman, and only secondly a terrorist. It is, so the insinuation follows, why she is a 'good' one.[94]

Alice might, at first glance, in her pity for the poor and dispossessed, seem to fit Fanon's model of the terrorist heroine.[95] But ideology, as one of the male protagonists reassures Alice, is not her line.[96] Alice is a 'housekeeper terrorist'; a role shared not just with the likes of Conrad's Winnie Verloc in *The Secret Agent*, but also the reluctant terrorist 'maids' depicted in Devlin's *Ourselves Alone*.[97] Her efforts are focused on nurturing a 'fug of comfort' in the kitchen.[98] Those she looks after are not terrorist martyrs or terrorist murderers. They are her little 'family'.[99] Whereas the patriarchs devote their evenings to pursuing the class struggle, or at least talking about it, Alice worries about paying the bills, working out how to get the water back on, and fixing the tiles on the roof.[100]

because its protagonist is female. But she also recognises it to be a compromised depiction. See M. Scanlon, *Plotting Terror: Novelists and Terrorists in Contemporary Fiction* (University Press of Virginia, 2001), 90–1, and also P. Widdowson, 'Terrorism and Literary Studies', *Textual Practice*, 2 (1988), 9.

[93] As Margaret Scanlon notes, as the novel progresses it becomes ever more apparent that, as a young girl, Alice must have suffered some form of acute sexual trauma, either physical or emotional. See Scanlon, *Terror*, 81–3.

[94] Another putative female terrorist, Caroline, studies 'handbooks on how to be a good terrorist'. The ironies compound. What makes a terrorist 'good'? Is Lessing's novel such a 'handbook'?

[95] See Widdowson, 'Terrorism', 15–16, suggesting that there is more than a little irony in the very idea of 'good' terrorism, and also aligning the 'fetishization of mundane terrorism' with a particularly 'perverse reflex of feminism'.

[96] GT, 102.

[97] For Devlin's critique of the terrorist maid, articulated in the voice of Frieda, see *Ourselves Alone*, 29. Depictions of women terrorists as housekeepers are prevalent in a number of contemporary accounts drawn from the 1970s and 1980s. Caron Gentry quotes one SDS member observing, 'For years we had run mimeograph machines, but not meetings, made coffee, but not policy'. See Gentry, 'Relationship', 281. For the idea of the woman as the 'token terrorist', see Greenhalgh, 'Bomb', 161, and also 163–8, discussing the extent to which literary images of the woman terrorist tend to be cast within a very definite matriarchal context. Greenhalgh focuses particularly upon the matriarchal image in the plays of Anne Devlin, such as *Naming the Names* and *Ourselves Alone*, both of which are set in the context of the Northern Irish 'troubles'.

[98] GT, 101.

[99] GT, 87, and also 185 expressing her 'happiness' at all her family sleeping peacefully in the kitchen one late evening, and 192–3 reflecting on how effective she had been in forging such a 'close tender group'.

[100] Something which, as Scanlon suggests, puts Lessing's novel in the 'best tradition' of Jane Austen, Emily Bronte and Virginia Woolf. See Scanlon, *Terror*, 87–9. Peter Widdowson suggests that this portrayal can be read as a 'practical expression of humanism'. See his 'Terrorism', 15. When one of the other female members of the 'family' chides Alice for being so domesticated, Alice decides that the best response is to make her a nice cup of tea, see GT, 112, 115. For Alice's various domestic anxieties, see GT, 15–16, 32–3, 42–3, 53, 86, 160, 226–30.

Alice only really gets angry if people fail to clear up their mess.[101] She seems to be just like one of us really.

Except that she blows people up. The final passages of *The Good Terrorist* see Alice and her associates detonate a car bomb outside a London hotel, in the process killing one of their number as well as four innocent passers-by.[102] The endless talk, the seeming irresolution, the ultimate incompetence; it is, as we shall see in the next chapter, a familiar narrative.[103] So too is the attendant sense of futility and doubt. As she scouts the hotel, Alice cannot look at other passers-by, 'the potential victims':

> Alice was thinking: but people might be killed … oh no, that couldn't happen! But inside her chest a pressure was building up, painful, like a cry – but she could not let it be heard. Like the howl of a beast in despair, but she could not reach it, to comfort it.[104]

The inability to articulate consumes Alice. It is a howling prescribed in the canon. Again, in part at least, it is why she is a good, even redeemable, terrorist.

The inability to articulate provides an alternative explanation for the otherwise aberrant presence of the woman terrorist.[105] At an extreme it leads to convenient assumptions that female terrorists are more readily susceptible to being 'zombified', being entranced by some kind of 'mass psychosis'.[106] The supposition was readily deployed in the case of Zarema Muzhakhoyeva, as it was for those who held hundreds of theatre-goers hostage in Moscow in 2002. They had all, survivors confirmed, seemed so polite, and so nice. It could only be, the waiting media confirmed, that the women had been driven to contemplate such unnatural violence through the experience of sorrow and grief; an impression reinforced by survivors who recollected 'widows' crying over pictures of lost children and husbands, even seeking out hostages to whom they

---

[101] GT, 167–9.

[102] A 'model of senseless violence', as Scanlon puts it. See Scanlon, *Terror*, 87. Participating in the discussion of putative targets for the bombing, Alice noted that the 'whole thing turned into a comedy'. The horrific and the comedic, as ever, run together. See GT, 343, and also 378–80 describing the actual bombing and the carnage that resulted.

[103] Scanlon suggests that there is an obvious genetic affinity between the 'conservativism' of Conrad and of Lessing. Both are suspicious of the 'language of public discourse', preferring instead to focus on the personal and private, on the impact of terrorism on the lives of ordinary terrorists and their victims. See Scanlon, *Terror*, 81, and also 90–1 musing on the curiosity of Lessing, a former Communist party member and active student radical herself, composing a novel that is so obviously sceptical of ideology and idealism. Widdowson also notes that the novel, and its politics, came as 'something of a surprise'. See his 'Terrorism', 14.

[104] GT, 377.

[105] See, K. Cunningham, 'Cross-Regional Trends in Female Terrorism', *Studies in Conflict and Terrorism*, 26 (2003), 171–2, and 187, exploring the limitations of these cultural prejudices in terms of actually better understanding the motivations of women terrorists.

[106] Discussing the particular case of Chechen women terrorists, Viv Groskop concludes that they are 'more likely to be forced, blackmailed or brainwashed to the deaths'. See her 'Chechnya's Deadly "Black Widows"', 33. Anne Nivat reaches a similar conclusion in her 'Black Widows', 418.

could tell their stories of personal tragedy.[107] And yet, there they were; walking up and down the aisles of the theatre, their bodies encased in explosive devices which, it seemed, they would detonate without hesitation at the simple behest of their male leaders.[108]

Similar stories emerged from the subsequent Beslan elementary school massacre. Here, of course, the transgression seemed to be all the more horrific; of grieving mothers blowing up a school full of children, simply to ensure that other mothers would experience a similar tragedy. Again, the media sought refuge in reports of female fighters mutinying, and refusing to detonate their bombs. Their male leaders, the media ventured, must have done the deed instead; assuming that fathers blowing up children was a marginally more palatable narrative for their horrified, if fascinated, audience.[109] Recent research suggests that personal revenge, for the loss of familial members, does indeed emerge as a stronger motive amongst female than male terrorists.[110] Less sure, though certainly as convenient as an explanation for their apparent transgression, is the collateral presumption that many such women have been led astray, for reasons of fear perhaps, or maybe admiration, even love, by delinquent patriarchs.[111] The women terrorist, we still prefer to surmise, is gullible and over-wrought, not evil, or worse still rational.

The tensions which colour images of female terrorists in the canons of western culture cause just as much consternation in radical Islam. Here, of course, it is a tension framed by broader anxieties regarding the relation of women and politics in the Koranic tradition. A number of recent contributions to an emergent 9/11 literary genre, a genre to which we will turn in greater detail in Chapter 6, tend to privilege this tension. Vexed sexuality propels John Updike's Ahmed in *Terrorist*, as it does Mohsin Hamid's 'frustrated terrorist' in his *The Reluctant Fundamentalist*.[112] The same tension finds a more prosaic expression in the testament of Mohammed Atta, one of the leaders of the 9/11

---

[107] In her essay on the Chechen terrorist, Zarema Muzhakhoyeva, Viv Groskop confesses her perplexity, concluding, rather uncertainly, that her 'motives' seem to 'lie somewhere between choice and coercion'. See Groskop, 'Chechnya's Deadly "Black Widows"', 32.

[108] See Groskop, 'Chechnya's Deadly "Black Widows"', 33. In a different account, of those who took part in the Moscow theatre attack, Groskop quotes a survivor who recalled that one of the female terrorists, when asked about her motivation, replied 'My whole family was killed. I have buried all my children. I live in the forest. I have nowhere to go and nothing to live for'. In V. Groskop. 'Women at the Heart of Terror Cells', www.observer.guardian.co.uk/print/0,3858,5008682-102275,00.html. See also Politkovskaya's reports on the motivation of Chechen fighters, male and female, in Pilger, *Lies*, 411–32, and also B. MacIntyre, 'Women are Deadlier than the Male in Terrorism's Propaganda War', at www.timesonline.co.uk/article/0..1068-1256260.00html.

[109] See Nivat, 'Black Widows', 415.

[110] K. Jacques and P. Taylor, 'Male and Female Suicide Bombers: Different Sexes, Different Reasons?', *Studies in Conflict and Terrorism*, 31 (2008), 307–8, 321–2.

[111] For the supposition, see Nacos, 'Portrayal', 441–2. For the doubt, see Jacques and Taylor, 'Suicide Bombers', 309–10.

[112] See J. Updike, *Terrorist* (Hamish Hamilton, 2006), and M. Hamid, *The Reluctant Fundamentalist* (Hamish Hamilton, 2007).

strike, who conspicuously demanded that there should be no women at his funeral.[113] In this at least, the 'western' tradition, alternatively Christian and Enlightenment, and the Islamic, have something in common; the assumption that the natural place of women is not to be located in politics, still less political violence.[114]

In an echo of ETA's early attitude to the idea of female terrorists, Article 17 of the Hamas 'Charter' states that 'Muslim women have no lesser role than that of men in the war of liberation; they manufacture men and play a great role in guiding and educating the new generations'.[115] The lines, however, quickly blur. Who, here, is responsible for whom? The role of the female Islamikaze causes especial consternation. The injunction of the Hamas spiritual leader, Sheikh Yassin, that female suicide-bombers must be chaperoned to the targets would be comical, if it was not so tragic, and so grotesque.[116] Equally grotesque is the tendency to address these tensions by stressing the romantic nature of the sacrifice; a tendency that carries not just a gender insinuation but also a textual and poetic, even pornographic, import.[117] Here, of course, it is not just those who seek to justify the self-immolation of the female terrorist who prefer recourse to poesy. The western media has always relished a pretty female terrorist. We have already encountered Idoia Lopez Riano. The famed Palestinian terrorist Leila Khaled was famed less for the bombs she detonated, and rather more for her 'delicate Audrey Hepburn face'. Three decades on, with Khaled elevated to the pantheon of freedom fighters, one interviewer felt moved to burble admiringly, 'You were the glamour girl of international terrorism. You were the hijack queen'.[118] By way of sharp contrast, no one burbled admiringly at Ulrike Meinhoff, with her blotchy skin and weight problems. No one likes an ugly terrorist.

The case of Wafa Idris, the first female Palestinian suicide-bomber, who blew herself up in Jerusalem in July 2003, is again instructive. Idris was glowingly cast by the radical Islamic press as a latter-day Joan of Arc, or Virgin Mary, or,

---

[113] For a comment on the significance of this, see Eisenstein, 'Feminisms', 93, concluding that there is 'too much silence on this point for it not to be important'.

[114] For an overview of this tension, see D. Cook, 'Women Fighting in Jihad?' *Studies in Conflict and Terrorism*, 28 (2005), 375–84.

[115] In Israeli, 'Palestinian Women', 82. Article 18 further emphasises that 'The women in the houses and the families of the Jihad fighters, whether they are mother or sisters, carry out the most important duty of caring for the home and raising the children upon the moral concepts and values which derive from Islam; and of educating their sons to observe the religious tenets, in preparation for the duty of Jihad awaiting them'.

[116] In Israeli, 'Palestinian Women', 85–6. For the supposition, necessarily contentious, that such absurdity, at once comic and tragedy, is symptomatic of a cultural 'misogyny' which, in large part, defines radical Islam, see M. Amis, *The Second Plane* (Jonathan Cape, 2008), 64–8.

[117] For a thorough discussion of this tension, see Israeli, 'Palestinian Women', 67–80, noting the extent to which this debate has taken hold in contemporary Islamic and Sharia scholarship. See also S. Jordan, 'The Women Who Would Die for Allah', *New Statesman*, 14 January 2002, 32.

[118] The interviewer was reporting for *Aviation Security International*, something which merely compounds the irony. See Nacos, 'Portrayal', 439.

alternatively, a Mona Lisa with 'dreamy eyes and the mysterious smile on her lips'. In sacrificing her life, *Al-Arabi* declared, Idris had become the 'most beautiful of women in the world', an 'illuminating spirit and purity for the generations to come'. As she walked to her final destination she carried in her suitcase 'the most beautiful prize any woman can possibly win', her martyrdom. 'Her spirit was raging, her heart filled with anger and her mind convinced', the paper concluded, dancing along the contradictions, 'by the calls of peaceful coexistence'. The only disappointment, the editor observed, was that Idris only managed to kill one old woman.[119] In fact, it transpired that Idris was motivated as much by a sense of personal alienation, having been left by her abusive husband, as by anything that might be termed, however loosely, ideological. But such prosaic personal misery rarely lends itself to idolisation. And so, rather than thinking deeply about what really drove Idris to commit such an act, we are left with the poetic fancy of a newspaper editor.[120] Brought up in an impoverished, patriarchal Palestinian society, abused by her husband, rejected by her family, Idris was as silenced in death as she undoubtedly was in life. Existential heroine, broken-hearted fantasist or deluded zombie? Most likely a bit of each.

The particular situation of the putative Islamic female terrorist is explored in Orhan Pamuk's recent novel, *Snow*; a text we encountered in Chapter 2. At its heart is the alignment of the three critical themes; religion, silence and violence.[121] The background to *Snow* is framed by a military coup in a city at the far east of Turkey. The officers justify the coup as a necessary response to growing Islamic terrorism in the region. At the pivot of the novel is a theatrical performance entitled 'My Fatherland, My Headscarf', presented by a company manager sympathetic to the military cause.[122] The deeper narrative is given by the poet Ka who has returned to his home city to investigate a spate of suicides amongst young girls. One of the female characters Ipek puts the reason starkly, 'The men give themselves to religion, the women kill themselves'.[123] Caught between the demands of their families and those of public authorities, including their schools, 'they see no course of action but to imitate suicidal martyrs'.[124] Or so the leader of the local terrorist group sees it.

---

[119] For a discussion of the Idris Wafa phenomenon, see Israeli, 'Palestinian Women', 84–8, and G. Foden, 'Death and the Maidens', www.guardian.co.uk/women/story/0,3604,1000647,00.html.

[120] The western media similarly preferred to eschew the simpler realities of Idris's life. Of course, they could not dwell on her 'spirit and purity'. So, instead, they focused on the abandoned, and apparently bewildered, husband, carefully ignoring the fact that they were already divorced, in large part because he had repeatedly beaten her over a period of years. Asked to explain what might have driven his wife to such an act, the husband preferred to ignore her personal misery, and hazarded the thought that she might have been a bit of a 'nationalist'. See Nacos, 'Portrayal', 440.

[121] For a broader discussion of Pamuk's novel, particularly its gender implications, see I. Ward, 'Shabina Begum and the Headscarf Girls', *Journal of Gender Studies*, 15 (2006), 119–31.

[122] A rewriting of Kyd's *Spanish Tragedy*.

[123] O. Pamuk, *Snow* (Faber and Faber, 2004), 35 [hereafter S].   [124] S, 77.

Of course, the picture is not so simple. Masks, as Shelley appreciated, are by definition elusive. The headscarf is an ambiguous semiotic, a critical 'deformation of fetishism', in the words of one commentator; for some an image of oppression and subjugation, for others an image of liberation and resistance.[125] The veil as a semiotic for terrorism, for the terrified and for the terrorist, was explored in Fanon's essay *Algeria Unveiled*; at once a 'technique of camouflage' and of 'struggle'.[126] It was also highlighted in Pontecorvo's seminal cinematic portrayal of the same political struggle, *The Battle of Algiers*. Rather more recently, the donning of the veil in Iran during the final years of the Shah's reign was interpreted as a form of domestic terrorism.[127] This ambiguity is reflected in the contemporary 'headscarf debates', most obviously in the context of French and Turkish principles of *laicite* or *laik*.[128]

Pamuk's narrative explores the same reaches. For one of the suicide girls, Teslime, 'the headscarf did not just stand for God's love; it also proclaimed her faith and preserved her honour'.[129] The two sisters whose fates lie at the heart of the novel betray very different attitudes to the headscarf. One, Ipek, is sceptical, at times even scornful of the ritual. But the other, Kadife, is not. In part, she sympathises with the sentiments expressed by Teslime. But for Kadife there is also a political dimension. She wears the headscarf as an act of 'rebellion', a 'revolutionary gesture' against the state, as well as a gesture of personal self-assertion.[130] Political resistance aligns with personal resistance.

Except that Kadife is in no position to resist, not really. She is, rather, a pawn in a far bigger game played out between rival sets of male protagonists, between Islamic terrorist leaders who seek to glorify her sacrifice and military officers and actor-managers who bully her into performing the symbolic removal of her headscarf in their play. As Kadife removes the headscarf on stage, she shoots her chief tormentor, the actor-manager Sunay; a final act of self-assertion, except that it is, again, one that was forced on her. Terrorist and counter-terrorist, Kadife is also very obviously victim, forced to live out a role, as woman and reluctant actor, of 'terrible pain'.[131] It is why, she observes, so many young girls in Kars kill themselves, 'to escape all forms of punishment'.[132] The alignment is familiar; silenced victim, woman terrorist.

[125] J. Decker, 'Terrorism (Un)Veiled: Frantz Fanon and the Women of Algiers', *Cultural Critique*, 17 (1990), 191. For a discussion of the broader cultural, and gendered, context, see Eisenstein, 'Feminisms', 88–90.

[126] F. Fanon, 'Algeria Unveiled' in H. Chevalier (trans.) *A Dying Colonialism* (Grove Press, 1967), 61.

[127] For an overview of these instances and their complexities, see Decker, 'Terrorism', particularly 180–3, 189–93, and also Cunningham, 'Terrorism', 173–5, speaking in particular to the Algerian context.

[128] For discussions of these debates, see N. Hirschmann, 'Western Feminism, Eastern Veiling and the Question of Free Agency', *Constellations*, 5 (1998), 345–68, and N. Moruzzi, 'A Problem with Headscarves: Contemporary Complexities of Political and Social Identity', *Political Theory*, 22 (1994), 653–72.

[129] S, 121.   [130] S, 116.   [131] S, 412–13.   [132] S, 406.

Kadife's tortured admirer Fazil captures the deeper nature of their tragedy, trapped amidst the miasma of terrorist and counter-terrorist mythology:

> No one will remember us; no one will care what happened to us. We'll spend the rest of our days here arguing about what sort of scarf women should wrap around their heads, and no one will care in the slightest as we're eaten up by our own petty, idiotic quarrels. When I see so many people around me leading such stupid lives and then vanishing without a trace, an anger runs through me because I know then nothing really matters in life more than love.[133]

Fetish destroys, not just our capacity to reason, but our capacity to care and respect too. The individual is sacrificed to cultural prejudice. The fact that such fetishes are used to construct the grander prejudices of terrorism is as tragic as it is perhaps inevitable. In an interview given just before the publication of *Snow*, Pamuk confirmed his belief that terrorism is the product, not just of big ideas but of smaller, intensely personal 'degradations'.[134] A state of degradation is a common experience for women, and not just those obliged to cover their faces for fear of offending the men who write their cultures. Pamuk also noted that the failure to listen roots the failure to comprehend these degradations. So long as the female voice stays silenced, excluded from the broader terrorist discourses, these degradations will never be erased, and political violence, at an extreme the violence of self-destruction, will remain the only escape from 'terrible pain'.[135]

Raising voices

As we have already noted, the critical consonance between women, silence and terror is endemic to the discourse of terrorism.[136] Terror finds its ultimate disarticulation in absence and silence; in denying presence and process, in silencing the subject and denying voice, in the threat of 'non-being'.[137] The same is true, of course, of power itself, and law.[138] It is also a particular, even a

[133] S, 294.
[134] O. Pamuk, 'The Anger of the Damned', *New York Review of Books*, 2001, available at www.nybooks.com/articles/14763.
[135] In their empirical study of female terrorist in Italy, Luisella Neuberger and Tiziana Valentini chronicle numerous expressions of precisely this motivation, to destroy self and others as a gesture of liberation. See their *Women and Terrorism*, at 83–6.
[136] See Eisenstein, 'Feminisms', 80.
[137] See Kubiak, *Stages*, 37–8, 155, and also 133–5 and 138–40, 146, specifically exploring the idea of terror as absence and silence in Beckett and Genet. See also Jean-Francois Lyotard suggesting in his *The Postmodern Condition: A Report on Knowledge* (University of Minnesota Press, 1984), at 63, that the 'theatrical terror' denotes the 'efficiency gained by eliminating, or threatening to eliminate, a player from the language game'. The same sentiment is presented by Ariel Dorfman in his essay *Letter to an Unknown Iraqi Dissident* and also in his comments to the UN on World Press Freedom Day, 2 May 1997, both in A. Dorfman, *Other Septembers, Many Americas: Selected Provocations 1980–2004*, (Pluto, 2004), at 23–8, and 231 respectively.
[138] See M. Constable, *Just Silences: The Limits and Possibilities of Modern Law* (Princeton University Press, 2005), 55, affirming that the 'absence of words … constitutes absence of power'.

defining characteristic of the condition of women in modern society; and in
ancient society too. In this context the female terrorist does indeed become a
semiotic, not just for women who engage in acts of extreme political violence,
but for all women.[139]

This critical relation, between terror and disarticulation has been brilliantly
explored by Franca Rame, one of whose monologues we have already encountered.[140] Two others, both of which address the fate of female members of the
Baader-Meinhoff terrorist gang, engage precisely the same ambiguities which
we have encountered from Euripides to Lessing to Pamuk. Their tone, however,
is altogether more intense.[141] The female protagonists of *I'm Ulrike – Screaming*
and *It Happened Tomorrow* embrace terrorist violence and all its implications;
something which can only challenge our capacity for sympathy.[142] It is not that
Rame, despite her own personal and much-chronicled radicalism, is sympathetic to terrorism, or that she wants us to be.[143] But she is sympathetic to the

---

[139] For this insinuation, see C. MacKinnon, *Are Women Human? And Other International Dialogues* (Harvard University Press, 2006), 259–77, suggesting that the day-to-day domestic violence faced by women in America and everywhere else in the world is every bit as much a terrorist experience.

[140] Rame is renowned for her pioneering work in the form of dramatic monologues. Maggie Guensberg suggests that the form is immediately suited to Rame's overarching desire to impress the autonomy, as well as the loneliness and isolation, of women in the public sphere. It is the autonomy which allows the performer and protagonist to retain a measure of control over her image. It also provides a vehicle for the articulation of the female voice. In both instances, the theatre is thereby more liberating than the ordinary spaces of political and public life. See Guensberg, *Gender*, 203–7, 212–16, 238–41, also J. Farrell, *Dario Fo and Franca Rame: Harlequins of the Revolution* (Methuen, 2001), 207, quoting Rame's belief, expressed in a dramatic prologue to *A Woman Alone*, that language, and by implication, theatre is the key to female liberation. 'We believe', she declared, 'that in this way we are emancipated, autonomous, avant-garde'.

[141] A tone the 'stark' nature of which is rooted in its 'straightforward, expository style', according to David Hirst, and possessed of a peculiar 'directness, a searing force'. See his *Rame*, 35, 110.

[142] Rame is not alone in seeking inspiration from the fate of Ulrike Meinhoff. Heiner Mueller's *Hamletmachine*, in which Ophelia destroys her own home as a means to reclaiming her own body, was also inspired by the writings, as well as the fate, of Meinhoff. See A. Teraoka, 'Terrorism and the Essay' in R. Boetecher Joeres and E. Mittman (eds.), *The Politics of the Essay: Feminist Perspectives* (Indiana University Press, 1993), 209, quoting the cataclysmic conclusion to Mueller's play, 'I smash the tools of my captivity, the chair, the table, the bed. I destroy the battlefield that was my home … I set fire to my prison … I walk into the street clothed in my blood'.

[143] The accusation has often been made, not just of Rame, but of her husband, the playwright Dario Fo. Rame's vocal and material support for Red Aid, which collected funds for political prisoners, including members of Red Brigades, provide much fodder for those who accuse her of sympathising with terrorism. Sympathy for terrorists, Fo and Rame have repeatedly countered, does not presume support for acts of terrorism. Rame's particular criticism of the patriarchalism of the Catholic Church has attracted especial opprobrium in her native Italy. For a broader discussion of Rame's work, and Fo's, within the particular context of Italian political theatre, see Hirst, *Rame*, 37–72, 156–202, and also Mitchell, *Fo*, 71–94. See also S. Taviano, *Staging Dario Fo and Franca Rame: Anglo-American Approaches to Political Theatre* (Ashgate, 2005), 19–32, emphasising its root in Communist activism during the 1960s and 1970s, and more particularly Fo's desire to develop a more specific Gramscian theatre which enjoys affinities both with classical Greek tragedy and the Commedia dell'Arte. Perceptively, Taviano stresses the universal

plight of terrorist victims; and Ulrike Meinhoff and Irmgard Moeller are victims too. Like Alice, like Kadife, like Pentheus's mother, they are women first. And they are terrorists because they are women.[144] The gender context confirms that their fate is 'obscenely tragic with the obscenity of our times'.[145]

This same critical tension, between women as terrorists, and women terrorists as victims, cuts across both monologues. Whilst Rame's Meinhoff articulates a bleak irony in observing that she has finally achieved a measure of equality, incarcerated in a 'men's prison', the greater tragedy lies in the tragic consequences of her attempt to break the shackles of her gender.[146] 'No', she declares, 'I don't want to be one of those women you manufacture and keep in cellophane wrapping. Frustrated! Exploited! A mother and a whore – both at the same time'.[147] The state, she implies, oppresses everyone. But it oppresses, and terrorises, women in a particular way. Fanon's provocation resonates once again. And the greatest tyranny, Rame's Meinhoff confirms, is the silence it demands:

> Silence. Silence from outside. Not a single sound. Not a noise. Not one voice, You can't hear anyone walking in the corridor. No doors opening or closing. Nothing.
> Everything white and silent. Silence inside my skull. White as the ceiling. White like my voice if I try to speak. White, the saliva clotting in the corner of my mouth. White and silence in my eyes, in my stomach, in my belly swollen with emptiness.
> I feel sick all the time.[148]

Rame wrote *Ulrike* precisely so as to lift the shroud of silence, and retrieve the voice of the female terrorist.[149] It is supposed to unsettle us.

---

nature of the themes that Fo and Rame have developed, by musing, at 113, on the immediate challenge that would be posed by resituating Fo's most famous play, *The Accidental Death of an Anarchist* as *The Accidental Death of a Terrorist* in the contemporary context of Guantanamo Bay. For a further commentary on the origins of Fo and Rame's work in the context of post-war Italian radicalism, and focusing particularly on the latter's role and influence, see Farrell, *Fo*, 194–210.

[144] In 1977 Rame published an essay in which she opined 'First we have to change class relationships: I believe women's liberation is tied to the class struggle. And, as well, we need to change men, make them learn to discover and respect our dignity. Then finally women will be really free'. Quoted in Hirst, *Rame*, 146. It is not difficult to trace the presence of Rame's own intensely gender-oriented political beliefs in the *Ulrike* monologue. For Rame, the fate of women was rooted in political disempowerment, rather than any innate characteristic of female physiology or psychology. Most immediately, according to Joseph Farrell, it remains rooted in her Marxism. See Farrell, *Fo*, 199–204, 208–9.

[145] Quoted in Hood, *Plays*, 179. See Mitchell, *Fo*, 82–3, suggesting that, whilst they are monologues that appear to be about the fate of terrorists, they are really far more about the fate of women. For a more measured conclusion, emphasising that Rame wanted to present the fate of women, whilst not resigning everything to a simplistic plea for pity, still less self-pity, see Farrell, *Fo*, 199.

[146] F. Rame *I'm Ulrike – Screaming*, in Hood, *Plays*, 181.   [147] *Ulrike*, 183.   [148] *Ulrike*, 182.

[149] See Greenhalgh, 'Bomb' 170, stressing the importance of the metaphor of silence in *Ulrike*. For a detailed discussion of the ideology that Meinhoff articulated in her various essays and writings, see Teraoka, 'Terrorism', 212–14. Teraoka follows Rame in seeking to impress that Meinhoff's terrorism was rooted in a particular ideology urgency. This knowledge does not detract from the horrific nature of the terrorism she promoted. But it does enable us to better understand what might otherwise be all the more terrible in its apparent meaninglessness.

The silencing of the voice is complemented by the torture of the body. Both are intensely gendered. *It Happened Tomorrow* opens with a harrowing description of the attempted murder of Irmgard Moeller:

> They stabbed me in the heart. Four times. As if they wanted to split it open. I couldn't scream at the first thrust of the blade. All that came out of me was a noise a rattle … One of them grabbed me from behind. By the hair. He twisted my right arm behind my back, forcing me to sit down on the chair. The other one held onto my left arm. He shoved a knee into my groin, making me spread my legs apart, as if I was having a back street abortion.[150]

There is much, again, that resonates, the deprivation of voice, the undertones of sexual masochism found in *Ulrike*. There are also echoes of the particular physical degradation suffered by the mother in *A Mother*, forced to undergo a brusque vaginal examination before being allowed to see her son in prison.[151] The violence of the female body is experienced, not just by terrorists, but by their mothers, by women precisely because they are women.[152] Moreover, the rape imagery has a further, and familiar, consonance; as we noted in the last chapter, in the context of testaments given before ICTY and the South African TRC. Feminists have long deployed rape as a critical measure of the need to access a new jurisprudential 'language', one that can better articulate 'women's experiences'.[153] Rape is precisely the kind of everyday terrorism which is peculiar to the female condition.[154] It is just that those who perpetuate the

---

[150] In *It Happened Tomorrow*, in Hood, *Plays*, 187.

[151] *Mother*, in Hood, *Plays*, 203. Rame performed *A Mother* in London in 1983. The brutality of the strip-search, as it was portrayed, complemented a campaign of the time to end strip-searching of visitors to Armagh gaol in Northern Ireland. See Mitchell, *Fo*, 82–3, rightly concluding that Rame's mother 'is representative of female rage at female impotence in a male-dominated system of repression'.

[152] For a commentary on this insinuation, made most explicitly perhaps, in *The Rape*, written with Fo but most famously performed by Rame, see Hirst, *Fo*, 196–7. As is invariably the case with literary and dramatic accounts of rape, it is the experience, as much as the physical event, which is so intensely portrayed in *The Rape*; the victim's sense of diminishment, and her feeling of being not just disempowered but also disarticulated. See *The Rape*, in Hood, *Plays*, at 86. For a broader discussion of the particular 'sexual charge' that Rame brought to performances of this and other plays written by herself and by Fo, see Farrell, *Fo*, 196–7.

[153] See C. Heilbrun and J. Resnick, 'Convergences: Law, Literature and Feminism', *Yale Law Journal*, 99 (1990), 1921 and 1927, and more recently E. Rackley, 'Representations of the (Woman) Judge Hercules, the Little Mermaid, and the Vain and Naked Emperor', *Legal Studies*, 22 (2002), 603–5. For a further insightful commentary, from the perspective of psychotherapeutic responses to the experience of rape, see L. Brown, 'Not Outside the Range: One Feminist Perspective on Psychic Trauma' in C. Caruth (ed.), *Trauma: Explorations in Memory* (Johns Hopkins University Press, 1995), 100–12.

[154] For the alignment of rape and terrorism, see K. Sarikakis, 'Violence, Militarism, Terrorism: Faces of a Masculine Order and the Exploitation of Women', *Feminist Media Studies*, 2 (2002), 152–3. For a broad, and justly renowned commentary on the 'experience' of rape, see S. Estrich 'Rape', *Yale Law Journal*, 95 (1986), 1087–184. For a similarly nuanced discussion of the 'discourse' as well as the 'experience' of rape, see C. Smart, 'Law's Power, the Sexed Body, and Feminist Discourse', *Journal of Law and Society*, 17 (1990), 194–210. For the quotidian banality of the terrorism inflicted upon women, see Eisenstein, 'Feminisms', 95–6.

conditions of this terror prefer not to call it terrorism. Rape, like terrorism, is an 'untellable story'.[155] Meinhoff died in Stammheim prison, as did two other members of the faction, Andreas Baader and Gudrun Ennslin. Moeller survived what was later termed a 'suicide attempt'. Suspicions remain.[156] Rame was certainly unconvinced, suggesting that their fate should be comprehended as part of a wider rhetorical strategy, intended to maintain an awed public in a 'state of constant panic', reminded time and time again that those who 'take to the streets shouting that they're defending the quality of life' are 'playing the terrorists' game'.[157]

In fact, of course, precisely the opposite is true. The degradation, and murder, of terrorists in prison, the pursuit of wars against fantastical opponents, the inflammation of febrile imaginations, in the streets of Kabul and Cairo, Baghdad and Bradford; that is playing the terrorist's 'game'.[158] Defending humanity, on the contrary; that is the mark of a civilised society, one that respects the rule of law as the distinguishing feature of the good society, and which fears the alternatives. In the process of defending his denunciation of the Italian government in his play *The Tragedy of Aldo Moro*, Rame's husband, Dario Fo, affirmed precisely this: 'What is needed is the courage to assess our contradictions, and to strive to understand at all costs'.[159] To write about terrorism and terrorists is not to 'play' the terrorist 'game'. It is to resist it, to engage the intellectual as well as the material challenges it makes, and in doing so strive towards the confirmation of a better, more just society. To ignore

---

[155] J. Balint, 'Law's Constitutive Possibilities: Reconstruction and Reconciliation in the Wake of Genocide and State Crime' in E. Christodoulidis and S. Veitch (eds.), *Lethe's Law: Justice, Law and Ethics in Reconciliation* (Hart, 2001), 135. Here Simone Weil's observation, that 'if a young girl is being forced into a brothel she will not talk about her rights', because in such a 'situation the word would sound utterly inadequate' retains its resonance. Quoted in D. McLellan, *Simone Weil: Utopian Pessimist* (Macmillan, 1950), 280.

[156] Meinhoff, Baader and Ennslin all died on the same day. Conceivably Meinhoff might have killed herself. Forensic expertise has cast doubt on whether the bullet wound that killed Baader, apparently at the back of the head, could have been self-inflicted. Similar doubt surrounds the possibility of Ennslin hanging herself in the manner alleged. Each might have been assisted, but it is not obvious by whom, except a prison employee. The manner of Moeller's 'suicide attempt', which involved repeated stab wounds to the chest, has attracted similar suspicion. One of those who protested his suspicions most loudly was Jean-Paul Sartre. Fo and Rame organised a petition in protest at the Stammheim 'suicides' in 1978. It too led to accusations that they were terrorist sympathisers. See Mitchell, *Fo*, 81–2. For a commentary on the 'myths of Stammheim', arguing that the three did indeed synchronise their suicides for maximum publicity, see Burleigh, *Blood and Rage*, 244–9 and 256.

[157] *Ulrike*, 184–5.

[158] For a sober warning against the dangers of 'playing the terrorists' game' in precisely this way, by indulging in orgies of counter-terrorist brutality, see M. Walzer, *Arguing About War* (Yale University Press, 2004), 65–6.

[159] Mitchell, *Fo*, 85. Fo's play approached the subject of the kidnapping and murder of Aldo Moro by the Red Brigades. It was fiercely critical of the government's refusal to negotiate with the kidnappers which, Fo alleged, was the primary cause of Moro's death. For further discussion of *Moro*, exploring its parallels with Shakespeare's *King Lear*, and the particular theme of the formerly great man unable to comprehend the nature of his fall, or his responsibility for it, see Hirst, *Rame*, 61–72.

terror, to ignore its 'obscenities', is to abrogate our responsibilities as human beings.[160]

Understood in this way, raising voices becomes the first constructive step in a credible counter-terrorist strategy. And the silencing of women takes on an altogether greater semiotic import, the most acute symptom, perhaps, of a wider complaint. The demon is described, and condemned. Any attempt to comprehend is discouraged, any suspicion of the merest tincture of sympathy or compassion, the subject of loud abhorrence. Terrorism is indeed presumed to be a man's 'world'. And the 'word' of terrorism is man's too. For two and a half thousand years, the politics of resistance and counter-resistance has been written by men. Indeed, as Susan Faludi has recently argued, the extent to which conservative commentators, in the aftermath of 9/11, presumed to blame feminists for emasculating America was striking. If women had remained passive, the logic ran, then the Twin Towers would never have collapsed. The complementary phallic insinuation, of iconic and political emasculation, is immediate.[161] Small wonder, she adds, that President Bush sensed, almost viscerally, that middle America would crave the reassurance of a reasserted 'John Wayne masculinity'; by the confirmation that he and his posse would go hunting asses to kick.[162] Post 9/11, women are silenced once again; women in Afghanistan and Iraq, women in Britain and America.[163]

The marginalisation of the female voice, of course, merely makes its momentary articulation all the more terrifying. It is not, of course, a peculiar terror.[164] It characterises modern legal and political discourse. The politics frames the silence, as Cora Kaplan affirms. For the feminist 'the literary is always/already political in very obvious and common sense ways'.[165] On these terms, and for very obvious reasons, the silencing of women has become a central issue in feminist legal studies.[166] It is definitive, describing the place of women in

---

[160] For the same sentiment, see G. Achcar, *The Clash of Barbarisms: The Making of the New World Disorder* (Saqi, 2006), 25.

[161] Faludi, *Dream*, 9, and confirming, at 21, that in 'some murky fashion, women's independence had become implicated in our nation's failure to protect itself'. See also 23–4, criticising Camille Paglia's observation that the US 'is not going to be able to confront and to defeat other countries where the code of masculinity is more traditional'.

[162] Faludi, *Dream*, 3–5, and also 200–16, exploring the extent to which the 'war on terror' can be comprehended within a distinctive and historically charged 'wild west' culture, one that is triangulated by savage Indians, heroic cowboys, and their helpless womenfolk, and 256, commenting that the supreme wild west hero Daniel Boone offered itself as a 'Simplicity pattern for every Rudy Giuliani and Donald Rumsfeld to follow'.

[163] Faludi, *Dream*, 35–9, confirming 'The silencing of women took place largely in silence', and also at 131–4 and 158–9, commenting on the government and media campaign designed to reaffirm classical icons of female domesticity. In sharp contradistinction to putative Democrat presidential nominee, Hillary Clinton, the First Lady Laura Bush was presented as the 'mother of all security Moms'.

[164] Charlesworth and Chinkin, 'Sex', 600–1.

[165] C. Kaplan, *Sea Changes: Culture and Feminism* (Verso, 1986), 59.

[166] For a commentary on the present, as well as the past and prospective future of feminist legal scholarship, see N. Naffine, 'In Praise of Legal Feminism', *Legal Studies*, 22 (2002), 71–101.

politics and before the law. Deploying a notably juristic metaphor, Luce Irigaray suggests that the male voice has 'raped' the female, violating it and taking possession of it.[167] Erica Rackley seeks recourse to a very different literary citation, Hans Christian Andersen's little mermaid, 'But if you take my voice, what shall I have left?'[168]

Of course, Andersen's fancy opens up a wider, and virulent, debate regarding the possibility of a female 'voice'. Anti-essentialists eschew the textual and conceptual imperialism which they perceive in the presumption that there is such a 'voice'.[169] Better, instead, it is countered, to think in terms of myriad female voices.[170] The deconstructive and ethical implication here is obvious. Drucilla Cornell explores it in her call for an 'alliance of deconstruction and feminism' which can liberate us from the gendered prejudices of positive law.[171] Essentialist or deconstructive; either way, the case against silence is deafening, or it should be.

The absence of these voices matters, not just because it betrays the gendered nature of the legal process, but because it evades the collateral supposition that such voices might be different both in form and substance; in their affinity, not just with a more testamentary form, but also with a more empathetic substance.[172] In defence of literary strategies in legal feminism, Robin West has gestured to precisely this, urging us 'to understand our laws not only as "texts" that embody our traditions and our cultural ideals, but also as interactive instruments of violence, violation, compassion or respect'. If the silencing, and the violence, are to be countered, what matters is 'the production of narratives about the impact of legal norms and institutions upon the subjective lives of those whom the legal textual community excludes'.[173]

---

[167] In 'Women's Exile: Interview with Luce Irigaray' in Cameron, *Critique*, 80–96.

[168] In Rackley, 'Representations', 602.

[169] For a commentary on the particular anxiety regarding the 'bogey of essentialism', see Naffine, 'In Praise', 88–90. For an early discussion of the alternative political and post-modern approaches to legal feminism, and their impact on 'law and literature' scholarship, see I. Ward, *Law and Literature: Possibilities and Perspectives* (Cambridge University Press, 1995), 119–28.

[170] For a strident critique of the feminist engagement with 'law and literature' founded on this anxiety, regarding the possible identity of a female 'voice' and its imperialist assumption see Heilbrun and Resnick 'Convergences', 1913–53. According to Heilbrun and Resnick, there is a peculiar irony in feminists deploying canonic literature as a means by which to retrieve a female voice. All too often, such texts, so often written by men, actually serve to suppress the female voice. Canonical literature is deployed instead of real female voices. A more recent echo can be found in Sandra Berns, *To Speak as a Judge: Difference, Voice and Power* (Ashgate, 1999), emphasising at 13 that too great a preoccupation with the subtleties of text can detract from the pressing need to reinvest a female 'right to participate authoritatively within "interpretive" communities'.

[171] D. Cornell, *Beyond Accommodation* (Routledge, 1991), 115.

[172] Perhaps the most renowned example here is the work of Patricia Williams. See, for example, her *The Alchemy of Race and Rights* (Harvard University Press, 1991).

[173] See R. West, 'Communities, Texts and Law: Reflections on the Law and Literature Movement', *Yale Journal of Law and the Humanities*, 1 (1988), 146–56. She reaches the same conclusion in 'Jurisprudence and Gender', *University of Chicago Law Review*, 55 (1988), at 71.

Speaking to the broader poethical aspiration, Melanie Williams agrees, arguing that the retrieval of female voices is a litmus test for a revitalised legal humanism, one that is prepared to 'think in terms of the spectrum of human tendencies and capabilities', and that aspires to nothing more than 'the greatest good that we can muster from the fragments we collect of our joint humanity'.[174] Such an aspiration defines a literary jurisprudence. The value of excavating the female voice, or voices, Maria Aristodemou agrees, lies in their innate capacity to articulate the emotional, as opposed to the purely 'cold' and rational.[175] The resonance here with Martha Nussbaum's broader assertion, that literature softens law, introducing a necessary component of compassion and empathy into the legal situation, is compelling. In the 'beginning', Aristodemou confirms, 'there was not logos but music, not utilitarian word but an image, not law but a feeling', and it is a feeling that 'promises continuity rather than closure, connectedness rather than competition, and eternity rather than death'.[176]

For this reason, whilst the patriarchal voice has historically laid claim to reason and truth, the female voice, the voice of emotion and empathy, has been cast in terms of myth and illusion. The jurisprudential implication is immediate. The despatch of the female voice to the realm of myth takes it outside the pretended realms of analytical jurisprudence. Less troubled by the apparent indeterminacies of law as myth or illusion, literature seems to be a more receptive, even more natural, home for a distinctive female experience.[177] The poethical resonance is immediate too, precisely because the supposedly natural affinity is so contrived. The female voice becomes the voice of the outsider, of the 'other', the voice which articulates a permanent challenge to patriarchal presumptions of universality. The voice that speaks compassion is also the voice that recognises the 'uniqueness and singularity' of the 'other'.[178] The original despatch of the female voice is, of course, demanded by precisely this challenge.

It terrifies, and the greatest terror of all is the terror of many voices; or at least it is for those who would presume to prescribe the parameters of our jurisprudence, and our cultural discourses of terrorism. The women of Lockerbie, women like Olive, are terrifying because they articulate an alternative voice of compassion and empathy. The women of Thebes are terrifying because they

---

[174] M. Williams, *Empty Justice: One Hundred Years of Law, Literature and Philosophy* (Cavendish, 2002), xxviii–xxx, 199, 214–18.

[175] See Aristodemou, *Law and Literature*, 4, arguing 'The male lawyer's preference for abstract language, reason, and intellectuality is also an attempt to deny the tactile, the bodily and the sensual, supposedly by overcoming, but instead by imitating with words, woman's capacity to procreate with her body', and also 270–1, concluding that 'While man was running away, or hiding in his own, self-created prisons, in labyrinths variously called law, reason, science, or God, woman, without fear, guilt, or shame, has travelled the world'.

[176] Aristodemou, *Law and Literature*, 28.   [177] See Aristodemou, *Law and Literature*, 4.

[178] See Aristodemou, *Law and Literature*, 206, arguing that ethical activity 'does not mean acting in accordance with a universal principle but responding to the needs and demands of the other in her own uniqueness and singularity'.

challenge the rule of men, and triumph a world of passion. The fate of George is no less worrying than the fate of Pentheus. And so terrifying images are conjured; of howling women and zombies and 'suicide girls'. Sensing the ultimate fear, that the contagion might spread, that women will begin to raise their voices, and that men might listen, those who seek to retain control of the discourse resort to a familiar strategy, to image and counter-image, myth and counter-myth. And the distinctions fade away.

5

Stark humanity

Writing in the *New York Times* in early 2004, the neo-conservative columnist David Brooks, despairing the apparent incompetence of US intelligence, advised that when it 'comes to understanding the world's thugs and menaces' his readers would be better advised to read a Dostoevsky novel.[1] The statement echoes one made thirty years ago, when a US Congressional committee urgently advised that all police officers in America should be made to read Joseph Conrad's novel *The Secret Agent*.[2] A similar injunction was placed on the FBI officers who sought the notorious Unabomber Theodor Kaczynski, between 1975 and 1998. Kaczynski was himself fascinated by Conrad's novel, and used it as something of a terrorist handbook.[3] Of course, there is a pragmatic edge to such injunctions, and the idea that counter-terrorists might be able to brush up their skills by reading Conrad or Dostoevsky may seem to smack of a certain naivety.

But there is rather more to it than this. Writing as long ago as 1977, the doyenne of terrorist studies, Walter Lacqueur, suggested that 'fiction holds more promise for the understanding of the terrorist phenomenon than political science' ever can.[4] More recently, Margaret Scanlon has attributed a vital shared affinity between the writer of novels and the terrorist, a common desire to destabilise and to deconstruct; and we shall encounter the same affinity in the next chapter when we engage Don DeLillo's novel *Mao II*. Exploring this canon, Margaret Scanlon describes a 'paradoxical affiliation' between literature and

---

[1] Cited approvingly by John Gray, in his *Black Mass: Apocalyptic Religion and the Death of Utopia* (Penguin, 2007), at 143–5.

[2] W. Lacqueur, *Terrorism* (Weidenfeld & Nicolson, 1999), 3, 173.

[3] The extent to which Kaczynski drew from *The Secret Agent* in his 'Manifesto', led the FBI to consult Conrad experts in their increasingly frantic investigation. It was surmised that Kaczynski modelled himself upon the professor in Conrad's novel. Of course, Kaczynski was also, at least until his capture, a figure of myth and fetish. According to the *New York Times*, on his capture, he was suddenly demoted from 'brilliant' if evil genius to 'nut'. See J. Guimond and K. Maynard, 'Kaczynski, Conrad and Terrorism', *Conradiana*, 31 (1999), 3–25, and also A. Houen, *Terrorism and Modern Literature: From Joseph Conrad to Ciaran Carson* (Oxford University Press, 2002), 14–16, and M. Scanlon, *Plotting Terror, Novelists and Terrorists in Contemporary Fiction* (Virginia University Press, 2001), 159–62.

[4] Even if it is, as he adds, 'no place for leisurely strolls'. See Lacqueur, *Terrorism*, 149–50.

terrorism, between 'actual killing' and 'fictional construct', between what is apparently fictional and what seems to be chillingly real.[5] The insinuation is clear; to catch the terrorist, set the writer.[6]

The Secret Agent is generally held to be the first of a distinctive genre of modern terrorist literature. And a canon of the genre too; an 'unquestionable' classic, according to F.R. Leavis; for Thomas Mann, a 'thrilling' and 'passionate' example of Conrad's 'narrative genius'; a novel of stunningly 'stark humanity', according to an early reviewer in the *New York Review of Books*.[7] Alongside *The Secret Agent*, at the origins of the genre, Scanlon places a second Conrad novel, *Under Western Eyes*, as well as Dostoevsky's *The Demons*.[8] All modern terrorist novels are written in their shadow, whilst the author of the latter, in particular, can be today regarded as the 'tormented prophet' of the 'coming apocalypse'.[9] Pre-eminent amongst contemporary contributions to the genre, Scanlon further suggests, is J.M. Coetzee's *Master of Petersburg*. The master in Coetzee's *Master* is, of course, Dostoevsky himself. It is his, and our, increasingly desperate attempt to comprehend the experience of terrorism, and the mind of the terrorist, that Coetzee describes. This chapter will move around Conrad's two novels, Dostoevsky's *Demons* and Coetzee's *Master*.

In his lecture, *The Novel Today*, Coetzee suggested that 'in times of intense ideological pressure', the novelist has two related responsibilities. One is 'supplementarity'. The other is 'rivalry'. Literature should supplement political discourse at the same time as it provides a critical alternative. Presenting this alternative, to the privileged narratives of presumed historical or political 'truth', is a primary ethical responsibility for any writer.[10] It is also the

---

[5] Scanlon, *Terror*, 2–3, 155–62. See also A. Teraoka, 'Terrorism and the Essay: The Case of Ulrike Meinhof' in R. Boetcher Joeres and E. Mitman (eds.), *The Politics of the Essay: Feminist Perspectives* (Indiana University Press, 1993), 220.

[6] Scanlon, *Terror*, 6.

[7] According to Barbara Arnett Melchiori, it is 'exquisite in its varying layers of subtlety'. See her *Terrorism in the Late Victorian Novel* (Croom Helm, 1985), 74. See also J. Zulaika and W. Douglass, *Terror and Taboo: The Follies, Fables and Faces of Terrorism* (Routledge, 1996), 47, 137, and the various modern reviews cited in I. Watt (ed.), *Conrad, The Secret Agent: A Casebook* (Macmillan, 1973), 66–85, 118–19, as well as Mann's observation, cited at 101. For the *New York Review of Books* citation, see Watt, *Conrad*, 56.

[8] Critical applause for *The Demons* has been similarly loud. For a general account of its critical reception, see W. Leatherbarrow, '*The Devils* in the Context of Dostoevsky's Life and Works' in W. Leatherbarrow (ed.), *Dostoevsky's The Devils: A Critical Companion* (Northwestern University Press, 1999), 3–59, quoting, at 55, an early review in *The Athenaeum* which appraised an 'extraordinary handling of psychological abnormality'. For a discussion of its possible influence on Conrad, who pointedly refused to mark any attribution, see, R. Matlaw, 'Dostoevskii and Conrad's Political Novels' in Leatherbarrow, *Dostoevskii and Britain* (Berg, 1995), 230–3, and 243–5, quoting at 230, Conrad's notorious observation, 'I don't know what Dostoevsky stands for or reveals, but I know he is too Russian for me'.

[9] Scanlon, *Terror*, 98.

[10] For a discussion of these unpublished comments, see D. Head, *JM. Coetzee* (Cambridge University Press, 1997), 10–12, and also 162 suggesting that *The Master* was composed as an expression of a potentially liberating 'idea of literariness', something designed to 'create an alternative expressive space' which is somehow supremely 'human' in its 'claim to independence, non-conformity, alterity'.

aspiration that lies at the heart of poethical jurisprudence, as we noted in our introductory chapter. By using literature, the poethical scholar hopes to access a 'new ethics' of 'otherness' in real, as well as imagined, jurisprudential contexts.[11] In doing so, it presents 'a mirror to ourselves', an optic of 'ethical modelling'.[12] Its aspirations are firmly humanistic.[13] It seeks to reinvest a sense of 'joint humanity'.[14] It makes, in short, for a more emotionally literate jurisprudence.

And, as we also noticed, the strategies of a jurisprudential 'poethics' complement the broader aspirations articulated by the likes of Martha Nussbaum, who see in literature the potential to rejuvenate political morality in terms of 'imagination, inclusion, sympathy and voice'.[15] It is the reading of literature that informs our 'larger sense of the humanity of suffering'.[16] This chapter is cast in this spirit; an overtly poethical engagement with the experience of terrorism. For nothing better represents this 'humanity of suffering' than the simple banal horror of terrorism, that particular 'heart of darkness', as Zulaika and Douglass term it, deploying a suitably Conradian metaphor, that lurking horror of a 'dehumanized world that has lost all touch with reason and morality'.[17]

Pests

A century ago, Europe was thrilled and terrified, in roughly equal measure, by the 'propaganda by deed' terrorism of the anarchist and nihilist gangs of Johannes Most, Sergei Nechaev and others.[18] It was Nechaev who first embraced the term 'terrorist' in the late 1860s.[19] The desire to 'remake the world by spectacular acts of terror' may indeed be a characteristic of the modern terrorist.[20] But it is not new, as we have already seen. The Powder Plot of 1605 was intended to be spectacular, as was the storming of Versailles in 1789.

---

[11] M. Aristodemou, *Law and Literature: Journeys from Her to Eternity* (Oxford University Press, 2000), 295. See also 2 and 225.

[12] M. Williams, *Empty Justice: One Hundred Years of Law, Literature and Philosophy* (Cavendish, 2002), xxiv, 180.

[13] For an account of this development, see I. Ward, 'Universal Jurisprudence and the Case for Legal Humanism', *Alberta Law Review*, 38 (2001), 941–59, and 'The Echo of a Sentimental Jurisprudence', *Law and Critique*, 13 (2002), 107–25.

[14] Williams, *Empty Justice*, 218.

[15] M. Nussbaum, *Poetic Justice: The Literary Imagination and Public Life* (Beacon Press, 1995), 73–8, 90–1, 115–20.

[16] M. Nussbaum, 'Compassion and Terror' in J. Sterba (ed.), *Terrorism and International Justice* (Oxford University Press, 2003), 231, 244–5, 249–51.

[17] Zulaika and Douglass, *Terror*, 25.

[18] The term, originally coined by the French anarchist, Paul Brousse, was officially introduced in 1876 at the Anarchist International; part, inevitably, of a wider rhetorical battle with the perceived forces of the state, including the media. See Lacqueur, *Terrorism*, 11–15, 49–53; Zulaika and Douglass, *Terror*, 17–18; Houen, *Terrorism*, 34; and also G. Guillaume, 'Terrorism and International Law', *International and Comparative Law Review*, 53 (2004), 538.

[19] Scanlon, *Terror*, 5–6.

[20] J. Gray, *Al-Qaeda and What it Means to be Modern* (Faber and Faber, 2003), 22.

Accordingly, the events of 9/11 and 7/7 have impacted upon our consciousness in much the same way as the anarchist assassination of Tsar Alexander II did 140 years ago, or indeed that of General Mesentzoff a couple of decades later. Mesentzoff's assassin, Stepniak, was fully attuned to the need, for the aspiring terrorist, of attaining the 'sublimities' of mythic 'grandeur' in his or her work.[21] The purpose of terrorism is not to kill, or at least not only. It is to terrorise the living.

Someone who fully appreciated this chilling truth was Joseph Conrad, whose two most overtly political novels, *The Secret Agent*, published in 1907, and *Under Western Eyes*, published in 1911, were both focused on the experience, and perverse thrill, of terrorism.[22] Both novels are, at once, about the universal and the immediate; the universal experience of terror, and the particular context of the Russian 'problem'. The Russian context is immediate in the case of *Under Western Eyes*, in which much of the action oscillates around exiled Russian anarchists in Geneva, and more remote in *The Secret Agent*, in which the action is centred in London, but where the trigger for violence comes from the Russian paymasters of the indolent double-agent Verloc.

For Conrad, as for most of his audience, this 'propaganda by deed' terrorism was perceived as part of a greater Russian 'problem', a problem which, it seemed, was spreading like a plague, not just to the more familiar terrorist haunts of Geneva or Paris, but even to London.[23] Whilst the instances of nihilist-inspired violence had, by the first decade of the twentieth century, substantially diminished, Conrad's audience, fed a steady diet of lurid newspaper reports depicting lurking Fenians and swarthy Slavs, remained, by and large, possessed of terrible fear that the next outrage was just round the corner.[24] Theirs was proclaimed an age of terror too.

---

[21] From his *Underground*, quoted in Houen, *Terrorism*, 57.

[22] The subtlety of these two political novels has long been appreciated. George Orwell would later acclaim their 'grown-upness and political understanding'. See E. Hay, *The Political Novels of Joseph Conrad* (Chicago University Press, 1963), 7. For a similar commentary, see O. Knowles, 'Conrad's Life' in J. Stape (ed.), *The Cambridge Companion to Joseph Conrad* (Cambridge University Press, 1996), 9–12, and also Z. Najder, *Conrad in Perspective: Essays on Art and Morality* (Cambridge University Press, 1997), 139–41.

[23] As the narrator in *Under Western Eyes* confirms, it is a 'story of Western Europe'. J. Conrad, *Under Western Eyes* (Penguin, 1996) 20 [hereafter UWE]. For a commentary on this dominant theme, see A. Busza, 'Rhetoric and Ideology in Conrad's *Under Western Eyes*' in N. Sherry (ed.), *Joseph Conrad: A Commemoration* (Macmillan, 1976), 109.

[24] See Lacqueur, *Terrorism*, 53, 227; Melchiori, *Terrorism*, 1–33; Houen, *Terrorism*, 21–33; and Watt, *Conrad*, 238, suggesting that the decades surrounding the turn of the nineteenth and twentieth centuries represented something of a 'golden age' for the terrorist *agent provocateur*. *The Times* was particularly inclined to regale its readers with reports of pending Fenian outrages, rejoicing, in suitably horrified tones, when one actually took place, on the occasion of the Westminster bombing in January 1895. Intriguingly, in its report of this bombing *The Times* drew a distinction between the 'cowardly' nature of this atrocity when compared to the more 'intelligible' acts of nihilist assassins on the 'Continent'. See Lacqueur, *Terrorism*, 34–5, 41–2, 92–5. The nature of the respective Fenian and Anarchist threats is also discussed, at length, in Michael Burleigh's *Blood and Rage: A Cultural History of Terrorism* (HarperCollins, 2008), in Chapters 1–3.

The Russian context was of enormous personal importance to Conrad. Like his father, he was active amongst Polish émigrés. Both argued virulently against Tsarist-sponsored state terrorism in their native land.[25] Conrad focused his critical attention on the 'problem' in his essay *Autocracy and War*, published in the wake of the 1905 revolution, in which he railed against the 'inhuman' despotism that characterised imperial 'autocracy', and the 'oppressive degeneration of legality' that it appeared to nurture. According to Conrad the Polish émigré, the Russian empire was 'simply the negation of everything worth living for'.[26] As he wrote *Under Western Eyes*, Conrad confessed that the 'question' of Russia 'haunted me'.[27] Conrad's protagonist, Razumov, is overcome with Russia's 'immensity'.[28] Neither he nor his creator was alone. The apparent demise of 'mother Russia' nourished its own particular and vigorous literary canon, nurturing, amongst many, Kravchinski's *Underground Russia*, Brzozowski's *Flames*, and, as we shall see shortly, Dostoevsky's *The Demons*.[29]

The plots of both novels, *Under Western Eyes* and *The Secret Agent*, were framed by real instances of spectacular acts of political violence. In *The Secret Agent*, that instance was Michel Bourdin's attempt to blow up Greenwich Observatory in 1894; an attempt that resulted only in his own destruction.[30] The bombing of the Observatory, the repository of what Conrad's shadowy

---

[25] The Korzeniowskis were members of the landowning gentry. Conrad's father aligned himself with the putatively revolutionary 'Reds'. Conrad eschewed such overt radicalism, but the nature of his sympathies, and his behind-the-scenes activities in *émigré* circles, should not be underestimated. See Hay, *Conrad*, 31–80; Knowles, 'Conrad's Life', 4–9; and M. Biskupski, 'Conrad and the International Politics of the Polish Question, 1914–1918: Diplomacy *Under Western Eyes*, or Almost *The Secret Agent*', *Conradiana*, 31 (1999), 84–98. Mikhail Bakunin famously referred to Russia as the 'wicked stepmother' to the masses, and centred his influential *Statism and Anarchy* on the associated questions of the demise of Russian autocracy and the cause of Polish liberty. See M. Bakunin, *Statism and Anarchy* (Cambridge University Press, 1990), 61.

[26] See J. Conrad, 'Autocracy and War' in *Under Western Eyes*, 324–6, discussed in Najder, *Conrad*, 123–5. Alexander Herzen famously echoed Conrad's sentiments, asking 'What is this monster called Russia, which demands so many offerings and which leaves to its children nothing but a sorry choice of either moral perdition within an environment hostile to everything humane, or death at the beginning of their lives?' In Najder, *Conrad*, 121. For many contemporaries, the 1905 revolution itself appeared to be 'terroristic', see Houen, *Terrorism*, 66. For a commentary on Conrad's particular distaste for this mask of mysticism, see Hay, *Conrad*, 267–8, 284.

[27] So much so that a novel, which he originally intended to write in just six weeks, in the end took over two years. It is to this agony of composition, and this 'haunting', that Conrad's breakdown of 1909–10 is often ascribed. See Houen, *Terrorism*, 72, and Knowles, 'Conrad's Life', 9–10.

[28] Discussed in Najder, *Conrad*, 131, and also Busza, 'Rhetoric', 110–1, arguing that *Under Western Eyes* is a pointed riposte to Dostoevsky's idea of Russia.

[29] Conrad's particular relationship with Dostoevsky was notoriously antipathetic; the latter being dismissed as 'too Russian for me', the expositor of 'fierce mouthings from prehistoric ages'. See Najder, *Conrad*, 126.

[30] Whilst debate continues to surround the extent to which he did so consciously, it is difficult to conceive that Conrad was unaware of the Bourdin 'plot'. Initially Conrad admitted the inspiration. 'This book is that story', he confessed in the 'Author's Note' to the first edition. Later, for no clear reason, he denied it. For a comprehensive discussion of Conrad's use of the 1894 Observatory bomb 'outrage', see N. Sherry, 'The Greenwich Bomb Outrage and *The Secret Agent*', *Review of English Studies*, 18 (1967), 412–28.

First Secretary terms the 'sacrosanct fetish' of time and certitude, carried an obvious semiotic charge; not unlike that represented by the Twin Towers.[31] In *Under Western Eyes*, the novel is founded on the murder of a prominent government official, 'Mr. de P'; an event that is clearly modelled on the notorious murder of the Russian Interior Minister, Plehve. The assassination of this official, the narrator of the novel emphasises, represents the 'moral corruption of an oppressed society where the noblest aspirations of humanity, the desire of freedom, an ardent patriotism, the love of justice, the sense of pity' have been 'prostituted to the lusts of hate and fear, the inseparable companions of an uneasy despotism'.[32]

The plots set, Conrad can then turn to what interests him most; the human experience of terror, those who perpetrate it and those who suffer it. This particular fascination, with the juxtaposition of ordinary people and extraordinary events, is one we have already encountered on a number of occasions; and we will do so again in the next chapter. Conrad's novels are famously character driven; their centre lying in the reaction of plot and character, and the extent to which this reaction, particularly at points of moral and political stress, can expose the innermost aspects of the human condition. It is for this reason that Conrad is often ascribed the broad soubriquet of realist or modernist.[33] And his protagonists, most obviously Razumov and Verloc, are intensely ordinary. Terrorists are ordinary. Killing is ordinary. It is just that both terrorists and counter-terrorists like to present it as something more.

Thus when the idealist Haldin tries to justify his assassination of 'Mr. de P', in terms of destroying those who 'destroy the spirit of progress and truth', it is Razumov who voices his suspicion of the 'fanatical lovers of liberty', and those 'visionaries' who 'work' their 'everlasting evil on earth'.[34] There is, he comes to realise, a hideous and overpowering futility, as well as inhumanity, in 'scattering a few drops of blood in the snow'.[35] It is a sensitivity born of ordinariness, and a desire to be ordinary.[36] Despite the extraordinary nature of the events within which he has become entrapped, Razumov remains convinced that the 'exceptional' cannot 'prevail against the material contact which make one day resemble another'. 'Tomorrow', he tells himself, 'would be like yesterday'; not today.[37]

---

[31] J. Conrad, *The Secret Agent* (Penguin, 2004), 24–5 [hereafter SA]. See Hay, *Conrad*, 243–4, and also C. Coroneos, 'Conrad, Kropotkin and Anarchist Geography', *The Conradian*, 18 (1994), 19.

[32] UWE, 7–8.

[33] See K. Graham, 'Conrad and Modernism' in Stape (ed.), *Conrad*, 204–5, and also A. Guerard, 'A Version of Anarchy' in Watt, *Conrad*, 150–1, and more recently still S. Skinner, 'As a Glow Brings out a Haze: Understanding Violence in Jurisprudence and Joseph Conrad's Fiction', *Legal Studies*, 27 (2007), 476–84, not only identifying Conrad's modernism, but also the place of violence across his literary corpus.

[34] UWE, 16, 37, 68.   [35] UWE, 45.

[36] His name is an epithet for reason as common sense, from the Russian *razumet*, to understand. See Hay, *Conrad*, 292.

[37] UWE, 40.

The ordinariness of Verloc, the protagonist in *The Secret Agent*, is just as pronounced. Indeed it verges on the contemptible.[38] His is not the thrilling life of the glamorous spy or the liberator of the masses.[39] *The Secret Agent* should be a novel of thrills and derring-do, of spies and terrorists, heroes and anti-heroes. But it is not. Instead, it is a novel about desperately 'normal people'.[40] And not only are they normal, but so too are they flawed, troubled, in many cases degenerate, and degenerating.[41] Conrad's Verloc is a seedy pornographer by trade, who pretends to be an *agent provocateur*, the kind of man, indeed, who 'generally arrived in London' from his sojourns on the continent 'like the influenza'.[42] Yet, whilst Verloc is repulsive, he is not diabolic. Verloc's is a very ordinary kind of degeneracy.[43] He is also indolent, possessed of a 'fanatical inertness'.[44] He is, characteristically, stunned by the Paymaster's suggestion that it is time he actually terrorised someone.[45]

The portrayal of Razumov is more sympathetic, precisely because he is more sensitive. Whilst Verloc too is both protagonist and victim, ultimately murdered by his own wife, Razumov's fate seems all the more tragic. For unlike Verloc, whose indolence appears to nullify his sensitivities, Razumov is fully aware of the 'naked terror', and 'true loneliness' of his existence.[46] In betraying Haldin, Razumov becomes the unwitting agent of the Tsarist regime, a double-agent indeed.[47] The idea of the state as an instrument of terror lies at the heart of both novels. In *Under Western Eyes*, it is a particular state, one that possesses the terrible 'aspect' of 'despotism', Tsarist Russia.[48] And Conrad is just as aware of the co-dependence of terrorist and counter-terrorist. They are both, as he has one of his terrorists in *The Secret Agent* observe, of the 'same basket'.[49]

The existential tone which shrouds Razumov is particularly acute in those moments when he explores his own guilt. As an émigré Conrad too admitted

---

[38] According to Irving Howe, appreciating the juxtaposition of ordinary and extraordinary, Verloc 'remains a dull-minded complying Englishman, a beef-and-ale patriot whose ordinariness has served, by a wild curve of irony, to place him beyond the limits of ordinary society'. From his *Politics and the Novel*, quoted in Watt, *Conrad*, 141. The ordinariness of Verloc was also cited by F.R. Leavis as one of the triumphs of Conrad's irony. See his comments from *The Great Tradition* quoted in Watt, *Conrad*, 121–2. One contemporary review, in *Country Life*, concluded that, in creating Verloc, 'Mr Conrad had set himself the impossible task of trying to make dullness interesting'. Again quoted in Watt, *Conrad*, 28.

[39] See Watt, *Conrad*, 77–8.   [40] Quoted in Watt, *Conrad*, 115.

[41] See Hillis Miller's observations, in *Poets of Reality*, discussing Conrad's depiction of the 'intrinsic absurdity' of human life, quoted in Watt, *Conrad*, 179–80, 186.

[42] SA, 5.   [43] SA, 10.   [44] SA, 10.

[45] SA, 17–22. Vladimir's harangue and Verloc's stunned silence represent, according to Thomas Mann, the 'satirical height' of the novel. See T. Mann, 'Joseph Conrad's *Secret Agent*' in Watt, *Conrad*, 108.

[46] UWE, 30.

[47] It is often suggested that part of Razumov's character appears to be based on the notorious double-agent and assassin, Azev.

[48] UWE, 34, and also 215–16.   [49] SA, 40, 48–52.

'the desperate shape of betrayal' as an intensely personal emotion.[50] And betrayal leads to confession. For Razumov this is an agonising experience. Whilst Conrad would later dismiss the confessional tradition, a 'discredited form of literary activity', it is no coincidence that Razumov's personal redemption only commences when, beneath the statue of the greatest exponent of literary confessional, Rousseau, he begins to write his testament of betrayal.[51] In doing so, he will finally prove himself 'capable of compassion', or so he hopes.[52] Razumov's confession, of course, carries a series of necessary ambiguities; part admission of guilt, part plea in mitigation, part rhetorical strategy. The narrator is clearly uncertain as to what the confession is, and how it should be treated. 'A mysterious impulse of human nature', he presumes.[53] Again, the fact that all the events surrounding Razumov and his confession will be filtered through this narrator introduces yet another refractory layer.[54]

Aside from their respective protagonists, both novels, *Under Western Eyes* and *The Secret Agent*, present a motley array of victims and conspirators. Of the latter, Conrad indulges in much caricature. Amongst Verloc's degenerate bunch of cronies can be found the 'ticket-of-leave apostle' Michaelis, generally thought to be an ironic mix of Marx and Kropotkin, with his 'enormous stomach and distended cheeks', and his endlessly dreary monologues on economic determinism, the 'toothless' Yundt, often cited as a caricature of Bakunin, self-styled 'terrorist', albeit a decrepit, and essentially passive one, a 'spectre' still possessed of an 'extraordinary expression of underhand malevolence', and the 'posturing' former medical student and 'wandering lecturer', Comrade Ossipon, a 'robust anarchist' who, it transpires, on actually coming across an act of violence, is 'terrified out of all capacity for belief or disbelief'.[55] And most degenerate of all, there is the sinister Nietzschean 'megalomaniac', the Professor, who so despises the 'idealistic conception of legality' and who is determined that 'public faith in legality' can only be confounded by acts of 'violence'.[56] The distinguishing feature of the Professor is his desire to actually terrorise, rather than merely talk about it. And so he makes bombs; though, as ever, he would prefer it if others actually carried out the bombings.

---

[50] Comment made in his *Personal Record*, and quoted in Hay, *Conrad*, 61. It has often been observed that much of Conrad's own personal agonies can be traced to his own burning sense of betrayal, and feelings of guilt at abandoning Poland. See E. Crankshaw, 'Conrad and Russia' in Sherry, *Conrad*, 91.

[51] See Najder, *Conrad*, 139, 142–3, 147–8.   [52] UWE, 131.   [53] UWE, 6.

[54] See J. Larson, 'Promises, Lies and Ethical Agency in *Under Western Eyes*', *Conradiana*, 29 (1997), 41, 48–9, and A. Fleishman, 'Speech and Writing in *Under Western Eyes*' in Sherry, *Conrad*, 119–28.

[55] SA, 31–2, 35–6, 38–9, 211–14. Together, as Thomas Mann observed, 'hardly lovable types' in Watt, *Conrad*, 107.

[56] SA, 54, 60–1. For a commentary on the Professor's character, and possible caricature, see E. Said, 'Conrad and Nietzsche' in Sherry, *Conrad*, 65. Most recently, Michael Burleigh has suggested, in his *Blood and Rage*, at 12–13, that the Professor might have been modelled on the notorious US-based *émigré* nihilist Professor Mezzeroff, who advertised courses in bomb-making for $30 an hour.

We are supposed to despise these 'fanatics'. Far from elite or dedicated, or even capable, Verloc's anarchists are as verbose and incompetent as they are physically degenerate.[57] As the Professor acerbically comments, 'you talk, print, plot, and do nothing'.[58] Even Verloc wonders precisely what could 'be expected' from 'such a lot'.[59] The destruction of this particular myth, of the dedicated clique, is central to Conrad's counter-terrorist strategy.[60] The émigré group which Razumov joins at Geneva is similarly populated. Their leader, Ivanovitch, the self-styled 'man of genius', so contemptuous of the ordinary 'dregs' of society, so convinced of his messianic importance, is variously thought to represent a mix of Kropotkin and Bakunin, with perhaps a dash of Rousseau's grand capacity for self-delusion.[61] Only Razumov refuses to be properly deluded, dismissing a self-promoting 'busybody' with the apposite observation that it is 'just as well to have no illusions'.[62]

It has been commonly remarked that the more interesting characters in Conrad's political novels tend to be the quieter, very often female, ones.[63] The figure of the female terrorist enjoyed a particular iconic status in nineteenth century literature, and caused especial consternation amongst the terrified and the thrilled.[64] As we noted in the last chapter, the idea of women terrorists has always engendered this kind of reaction in the popular imagination. M. de S. the 'dilettante spiritualist' and a confessed 'supernaturalist', who flitters around the Geneva émigrés in *Under Western Eyes*, with her terrifying fixed 'stare' of 'murderous hate' is perhaps more of a caricature, but the characters of Sophia Antonova, possessed of the 'true spirit of destructive revolution', and Natalie Haldin are rather more complex.[65] The latter's fervour is altogether more ethical and idealistic, and therefore, Conrad would have us sense, more troubling.[66] Natalie believes in the 'power of the people's will to achieve anything'. The role of the revolutionist does not lie in destroying things, but in changing

---

[57] According to Irving Howe, in describing the bunch, Conrad 'drops to a coarse-minded burlesque', quoted in Watt, *Conrad*, 145. Conrad was not alone in being fascinated by the grotesque in terrorism. Similar portrayals can be found in Dostoevsky, Zola, Stevenson and James. See Lacqueur, *Terrorism*, 153–4, and also Guerard quoted in Watt, *Conrad*, 158–60.

[58] SA, 54.   [59] SA, 39.

[60] Though in portraying his terrorists in this fashion, as grotesques and degenerates, Conrad is himself engaging in a rhetorical strategy common to counter-terrorism. See R. Leeman, *The Rhetoric of Terrorism and Counter-Terrorism* (Greenwood Press, 1991), 72–5, and Zulaika and Douglass, *Terror*, 112–13.

[61] UWE, 105, 110–13, 150. For a broad discussion of Ivanovitch, see K. Carabine, 'From *Razumov* to *Under Western Eyes*', *Conradiana*, 25 (1993), 3–29, arguing that Conrad retreated from an original intention, clear from earlier drafts, to insinuate an allusion between Ivanovitch and Dostoevsky. Ivanovitch's apparent 'escape' from captivity in Tsarist Russia most obviously resonates with Bakunin's similar experience, though the actual philosophy he appears to espouse is more ambiguous. See also Najder, *Conrad*, 147–8, and Coroneos, 'Conrad', 22–3.

[62] UWE, 91, 147.   [63] See P. Kirschner, 'Introduction' to UWE, xxii.

[64] See Houen, *Terrorism*, 60–6 and Burleigh, *Blood and Rage*, 29–30.

[65] UWE, 158, 176, 185. The most obviously grotesque figure in the novel is Ziemanitch, the drunk peasant who was supposed to aid Haldin's escape.

[66] UWE, 93.

minds, in countering the 'cruel', and in promoting an 'era of concord and justice'. The 'will must be awakened, inspired, concentrated'.[67]

And then there is Winnie, Verloc's long-suffering wife, commonly regarded as one of the most perplexing figures in Conrad's entire corpus. Quieter, and more troubling, even than Natalie Haldin, it is Winnie who finally emerges as the one character of destructive resolution in *The Secret Agent*. It is Winnie who, driven by an all-consuming if undetected hatred, finally rises up to murder her husband.[68] For this reason, it has often been suggested that Winnie is the true anarchist; at least insofar as she visits an apocalyptic destruction on her own domestic world.[69] She certainly reinforces Conrad's fear that real violence is the complement of 'immoderate' emotions. It is listening to Verloc's heartless report of her nephew's death, whilst carrying the bomb for her idle husband, which triggers Winnie's sudden moment of supreme violence. She is overcome with 'rage and despair, all the violence of tragic passions'.[70]

It is the unpredictability of violence that terrifies us, the thought that the seeds of destruction should lie deep within Winnie, and by implication, the rest of us. Conrad's portrayal of her nephew, 'poor Stevie', carries a similar insinuation.[71] Whilst his aunt's passions remained constrained, at least until she plunges her knife into Verloc's back, Stevie's 'convulsive sympathy', and the 'pitiless rage' which it inspires, is clear for all to see.[72] The eager-to-please Stevie is just the sort of naïf whose life can be so easily destroyed by witless self-delusion; 'blown to fragments in a state of innocence and in the conviction of being engaged in a humanitarian enterprise'.[73] Stevie is only innocent in the sense of being naive. He is also a terrorist, albeit a bumbling one.

In terms of plot, and context, and in the presentation of events and character, there is then much that is common to both *The Secret Agent* and *Under Western Eyes*. Conrad's politics remain consistent, and uncompromisingly conservative. *The Secret Agent*, as more than one critic has observed, is a 'defence of the Establishment'.[74] So is *Under Western Eyes*. Conrad loathed those who thought

---

[67] UWE, 96, 233.

[68] Something which, according to the critic Edward Garnett, makes her the 'real heroine of the story'. Garnett's comment was made in his famous review of *The Secret Agent*, published in *The Nation* in September 1907, and quoted in Watt, *Conrad*, 44. For Conrad's own admission, that Winnie emerged as the pivotal character in the novel, see his 'Note' in SA, 231. David Mulry has described the extent to which Conrad revised earlier drafts of the novel in order to give greater substance to Winnie's character. See his 'Patterns of Revision in *The Secret Agent*', *The Conradian*, 26 (2001), 52–4. For a broad discussion of Winnie's 'story', see E. Harrington, 'The Anarchist's Wife: Joseph Conrad's Debt to Sensation Fiction in *The Secret Agent*', *Conradiana*, 36 (2004), 51–63.

[69] See Houen, *Terrorism*, 54 and also, lauding the murder scene as one of 'genius', F.R. Leavis, quoted in Watt, *Conrad*, 123.

[70] SA, 156.   [71] SA, 6–8.   [72] SA, 124.   [73] SA, 195.

[74] See Melchiori, *Terrorism*, 81, and also Watt, *Conrad*, 245, describing Conrad as an 'arch-reactionary' as a young man, and only marginally milder as an older one. Irving Howe wondered if Conrad could be termed a 'Tory anarchist', but concluded that he was probably better described as a 'Tory with repressed affinities for anarchism', quoted in J. Surgal, '*The Secret Agent*: A Simple Tale of the XIX Century?', *Conradiana*, 29 (1997), 130.

that violence was a legitimate political strategy.[75] The broader debate regarding the legitimacy of political violence was a virulent one.[76] Some, such as Bakunin, remained uncertain as to the role, and legitimate extent, of political violence.[77] The assassination of a hated monarch or minister might have a reasonable chance of currying popular sympathy. Mass slaughter of the innocent, it was feared, would not.[78] 'Propaganda by deed' terrorism tended to oscillate unpredictably between the alternatives.

Conrad did not. The First Secretary's pronouncement on the 'philosophy of the bomb' in *The Secret Agent*, is intended to arouse our revulsion.[79] The great virtue of the bomb, according to the Secretary is that it has 'all the shocking senselessness of gratuitous blasphemy'.[80] But there is nothing particularly thrilling, or virtuous, about a science that can effect, in the words of Chief Inspector Heat, 'ages of atrocious pain and mental torture' that can 'be contained between two successive winks of the eye'.[81] The juxtaposition between self-justifying rant and human compassion and horror is stark. Conrad intends it to be.[82] Terrorism is contemptible, not because it favours or disfavours any particular politics or ideology, but because it destroys human beings. The thrill of blowing people up, or assassinating them, is a 'sort of terrible childishness', a grotesque immaturity born of a failure to empathise. Conrad deploys the same metaphor of juvenility in both novels.[83]

It is humanity that matters, not politics, and certainly not ideology. It is Chief Inspector Heat, once again, musing on the 'shattering violence of destruction'

[75] The narrator in *Under Western Eyes* is a consistent critic of those who seek to justify violence in terms of ideology. V.S. Pritchett referred to Conrad as a 'fixed reactionary', and discussed the nature of his dilemma in 'An Émigré' in Watt, *Conrad*, 133–9. See also Carabine, *Under Western Eyes*, 132–3.

[76] See C. Hamilton, 'Revolution From Within: Conrad's Natural Anarchists', *The Conradian*, 18 (1994), 31–48.

[77] See Lacqueur, *Terrorism*, 27–30, suggesting that Bakunin would have recoiled from the kind of mass slaughter effected in September 2001.

[78] Marx and Engels famously used terrorism as a stick to beat Bakunin's anarchists, arguing vigorously that the resort to violence could only be counter-productive and could only dilute radical energies that would be better channelled into fomenting the revolution of the proletariat. For a discussion, see Lacqueur, *Terrorism*, 63–9, 104–5, 124–7.

[79] Though Conrad was himself fascinated by physics, he was not uncritical of it, and he was determinedly sceptical of the hyperbole which characterised much late Victorian commentary on the subject. See Houen, *Terrorism*, 38–49, and also M. Whitworth, 'Inspector Heat Inspected: *The Secret Agent* and the Meanings of Entropy', *Review of English Studies*, 49 (1998), 40–59, discussing Conrad's particular interest in thermodynamics.

[80] SA, 25   [81] SA, 65. For a commentary, see Hamilton, 'Revolution', 42–3.

[82] See Skinner, 'Conrad's Fiction', 480–2, discussing Conrad's strategy in presenting 'brutal' depictions of physical destruction in order to shock his audience into contemplating rather more deeply the horror of inter-human violence.

[83] UWE, 24. The same metaphor is again deployed by the narrator, at 79, when he observes 'To us Europeans of the West, all ideas of political plots and conspiracies seem childish, crude inventions for the theatre or a novel'. It is also found in *The Secret Agent*, at 101, where the Secretary of State, who would prefer not to be troubled by the 'details' of terrorist atrocities, dismisses the anarchists as 'nasty little children'.

which had reduced Stevie's body to a 'heap of nameless fragments', who articulates Conrad's own despair at the particular 'absurdity' of terrorist killing.[84] Verloc identifies two types of terrorist. There are the 'fanatics' who operate out of a 'sense of justice'. And then there is the rest, the 'remaining portion of social rebels', their motivation 'accounted for by vanity, the mother of all noble and vile illusions, the companion of poets, reformers, charlatans, prophets, and incendiaries'.[85] The fanatic, and the deluded; both fail to anticipate the misery that their haphazard violence will cause to real people, that spectacular public acts can only lead to devastating private consequences.

At first glance it might seem that the sharpest distinction between the two novels lies in the parting images. *The Secret Agent* ends with the Professor, undeterred by the bungled bombing of the Observatory, busying himself in his laboratory making new bombs, and scurrying around the streets of London with them strapped to his body, 'like a pest in the street full of men'.[86] There will, it seems, always be pests. As he imagines the Professor abroad in the streets of London, Ossipon contemplates this unpredictability, and the 'madness and despair' wrought by just one bomb.[87] *Under Western Eyes* appears to close rather more hopefully, with Natalie Haldin's declaration that a 'new sun is rising', a moment when the 'anguish of hearts shall be extinguished in love'. But the dominant image, once again, is one of uncertainty and unpredictability. The narrator applauds Natalie's sentiment, but betrays an essential scepticism; love, a 'word of wisdom, a word so sweet, so bitter, so cruel sometimes'.[88] Conrad, famously, found the writing of *The Secret Agent* excruciating.[89] He wants us to be tortured too, denied certainty, haunted by the thought that the Professor might be walking the same street as us, that the nice young girl at the bottom of the road might be consorting with fanatical terrorists. He is not the only one who would have us contemplate such fantasies, as we have already seen.

Demons

The novel and the terror are mutually sustaining. As well as Conrad's novels, the late Victorian and Edwardian connoisseur of terrorist fiction could also find contributions by the likes of Henry James, Robert Louis Stevenson, and, of course, Feodor Dostoevsky.[90] Terrorism, as we noted before, was prominent in the popular consciousness, and the subject had a ready audience. For much of the first part of the twentieth century, however, as attention turned to an

---

[84] SA, 65, 68–72.   [85] SA, 39.

[86] SA, 227. For a commentary on the 'terrifying simplicity' of the Professor's 'madness', see S. Kim, 'Violence, Irony, and Laughter: The Narrator in *The Secret Agent*', *Conradiana*, 35 (2003), 84–5.

[87] SA, 226–7.   [88] UWE, 264.

[89] Just as he found writing *Under Western Eyes*, and pretty much everything he wrote at the time. For an account, see I. Watt, 'The Composition of *The Secret Agent*' in Watt, *Conrad*, 13–25.

[90] Henry James's contribution to the genre being *Princess Casamassina*, and Robert Louis Stevenson's being *The Dynamiters*.

alternative kind of horror, the terrorist novel fell into abeyance. Today, how-ever, for reasons that are all too obvious, terrorism sells once more.[91] One of the most compelling contributions to this now revitalised genre is Coetzee's *The Master of Petersburg*; itself an overt homage to one of the founding novels of the tradition, Dostoevsky's *The Demons*.[92]

Dostoevsky's novel describes the devastating impact of a pair of young radicals, Nikolai Stavrogin and Pyotr Verkhovensky, who descend from Petersburg on a sleepy provincial town. The two, who have family roots in the town, insinuate themselves into local radical politics, whilst the latter in particular devotes his particular skills of duplicity and dissimulation to incite the murder of a former, but now disillusioned, revolutionary, Shatov. As with Conrad's two political novels, the plot Dostoevsky weaves is again based on a historical event, the murder, by some of Nechaev's followers, of a young student at Petersburg Agricultural Academy in 1869.[93] The immediate political context, of anarcho-nihilist terrorism spreading abroad, is, of course, the same as that which Conrad exploited for his two political novels; except that Dostoevsky perceived the infection to be coming from western Europe and infecting the Russian body politic.[94] Stavrogin and Verkhovensky may have come from Petersburg, but the ideological infections, which have already corrupted their

---

[91] See Scanlon, *Terrorism*, 11–12, and also P. Widdowson, 'Terrorism and Literary Studies', *Textual Practice*, 2 (1988), 8–20 tracing a similar re-emergence of the genre.

[92] For an overview of Coetzee's work, see Head, *Coetzee*, particularly Chapter 1. As a homage to Dostoevsky, *The Master of Petersburg* confirms, as Scanlon puts it, an 'inevitable logic'. See Scanlon, *Terrorism*, 14, and also 83 and 133, appraising, in turn, the position of Lessing's *The Good Terrorist* and Duerrenmatt's *The Assignment* also within this genre.

[93] For a commentary on the background to *The Demons*, see J. Jones, *Dostoevsky* (Oxford University Press, 1983), 239–40, 251–2. For a specific discussion of the murder of the student Ivanov, see D. Offord, '*The Devils* in the Context of Contemporary Russian Thought and Politics' in Leatherbarrow, *Critical Companion*, 68–9. For a broad discussion of Nechaev and his presence in Dostoevsky and contemporary radical culture, see Burleigh, *Blood and Rage*, 36–40.

[94] Dostoevsky had attended radical circles in Geneva, the recognised haven for exiled putative plotters for much of the nineteenth century, at least until London assumed that symbolic role. Interestingly Dostoevsky did so at the same time as Nechaev, though there is no evidence that they actually met. Earlier events in Geneva haunt *The Demons*, most importantly Shatov's insulting and striking Verkhovensky. The insinuation that the latter's apparently laudable objective, to protect the integrity of the political cause, merely exists to mask a more personal and visceral hatred, runs throughout the novel. In convincing an uncertain Nikolai as to the necessity of killing Shatov, Verkhovensky further evidences his particular capacity for lying to his closest comrades; a skill defended by the likes of Nechaev in his revolutionary *Catechism*. There was, Nechaev repeatedly advised, no room for sentiment, still less friendship, in the politics of nihilism and revolution. Following the murder of Shatov, a troubled Stavrogin flees to Geneva, only to return to his own suicide. See F. Dostoevsky, *Demons* (Alfred Knopf, 2000), 76, 612–13, 674–8 [hereafter D]. For a commentary, see Jones, *Dostoevsky*, 241–2, and J. Frank, *Dostoevsky: The Miraculous Years 1865–1871*, (Princeton University Press, 1995), 435–8 and 443–4, inves-tigating the extent to which Dostoevsky tried to present his novel, and particularly its portrayal of Nechaev and his anarchist cronies, as pastiches and ironic caricatures, rather than precise representations, and also 445–6 and 451–2, discussing the original murder of the student Ivanov which provided the model for Shatov's demise.

own personalities, come from beyond Russia, from a Europe gripped by a diabolic atheism.[95]

And as was the case with Conrad's motley gangs of revolutionaries, prior to the arrival of the two 'demons' from Petersburg, the members of the Virginsky 'circle' of radicals had been more than happy to potter about penning tracts that nobody read and muttering about the possibility of insurrection, one day far into the future.[96] No one really wanted to murder anyone. It took a peculiarly demonic impetus to set in motion the events that would lead to Shatov's death. When the circle discusses Shatov's case, one of their number expresses a preference for a 'humane solution'. None, Verkhovensky replies, is possible.[97] Barely comprehensible murder, Dostoevsky implies, the ultimate expression of terrorism, is the product of a demonic inhumanity.[98]

Verkhovensky, whose father Stepan Trofimovich was a leading intellectual figure amongst the more idealistic radicals of the previous generation, assumes the role of Nechaev in Dostoevsky's novel.[99] Trofimovich, a man of 'extreme kindness' and possessed of a 'gentle and unresentful heart', articulates Dostoevsky's despair.[100] Stepan simply cannot understand either his son's motivation or his politics. The novel presents an uncompromising denunciation of the younger generation, and

---

[95] They are not the only ones infected, of course. Stepan Trofimovich's constant recourse to French linguistic mannerisms emphasises the extent to which Dostoevsky fears the perversion and abandonment of that which ultimately defines Russia, its language. See Offord, 'Context', 88–9. For a discussion of Dostoevsky's particular distrust of 'western' ideology, and its demonic presentation, see Leatherbarrow, 'Life and Work', 9–11, 16–23, suggesting that Shatov emerges as the epitome of Russia and Russian-ness, and its pending demise, and also 39–40.

[96] For an account of the circle's seemingly endless discussion of procedure, and its invariable tendency to assume that actually doing something would be too impetuous, see D, 292–400. For a commentary, see Jones, *Dostoevsky*, 243–4.

[97] His contemptuous dismissal of the circle, 'what trash these people are though', articulates precisely the same emotion as that which Razumov came to feel, and which Conrad clearly intended the audience of both his novels to feel too. See D, 609.

[98] Dostoevsky's use of the demonic theme in *The Demons* gives his novel a critically different edge when compared with Conrad's. For the latter, terrorism was defined by its ordinariness. Dostoevsky's demonism, however, is a distinctly metaphysical inflection. In his study of Dostoevsky's composition of *The Demons*, Joseph Frank discusses Bakunin's well-known 'letter' on Nechaev, in which he sought to warn erstwhile fellow political travellers that the newer breed of revolutionary, like its most famous protagonist, were dangerous precisely because they were 'devoted fanatics'. Bakunin suggested that this explained what might otherwise seem to be incomprehensible violence. Whether or not Dostoevsky was aware of this letter at the time of composing his novel is uncertain. See Frank, *Dostoevsky*, 439–43.

[99] Stepan Trofimovich idealises himself as an 'ancient pagan', like Goethe. See D, 37. For Verkhovensky as Nechaev, see Jones, *Dostoevsky*, 251–2, Frank, *Dostoevsky*, 238–44 and Scanlon, *Terror*, 96–7.

[100] D, 11. For Trofimovich as a 'representative of the good', and a supremely human incarnation, see R. Davison, 'Dostoevsky's *The Devils*: The Role of Stepan Trofimovich Verkhovensky' in Leatherbarrow, *Critical Companion*, 124–5, 130–1. The classical interpretation sees Stepan Trofimovich as modelled on Timofei Granovsky, a leading liberal professor at Moscow University, and someone whose work fascinated Dostoevsky. See Leatherbarrow, 'Life and Work', 33–4, and Jones, *Dostoevsky*, 269–71 appraising one of the most memorable and deeply-layered of all his creator's characters, and also 288–9 emphasising the extent to which Trofimovich's 'aesthetic convictions' are Dostoevky's.

the havoc their essentially self-serving and vainglorious activities have on the ordinary lives of ordinary Russians. They are 'demons', possessed of a myriad barely comprehensible impulses, most of which seem determined to destroy and to mutilate; impulses which, ultimately, only result in a spiralling urge to self-destruction and the murder of the unfortunate Shatov.[101]

The Demons confirmed Dostoevsky's turn away from politics, his abjuration from the kind of radicalism which had resulted in his own exile to a penal colony in Omsk in 1850, and his desire to argue the case for a revitalised sense of Russian cultural identity, and theology, against what he perceived to be the demonic infection of western ideology.[102] It also attracted the visceral condemnation of the younger generation; one not dissimilar perhaps, though altogether more robust, than the condemnation which J.M. Coetzee attracted as a result of a perceived refusal to engage with anti-apartheid politics in his native South Africa.[103]

For Coetzee, the responsibility of the author, particularly the post-colonial one, has always resisted an easy political determination. His novel *The Master of Petersburg* is a multilayered exploration of this responsibility; one which carries an ultimate, and itself chilling, ethical charge.[104] The writer, and by implication the audience, Coetzee insinuates, are complicit in terror, whether it be the kind visited by anarchists like Nechaev or by apartheid racists. They are partners in a process of textual 'negotiation'. In chronicling terror, they attest to it and confess it too. Coetzee's Dostoevsky does precisely this; and so too, does his creator.[105] We shall encounter Don DeLillo exploring precisely the same theme, in *Mao II*, in the next chapter.

Coetzee's novel is about Dostoevsky and his demons, those which possessed him and those he wrote about. Ultimately *The Master of Petersburg* concludes with the blurring of Dostoevsky's own identity, as he becomes, not just his progenitor, the author of *The Demons*, but his own dead son too.[106] It describes Dostoevsky's journey to Petersburg to try to understand the death of his

---

[101] See Head, *Coetzee*, 145, suggesting that the demons of ideology and impulse align to present a peculiarly volatile impulse.

[102] During the late 1840s, Dostoevsky had become part of the Petrashevsky 'circle'. Its eponymous leader was an eccentric socialist intellectual, who rather vaguely argued the case for social and legal reform. The 'circle' was broken up in 1849, and its members convicted of subversion and sentenced to death. At the last minute, their sentences were commuted to hard labour and exile. In later correspondence, Dostoevsky referred back to the experience and confessed 'I was a man with a spiritual illness (I admit that now) before my journey to Siberia, where I was cured'. See Leatherbarrow, 'Life and Works', 6–8.

[103] See Scanlon, *Terror*, 95.

[104] A novel of supreme 'metafictional complexity' according to Dominic Head. See his *Coetzee*, 144.

[105] For an exploration of this thesis, see Head, *Coetzee*, 5, 10–12, 18–20, 157–8. For a similar statement regarding the 'implied contract', between author and audience, that the presence of a narrator creates in *The Demons*, see M. Jones, 'The Narrator and the Narrative Technique in Dostoevsky's *The Devils*' in Leatherbarrow, *Critical Companion*, 102. The same, of course, holds for the role of the narrator in Conrad's *Under Western Eyes*.

[106] J. Coetzee, *The Master of Petersburg* (Vintage, 1999), 250 [hereafter MP].

stepson, Pavel. It is rumoured that Pavel, who associated with radical groups, and was implicated in certain terrorist activities, was murdered, either by the police or by his fellow conspirators. The plot clearly echoes the real Dostoevsky's own personal anxieties regarding his own son, and his own earlier associations with radical groups, as well as the narrative which he crafted and which runs through *The Demons*. It also resonates, very obviously, with the particular tradition of 'father and son' novels, to which *The Demons* was a foremost satirical riposte.[107]

Demons are pervasive; demons that haunt grieving fathers, devils that possess deluded revolutionaries, spirits of dead children.[108] Coetzee's Nechaev, the radical for whom Pavel appears to have sacrificed his life, is possessed by a 'demon', by a 'dull, resentful and murderous spirit'. It is this dullness, this acute ordinariness, which indeed makes him so demonic.[109] And the emptiness; one which the historical Nechaev confirmed in his notorious *Catechism*, in which he opined that the true anarchist revolutionary should have 'no personal interests, no business affairs, no emotions, no attachments, no property, no name'.[110] The same demonic vacuity characterises Verkhovensky in *The Demons*, someone so possessed by a 'satanic flatness', his fascination with a prospectively Nietzschean 'man-God' clearly generated by this sense of inner, existential absence.[111] It is the realisation of his own ultimate emptiness, his almost de-human existence, which finally propels Stavrogin to take his own life in the final passages of *The Demons*.[112]

As physically degenerate as Verloc, as deluded and empty as Verkhovensky, it is, once again, the acute ordinariness of Coetzee's Nechaev that is so terrifying. And his childishness. Coetzee's Dostoevsky recalls an earlier observation. Nechaev 'may be the *enfant terrible* of anarchism, but really, he ought to do something about those pimples'.[113] The same is true of the young Kerri, another who is deluded into sacrificing her life for an ideology that she barely seems to comprehend, a 'child in the grip of the devil', possessed of a demon 'inside her twitching, skipping, unable to keep still'.[114] The image of a child possessed, as Conrad repeatedly noted, intensifies the sense of horror.[115] 'A child can kill as

---

[107] The character of Karmazinov in *The Demons* is a very obvious caricature of Turgenev, whose novel *Fathers and Sons* is commonly presented as the founding contribution to the genre. For this theme in MP, see 189–90, 239. Stepan Trofimovich muses on Turgenev, and the theme of 'father and sons', in D, at 215. See also Scanlon, *Terror*, 7–8, Jones, *Dostoevsky*, 248–9 and Frank, *Dostoevsky*, 453–8 and 463–5 discussing the 'father and sons' genre in Russian literature, and suggesting that *The Demons* represents perhaps the supreme satiric response.

[108] As, of course, they are in Dostoevsky's novel, wherein the deployment of diabolic metaphors is even more striking. See Leatherbarrow, 'Life and Works', 36–42.

[109] MP, 44, and also 112–13.   [110] Quoted in Burleigh, *Blood and Rage*, 37.

[111] D, 220–1, 238, and also 527 appraising an image of 'one splendid, monumental, despotic will'. For the reference to his 'satanic flatness', see Jones, *Dostoevsky*, 251.

[112] D, 674–8. See Offord, 'Context', 86–7, and also Jones, *Dostoevsky*, 255–7 revealing the extent to which Dostoevsky was determined to portray this emptiness in the notebooks which charted the composition of the novel.

[113] MP, 101.   [114] MP, 92.

[115] See also Jones, *Dostoevsky*, 247–8, identifying the theme of childishness in *The Demons*.

dead as a dead man can, if the spirit is in him'.[116] There is a terrible childishness about terror, and terrorism; the innocence and the unpredictability, and the apparent lack of witting evil.[117] The responsibility of society, of previous generations, seems all the greater. Stepan Trofimovich at least dimly comes to this realisation.[118] And it is this guilt that terrifies Coetzee's Dostoevsky, more than anything.

The relation of the guilt-ridden father and his dead child is the central theme of Coetzee's *Master*. As is the case in *The Demons* and Conrad's two terrorist novels, moments of terrorist violence are incidental, levers with which to stretch the essential tension between protagonist and victim, father and son. The fact that Coetzee's Dostoevsky emerges as the most tortured victim of his son's violence gives the tension an added dimension. Trofimovich's same agonies provided the literal, as well as metaphorical, heart of *The Demons*. It is the primary means by which both Dostoevsky and Coetzee can stress the intensely personal, and human, nature of this kind of horror. When Coetzee's Dostoevsky lies on his dead son's bed, and realises that he is 'the one who is dead', the full depth of this horror is apparent.[119]

The identification of language as an instrument with which to ameliorate terror is central to Coetzee's endeavour. His Dostoevsky is, of course, a writer, and he clings to the hope that 'Poetry might bring back his son'.[120] It is not, however, that simple. For language is the recourse of the forger and the dissimulator, as well as the aspiring chronicler of truth. We have already encountered Burke and Shelley and Shakespeare musing on precisely this, and we shall find Don DeLillo investigating the same essential paradox in the next chapter. Any writer, as Coetzee's Dostoevsky acknowledges, is a practitioner of these darker arts, of the 'sensual pleasure' that comes with the 'dance of the pen'.[121] Dostoevsky's Stepan admits precisely this, teasing the narrator of the novel, 'My friend, the real truth is always implausible, did you know that? To make the truth more plausible, it's absolutely necessary to mix a bit of falsehood with it. People have always done so'.[122]

And so language carries a destructive potential too; as readily an instrument of value to the terrorist as it is one that might be used to counter terrorism, or to comprehend it.

---

[116] MP, 112.

[117] The theme is revisited elsewhere in the terrorist 'genre'. See, for example, J.G. Ballard's description of the middle-class terrorists of Chelsea Marina, dismissed as a 'playgroup' that has run 'out of control'. In his *Millennium People* (HarperCollins, 2004), at 191.

[118] See Offord, 'Context', 79–80.

[119] MP, 19, and perhaps most poignantly reaffirmed in the agonies he experiences in visiting his son's grave. See Scanlon, *Terrorism*, 99.

[120] MP, 17.

[121] MP, 200–1, 236, 245. For a commentary on this irreducible ambivalence, see Scanlon, *Terror*, 104–5 and Head, *Coetzee*, 146, quoting John Bayley's review of *The Master*, in which he argued that Coetzee's novel reinforces the view that 'whatever truth the writer utters can be twisted'.

[122] D, 216.

Pavel, as his father comes to realise, had drafted a novel; the existence of which, according to the police, clearly implicated him in revolutionary activities.[123] The desire to narrate appears to be the one thing that father and son had in common. But the draft serves to condemn Pavel, not because of what it says, but because of what it does not say. It is for this reason that Dostoevsky can barely bring himself to read it. Deep down, Coetzee's Dostoevsky is haunted by the suspicion that terrorists are possessed by personal demons, not ideologies; demons, moreover, that might have a familial, even genetic, root. The unthinking, and unfeeling nature of the terrorist enterprise is admitted by Nechaev: 'We aren't soft, we aren't crying, and we aren't wasting our time on clever talk… We don't talk, we don't cry, we don't endlessly think on the one hand and on the other, we just do!'[124] Dostoevsky's Nechaev, Pyotr, articulates the same desperate justification. His dismissal of 'too much goodness' in liberal politics is equally chilling.[125]

Language carries this innate ambivalence; a medium of redemption as well as tool of destruction. It charts the 'dark places' of the 'heart', as well as the lighter.[126] It is the failure of literature to effect social reform which haunts the author of The Demons. When Stepan is dragged off the stage at Yulia's fete, his defence of literature howled down by an audience whose faith in rioting is now greater than its faith in the power of poetry, it presages the bombing of the town and the deaths that follow.[127] Shatov's final musings, as he prepares to venture out to his unknowing death, betray his realisation that literature provides both the germ of terror, and its antidote.[128] The innate paradox of language describes the essential, defining ambivalence of those who seek to deploy it, including, of course, Dostoevsky and Coetzee.

Language permits remembrance. In this it provides a measure of redemption. The author of The Demons was famously entranced by the idea of redemption. Stepan Trofimovich's final hallucinatory moments are devoted to the possibility.[129] And it allows Coetzee's Dostoevsky to remember, and in doing so, perhaps, to exorcise some the demons, of guilt and failure, that possess him.[130] But language also raises spectres. It possesses Coetzee's Dostoevsky, luring him into contributing to Nechaev's radical presses.[131] And it confirms his deepest

---

[123] MP, 40.   [124] MP, 104.

[125] D, 316. See Frank, Dostoevsky, 447, discussing the portrayal of Nechaev as one of 'total negativism'.

[126] MP, 144. As Dominic Head suggests, Coetzee's Dostoevsky is driven to the edge of madness by the realisation that everything he writes, everything he seeks to chronicle as a truth, 'contaminates' itself. See his Coetzee, 148–9

[127] D, 487–9, and also 508, for an ironic dismissal of the 'quadrille of literature' which had been brought to such an abrupt and violent end. For a discussion of the quadrille, and Dostoevsky's use of the metaphor to ridicule the pretences of liberal aesthetics, see Offord, 'Context', 74–5.

[128] D, 578–9.

[129] For Dostoevsky, and Stepan Trofimovich, the redemption is more obviously theological of course. But that did not make its consideration any less textual. See Jones, Dostoevsky, 262–3.

[130] MP, 5, 14–15.   [131] MP, 181–82, 197–8, 201–2.

horror, his own guilt, as the inspiration, according to Nechaev, for much of what he, and by implication Pavel, believed should be done.[132] The father raised the demon which possessed his son.[133]

And it confirms, necessarily, Pavel's guilt too. There is nothing in Pavel's novel, or indeed in the chronicle of his final weeks, days and hours, which can explain, still less justify, what he did. The 'same demon', Dostoevsky admits, 'must have been in Pavel'. 'It's nice to think that Pavel was not vengeful. It's nice to think well of the dead. But it just flatters him. Let us not be sentimental'.[134] Pavel was a human being, a flesh and bones person, albeit one consumed apparently with a barely comprehensible demonic impulse to destroy. 'By giving him labels', calling him an anarchist or a nihilist or a terrorist, 'you miss what is unique about him', and you fail to comprehend the demons that possessed him.[135] Ultimately Stepan Trofimovich comes to realise the same about his own son.

Doestoevsky's *The Demons* closes with Trofimovich's lingering death, his final delirious thoughts oscillating between moments of high optimism and deep despair, between the thought that his body might be purged of its own 'demons', and the horrific realisation that it might not, and that the demons will devour his own being.[136] There is to be no ultimate purgation, no final consolation. Coetzee's *Master of Petersburg* must deny this too.[137] There is no resolution to the lesser questions, how did Pavel die and who killed him?[138] And there is no resolution to the more important one either, why did he die? The only truthful account, Coetzee's Dostoevsky realises, is the one he prefers. The search for greater certitude is itself a kind of demonic possession, a 'plague of devils'.[139] The more he searches for explanations, the greater the 'perversion' that seems to possess him, and all those whom he encounters.[140]

There is no end to terror; except in the fantastical rhetoric of those who pretend that such demons might be defeated in some sort of 'war'. Nechaev's uncompromising nihilism leaves us with a similar image as to that which closed Conrad's *The Secret Agent*. More sons will be deluded by idealism, more will be killed, and more parents will grieve. Coetzee's Dostoevsky is haunted by the

---

[132] MP, 183–4, 186, 189, and at 201, with Nechaev suggesting that he has taken Raskolnikov, the protagonist of Dostoevsky's *Crime and Punishment* as a precise inspiration.

[133] We encountered the same parental theme, though focusing more on maternal than paternal guilt, in the previous chapter.

[134] MP, 113.   [135] MP, 113–14.

[136] D, 654–5. For a commentary, see Jones, *Dostoevsky*, 274–5.

[137] See Scanlon, *Terror*, 86–7, 91, 107. Coetzee is not of course alone amongst more recent contributors to the genre in denying closure. As we have already seen, the end of Doris Lessing's, *Good Terrorist* has a decidedly ambivalent, almost Beckettian, feel about it. Just as Conrad's Professor roams the streets with his bombs, Lessing's protagonist just drifts away, her personal confusions and anxieties no more resolved than they were at the outset of the novel.

[138] MP, 122–3.   [139] MP, 125.

[140] MP, 235. The realisation comes shortly after the scene in which Dostoevsky 'possesses' his son's landlady. At 'the instant at the onset of the climax when the soul is twisted out of the body and begins its downward spiral to oblivion', she whispers 'devil'. MP, 230–1.

thought that his son killed other sons, or at the very least was prepared to do so.[141] There is no end to the sorrow and the guilt, and to the sense of abandonment. 'Mourning for a dead child has no end'.[142] And no meaning either. Coetzee's Dostoevsky struggled to comprehend, but could only conclude 'God said: Die'.[143] So did the author of *The Demons*, whose Kirillov kills himself because he realises that God does not care whether he lives or dies.[144]

Death, as the narrator of *The Demons* concludes, is the 'measure of our absurdities'.[145] Shatov's death is horrific precisely because it seems so ordinary and unremarkable and unnecessary, a minor paragraph in the deeper recesses of a morning paper; which is, of course, where the author of *The Demons* first encountered the reported murder of an obscure agriculture student by a bunch of shadowy terrorists.[146] It is, famously, this absurdity that characterises the existential genre with which Dostoevsky, and to a degree Conrad and Coetzee, are so readily identified.[147] And terrorism, an expression of ultimate, seemingly incomprehensible destruction, is the compelling metaphor. 'Death is a metaphor for nothing', as Coetzee's Dostoevsky realises with an ultimate horror, 'Death is death'.[148] It is his sickness, as it was Stepan Trofimovich's. It is the final 'darkness'; terrorism an ultimate expression of the humanity which suffers it.[149]

Stark humanity

At the outset of this chapter, and indeed this book, it was suggested that a poethical strategy might allow us to approach a jurisprudence that is more sensitive to the kinds of challenges that terrorism presents. If ever there was a need for a literary 'supplement' to more formal texts, it is here, in a jurisprudence that is, otherwise, so strikingly short of definition and substance. The very idea of a law of terrorism is questionable, whilst the relation between law and terrorism remains similarly uncertain and contentious. Here, as we have also intimated on more than one occasion, in the absence of a primary text, the supplementary text becomes more than desirable. It becomes vital. But what, more precisely, might Conrad's novels, and Dostoevsky's and Coetzee's, tell us

---

[141] MP, 99.   [142] MP, 75.

[143] MP, 75. A conclusion that has a resonance in the context of Dostoevsky's own struggles with religion, and a collateral, and corrosive, sense of abandonment. In correspondence, an agonised Dostoevsky later wrote, 'The Antichrist is coming among us! And the end of the world is close – closer than people think!' The observation, from 1873, is quoted in Leatherbarrow, 'Life and Work', 42.

[144] D, 618–19. See Jones, *Dostoevsky*, 280–1, arguing the critical view that Kirillov kills himself in revenge for God abandoning him. In killing himself, the putative Nietzschean presumes that he can kill God in return. There is, as Jones suggests, a distinct 'whiff of Kafka'.

[145] D, 610.   [146] See Jones, *Dostoevsky*, 245–6.

[147] For an identification of Coetzee's post-modern textuality with the existential tradition, see Jones, *Coetzee*, 6–7, 148–9, 154–6.

[148] MP, 118.   [149] MP, 234–5.

about law and terrorism? What is their poethical import? How can they serve as necessary supplements?

First they can help us to strip away the mythologies and the fetishes, to remove the 'masks of anarchy' which the perpetrators of violence, terrorist and counter-terrorist alike, invariably assume.[150] In simple terms, they can help us pick our way through what Norman Mailer rather bluntly terms the 'crap'. As Conrad confided in correspondence, the characters he presented in novels such as *The Secret Agent* were not 'revolutionists' or counter-revolutionists, the 'true anarchists' as he abruptly termed them. They were, rather, nothing more than 'shams'.[151] The same is just as true of Dostoevsky's Pyotr Verkhovensky and Coetzee's Nechaev. We encountered similar examples, albeit in rather more sympathetic form, in the previous chapter, most obviously perhaps in Doris Lessing's *The Good Terrorist* and Orhan Pamuk's *Snow*. And we shall again in the next chapter too, when we take a closer look at some of the emergent 9/11 genre of literature. The mythic engagement of 'martyrs and monsters' benefits the terrorist and the counter-terrorist alike; but no one else.[152] Fiction can help to deconstruct this mythology.

In the context of our present 'age of terror', this conclusion has obvious implications. Most obviously it confirms that the pressing need is not to pursue a war against terrorism, a war that will never, by definition, actually be won. It is, rather, to engage a process of 'de-mythification' or 'de-canonisation', to shatter the ring of enchantment.[153] This is what Conrad and Dostoevsky and Coetzee, and Lessing and Pamuk, in their different ways, endeavour to do, to reach past the politics of 'hyperbole' and nurtured fear.[154] If we can do this, we might just make a first step towards countering the inherent inhumanity that terrorism, and indeed counter-terrorism, represents and nourishes.

This leads us to a second insight, one that carries a clear poethical resonance. Behind the rhetoric of the terrorist zealot, and the counter-rhetoric of the public official, there will always be human tragedy.[155] It is important that this simple truth is not forgotten. There will always be troubled children and haunted parents. Again, the particular agonies that terrorism inflicts upon the parental relationship has emerged as a distinctive characteristic in 9/11 literature. It finds, most obviously perhaps, a voice in Oskar, the nine-year-old protagonist of Jonathan Safran Foer's *Extremely Loud and Incredibly Close*. The 9/11 attack killed Oskar's father. And it 'crushed' Oskar; so much so that a year later, still

---

[150] For the original use of this metaphor, see P. Shelley, 'The Mask of Anarchy' in P. Shelley, *Complete Poetical Works* (Oxford University Press, 1971), ll.30–7.

[151] Correspondence with Cunninghame Graham. In Watt, *Conrad*, 230.

[152] See Zulaika and Douglass, *Terror*, 119, and in the specific context of Conrad's novels, W. Moseley, 'The Vigilant Society: *The Secret Agent* and Victorian Panopticon', *Conradiana*, 29 (1997), 59–78, suggesting that Conrad shrouded *The Secret Agent* in a pervasive, ultimately corrosive, atmosphere of suspicion and counter-suspicion.

[153] See Zulaika and Douglass, *Terror*, 150, 226, 239.   [154] Houen, *Terrorism*, 5–7.

[155] See Burleigh, *Blood and Rage*, x.

haunted by nightmares of burning towers and falling men, he is unable, even unwilling, to reconcile the absence; 'It's the tragedy of loving, you can't love anything more than something you miss'.[156] The devastation reaches through generations.

It is for this reason that 9/11 is indeed an 'event of historical importance'; not just because of its scale, or because of its impact upon public consciousness, but because it shattered thousands of lives and affronted the ethical pretences of those it left behind.[157] George Steiner's observations regarding our forgotten capacity to 'bring sweetness and light to men' are immediately resonant.[158] We shall revisit these observations, and their deeper insinuations shortly, in our concluding chapter. And the same is true of Natalie Haldin's closing observations in *Under Western Eyes*, as is the collateral scepticism of Dostoevsky's narrator. According to critics such as Zdizislaw Najder, novels written in the loosely existential tradition of Conrad and Dostoevsky are best understood as exercises in 'unabashed emotionalism'. The politics that they portray is one in which the central struggle is not legalistic or even rational, but is, instead, intensely emotional; the struggle between 'hatred' and 'compassion'.[159]

As Razumov came to realise, the 'real drama' is 'not played on the great stage of politics', but in private lives, in the ordinary struggles of ordinary people against the innately destructive ravages of those who represent the state, and those who seek its dissolution.[160] And it is defined by its ambiguity; for humanity is defined by its contradictions. As Conrad wrote in a letter to the *New York Times* in 1901, 'The only legitimate basis of creative work lies in the courageous recognition of all the irreconcilable antagonisms that make our life so enigmatic, so burdensome, so fascinating, so dangerous – so full of hope'.[161]

The aspiration was fully appreciated in an early review of *The Secret Agent* published in the *Times Literary Supplement*:

> To show how narrow the gulf is fixed between the maker of bombs and the ordinary contented citizen has never before struck a novelist as worth while, the subterranean world in which the terrorists live having up to the present been considered by him merely as a background for lurid scenes and hair-raising thrills. And then comes Mr Conrad with his steady, discerning gaze, his passion for humanity, his friendly irony, and above all his delicate and perfectly tactful art, to make them human and incidentally to demonstrate how monotonous a life can theirs also be.[162]

The precise theme of the review focused on the familiar Conradian juxtaposition of extraordinary circumstance and ordinary people. The same theme, of

---

[156] J. Safran Foer, *Extremely Loud and Incredibly Close* (Penguin, 2006), 74–5, 208, 230, 256–7.

[157] See M. Ignatieff, *The Lesser Evil: Political Ethics in and Age of Terror* (Edinburgh University Press, 2005), 125–8.

[158] G. Steiner, *In Bluebeard's Castle: or Some Notes Towards a Redefinition of Culture* (Faber and Faber, London, 1971), 17–18, 31–2, 47–8, 64–5, 105.

[159] Najder, *Conrad*, 110–11, 117.   [160] UWE, 238.

[161] In Carabine, '*Under Western Eyes*', 122.   [162] In Watt, *Conrad*, 33.

course, pervades *The Demons* and *The Master of Petersburg*. It has, of course, already pervaded much of the literature we have encountered in previous chapters, and we shall encounter it again in the next chapter too.

Those who perpetrate terrorist acts, like those who suffer and experience them, do so emotionally, even viscerally. It is here that Burke's insight is prescient again; that terror is an expression of the sublime. In his *Millennium People*, a novel to which we can readily ascribe an existential genus, J.G. Ballard has his protagonist, placed in a position akin to that of Conrad's Stevie, contemplate the apparently 'limitless… allure and sensual potency of primed Semtex'.[163] We encountered Doris Lessing's Alice contemplating much the same in the previous chapter too. The terrorists which populate all these novels, and their victims, are defined, not by their ability to reason, but by their capacities for pain and fear, love and compassion. Safran Foer's young Oskar, when challenged by his psychiatrist to explain what he means by life becoming 'impossible', replies that he feels 'constantly emotional'; 'sadness, happiness, anger, love, guilt, joy, shame', all of them all the time.[164]

And so do we, sometimes more intensely, sometimes less so; but all, nonetheless, all the time to some degree. The morality that counts, in this analysis, is the morality identified by Martha Nussbaum as a 'morality of compassion', and by Richard Rorty as a morality of 'feelings and ideas', 'cruelty' and 'kindness', rather than presumed absolutes of truth and falsehood, right and wrong.[165] It is a morality which is, also, so complex and yet also so simple.[166] Here, as Dostoevsky's Stepan Trofimovich confirms, can be found the 'real fruit of all mankind', its capacity to express love and compassion for the fate of others.[167] And it is here, again, that literature, novels such Conrad's and Dostoevsky's, and Lessing's and Safran Foer's, become so vital. They engage our emotions, nudging them ever more closely to the sufferings of those who experience more immediately the horrors of terror and terrorism.

The fashioning of a 'morality of compassion' is made possible only if the truly human, even existential, nature of terrorism, and our experience of it, is properly appreciated. Terrorism, Conrad opined in correspondence, represents a 'general manifestation of human nature'.[168] It is an intrinsic expression of human nature, albeit an extreme one.[169] It is humanity that we must come to understand better, if we are to approach, in any sensible way, a resolution to the

---

[163] See Ballard, *Millennium People*, 188, and also 261 and 292 exploring the more obviously Nietzschean and existential themes.

[164] Safran Foer, *Loud*, 201.

[165] See Nussbaum, 'Compassion', 231, 249–51, and R. Rorty, 'Human Rights, Rationality, and Sentimentality' in S. Shute and S. Hurley (eds.), *On Human Rights: The Oxford Amnesty Lectures 1993*, (Basic Books, 1993), 130, and also *Philosophy and Social Hope* (Penguin, 1999), 96–7, 122.

[166] For a reflection on this obvious paradox, see the closing observations of Safran Foer's Oskar, in *Loud*, 324.

[167] D, 485. See also Frank, *Dostoevsky*, 460.

[168] Quoted in J. Berthoud, 'The Secret Agent' in Stape, *Conrad*, 100–21.

[169] See Kim, 'Violence', 93, concluding that Conrad 'yields ultimately to a faith in humanity'.

challenges posed by terrorist violence. And a law of terrorism, even if such a thing can be sensibly discerned, will help us little in this endeavour. Law is an instrument only; and a blunt one.

It will achieve nothing, not just in countering terrorism, but in mitigating its causes, unless we can, at the same time, reinvest what Vaclav Havel has termed our trans-cultural 'moral sensitivity'.[170] And it is here, as Havel reaffirms, that literature is indeed so vital, not just as a supplement, but as the necessary supplement. The dictates of 'law', as Jacques Derrida famously advised, leave no 'place for justice or responsibility'.[171] Writing again in the immediate wake of 9/11, Derrida invoked a prospective spectre, of a 'democracy to come', a 'cosmopolitan' democracy of 'justice' founded on effective and compassionate engagement across increasingly porous and ultimately meaningless state boundaries. At the heart of such an idea of justice lies the idea of simple friendship and association, or reciprocal kindness and respect and 'unconditional hospitality'.[172]

The aspiration, as Derrida confessed, is both Aristotelian and post-modern. It presumes a politics, and a jurisprudence, that 'amounts to creating (to producing, to making etc) the most friendship possible'.[173] Friendship is the primal characteristic of humanity, its politics and its jurisprudence. It gears, not just 'democracy', but also 'truth, freedom, necessity and equality'. It defines the strength of any political community, its politics and its morality.[174] It is also, most importantly, a Conradian politics; a politics of 'friendly irony', of private human relations rather than public posturing or ideological pretensions. It is the politics to which Natalie Haldin gestures, where the 'revolutionist and reactionary' will both be 'pitied and forgotten; for without that there can be no union and no love'.[175] It is furthermore the politics which can help us to meet Camus's challenge, which might help us to discern once again 'beauty in the world and in human faces'.[176]

The stakes are indeed high, even if not quite so high as the more hyperbolic would have us believe. The taking of life indiscriminately is an evil, 'immoral', an affront to the moral idea of humanity.[177] It is also an affront to political

---

[170] V. Havel, *The Art of the Impossible: Politics as Morality in Practice* (Fromm International, 1998), particularly 74, 100–1, 125–7, 166–9.

[171] J. Derrida, 'Autoimmunity: Real and Symbolic Suicides' in G. Borradori (ed.), *Philosophy in a Time of Terror: Dialogues with Juergen Habermas and Jacques Derrida* (Chicago University Press, 2003), 128–9, 134–5. For a similar observation, see Derrida, 'On Forgiveness' in J. Derrida, *On Cosmopolitanism and Forgiveness* (Routledge, 2002), 28.

[172] J. Derrida, 'Dialogue' in Borradori, *Terror*, 120, 128–30, 133.

[173] J. Derrida, *Politics of Friendship* (Verso, 1997), 8.   [174] Derrida, *Politics*, 100.

[175] UWE, 248. Inevitably, Conrad casts an ironic sheen over Natalie's observations, insinuating their naivety. But the suspicion remains, as critics have alleged, that Conrad betrays a certain grudging sympathy for the sentiment. For a commentary, using this passage as an exemplar of Conrad's determination to set in stone the dynamic 'confrontation' between 'autonomous reason' and 'dependent suffering', see Berthoud, 'The Secret Agent', 119.

[176] A. Camus, *Between Hell and Reason* (Wesleyan University Press, 1991), 117–18.

[177] See C. Gearty, 'Terrorism and Morality', *European Human Rights Law Review*, 4 (2003), 378.

principles of toleration and democracy; it is meant to be.[178] If terrorism, the terrifyingly indiscriminate taking of life, is to be countered, we need to engage more nuanced debate as to what it is, and why it is. And it must be a poethical as well as political or legal debate. On the one hand it must carve out a space for human engagement. 'Contemplating, literally and figuratively, the faces of the effaced activist and his or her intimates', it is rightly urged, 'becomes a condition for understanding the inferno of action'. Such a 'confrontation rescues us from obfuscating allegory and representation'.[179]

On the other, it must also press the case for an ethics that properly understands the vitality of human emotions. It is emotion, as Ted Honderich argues, far more than cold juristic reason, which takes us 'closer to the reality' of our 'experience' of political violence, in all its forms.[180] Again we shall revisit this idea in due course in our concluding chapter. We need to contemplate an alternative ethics, and an alternative jurisprudence, one that owes at least as much to feeling and compassion as it does to reason and the pretences of certitude. We have far less need of a 'law' of terrorism than we do a better developed sensitivity to the tragedies that it engenders.

Referring to his canon as a whole, D.H. Lawrence famously observed, 'I can't forgive Conrad for being so sad and for giving in'.[181] Sometimes, though, sadness is appropriate. The events of 9/11 should evoke feelings of sadness, as well as compassion; and it is to this supposition that we will turn in the next chapter. And the same is just as true of the myriad other terrorist tragedies that came before, and which have come since. But Lawrence is right in condemning the 'giving in'; the giving in to hyperbole and vitriol, and to fear and despair, and to the simplistic supposition that the writing of a 'law' of terror or the winning of a 'war' against terror will somehow obviate our collective need to think and to care.

---

[178] As John Gray confirms, there 'cannot be tolerance so long as terrorism goes unchecked'. See Gray, *Al-Qaeda*, 115. The sentiment finds an echo in Derrida, 'Dialogue', 125–8.

[179] Zulaika and Douglass, *Terror*, 217.

[180] T. Honderich, *Terrorism and Humanity: Inquiries in Political Philosophy* (Pluto, 2003), 4, 13–14.

[181] Quoted in J. Lyon, 'Introduction', to *The Secret Agent*, xxxiv.

6

The stuff of nightmares

Far away in Cuba there is a small plot of land leased by the US government from the Cuban state. The rent is minimal, derisory even; and the Cuban government treats it with suitable contempt.[1] For much of the last 5 years, around 650 alleged terrorists, the 'worst of a very bad lot', in the words of US Vice-President Cheney, have resided at Guantanamo.[2] Their degradation is deemed to be essential to the 'life of the nation'. These men, and boys, 'the most dangerous, best-trained vicious killers on the face of the earth', according to former Secretary of State Donald Rumsfeld, are so terrifying that they must exist 'beyond' the reaches of the law.[3] Those incarcerated at Guantanamo are, quite literally, outlaws. As one who purports to defend this state of affairs confirms, they are pirates and bandits and nihilists.[4]

Guantanamo is a 'law-free zone', a semiotic for the extra-judicial 'war on terror', a visceral expression of a nation that is troubled, not just by feelings of impotence and rage, but of guilt too.[5] We are, once again, adrift amongst the

[1] The Cuban government refuses to cash the annual rent 'cheques', and has condemned Guantanamo as a 'concentration camp'. See K. Raustiala, 'The Geography of Justice', *Fordham Law Review*, 73 (2005), 2537, and A. Roberts, 'Righting Wrongs or Wronging Rights? The United States and Human Rights Post-September 11', *European Journal of International Law*, 15 (2004), 731.

[2] D. Rose, *Guantanamo: America's War on Human Rights* (Faber and Faber, 2004), 8.

[3] In the context of post-9/11 jurisprudence, Phil Thomas suggests an analogy with the notion of *homo sacer* from Roman law. The terrorist is rendered a 'non-person: game to be hunted and destroyed'. See P. Thomas, '9/11: USA and UK', *Fordham International Law Journal*, 26 (2003), 1225. For Rumsfeld's observation, see Roberts, 'Righting Wrongs', 725.

[4] See R. Wedgwood, 'Al-Qaeda, Terrorism, and Military Commissions', *American Journal of International Law*, 96 (2002), 328–9.

[5] As Judith Butler has recently observed, the writ of law 'is effectively suspended'. See J. Butler, *Precarious Life: The Powers of Mourning and Violence* (Verso, 2004), 51. Philippe Sands quotes Michael O'Hanlon, senior fellow at Brookings Institute. Accordingly to O'Hanlon, 'We can sort of do what we want there. It's on foreign soil and yet the foreign government doesn't have much say in how we use the place.' See P. Sands, *Lawless World: America and the Making and Breaking of Global Rules* (Penguin, 2005), 158. See also Rose, *Guantanamo*, 22, 32–3, and M. Ratner, 'Moving Away from the Rule of Law: Military Tribunals, Executive Detentions and Torture', *Cardozo Law Review*, 24 (2003), 1518. Of course, much depends here upon classical notions of sovereignty, and the fiction that as Guantanamo is not part of US sovereign territory, those who reside there are not subject to US law; a state of affairs that the protocol to the third Geneva Convention was expressly created to prevent. For a commentary on Guantanamo as an expression of anger, and of 'the

images and the metaphors. In the discourse of terrorism, as we have already noted, it is always thus. The law vanishes and in its place comes linguistic and metaphysical allusion. In the context of Guantanamo, there are lots of allusions to gulags and concentration camps.[6] And lots of references to Kafka too.[7] US military and State Department officials can be found talking about the need to conceptualise a 'vanishing point' of the law, or to locate a 'legal equivalent of outer space'.[8]

The astrophysical allusion has been famously deployed, in slightly different form, by the former British Law Lord, Lord Steyn. Guantanamo, according to Steyn, is a 'black hole', a 'stain on American justice', an 'utterly indefensible' affront to the very ideas which are supposed to define Anglo-American juris-prudence, due process, the rule of law, human rights.[9] It is also, he adds, rather more prosaically, just plain stupid; revealing claims to a superior jurisprudence to be nothing more than 'self-serving hypocrisy'.[10] It is a common perception; one enjoined more recently by David Dyzenhaus who has further suggested that Guantanamo should indeed be comprehended as just one, albeit perhaps the darkest, of a 'variety of black holes' deposited by the 'war on terror'.[11] It has

impotent acting out', see S. Zizek, *Welcome to the Desert of the Real* (Verso, 2002), 35, 37. Similar suggestions can be found in A. Dorfman, *Other Septembers, Many Americas: Selected Provocations 1980–2004*, (Pluto, 2004), 10. For the suggestion that it is also an expression of guilt, see G. Achcar, *The Clash of Barbarisms: The Making of the New World Disorder* (Saqi, 2006), 43, arguing that the American political elite is haunted by the thought that Al-Qaeda is a Frankensteinian monster, built to destroy the Soviet Union, but which has turned upon its creator. For similar views, see also W. Lacqueur, *No End to War* (Continuum, 2004), 127, and Tariq Ali, *Bush in Babylon: The Recolonization of Iraq* (Verso, 2003), 152–3.

[6] The gulag reference, articulated by Amnesty, is given in M. Begg, *Enemy Combatant* (Free Press, 2006), 389.

[7] Invocations of Kafka are many. It is found, for example, in the account of detainee Moazzam Begg, who comments 'I hadn't read Kafka, but I knew the expression Kafkaesque. It was happening to me'. See his *Enemy Combatant*, 155. For an alternative invocation, see B. Ackerman, *Before the Next Attack: Preserving Civil Liberties in an Age of Terrorism* (Yale University Press, 2006), 70, suggesting that the fate of those incarcerated at Guantanamo can be compared with Kafka's famous parable of the doorkeeper in *The Trial*. For a discussion of the possible jurisprudential interpretations of this particular parable, see I. Ward, *Law and Literature: Possibilities and Perspectives* (Cambridge University Press, 1995), 144–5

[8] See Rose, *Guantanamo*, 23, quoting Marine Colonel William Lietzau, and also C. Stafford Smith, *Bad Men: Guantanamo Bay and the Secret Prisons* (Weidenfeld & Nicolson, 2007), 243.

[9] J. Steyn, 'Guantanamo Bay: The Legal Black Hole', *International and Comparative Law Quarterly*, 53 (2004), 1–15, and more recently 'Democracy, the Rule of Law and the Role of Judges', given as the 2006 Attlee Lecture, and published at www.attlee.org.uk/Transcript-Steyn. doc. The same sentiment can be found in Lady Justice Arden, 'Human Rights in an Age of Terrorism', *Law Quarterly Review*, 121 (2005), 604, reflecting on the nature of the 'challenge' which Guantanamo poses to precisely these principles, and also Ratner, 'Rule of Law', 1521, commenting 'I do not care whether we love or hate these people, every human being is guaranteed certain fundamental rights'.

[10] Observations in his 2006 Attlee Lecture, at www.attlee.org.uk/Transcript-Steyn.doc.

[11] D. Dyzenhaus, *The Constitution of Law: Legality in a Time of Emergency* (Cambridge University Press, 2006), 1–3, 202–10.

certainly bequeathed a virulent and violent testament, one that is destined to be written in blood.[12] It has been thus far.

It very quickly becomes apparent that Guantanamo is also a semiotic as well as metaphorical construct, a hideous 'spectrum of unsettling images'.[13] The orange jump-suits seem peculiar, the shackles, goggles, headphones and surgical masks rather more disturbing and the cages, in which crouching detainees were initially kept in the red hot sun, more disturbing still. And as an icon, it is, of course, cherished by both terrorist and counter-terrorist. For the former it describes a drama of post-colonial oppression. For the counter-terrorist, it represents a dramatic statement of intent, of how the 'war on terror' will be conducted, of what 'shock and awe' is supposed to mean.[14] Images of terrified Abu Ghraib inmates, shocked and awed to an appropriate level, tethered like dogs, forced to suffer sexual degradation or made to pose in mock crucifixion, make pretty much the same statement; even if their publication was unwitting.[15] The theatre of terror, like the rhetoric, is all consuming.[16] It threatens to devour our jurisprudence, as it does our better selves.

Previous chapters have addressed alternative experiences of terror and terrorism, ranging from ancient history through to the Balkan wars. The purpose of this chapter is to investigate our more immediate legal and literary responses to 9/11. In doing so we will be addressing an experience that is more particular, but which also, as we shall see, reveals a number of rather more familiar aspects. In due course we will focus more particularly on literary chronicles of the two

---

[12] See Rose, *Guantanamo*, 12, also 133. As former hostage Terry Waite confirms, the melancholy truth is that Guantanamo Bay 'represents a victory for the terrorists'. In M. Ratner and E. Ray, *Guantanamo: What the World Should Know* (Arris, 2004), x. For similar sentiments, see B. Barber, *Fear's Empire: War, Terrorism and Empire* (Norton, 2003), 24–6, commenting on the 'toxic combination of powerlessness, resentment and humiliation' that US foreign policy, particularly its most recent wars in Afghanistan and Iraq have nurtured amongst a generation of disaffected Islamic youth, and also 80–1.

[13] See Achcar, *Barbarisms*, 86, Rose, *Guantanamo*, 11, and D. Amann, 'Guantanamo', *Columbia Journal of Transnational Law*, 42 (2004), 264. See also Ratner and Ray, *Guantanamo*, 36, and Arden, 'Human Rights', 621, regretting that Guantanamo 'constitutes one of the most enduring images of President Bush's war on terror'.

[14] See M. Walzer, *Arguing About War* (Yale University Press, 2005), 60–2, emphasising the extent to which 'cycles' of terrorism and terroristic counter-terrorism are mutually sustaining. Terrorists, he observes, crave 'counter-terrorism', the more brutal the better.

[15] See A. Soueif, *Mezzaterra: Fragments from the Common Ground* (Anchor, 2004), 163–7, placing the pictures within the history of the 'pornography' of colonial occupation, at the heart of which has always lain the strategy of diminishing the conquered 'other'. A similar conclusion is reached by Joseph Pugliese, in 'Abu Ghraib and its Shadow Archives', *Law and Literature*, 19 (2007), 247–76, arguing that the images capture a pervasive anti-Islamic cultural prejudice, what he terms a 'codified imperial-fascist aesthetics', and concluding at 272, that the 'geocorpographic' images of raped and abused prisoners become 'metonymic adjuncts of the external terrain of Iraq – as territory to be raped, mutilated into submission and conquered.' See also J. Bacchus, 'The Garden', *Fordham International Law Journal*, 28 (2005), 314–16, and Achcar, *Barbarisms*, 120–1, suggesting that the impact of the Abu Ghraib images was like an 'electric shock', not just on Islamic public opinion, but on that in the west too.

[16] For a similar observation, see Achcar, *Barbarisms*, 119, suggesting that barbarism feeds on the 'spectacle' of still greater barbarisms.

key semiotics of our present 'age of terror', Guantanamo and 9/11. First, however, we need to gauge the limitations of our jurisprudential discourse; for, as we have already noted on more than one occasion, it is at times like these, when the jurisprudence is so incoherent and so impoverished, that the need for the literary chronicle and supplement becomes so pressing.

Tyrants and tyranny

The official line remains. Guantanamo is necessary. It is necessary if the threat of global terrorism is to be defeated, if the war is to be won. This fantastical war provides the inevitable backdrop. A new age of empire and of 'imperial presidency' has arrived, replete with its quasi-jurisprudence of ass-kicking.[17] America is at war, an exceptional event which is supposed to justify an exceptional abrogation of both domestic and international law. For this reason, existing provisions of international and humanitarian law must be suspended.[18] When organisations such as the Red Cross complain about allegations of torture at Guantanamo, allegations which might suggest a fundamental breach of the Geneva and Torture Conventions, such allegations are dismissed by the US Attorney-General as 'quaint' and 'obsolete'. They are, we are constantly reminded, not just the 'hardest of the hard', as Donald Rumsfeld would have us believe, or 'killers all' as his president parroted, but 'unlawful combatants' too; a juristic convenience which was able to magic away the apparent relevance of the ordinary laws of war.[19]

American constitutional law will not be allowed to get in the way either; after all, 9/11, the President advised, ushers in a 'new paradigm' of jurisprudence.[20] Instead, it will be rewritten.[21] Convenient legal precedent will be used.[22] Inconvenient precedents will be ignored. Executive fiat, in the form of presidential orders, will be deployed to authorise the establishment of detention camps and associated tribunals.[23] Above all looms the vast USA PATRIOT Act,

[17] See R. Blackburn, 'The Imperial Presidency, the War on Terrorism, and the Revolutions of Modernity', *Constellations*, 9 (2002), 6–11.

[18] It is, in effect, a 'human rights free zone'. See P. Hoffman, 'Human Rights and Terrorism', *Human Rights Quarterly*, 26 (2004), 945.

[19] See Hoffman, 'Human Rights', 943–5, Rose, *Guantanamo*, 24 and Thomas, '9/11', 1216, and also Amann, 'Guantanamo', 268–9, quoting Rumsfeld confirming that 'unlawful combatants' just 'don't deserve the same guarantees' as everyone else.

[20] For a general commentary and critique of the associated measures, see K. Roach and G. Trotter, 'Miscarriages of Justice in the War Against Terror', *Pennsylvania State University Law Review*, 109 (2005), 973, 1015–31, 1036.

[21] According to Deputy Assistant Attorney-General John Yoo, the 'war on terror' necessitates the creation of a 'new legal regime'. Quoted in Amann, 'Guantanamo', 286, and Sands, *World*, 153–4. See also E. Saar and V. Novak, *Inside the Wire* (Penguin, 2005), 161.

[22] The most convenient is *Quirin* (1942) 317 US 1.

[23] The presidential orders are founded on the assumed Congressional Authorization for the Use of Military Force order (AUMF). It is argued that the AUMF vests in the President a power to capture and detain enemy combatants by whatever means. For the most compelling defence of

that 'symbolic shake of the collective fist', as Bruce Ackerman terms it; legislation which was intended to redefine 'homeland security' and which was accepted, in startled haste, by Congress as a vital 'tool' in winning the 'war on terror'.[24] At the heart of the Act was the statement that continual detention of terrorist suspects would be permitted if the Attorney-General had 'reasonable grounds to believe' that such detention was necessary for national security.[25] And in case anyone should doubt the need, there was much raising of spectres, of trained killers wandering the streets of America.[26]

Many jurists expressed their horror at such dangerous nonsense. Ronald Dworkin condemned Guantanamo as resonant of the 'most lawless of totalitarian dictatorships', and criticised his fellow Americans for having given up on 'fair play'.[27] But many did not; entranced, it seems, by the rhetoricians and the equivocators. A number, immersing themselves in the texts of the infamous Nazi *Kronjurist* Carl Schmitt, unearthed the doctrine of the exception, which argues that, in moments of acute danger, the sovereign has a duty to act extralegally.[28] Notorious texts such as the Yoo and Bybee memoranda, which sought to justify the use of torture techniques at Guantanamo, in apparent breach of international Torture Conventions, tend to be defended in these terms.[29] The

this view see C. Bradley and J. Goldsmith, 'Congressional Authorization and the War on Terrorism', *Harvard Law Review*, 118 (2005), 2048–2133. For alternative views, see R. Goodman and D. Jinks, 'Replies to Congressional Authorization: International Law, US War Powers and the Global War on Terrorism', *Harvard Law Review*, 118 (2005), 2653–62 and M. Tushnet, 'Controlling Executive Power in the War on Terrorism', *Harvard Law Review*, 118 (2005), 2673–82.

[24] See Ackerman, *Attack*, 2 and also 18, suggesting that Congress passed the 'buck', and also O. Gross, 'What Emergency Regime?', *Constellations*, 13 (2006), 79–83, noting in passing, at 76, that 'violent emergencies tend to bring about a rush to legislation', and quoting Plato's observation that 'no man ever legislates at all. Accidents and calamities occur in a thousand different ways, and it is they that are the universal legislators of the world.'

[25] The Act runs to 342 pages, covers 350 subject areas and carries no less than 21 legal amendments. Amongst its myriad provisions, some of the most controversial relate to the redefinition of 'domestic terrorism' and the collateral permission, under section 412, to detain immigrants and non-citizens for an indefinite period. See Thomas, '9/11', 1209–10, and also E. Verdeja, 'Law, Terrorism and the Plenary Powers Doctrine: Limiting Alien Rights', *Constellations*, 9 (2002), 93.

[26] See J. Margulies, 'A Prison Beyond the Law', *Virginia Quarterly Review*, 80 (2004), 44–5, suggesting that the camps were established in the context of a rhetorical 'hysteria that periodically grip[s]' American at moments of perceived threat. For a similar conclusion, see S. Babb, 'Fear and Loathing in America: Application of Treason Law in Times of National Crisis and the Case of John Walker Lindh', *Hastings Law Journal*, 54 (2003), 1721–2, and at 1735, commenting on the 'rolling rhetoric of patriotism and anger' that gripped America post-9/11.

[27] R. Dworkin, 'The Threat to Patriotism', *New York Review of Books*, 49, 3 (2002), at www.nybooks.com/articles/15145.

[28] For accounts of Schmitt's thesis in the context of contemporary terrorism, see Ackerman, *Attack*, 56–7; Dyzenhaus, *Constitution of Law*, 34–54; T. Kochi, 'The Partisan: Carl Schmitt and Terrorism', *Law and Critique*, 17 (2006), 267–95; and also William Scheuerman, 'Carl Schmitt and the Road to Abu Ghraib', *Constellations*, 13 (2006), 112–14, investigating more closely Schmitt's idea of the partisan, and concluding in this context that, whilst those who attacked New York in September 2001 might be termed terrorist, those who are presently castigated as 'insurgents' in the Iraq war should be more accurately understood as 'partisans'.

[29] For a critique of this position, see Scheuerman, 'Schmitt', 118–20, and S. Levinson, 'Preserving Constitutional Norms in Times of Permanent Emergencies', *Constellations*, 13 (2006), 69–70.

obvious problem is temporal. The threat that concerned Schmitt, presented by rival Marxist and fascist street-gangs, was passing. The nature of the threat today is rather different. It may be intermittent, but it is also indeterminate. We are clearly not experiencing a moment of exception. Precisely the opposite is true, and in an indefinite state of emergency the state of exception becomes the state of normality.[30]

The economic analyst provides a further variant. Eric Posner and Adrian Vermeule argue that politicians rather than judges are best equipped 'at striking the correct balance between security and liberties during emergencies'. The 'trade-off thesis' has served the interests of Americans well for centuries. The test of counter-terrorist efficacy lies not in its accordance to constitutional principle, but whether it is 'cost-justified'.[31] It is, of course, a curiously dyslexic perception of pragmatics; the sacrifice of centuries of hard-earned liberties in response to one isolated terrorist attack, and the vague threat of more to come. The incoherence of such an approach, moreover, is evinced in the alternative argument, presented by alternative economic analysts, that the kind of balances ventured by Posner and Vermeule are unjustified, not simply as a matter of principle, but because they are disproportionate, and likely in the longer term to be counter-productive.[32] There is little here that is terribly convincing.

It is, however, the lack of concern for principle which is so striking. It invites the kind of juristic aberrations represented in Guantanamo and Abu Ghraib.[33] A depleted jurisprudential culture nurtures disillusion and indifference to those principles which define a liberal democratic society. The fall of the Twin Towers was an appalling tragedy. But the fall of our belief in justice would be a far greater one.[34] 'The greatest threat', Ackerman concludes, 'is the implosion of liberal democratic values in the heartland, not their destruction by hostile forces from the periphery'.[35] But even he is prepared to abrogate the ordinary processes of law, even if only for a more limited moment, one circumscribed by an 'emergency constitution'.[36]

It is perhaps hardly surprising given the apparent confusion in academic circles that the US judiciary should appear to be equally uncertain. The validity of legal provisions, and executive orders, regarding the status of detainees at Guantanamo and elsewhere, has come before the US courts on a number of occasions.[37] Similar provisions, as we shall shortly see, have also been reviewed

---

[30] See G. Agamben, *The State of Exception* (Chicago University Press, 2005), 2–3, and arguing the same; Ackerman, *Attack*, 17–18; Gross, 'Regime', 74–88; and Levinson, 'Emergencies', 67–9.

[31] E. Posner and A. Vermeule, *Terror in the Balance: Security, Liberty, and the Courts* (Oxford University Press, 2007), 5–6, 39.

[32] C. Aradau and R. van Munster, 'Governing Terrorism Through Risk: Taking Precautions (un) Knowing the Future', *European Journal of International Relations*, 13 (2007), 106.

[33] Scheuerman, 'Schmitt', 120–1.

[34] See Levinson, 'Emergencies', 72, insinuating the same conclusion.

[35] Ackerman, *Attack*, 169.   [36] Ackerman, *Attack*, 3–5, 35, 77–80.

[37] For a recent and broad overview, focusing on the question of jurisdiction in particular, see F. de Londras, 'Guantanamo Bay: Towards Legality?' *Modern Law Review*, 71 (2008), 36–58.

in the UK. The first judgements reached by the US Supreme Court were notable precisely for their fragmentary and inconsistent form; and for their general preference for deference. In both *Rasul* and *Hamdi*, the Court was prepared to assert its jurisdiction, but having done so seemed altogether less sure what to do with it.[38] In the former case, Justice Scalia condemned his colleagues for even going this far. It was not a time, he railed, for 'judicial adventurism'.[39] A marginally greater sense of disquiet was detectable in *Hamdi*, just.[40] Justice Souter mused upon the 'tradition' of Magna Carta, whilst Justice O'Connor felt moved to warn against the dangers of an 'unchecked system of detention', but not so moved that she was inclined to bother checking the one in question.[41]

The only exception in this depressing narrative of what Owen Fiss terms 'judicial cowardice' can be found in Justice Stevens's opinion in a subsequent case to reach the Court, *Padilla*.[42] 'At stake, Stevens opined:

> is nothing less than the essence of a free society. Even more important than the method of selecting the people's rulers and their successors is the character of the constraints imposed on the Executive by the rule of law. Unconstrained Executive detention for the purpose of investigating and preventing subversive activities is the hallmark of the Star Chamber.

There are occasions when such detention might, as a temporary measure, be acceptable. This was not such an occasion:

---

[38] *Rasul v Bush* 124 S. Ct 2686 (2004), and *Hamdi v Rumsfeld* 124 S. Ct.263 (2004). The decisions were reached together. Writing for the plurality in *Rasul*, Justice Stevens affirmed, at 2696, that such detainees were held within US 'territorial jurisdiction', since it exercised 'complete jurisdiction and control'. Given the peculiar circumstances of Rasul's detention, his is probably the only case in US constitutional history in which a litigant was unaware that his fate was being considered by the Supreme Court. The supposition is made by one of Rasul's lawyers, Joseph Margulies, in 'Beyond the Law', 40. See also de Londras, 'Legality', 42–3, detecting a prospective willingness to not just assert jurisdiction, but to act on it.

[39] *Rasul*, 2706–7 and 2710–11. For the *New York Times* observation, see Ratner and Ray, *Guantanamo*, 162. For a dismissal of the *Rasul* judgement as one of pitiful 'timidity', see O. Fiss, 'The War Against Terrorism and the Rule of Law', *Oxford Journal of Legal Studies*, 26 (2006), 256.

[40] See Ackerman, *Attack*, 27–31, expressing some reservations with regard to the popular perception that the *Hamdi* judgement represented a victory for liberty, concluding that 'only a modern-day Kafka could do justice' to the bland nature of judicial reasoning in the face of such fundamental questions of liberty and humanity. For a similar conclusion, albeit for very different reasons, on this occasion of cost-benefit efficacy see Posner and Vermeule, *Terror in the Balance*, 50.

[41] For Souter's comments, see *Hamdi v Rumsfeld*, at 2659, and also 2655 referring to the 'constant tension between security and liberty' which the Supreme Court must acknowledge. For O'Connor's, see 2647, and also 2648 stressing the overarching importance of 'striking a proper constitutional balance'.

[42] *Rumsfeld v Padilla* 124 S. Ct.2711. (2004). The Court restricted its substantive judgement to the matter of wrongful direction of an original writ of *habeas corpus*. For an interesting account, from the perspective of Padilla's lawyer, both of the proceedings and the frustrations, see J. Martinez, 'Jose Padilla and the War on Rights', *Virginia Quarterly Review*, 80 (2004), 56–67. For Fiss's comment, see his 'War', 239.

It may not, however, be justified by the naked interest in using unlawful procedures to extract information. Incommunicado detention for months on end is such a procedure. Whether the information so procured is more or less reliable than that acquired by more extreme forms of torture is of no consequence. For if this nation is to remain true to the ideals symbolized by its flag, it must not wield the tools of tyrants even to resist an assault by the forces of tyranny.[43]

Whilst the Court subsequently struck down the proposed Guantanamo Military Commissions in *Hamdan*, the lack of similar appeals to principle remains conspicuous. It too is a fragmented judgement, and rather less obviously a defeat for the doctrine of the exception than was initially surmised.[44] Not least, perhaps, because a supine Congress immediately accepted a new Military Commissions Act which reversed the Court's decision.[45]

Serial contempt for judicial propriety appears to have become endemic, and not just in the US. Historically British courts have adopted a broadly deferential position in matters of supposed national security.[46] However, post-9/11, and in seeming contrast to the evasive uncertainties of the Supreme Court, the judicial mood in British courts has changed quite noticeably. In *Abbasi*, for example, in which the Court of Appeal was invited to grant a declaration urging the government to make representations on behalf of a British citizen held in Guantanamo, Lord Phillips invoked the 'great legal tradition' of Anglo-American jurisprudence in order to confirm the aberrant nature of the applicant's fate. Such extra-judicial detention 'in apparent contravention of fundamental principles of law' in a territory over which the US plainly had 'exclusive control', was a matter of 'deep concern'.[47] For reasons of practicality the Court felt unable, however, to approve the application; which saved the British government the embarrassment of having to pretend to complain.[48] *Abbasi*, it has been suggested, is one of 'two rays of light'.[49]

---

[43] *Rumsfeld* v *Padilla*, at 2735.

[44] *Hamdan* v *Rumsfeld* 126 S. Ct.2749. The judgement emphasised, most painstakingly in Justice Steven's opinion, the lack of various constituent legal rights to which Hamdan, as a detainee, should have been entitled, including a copy of the charge against him, a presumption of innocence, various rules of evidence, and so on. For commentaries, see Posner and Vermeule, *Terror in the Balance*, 51, 272, and de Londras, 'Legality', 45–8.

[45] The constitutionality of the 2006 Military Commissions Act by the Supreme Court is a matter of ongoing consideration. For a prospective commentary, see de Londras, 'Legality', 51–3. For a reflection on the Supreme Court's jurisprudence in this line of jurisdiction cases, and a particularly sceptical view of the determination of President Bush and his Congress to legislate away its implications, see A. Chaskalson, 'Counter-Terrorism, Human Rights and the Rule of Law', *Cambridge Law Journal*, 67 (2008), 80–3.

[46] See most obviously, and most recently, *Home Secretary* v *Rehman* [2001] 3 WLR 877.

[47] *R (Abbasi)* v *Sec. of State for Foreign and Commonwealth Affairs*, [2002] EWCA Civ 1598, paras.15, 59–60, 66, 107. For an account of the case, see Sands, *World*, 165–6.

[48] The same result, essentially grounded on practicalities, as well as a due measure of deference, was achieved in a similar case, involving a non-UK national who was resident in the UK, in *R (on the Application of Al Rawi)* v *Sec. of State for Foreign and Commonwealth Affairs*, [2006] EWCA Civ 1279.

[49] See Dyzenhaus, *Constitution of Law*, 162.

The other, brighter still perhaps, is the case of *A (no.1)*; a case which has been lauded as 'monumental', a 'powerful statement' as to 'what it means to live in a society where the executive is subject to the rule of law'.[50] *A* was held, along with a number of other suspected terrorists, in Belmarsh prison under the provisions of the 2001 Anti-Terrorism, Crime and Security Act (ATCSA), which in Section 21.2 of Part 4 allowed for the indefinite detention of suspected terrorists on the grounds of perceived 'risk to national security'.[51] Invoking the familiar metaphor, Amnesty described their fate as 'Kafkaesque'.[52] The legislation attracted widespread criticism.[53]

The narrow question in *A (no.1)* related to the possible discrimination between UK and non-UK nationals in contravention of Article 14 of the European Convention.[54] The Court of Appeal preferred the course of 'considerable

---

[50] See Arden, 'Terrorism', 622, 625. See also A. Tomkins, 'Readings of *A v Secretary of State for the Home Department*', *Public Law* 2005, 263–4, suggesting that the decision might presage the beginnings of a much-belated judicial awakening to the fact that even in the context of national security the courts have a responsibility to 'ensure that the rule of law is respected', adding that it has been a 'long time coming, to say the least'.

[51] Section 21.2 then defines a 'terrorist' as someone who 'is or has been concerned in the commission, preparation or instigation of acts of terrorism'; an obvious tautology. The definition is expanded to include anyone having 'links' with a group of terrorists, which includes, according to section 21.4, anyone who 'supports or assists' such a group. Section 21.5 makes further definitional reference to section 1 of the 2000 Terrorism Act, which defines a terrorist threat as one made 'for the purpose of advancing a political, religious or ideological cause' which is 'designed to influence a government or to intimidate the public or a section of the public'. For an overview of the Act, see C. Gearty, '11 September 2001, Counter-terrorism and the Human Rights Act, *Journal of Law and Society*, 32 (2005), 22–7.

[52] It also condemned Belmarsh as the UK's 'Guantanamo Bay in its Own Backyard'. In D. McGoldrick, *From 9–11 to the War on Terror* (Hart, 2004), 37–8.

[53] The UK was one of the first to rush to legislate in order to give effect to the UN's panicky Resolution 1373, which required 'all States to take measures to prevent the commission of terrorist acts, including by denying safe haven to those who finance, lend, support or commit terrorist attacks'. 'In a long record of shaming fealty to whips', Hugo Young observed, 'never have so many MPs showed such utter negligence towards so impressive a list of fundamental principles'. See his comments in 'Once Lost, these Freedoms will be Impossible to Restore', the *Guardian*, 11 December 2001. For a commentary on the UN response to 9/11, see R. Talbot, 'The Balancing Act: Counter-terrorism and Civil Liberties in British Anti-terrorism Law' in J. Strawson (ed.), *Law After Ground Zero* (Glasshouse Press, 2002), 131–2, and also McGoldrick, *9–11*, 24–5. Of course, perhaps more than anyone, the UK should have been aware of the hazards of detention and internment. The policy had singularly failed in Northern Ireland. See Roach and Trotter, 'Miscarriages', 973–98. Interestingly, as ATCSA passed through Parliament, the Home Secretary had admitted that there was 'no immediate intelligence pointing to a specific threat to the United Kingdom'. In A. Tomkins, 'Legislating Against Terror: The Anti-Terrorism, Crime and Security Act', *Public Law* 2002, at 216, further observing at 205 that the legislation was the 'most draconian' ever passed by a 'peacetime' Parliament. For a further commentary on ATCSA, see H. Fenwick, 'The Anti-Terrorism, Crime and Security Act 2001: A Proportionate Response to 11 September?', *Modern Law Review*, 65 (2002), at 724 and 762, criticising in particular the lumping together of 'extremely disparate' aspects of terrorism, crime and security, and asylum and immigration.

[54] *A,X and Y v Secretary of State for the Home Department*, [2002] EWCA Civ 1502, paras.1–10, 37–8.

deference'.[55] The House of Lords did not.[56] And it was the tone of the judgement that was so startling.[57] The rule of law, Lord Bingham held, could never be abrogated 'even in a terrorist situation'. The European Convention, now incorporated into English law, confirmed this, and so did centuries of 'libertarian tradition'.[58] Detentions should never be excessive, and could never be indefinite.[59] He was not alone in this view, or in the tone of his judgement.[60] According to Lord Nicholls, such forms of 'indefinite' detention were 'anathema in any country which observes the rule of law'. Only the most 'exceptional' circumstances could justify it, and there was little reason to believe that such circumstances were then present.[61]

Lords Hope, Rodger and Scott articulated a similar scepticism.[62] According to the latter, the notion that people might be imprisoned indefinitely on little more than some kind of unwarranted and undisclosed 'denunciation' was 'the stuff of nightmares, associated whether accurately or inaccurately with France before and during the French Revolution, with Soviet Russia in the Stalinist era'.[63] Equally caustic was Baroness Hale, who agreed that such forms of 'executive detention' are the 'antithesis of the right to liberty and security of person', whilst 'unwarranted declarations of emergency', she added pointedly, 'are the familiar tool of tyranny'.[64] More contemptuous still was Lord Hoffmann. 'Nothing', he opened, 'could be more antithetical to the instincts and traditions of the people of the United Kingdom' than the idea of indefinite extra-judicial detention. People should not be locked up, and cast beyond the law, just because some

---

[55] See paras.40, 44, 47, 52, 64. Lord Brooke expressed rather greater suspicion with regard to the competence of government agencies to actually discern which alleged terrorists were actually terrorists, but was not prepared to translate his suspicion into a substantive dissent. See paras.86–7.

[56] The derogation could not, Lord Bingham confirmed starkly, be 'justified'. Para.68. For substantive commentaries on *A*, see Tomkins, 'Readings', 259–66, Arden, 'Human Rights', 605–18, and also C. Walker, 'Prisoners of "War All The Time"', *European Human Rights Law Review*, 1 (2005), 61–8.

[57] Virtually 'unprecedented', as Tomkins suggests in 'Reading', at 259.

[58] Paras.36, 41. Thus rejecting the Attorney-General's argument that a declaration against the legality of ATCSA would be 'undemocratic'.

[59] Para.9. For a discussion of the proportionality issue in the judgements, see Arden, 'Human Rights', 608.

[60] Only one member of the panel, Lord Walker, dissented.

[61] Paras.74, 78, 80. The government had sought to argue that the present threat of terror amounted to a 'time of war or other public emergency' as defined by Article 15 of the European Convention, and was thus sufficient to trigger a derogation from the Convention itself. The sceptical view is also taken by David Bonner, in his 'Managing Terrorism While Respecting Human Rights? European Aspects of the Anti-Terrorism, Crime and Security Act 2001', *European Public Law*, 8 (2001), at 517, and also Adam Tomkins, in 'Terror', at 216.

[62] Para.155. The tone of Scott's remarks were, according to one commentator, particularly 'memorable'. See B. Dickson, 'Law Versus Terrorism: Can Law Win?' *European Human Rights Law Review*, 1 (2005), 22.

[63] Para.155.   [64] Paras.222, 226.

government officer might think them to be a 'supporter' of terrorism.[65] Individual terrorist acts could not, he continued, threaten the 'life of the nation', merely, perhaps, the lives of certain citizens. 'Terrorist violence', accordingly, 'serious as it is, does not threaten our institutions of government or our existence as a civil community'.[66] And he concluded:

> The real threat to the life of the nation, in the sense of a people living in accordance with its traditional laws and political values, comes not from terrorism but from laws such as these. That is the true measure of what terrorism may achieve. It is for Parliament to decide whether to give the terrorists such a victory.[67]

The government, however, was not to be chastened. A couple of days later, the Home Secretary Charles Clarke reassured the nation that he had no intention of letting anyone out of Belmarsh prison, no matter what their Lordships might have thought of his legislation.[68] A new Prevention of Terrorism Act, rushed through Parliament, set in place a system of 'control orders' as an alternative to detention.[69] They too received a frosty judicial reception, something which merely led to Clarke's successor, John Reid, announcing, in a suitable tone of despair, that the judges 'just don't get it'.[70]

And still they do not, it seems. And for this we should be thankful. Control orders have been struck down on a number of occasions.[71] More recently still, in *A (no.2)*, the House of Lords confirmed an exclusionary principle that prevents the admission of torture evidence in immigration hearings, irrespective of where the evidence was obtained, and regardless of whether the

---

[65] Paras.86–7. For a concentrated examination of Hoffmann's judgement, see T. Poole, 'Harnessing the Power of the Past? Lord Hoffmann and the *Belmarsh Detainees* Case', *Journal of Law and Society*, 32 (2005), 534–61. Poole rightly notes the extent to which Hoffmann's rhetorical strategy focused on the idea of common law rights, rather than Convention rights, precluding the legality of Part IV of ATCSA. For a more critical commentary on Hoffmann's rhetoric, see D. Dyzenhaus, 'An Unfortunate Burst of Anglo-Saxon Parochialism', *Modern Law Review*, 68 (2005), 673.

[66] Para.91.   [67] Para.97.

[68] For which reason it might be agreed that the Human Rights Act is indeed an act of ultimate jurisprudential 'futility'. See K. Ewing, 'The Futility of the Human Rights Act', *Public Law* 2004, 829.

[69] The Act repealed sections 21–32 of ATCSA. Control orders can include a variety of restrictions on movement and communication, including tagging. It has been suggested that senior members of the 'legal profession' have 'concerns' regarding control orders. See comments in John Kampfner's interview with the UK DPP Ken Macdonald in the *New Statesman*, 7 February 2005, 35. Arthur Chaskalson pointedly aligns the 'control orders' with similar measures deployed in apartheid South Africa. See his 'Counter-Terrorism', 86. We have already encountered this statute, in Chapter 1, when we mused upon the notion of an offence of 'glorifying' terrorism.

[70] See K. Starmer, 'Setting the Record Straight: Human Rights in an Era of International Terrorism', *European Human Rights Law Review* 2007, 127.

[71] Notable reversals on the matter of control orders include *MB*, [2006] EWCH 1000, [2006] HRLR 29 and *JJ*, [2006] EWHC 1623 (Admin), EWCA Civ.141. For an overview, see Starmer, 'Record', 123–32 and also C. Walker, 'The Treatment of Foreign Terror Suspects', *Modern Law Review*, 70 (2007), 432–3.

deponent in the hearing was suspected of presenting a threat to national security.[72] The need to torture has emerged as one of the less edifying discursive sub-cultures in the present 'war on terror'.[73] Its very existence is, of course, suggestive, not least of the fragility of our moral confidence in the face of an essentially delusive danger.[74] As Lord Hoffmann affirmed in *A (no.2)*, 'The use of torture is dishonourable. It corrupts and degrades the state which uses it and the legal systems which accept it'.[75] The argument in favour of torture, and the use of torture evidence in legal hearings, has no defence in principle, whilst its practical efficacy has long been questionable.[76]

It is easy to be critical of judges, so often presented as semi-detached by a disapproving media and a despairing executive alike. Comedic instances of otherworldliness are easily seized upon, insinuations of irresponsibility just as easily made. More serious commentators such as John Griffith express a related anxiety regarding the propensity for judges to act as 'philosopher-kings', in disregard of democratic imperatives.[77] But there are times when the executive ambition must be checked, lest it does indeed fall into the temptations of tyranny.[78] This, it seems, is just such a moment.[79]

The ordinary and the extraordinary

Of course, Guantanamo is not really necessary at all. This much has become ever more obvious. A leaked CIA report, acquired by the *New York Times* in June 2004, admitted that 'only a relative handful' of those detained at Guantanamo were likely to be even militant, never mind terrorist.[80] Even strident defenders of Guantanamo are increasingly prepared to concede this

---

[72] *A v Secretary of State for the Home Department (no.2)* [2005] UKHL 71. For comments on *A (no.2)*, see Walker, 'Treatment', 449 and C. Gearty, 'Terrorism and Human Rights', *Government and Opposition*, 42 (2007), 355–6.

[73] For a criticism of the emergent 'apologetics for torture', see R. Weisberg, 'Loose Professionalism, or Why Lawyers Take the Lead on Torture' in S. Levinson (ed.) *Torture: A Collection* (Oxford University Press, 2004), 303–4.

[74] See Martin Amis, *The Second Plane* (Jonathan Cape, 2008), commenting at 142, that 'Torture is always the first recourse of a terrorised state'.

[75] *A (no.2)* Para 85.

[76] See Gearty, 'Terrorism', 360, and more generally P. Sands, *Torture Team: Deception, Cruelty and the Compromise of Law* (Penguin, 2008), particularly 214–15 and 270–5. For the alternative view, see A. Dershowitz, *Why Terrorism Works: Understanding the Threat, Responding to the Challenge* (Yale University Press, 2002), 124–5, 134–9, 152–63.

[77] See J. Griffith, 'The Brave New World of Sir John Laws', *Modern Law Review*, 63 (2000), 165. A similar sentiment can be detected in R. Ekins, 'Judicial Supremacy and the Rule of Law', *Law Quarterly Review*, 119 (2003), 144.

[78] See Gearty, 'Terrorism', 347–9 and 353, cautioning against allowing the 'discourse of counter-terrorism' to be used to justify the erosion of basic legal and human rights.

[79] As both David Dyzenhaus and Arthur Chaskalson have recently argued with vigour. See their *Constitution of Law*, 3–11, and 'Counter-Terrorism', 90–1, respectively.

[80] In Rose, *Guantanamo*, 42. A confession confirmed by a former camp commandant General Hood who, in the *Wall Street Journal* in 2005, admitted that 'we just didn't get the right folks', quoted in Stafford Smith, *Bad Men*, 163.

reality.[81] Included amongst those released so far, the worst of the worst, or perhaps the not-quite-so-bad-after-all, have been one man of 90 years old, and another who claimed to be 105 years old, and was described as 'babbling at times like a child'.[82] Many of the actual children remain.[83] Their misery compounds that of the tens of thousands of children who starved to death in Iraq during the 1990s, and the tens of thousands who have been killed, maimed, and orphaned since in our frenzied pursuit of the 'war on terror' there and elsewhere over the past few years. A few more will have died this week.

But if it is not of much value in actually pressing a 'war on terror', Guantanamo is of enormous value as a semiotic of it; not least insofar as it encourages us, ever more so as time passes, to try to comprehend what it says about the strength of our jurisprudential culture. Most obviously, for the reasons we have just encountered, it underlines the fragility of this culture, the readiness with which our political leaders would have us abrogate our most dearly held principles of justice, and the uncertain manner in which many judges and jurists respond. It is, as we have repeatedly argued, at this point, where the primary jurisprudential texts seem, once again, to fail, that the case for looking to supplementary accounts, testamentary, dramatic, fictive, becomes compelling.

Testamentary chronicles, of the kind we considered in Chapter 3, provide one such supplementary form; and a number of such texts, focused on the particular experience of Guantanamo, have emerged in recent years. On occasion they can provide a peculiarly intense insight. One such example is given in Clive Stafford Smith's account of serving as a defence lawyer at a Military Commission. There is something peculiarly apposite in his account of all parties being handed 'scripts' which were intended to prescribe the forthcoming events.[84] Rather different, but equally revealing, is his recounting his receipt of an injunction demanding that detainee suicides should be termed, for the benefit of public consumption, 'asymmetrical acts of war'; a linguistic equivocation of peculiarly grotesque proportions.[85]

---

[81] Most, former US Deputy Defence Secretary Paul Wolfowitz admits, are likely to 'turn out to be completely harmless'. But then it is so difficult to tell, and 'if we put them in the Waldorf Astoria', he added with a certain grim, if not grotesque, humour, 'I don't think we could get them to talk'. Not that many have, it seems, had much to say; probably because they are indeed harmless. There is a certain absurd circularity to the argument. For Wolfowitz's comments, and their innate idiocy, see Barber, *Fear's Empire*, 112.

[82] As reported by David Rhode of the *New York Times*. In Roach and Trotter, 'Miscarriages', 1012–13, and Ratner, 'Rule of Law', 1519, and more recently in the *Guardian*, 22 September 2006, 25.

[83] It is alleged that boys as young as thirteen have been detained at Guantanamo. See Amann, 'Guantanamo', 267, and also Stafford Smith, *Bad Men*, 144–51, discussing the controversy that surrounds the detention of juvenile detainees, and in particular the case of a young boy called Yusuf who, the authorities alleged, was a senior Al-Qaeda financier, at least until the notion became so obviously absurd. It transpired that Yusuf's apparent confession to being a money-trader was actually a mistranslation. In his dialect, the critical word, *zalat*, meant salad, not money. Pakistani authorities had picked up a fourteen-year-old roadside tomato seller.

[84] Stafford Smith, *Bad Men*, 95–107.   [85] Stafford Smith, *Bad Men*, 219.

Accounts of released detainees such as Moazzam Begg have a similar value; chronicles which describe the sheer existential horror, not just of being incarcerated indefinitely, not just of being systematically beaten and tortured, but of recognising the common spiral of 'depression and hopelessness' into which all involved parties seemed to fall.[86] We need to know Begg's story, just as we need to know those of Hamdo Kharimanovic and Drazen Erdemovic. These narratives are narratives of both testament and resistance. They chronicle injustice, and they invite us to consider it. And we have a responsibility to do so. The need to chronicle and the urge to excavate the deeper ethical questions run together.

The re-emergence of a distinctive genre of verbatim theatre in direct response to 9/11 and subsequent events presents a striking example of how the two strategies can be aligned.[87] We have already encountered an example of the genre with David Hare's critique of the 'war on terror', *Stuff Happens*. According to Hare the form of verbatim drama minimises 'interpretive gloss', whilst also more urgently demanding the reflective participation, and complicity, of the audience.[88] It seeks, most obviously, to chronicle actuality, to replicate 'images of real violence' that might otherwise be obscured.[89] Of course, the aspiration, to present reality, is inherently 'elusive'.[90] For theatre can also articulate terror, perhaps even glorify it. It has always done this, since the days of Euripides.[91] 'I had a role to play', the sometime poster-girl of 1970s' terrorism, Patty Hearst, once recalled of her appearances in court, 'and I knew

---

[86] Begg, *Enemy Combatant*, 188.

[87] Verbatim theatre re-presents the actual comments of political protagonists in dramatic form. For discussions of early verbatim theatre, and the particular roles of Hare and also Howard Brenton, see R. Boon, 'Politics and Terror in the Plays of Howard Brenton' in J. Orr and D. Klaic (eds.), *Terrorism and Modern Drama* (Edinburgh University Press, 1990), particularly 138–9 and also *About Hare: the Playwright and the Work*, (Faber and Faber, 2003), 18–20, 62. See also Hare's own observations, in *Obedience, Struggle and Revolt* (Faber and Faber, 2005), at 18–20.

[88] As Hare's much-maligned UN weapons' inspector, Hans Blix, confirms in *Stuff Happens*, 'I was an amateur actor when I was a student. Theatre teaches you the value of collaboration, of getting on with people'. See D. Hare, *Stuff Happens* (Faber and Faber, 2004), 9. For Hare's comments on the value of verbatim drama, see Boon, *Hare*, 157, and also D. Hare 'On Factual Theatre' in R. Soans, *Talking to Terrorists* (Oberon, 2005), 111–3, arguing that the deployment of 'real-life dialogue' necessarily removes a play from the relatively narrow cognitive confines of a 'metropolitan' theatrical 'elite', a 'welcome corrective' indeed 'to the cosy art-for-art's sake racket which theatre all too easily becomes'. See also Hare, *Obedience*, 4 and 118–19 discussing the implications of participation and complicity. For a glowing review of this dramatic strategy of 'constructive montage', see Michael Billington's review of Soans's play in the *Guardian*, 6 July 2005, 26. 'At moments like this', Billington concludes, 'verbatim drama achieves the emotional power of high art'.

[89] To overcome, accordingly, the 'seeming disintegrations of the modern theatre'. For a discussion of these 'disintegrations', which he roots in the post-Enlightenment critique of Nietzsche and others, see A. Kubiak, *Stages of Terror: Terrorism, Ideology and Coercion as Theatre History* (Indiana University Press, 1991), 118–19, 123–8, 144–5.

[90] As Harold Pinter observes. See his Nobel lecture, published in the *Guardian*, 8 December 2005, G2, at 9. See also Kubiak, *Stages*, 9, referring to the 'true illusion' that is raised in any dramatic performance.

[91] See Kubiak, *Stages*, 1–2, 5, 21, 26, 54, declaring that the 'history of theatre' is the 'history of terror'. For similar sentiments, see J. Orr and D. Klaic, 'Terrorism and Drama: Introduction' in Orr and

my part well'.[92] In order to become an effective terrorist, as one character in Robin Soans's contribution to the genre, *Talking to Terrorists*, confirms, it is necessary to 'assume a new role' until 'it becomes second nature'.[93]

To a degree, of course, verbatim theatre is no exception. It is still theatre. Hare confesses as much, admitting that whilst the 'driftwood' is there to be found, it must still be carved and painted 'to make it art'.[94] Like any drama it is impressionistic, it seeks to represent, and to persuade.[95] Equivocation lurks behind the lines of verbatim drama, as it does any form of literature, or politics. In creating a 'site' of 'theatrical imaginative interiority', as Antony Kubiak terms it, theatre also provides a site of 'false consciousness', where terrorist and counter-terrorist can spin illusions and counter-illusions of truth and fear.[96] The insinuation is innately violent, as Shakespeare recognised. Unmasking equivocation imports its own terrors.[97]

In early 2004, another contribution to the verbatim genre ran to critical acclaim in London. *Guantanamo*, written by Vera Brittain and Gillian Slovo, has a dual ambition. On the one hand the play serves to present a chronicle before the 'bar of informed international opinion', to use Lord Steyn's analogy.[98] On the other, it also facilitates the raising of voices, those stories identified by Ariel Dorfman as lying at the 'bottom of the rivers of silence'.[99] Its immediate focus is the fate of five British detainees, three of whom, the so-called 'Tipton Three', attracted particular media interest when it became apparent that they had been employed in an electrical store near Birmingham at the time when it was

---

Klaic, *Terrorism*, 2–3, and 8 arguing that terrorism is, as such, 'paratheatrical', and 11 describing the particular and myriad impact of different forms of dramatic terror in 'our audio-visual lives' today. For further discussion of the idea of terrorism as 'paratheatrical', see Aida Hozic, 'The Inverted World of Spectacle: Social and Political Responses to Terrorism' in Orr and Klaic, *Terrorism*, 64–5, 72, and also L. Kralj, 'Terror in German Expressionist Drama', also in Orr and Klaic, *Terrorism*, 96–7.

[92] Quoted in J. Martin, 'The Fictional Terrorist', *Partisan Review*, 51 (1988), 75. Martin also cites, at 81, a passage from John le Carre's *The Little Drummer Girl*, wherein the terrorist Khalil admits 'Terror is theatre. We inspire. We frighten, we awaken indignation, anger, love. We enlighten. The theatre also. The guerrilla is the great actor of the world'.

[93] Soans, *Talking*, 82.

[94] In Hare, *Obedience*, 29, and at 78–9 making similar observations, and 84 commenting, somewhat defensively perhaps, that 'the editing and organisation of reality is a genuine skill'.

[95] See Kubiak, *Stages*, 162, suggesting that we cannot 'escape representation'.

[96] Kubiak, *Stages*, 100, 147–9, discussing the shared aspiration of dramatist, terrorist and counter-terrorist, to create a community of the terrified.

[97] Kubiak, *Stages*, 26–48, exploring this thesis in the specific context of Senecan and Euripidean drama, and also 45–7. See also D. Orr, 'Terrorism as Social Drama and Dramatic Form' in Orr and Klaic, *Terrorism*, 48–9.

[98] Steyn, 'Black Hole', 8, and also 14, emphasising that the chronicle 'will not be neutered'.

[99] And nothing, as Hare confirms, is more 'important' than this. See his comments, made in the context of an earlier verbatim work, *Via Dolorosa*, in *Obedience*, 201, and also his observation that 'theatre is the best court that society has', in Boon, *Hare*, at 79, and that the need for 'sustained and serious scrutiny' has never been greater than it is today, in *Obedience*, at 28. Similar comments can be found in Kubiak, *Stages*, 157. For Dorfman's observation, see *Other Septembers*, 232.

suggested by US authorities that they had been attending an Al-Qaeda training camp.[100] The farce chased down the tragedy.[101]

Framed by Lord Steyn's excoriating critique of the 'black hole' of Guantanamo, the high politics of the play is provided by the usual suspects, various lawyers and bureaucrats, foreign ministers and secretaries of state. It is also present in the bigger questions which *Guantanamo* explores, the careless pursuit of a 'war on terror' that so easily takes the appearance of being a 'war on Islam', the sheer brute idiocy of alienating 'one billion Muslims around the world', the real danger which the abrogation of legal principle presents to all of us, and the increasingly uneasy sense that when it comes to dealing with 'others' there is indeed little 'difference' between 'Saddam Hussein and Bush and Blair'.[102]

But it is the fate of the detainees which dominates, their personal despair, their sense of loss, the agony of their families, their hitherto intensely ordinary lives and experiences; 'hardly the stuff of terrorism' as one of their campaigners observes, hardly the stuff of 'trained vicious killers'.[103] In the opening act of the play, the father of one of the detainees recounts how his son was seized in his house in Pakistan, 'bundled up' and thrown into the boot of a car in front of his child.[104] The emotional heart of the play can be found in their correspondence, their shared sense of bewilderment and despair.[105] It is a vital strategy; for whilst few in the audience are likely to have been kidnapped and bundled into cars, or tortured into making false confessions, many are likely to have experienced the peculiar love, and attendant anxieties, shared by parents and their children.

Discussing her clients, one defence lawyer observes:

> The boys are three young British lads who are like all our children – they're people who are very familiar, very easy to feel immediately comfortable with. And yet the story they tell us is one of terrible stark medieval horror. It's like going back in time to something unimaginable from beginning to end of what they say... I think perhaps we're very calloused. We read, we watch, we hear about atrocities – we know what man's inhumanity to man consists of, we know all that, but we don't sufficiently register it. We don't have the capacity to take it in and react in the way we should as human beings. But when you have in front of you men you're getting to know and they're talking about it, not because you're interrogating them, but it's tumbling out and they're reminding each other,

---

[100] Rose, *Guantanamo*, 118–19.

[101] Something that speaks volumes, in passing, to the argument that evidence extracted by torture should always be treated with the utmost scepticism, for reasons of practice as well as principle. See Roach and Trotter, 'Miscarriages', 981–2, and also Rose, *Guantanamo*, 114–17, 121–4.

[102] V. Brittain and G. Slovo, *Guantanamo* (Oberon, 2004), 43 [hereafter G].

[103] G, 19–20, 34. For a collateral account, focusing on the 'Tipton Three', see Rose, *Guantanamo*, 12–14, 38–9, and also more generally 134–5.

[104] G, 23. The account is authenticated by Begg's lawyer, Michael Ratner, in Ratner and Ray, *Guantanamo*, 57–8.

[105] See G, 29. As James Bacchus puts it, detainees like Moazzam Begg became the new 'disappeared'. See his 'Garden', 316–18.

they're telling things that they haven't told anyone. Maybe it's the testimony of every survivor from a concentration camp or a massacre…

… It's a complete ordinariness of where they are now, suddenly, from something so extraordinary.[106]

Guantanamo is about the relation of the ordinary and the extraordinary. Like any drama, it humanises the experience of those whose experiences could not otherwise be readily comprehended.[107] It makes injustice stark. It describes the failure of justice, and it makes us, the audience, complicit in this failure. It should make us angry.[108]

It certainly makes Tom Clark angry. Tom lost his sister in the Twin Towers; something which, given her interest in the peculiar injustices which afflict the Middle East, inheres its own poignant irony.[109] And he readily acknowledges his struggle with hatred; a hatred that is directed, increasingly, not just at the terrorists, but at those who pretend to justify their reciprocal injustices as a proportionate response:

I'm furious at the length of detention of these people, furious because those who are innocent have lost three years of their life, much as I lost, as I've been living in a sort of private hell since my sister was murdered, and although at least I've been able to recover and get over it and deal with, and still sort of have my life, they've had theirs taken away. And that's… and they'll never get it back and I'd buy them a drink if I met them, you know, if in truth they had done nothing wrong. I can't imagine a worse thing for any person, they deserve all our sympathies and all of our efforts to sort of make sure they do actually get the justice they deserve.[110]

With a nice though unwitting sense of irony, two of the detainees were returned just days before *Guantanamo* opened. The observations of one of the released is reproduced in the play, 'If I am the worst of the worst, and obviously the scum of the earth, and people should fear me, of course, why then have I been released?'[111] Indeed.

Falling

Tom Clark's voice is a vital one. It invites, most obviously, the grander narrative context of 9/11. But it also aligns the suffering, of all those who have suffered

---

[106] G, 51–2.

[107] Lucia Zedner has recently emphasised the value of applying the faculty of political 'imagination' in such circumstances, suggesting that 'To posit our loved ones or ourselves as possible subjects of security measures is no abstract act of jurisprudential conjecture'. See L. Zedner, 'Securing Liberty in the Face of Terror: Reflections from Criminal Justice', *Journal of Law and Society*, 32 (2005), 515.

[108] See Hare, *Obedience*, 77, commenting on the 'anger' that can be 'painted' in dramatised accounts of legal and quasi-legal tribunals and institutions. He was commenting more immediately on Richard Norton-Taylor's dramatisation of the Lawrence Inquiry, entitled *The Colour of Justice*. A projected film of the experiences of the 'Tipton Three' should widen feelings of anger still further. See the *Observer*, 23 January 2005, at 6.

[109] G, 28–29.   [110] G, 45–6.   [111] G, 48.

because of 9/11, in New York, or in Cuba, or indeed Afghanistan or Iraq. Literature, to repeat, has a responsibility to respond to 9/11, to nurture what Agnes Heller has termed a necessary 'discourse of understanding'.[112] We need to engage with 9/11 and the war on terror and Guantanamo. To this end we must also engage further sites of resistance and further strategies of resistance too. We must seek out alternative voices, alternative texts. It is in this context that Martin Amis's confession of momentary doubt in the aftermath of 9/11, a sudden feeling of 'gangrenous futility', becomes so threatening.[113] This moment of silence, a poetic equivalent to the juristic moment of exception, threatened just the same kind of mute tyranny. It had to be resisted. The failure to narrate would have been a further defeat for the possibility of hope.

The problem, of course, is that of sensitivity; to condemn our political response to 9/11 whilst in no way diminishing its tragedy. This, to follow Heller's lead, can be termed the paradox of understanding. Literature must take sides, and the side it must take is that of humanity. It must, of course, do so sensitively.[114] Lives were devastated. As Susan Buck-Morss puts it, the 'psyche' of an entire nation, an entire culture, was 'ripped'; but in ways that were also intensely personal and particular.[115] One way of doing this is by seeking to deconstruct the grander political meta-narratives, and instead concentrate on the reality of human loss as a foil to political pretension. Such a strategy can touch depths that the rhetoric and the politics of 'ass-kicking' never could. It can nurture a sense of humanity, of care and compassion.[116]

In this context, the emergence of a distinctive genre of 9/11 literature is striking, and its common determination to bring together, once again, the ordinary and extraordinary, more striking still. We have already encountered some examples of this literature, most obviously in the previous chapter. It speaks to the Conradian aspiration; to excavate 'stark humanity'. What is so immediately striking about novels such as Don DeLillo's *The Falling Man* or Jay McInerney's *The Good Life* or Safran Foer's *Extremely Loud and Incredibly Close* is their shared determination to reinvest the experience of loss and suffering, and in doing so to deconstruct all the mythologies and rhetorical strategies that pervade the higher political and jurisprudential discourses of

---

[112] A. Heller, '9/11, or Modernity and Terror', *Constellations*, 9 (2002), 53.

[113] See *Guardian Review*, 19 May 2007, 4, also citing the similar sentiments of Jay McInerney and Ian McEwan.

[114] David Held contemplates this dilemma, citing his own reaction to reading Barbara Kingsolver's article in the *Los Angeles Times* twelve days after 9/11, in which, in the cause of seeking to provide some sobering perspective, she observed 'It's the worst thing that's happened, but only this week'. See D. Held, 'Violence, Law and Justice in a Global Age', *Constellations*, 9 (2002), 74. Andrew Arato relates a similar dilemma, 'was September 12 the right day to resume laughing' at George Bush? See A. Arato, '*Minima Politica*: September 11', *Constellations*, 9 (2002), 46.

[115] S. Buck-Morss, *Thinking Past Terror: Islamism and Critical Theory on the Left* (Verso, 2003), 24–5.

[116] See Buck-Morss, *Terror*, 25, suggesting that the appearance of such emotions in the days that followed 9/11 gave her 'courage to write'.

terrorism. In these novels, the events of 9/11 provide a backdrop to the altogether more essential play of human emotions.

The over-arching aspiration of McInerney's novel, its determination to strip away the fragile masks of 9/11 mysticism in order to reveal the deeper measures of human suffering that lurk beneath, is acutely Shelleyan. It finds a compelling encapsulation in the image McInerney presents of a distraught relative railing against those who prefer to post pictures of missing relatives:

> What's the matter with you people? They're fucking gone. They're already cremated, crushed, incinerated like garbage, and we won't even have a fucking bone to bury. It doesn't have to make sense. People die... My mother died a nasty, horrible death, leaking out of every orifice. Was that fair? Did that make sense? Did I make a fucking poster?[117]

For some, the nascent iconography, the 'fiction of the missing', comforts.[118] For others it offends deeper sensitivities. Suffering is a variable experience; but it is also a common one. And if there is redemption to be had, it is found in distraught relatives comforting other distraught relatives, in those who placed their lives on hold in the days that followed 9/11 in order to work in soup kitchens and the like, 'smearing peanut butter on the wounds of the city'.[119] If there is anything noble or inspiring to be retrieved from the events of that day it will be found here. It will not be found in the preposterous rhetoric which invokes an ultimately vacuous 'war on terror'.

There is, of course, a necessary paradox here; one that lies at the heart of McInerney's novel, and one that cannot be easily exorcised. It is impossible to excavate the experience of 9/11 without first invoking the iconography of 9/11. It finds a further expression in *The Good Life* when one of the protagonists recalls first seeing his rescuer:

> I walked out of the smoking ruins and there she was. I can't tell you what it was like that day. It was like the world had come to an end. You can't believe some of what I saw down there. There was a woman with her face burned off. And suddenly there was this new face. It was like seeing Botticelli's Venus in the Uffizi, like the reinvention of the world. I actually thought, in my delirium, she might have been an angel.[120]

The resonance of the Burkean sublime presses as hard as the Shelleyan urge to unmask. The two exist in a necessary tension, and it is the desire to explore, and deconstruct, this tension which impels poethical jurisprudence.

One of the most heavily laden of such icons is that of the falling man, and it is found frequently in this emergent post-9/11 genre. It is, as we shall shortly see, most heavily engaged in DeLillo's *Falling Man*. But it can also be found in McInerney's imagery of 'bodies raining down on the plaza'.[121] And it also finds expression in Safran Foer's Oskar reordering a sequence of pictures of a falling

---

[117] J. McInerney, *The Good Life* (Bloomsbury, 2007), 145.
[118] McInerney, *Good Life*, 144 [hereafter GL].   [119] GL, 125.   [120] GL, 309.   [121] GL, 71.

man in *Extremely Loud and Incredibly Close*, in order to conjure his father's imaginative resurrection; an exercise that is so poignant precisely because it is so desperate and so futile.[122]

The metaphor speaks, of course, at a number of levels. In his novel *The Fall*, for example, Albert Camus famously used an apparent suicide-jumper as a metaphor for exploring the idea of descent into nothingness.[123] His lawyer protagonist is haunted by the memory, reinforcing all his nascent anxieties about his own alienated condition. Whilst the suicide might have meaning for the jumper, it has none for him. It is rather an expression of the terrible unpredictability of human existence. As he wrestles with the implications of this initial appreciation, he comes to realise that it can only be comprehended within a personal philosophy that cherishes human particularity. 'We are all', Camus confirms, 'exceptional cases'.[124]

Of course, the image of the falling man carries an immanent danger. As we noted before, the collective imagery of 9/11 is all consuming, a transcendent, even sublime, moment; one that provokes a sense of mourning, not just in those who really suffered loss, but in those who watched it.[125] The paradox is immediate, and unavoidable, the danger of entrancement obvious. For this reason, whilst the image remains central, a vital strategy indeed for stimulating the consciousness of an audience, it must also be resisted. Otherwise it will blind us. It adds a further dimension of authorial responsibility; one of which Camus was only too aware. The writer fetishises, just as he or she seeks to deconstruct the fetish; a paradox which, of course, can only exacerbate the sense of hopelessness against which Camus's protagonist struggles. The writer writes to entrance, to 'enslave' an audience; and the audience reads in the hope of being entranced and enslaved. It is a 'dreadful', but inevitable, pact; of the kind all too readily appreciated not just by Camus, but, as we have seen, by the likes of Burke and Shakespeare too.[126]

This same awareness lies at the heart of DeLillo's earlier novel about terrorism, *Mao II*. On a superficial level there is much in *Mao II*, published in 1992, that is eerily prescient of events that would occur a decade later.[127] The 'fallen' state of New York is a prevalent theme, whilst the construction of towers and skyscrapers is taken to be representative of a rather greater moral and aesthetic degradation.[128] It is, however, the presentation of the writer as terrorist which advances the deeper questions; of the kind, interestingly, which we encountered in the last chapter in Coetzee's haunted Master. 'There's a curious knot that binds novelists and terrorists', DeLillo's protagonist Bill notes, a relationship

---

[122] See J. Safran Foer's *Extremely Loud and Incredibly Close* (Penguin, 2005), 325–6.
[123] Camus, *The Fall* (Penguin,1990), 52.   [124] Camus, *Fall*, 60.
[125] F. Dallmayr, 'Lessons of September 11', *Theory, Culture and Society*, 19 (2002), 137.
[126] Camus, *Fall*, 97–8.
[127] On this, see A. Thurschwell, 'Writing and Terror: Don DeLillo on the Task of Literature after 9/11', *Law and Literature*, 19 (2007), 278–9 and 293–6.
[128] D. DeLillo, *Mao II*, (Vintage, 1992), 23, 39 [hereafter M].

that is 'intimate and precise'.[129] No one better 'knows in his soul what the terrorist thinks and feels', no one better shares an 'affinity for the violent man'.[130] Sadly, however, the authority of the writer is no longer secure. 'Years ago I used to think it was possible for a novelist to alter the inner life of a culture. Now bomb-makers and gunmen have taken that territory'. The ability to terrorise has been sequestered. It is the terrorist who can most readily satisfy our craving for apocalyptic narratives; the 'darker the news, the grander the narrative'.[131] Burke would have nodded.

Projecting forward to 9/11, it is precisely this moment of self-doubt which silenced Amis's typewriter; the 'eloquence' of the 'withheld' word, as Bill puts it.[132] In writing the *Falling Man*, DeLillo seeks to counter this pessimism, to reassert the role of the writer as terrorist, the purveyor of critical deconstruction. The sublimity of the image, its power to stimulate, is undoubted; the irreducible alignment of 'Beauty, grief, terror, the empty desert, the Bach cantatas'.[133] In the words of DeLillo's Lianne:

> It hit her hard when she first saw it, the day after, in the newspaper. The man headlong, the towers behind him… The man with blood on his shirt, she thought, or burn marks, and the effect of the columns behind him, the composition, she thought, darker stripes for the nearer tower, the north, lighter for the other, and the mass, the immensity of it, and the man set almost precisely between the rows of darker and lighter stripes. Headlong, free fall, she thought, and this picture burned a hole in her mind and heart, dear God, he was a falling angel and his beauty was horrific.[134]

It is a stunning image. However, the iconography must also be resisted; and it is, distracted by the periodic intervention of a stunt man who pops up across the city seemingly to remind New Yorkers of what they can never forget.[135]

Against it, yet also stimulated by it, the *Falling Man* presents a narrative of human redemption and reconciliation, in its primary form a narrative of inquiry and introspection.[136] This speaks to another of the most obvious metaphorical resonances; with a biblical fall. When one of DeLillo's characters, Martin, reflects on the danger of 'closed' theologies and closed societies, the allusion is clear.[137] Theology, as we can see in Lianne's evocation of the falling man, hovers constantly, the sense of fall and abandonment, the questioning of faith, on the part of both terrorist and victim. 'Ashes and bones' is all that is left.[138] The depiction of 'organic shrapnel', the bits of bodies that float in the

---

[129] M, 41, 157. For a commentary on the affinity, which can be traced back at least as far as Maurice Blanchot's idea of literary terrorism, see Thurschwell, 'Writing', 281–6.

[130] M, 130.   [131] M, 41–2.   [132] M, 49.

[133] D. DeLillo, *Falling Man* (Picador, 2007), 234 [hereafter FM].   [134] FM, 222.

[135] FM, 33, 164–5, 168, and also 49 for Lianne's confession that whatever she looks at, even in the kitchen, what she sees is the Twin Towers. The death of the stunt man at the end of the novel, at 219–21, carries an obvious significance.

[136] See, for example, FM, 191–3, exploring the nature of self-loathing.   [137] FM. 47.

[138] FM, 60–1, 64, 90.

New York air, so evocative of John Donne's famous St. Paul's sermon in which he invoked an image of a congregation bound by the 'dust' of the deceased which they breathe, is compelling in its concurrent ability to reinforce a sense of humanity bound by its common fragility.[139]

To stretch the biblical metaphor, the original sin is a failure to listen to stories, to experiences of suffering and devastation. The comment that New Yorkers are buying English language versions of the Koran in an effort to better understand the terrifying 'other' is a shaft of brilliant hope.[140] So too is the urge to contemplate the mind of a hijacker; a mind possessed, not just by 'sacred words', but by recollections of 'Shia boys' slaughtered on the battlefield of Shatt al Arab.[141] He too has his images of devastation and horror. The tragedy is that, in his case, they bred a pathological hatred. Recollection is a vital, yet potentially devastating, capacity. DeLillo's victims constantly try to recollect what happened, some haunted as much by what they did not see, as what they did.[142] The need to talk about 9/11, about the terrorists as well as the victims, is urgent, the need to exchange imaginations. Becoming 'talkative' again is the first vital stage of redemption.[143]

Since 9/11 'all life has become public', as one of DeLillo's characters attests. The 'stricken community pours forth voices and the solitary night mind is shaped by the outcry'.[144] The observation is made during an anti-war march; symbolic of a broadening political discourse, and of the temporal fluidity of 9/11. Comprehending 9/11 is not just necessary for the reconciliation of those left behind. It is also necessary for the redemption of the society in which they presently live, in which we live too. As DeLillo acknowledged in his essay *In the Ruins of the Future*, written in the aftermath of 9/11, nurturing this 'counter-narrative' is the primary responsibility of the writer.[145] Here, the text becomes an essential site of resistance, the deployment of 9/11, not as a justification for a 'war on terror', but as an icon which deconstructs the mythologies upon which this war, and its collateral expressions of injustice, depends.

Novels such as *The Falling Man* can be placed alongside *Guantanamo* in their facility for providing further sites of engagement, and resistance. They do what DeLillo's editor in *Mao II* says they should: 'The state should want to kill all writers. Every government, every group that holds power or aspires to power should feel so threatened by writers that they hunt them down, everywhere'.[146] It is the writer's responsibility to terrorise those who seek to terrorise us. A free

---

[139] FM, 16. For Donne's invocation, see his *Selected Prose* (Penguin, 1987), 229–30.   [140] FM, 231.

[141] FM, 238. The urge is also joined by Martin Amis in his short story 'The Last Days of Muhammed Atta', published in *The Second Plane*, at 94–124. Once again at the heart of Amis's account is a determination to present Atta as a supremely ordinary person, defined as much by his headaches and constipation as by his desire to destroy tall buildings.

[142] See, for example, FM, 55, and also 61 for Rosellen's sad lament for what she never saw, 'I didn't see them holding hands. I wanted to see that'.

[143] FM, 63–4, 205.   [144] FM, 182.   [145] See Thurschwell, 'Writing', 280–1.   [146] M, 97.

society needs 'internal dissent'.[147] Literature provides it, in a way that the discipline of jurisprudence only rarely does. We need Bill and his dissent. The temptation is real; the temptation to sit in stunned silence, to give in. It would be the ultimate act of self-destruction, the ultimate victory for Osama bin Laden and his motley gang. The purpose of 'stories', as Bill comes to realise, is to 'absorb our terror', to allow us to digest and comprehend, and then to move forward, to reassert our own critical faculties.[148]

Those who effected the 9/11 attack hoped that those afflicted would be blinded by the semiotic, the image of the event itself. It was an act intended not to communicate, but to 'explode understanding'.[149] In such a febrile moment, bin Laden and his acolytes hoped we would react wildly, would go hunting asses to kick. They hoped that the trauma would be so great that rather than being healed, rather than it promoting a greater sense of care and trust amongst those afflicted, it would fester, building into a cycle of recurring violence, hatred and distrust.[150] They hoped, in essence, that the iconography of 9/11 would mutate into the iconography of Guantanamo. Thus far, it seems, their hopes have come to pass. If anyone is winning a 'war on terror', it is not us.

---

[147] M, 159.   [148] M, 140.   [149] See Buck-Morss, *Terror*, 24.
[150] See E. Zaretsky, 'Trauma and Dereification: September 11 and the Problem of Ontological Security', *Constellations*, 9 (2002), 98–104.

Conclusion: The Devil's big day

At the close of his verbatim drama, *Talking to Terrorists*, Robin Soans ascribes the following comments to a Bethlehem schoolgirl:

> This year things are getting worse. Last April… the saddest day; one of the girls in the form below me, Christine, was killed by an Israeli sniper. The Israelis said it was a mistake, but they can't bring her back, can they?
>
> When I first saw the Twin Towers on television, I felt sorry. But now I feel happy that they died. It's their turn to suffer. I could see many thousands of them die. I wouldn't feel a thing.[1]

There is much here to ponder, and not just the question of why a young girl should feel such hate that she relishes the suffering of thousands of people she has never met, and never now will.[2] The girl's hatred should chill us.[3] It is one of those moments identified by Albert Camus, when it suddenly seems difficult to be 'hopeful' about humanity.[4]

Writing in 1971, George Steiner asked 'How is one to address oneself without a persistent feeling of fatuity, even of indecency, to the theme of ultimate inhumanity?' It is an ultimate question. And it is hard, as Ariel Dorfman has rather more recently confirmed, 'not to despair'.[5] The more immediate focus of Steiner's reflection was, of course, genocide. But the question loses nothing of its

---

[1] R. Soans, *Talking to Terrorists* (Oberon, 2005), 96–7.

[2] As Judith Butler comments, such observations should make us 'ask what scenes of pain and grief' are conveyed by these kinds of images, in this case of 9/11 and of Israeli snipers shooting schoolgirls. See J. Butler, *Precarious Life: The Powers of Mourning and Violence* (Verso, 2004), 143.

[3] See A. Dorfman, *Other Septembers, Many Americas: Selected Provocations 1980–2004*, (Pluto, 2004), 218–20, emphasising the responsibility of the dramatist to disturb his or her audience, to leave it 'unsettled and uncertain', troubled above all, by a sense of guilt and complicity.

[4] A. Camus, 'Hope and the Absurd in the Work of Franz Kafka' in *The Myth of Sisyphus* (Penguin, 1975), 124. A more recent echo can be discerned in Ariel Dorfman's regret for 'the damaged brotherhood we call humanity', in his *Other Septembers*, at 100.

[5] Dorfman, *Other Septembers*, 123, and 217 asking the equally simple question, 'Why is there so much needless suffering in the world today?' If there is an answer, he muses, it will certainly not be a simple one. The reduction of 'complex issues to simple and heroic answers' solves nothing, no matter how strenuously our political leaders might persuade us otherwise.

pertinence in the context of mass terrorist atrocities. And neither does his sorry conclusion; that whilst we might have acquired the 'technical competence to build Hell on earth', we have lost the capacity to 'bring sweetness and light to men'.[6]

In trying to comprehend the challenges that terrorism presents, and the veracity of those strategies that our political leaders vouch as a necessary counter, the greatest mistake we can make is failing to think in terms of individual experience. Terrorism, as Jean-Paul Sartre emphasised in his notorious Preface to Fanon's *Wretched of the Earth*, is a human experience, something conceived in the 'weariness of the heart'.[7] The implications are immediate. Whereas the event of terrorism might remain frustratingly indeterminate, the experience of terrorism embraces this indeterminacy. People suffer in different ways. The confused, indeed hysterical, nature of so much counter-terrorist rhetoric, and its popular reception, is, in large part, a testimony to our discomfort with regard to indeterminacy.[8] Surely, if anything is simple, it is the proscription of terrorism. And it is; but only at the most superficial level, the level of condemning the taking of innocent life. Thereafter, as has become all too apparent in previous chapters, it gets altogether more difficult.

Moreover, in terms of jurisprudence, the need to reconcile indeterminacy requires of us something more. An understanding of terrorism as an experience engages a rather different ethics, and a rather different jurisprudence. The preceding chapters have again sought to address this need. The purpose of this conclusion is to flesh out a little further what its implications may be. What is needed, in short, is a jurisprudence that embraces the indeterminacy of impression and experience, a jurisprudence that appreciates its narrative, poetic and dramatic form.[9] As we noted in our Introduction, half a century ago Camus sensed that the twentieth century would be chronicled as 'the century of fear'. 'We live', he projected, 'in terror because dialogue is no longer possible', because we can no longer discern 'beauty in the world and in human faces'.[10] The aspiration of this book has been to address this failing; to reintroduce the human face, and the human voice, in the jurisprudential discourse of terrorism.

---

[6] G. Steiner, *In Bluebeard's Castle: or Some Notes Towards a Redefinition of Culture* (Faber and Faber, 1971), 17–18, 31–2, 47–8, 64–5, 105.

[7] J.-P. Sartre, Preface to F. Fanon, *The Wretched of the Earth* (Penguin, 2001), 20.

[8] For a commentary on the infection of political discourse by panic, see B. Ackerman, *Before the Next Attack: Preserving Civil Liberties in an Age of Terrorism* (Yale University Press, 2006), 1–2.

[9] It is, as Simone Weil observed half a century ago, the human voice that we need to hear, not the 'shrill nagging' of legal pedants. S. Weil, 'On Human Personality', quoted in D. MacLellan, *Simone Weil: Utopian Pessimist* (Macmillan, 1950), 280. For a similar observation, written in the context given by the experience of the South African Truth and Reconciliation Commission, see J. Balint, 'Law's Constitutive Possibilities: Reconstruction and Reconciliation in the Wake of Genocide' in E. Christodoulidis and S. Veitch (eds.), *Lethe's law: Justice, Law and Ethics in Reconciliation* (Hart, 2001), 147.

[10] A. Camus, *Between Hell and Reason* (Wesleyan University Press, 1991), 117–18.

Thinking about terrorism

Alongside the need to reinvest a jurisprudence of discerning and listening, a physiognomic jurisprudence, it was also suggested from the very beginning that the conjunction of law and literature might make us think and feel rather more, not just when it comes to comprehending the limits of law, but also the possibilities of justice. It is this which underpins the inevitably ethical aspiration of poethics. Of course to think about terrorism is itself to transgress. As we noted earlier, we are not supposed to think too much about terrorism, still less voice any disquiet with regard to how we might best counter it; the 'implosion of the Twin Towers' followed by the 'explosion of silence'.[11] We are supposed to listen, at least to our leaders. It is the necessary complement of what US Defence Secretary Rumsfeld termed 'message discipline'.[12] The government and military will speak with one voice, and the awed citizenry will listen, and comprehend appropriately. We are not supposed to think and we are certainly not supposed to criticise. If we do, such a transgression will be dismissed as naive. It is part of the 'miasma of so-called realpolitic'.[13]

But as Ted Honderich rightly observes political 'realism' is itself a matter of moral judgement, of the 'morality of relationship'. The fact that the relationship in question might be that of terrorist and victim makes no difference.[14] Thinking, questioning in particular, is what responsible liberal citizenship is about. We should think about terrorism. We should challenge extra-legal aberrations such as Guantanamo, just as we challenge the fantastical rhetorical nonsense which finds its absurd expression in the 'war on terror', and the quasi-juristic fictions of 'extraordinary rendition' or 'unlawful combatants'. We need to nurture the 'kind of citizenship that questions' rather than 'simply applauds', the kind that embraces indeterminacy, the 'real variety and complexity' of life, and that reconciles itself to it.[15]

On the one hand, the core question, as articulated by the likes of Camus and Steiner, is considerable. On the other, the answer it demands could not be more particular or more precise. It demands an engagement with humanity, not just the idea of personhood, but the peculiar nature of individual suffering. A terrorist atrocity remains just that. Behind the rhetoric of the terrorist zealot,

---

[11] On the need to think and to resist the rhetoric of simplistic injunction, see U. Beck, 'The Terrorist Threat: World Risk Society Revisited', *Theory, Culture & Society*, 19 (2002), 39, and also S. Scheffler, 'Is Terrorism Morally Distinctive?', *Journal of Political Philosophy*, 14 (2006), 10–11.

[12] R. Jackson, *Writing the War on Terrorism* (Manchester University Press, 2005), 26.

[13] T. Franck, 'What Happens Now? The United Nations After Iraq', *American Journal of International Law*, 97 (2003), 607.

[14] See T. Honderich, *After the Terror* (Edinburgh University Press, 2002), 10–11, 59–61. For a similar conclusion, see M. Ignatieff, *Lesser Evil: Political Ethics in an Age of Terror* (Edinburgh University Press, 2005), 167–8, and also T. Seto, 'The Morality of Terrorism', *Loyola of Los Angeles Law Review*, 35 (2002), 1262.

[15] See M. Nussbaum, *Cultivating Humanity: A Classical Defence of Reform in Liberal Education* (Harvard University Press, 1997), 84.

and the counter-rhetoric of the public official, there will always be human tragedy. It was the desire to press this one salutary, overriding truth that drove Conrad to write *The Secret Agent* and Dostoevsky his *Demons*, and it is the same aspiration which underlies the more recent contributions to the genre presented by the likes of Lessing and Coetzee and DeLillo. It is for this reason that 9/11 is indeed an 'event of historical importance'; not just because of its scale, or because of its impact upon public consciousness, but because it is an affront to our ethical pretences.[16] When all is said and done, as Michael Walzer simply states, the 'murder of innocent people is not excusable'.[17] It displays a fundamental insensitivity to our concept of the human.[18] The worst mistake we can make is to become blinded by all the moral and jurisprudential imponderables, and deluded by all the masks of legitimacy parroted by terrorists and counter-terrorists alike. Murder is inexcusable. We must never lose sight of this simple truth.

Another large question presented by terrorism is addressed to those who like to presume an affinity between law and reason.[19] Terrorism, itself constantly evading the reach of reason, disrupts this affinity. It drives us to the kind of indeterminacy which a liberal citizen must embrace. As we have already seen, on more than one occasion, the world in which the modern terrorist, and the modern counter-terrorist, works is one of 'collective enchantment'.[20] Terrorism deals with impression, and emotion, not reason.[21] In so doing it displays an 'ultimate tendency to make life absurd'; something which just makes our responses all the more frantic.[22]

The first step towards countering terrorism is the refusal to be enchanted, to actively embrace a politics of impression, rather than remain catatonically entranced by it. Such a politics must, of necessity, be an unstable politics, a kaleidoscopic politics indeed, of constantly shifting images and patterns. As such it will always play on our uncertainties, our residual fear of the apparently indeterminate. Camus noted this, and placed it at the heart of his allegory of temptation, *The Fall*. And he also noted how critical it would be for future generations to resist this temptation. Put simply, terrorism demands that we

---

[16] See N. Chomsky, *9–11*, (Seven Stories, 2001), 119, and also C. Gearty, 'Terrorism and Morality', *European Human Rights Law Review* 2003, 378, agreeing that terrorism is 'immoral'.

[17] M. Walzer, *Arguing About War* (Yale University Press, 2004), 135.

[18] See W. Sofsky, *Violence: Terrorism, Genocide, War* (Granta, 2003), 53.

[19] Wolfgang Sofsky refers to this unpredictability as the 'temporal law of terrorism'. See his *Violence*, 104.

[20] See J. Zulaika and W. Douglass, *Terror and Taboo: The Follies, Fables and Faces of Terrorism* (Routledge, 1996), 183.

[21] A. Dershowitz, *Why Terrorism Works: Understanding the Threat, Responding to the Challenge* (Yale University Press, 2002), 2.

[22] See N. Mailer, *Why Are We At War?* (Random House, 2003), 18, 20, and also W. Lacqueur, *No End to War: Terrorism in the Twenty-First Century* (Continuum, 2004), 230–1, suggesting that it leads us inexorably into a state of 'growing madness'. In like spirit, Bill Durodie has explored the extent to which the real terror lies in its failure to admit reason. See his 'Fear and Terror in a Post-Political Age', *Government and Opposition*, 42 (2007), 427–31.

reconcile ourselves to indeterminacy; not just textual indeterminacy of the kind which we have encountered in various preceding chapters, but also the political and existential indeterminacy which the textual determinacy betrays. We must reconcile ourselves to the reality that the society in which we live is becoming more, not less, prone to 'uncontrollable risks'.[23] In this context, once again, the absurdity that there is a 'war against terror' that might be won becomes painfully obvious; a rhetorical gimmick designed to keep an intermittently awed audience in a state of lingering fear and unquestioning obedience.[24]

And, alongside the more prosaic reconciliation with the reality of political uncertainty, there comes the need for a further reconciliation with an even more illusive indeterminacy, ethical indeterminacy. We cannot detach ethics from the politics and the experience of terrorism. Some jurists seek to do so, as we saw in the previous chapter. They do so by seeking to focus legal attention on particular terrorist events. But terrorism, as we know, is an experience too. 9/11 was an event, of course. But it was also an experience. It is precisely the experience of 9/11 which makes us so frenetic, so willing to abrogate our most deeply held legal and political rights; a subject to which we shall return shortly. And it is the experience of 9/11 which makes us care, about the lives of those destroyed, and the lives of those who chose to destroy. It is experience which demands that we comprehend the deeper ethical questions.[25]

The moral injunction is joined by Michael Ignatieff:

> All battles between terrorists and the state are battles for opinion, and in this struggle ethical justifications are critical, to maintain the morale of one's own side, to hold the loyalty of populations who might otherwise align with terrorists, and to maintain political support among allies.[26]

Ethics is difficult terrain, and terrorism presents more than its fair share of dilemmas, of what is 'morally problematic'.[27] But that is not an excuse for ethical disengagement; quite the reverse.

The ethical problematic demands of us two irreducible and associated commitments; to reconciliation and to responsibility. As we reconcile ourselves to the indeterminacy of our lives, to what Melanie Williams terms 'the absence of a

---

[23] See Beck, 'Terrorist Threat', 41–2, and also M. Rasmussen, 'Reflexive Security: NATO and International Risk Society', *Millennium*, 30 (2001), 308. For a similar argument, but one which prefers to suggest means in which the risk might be managed through the employment of the precautionary principle, see A. Aradau and R. van Munster, 'Governing Terrorism Through Risk: Taking Precautions (un)Knowing the Future', *European Journal of International Relations*, 14 (2007), particularly 102–9.

[24] Beck, 'Terrorist Threat', 44–5 and Aradau and Munster, 'Governing Terrorism', 108, commenting on the strategy of inculcating fear.

[25] See C. Blakesley, 'Ruminations on Terrorism and Anti-Terrorism Law and Literature', *University of Miami Law Review*, 57 (2003), 1143–6.

[26] Ignatieff, *Lesser Evil*, 19.

[27] Ignatieff, *Lesser Evil*, 18 and also 21. As Honderich observes, in *Terrorism for Humanity: Inquiries in Political Philosophy* (Pluto, 2003), 180–4, ours is a world in which 'moral necessities sometimes conflict'.

certain God', we must also embrace the responsibility that projects, for 'if no one will come to our rescue, we must build in empty space from our frailties and our moral strengths as we come to know them, aspiring to the greatest good that we collect of our joint humanity'.[28] It is, of course, an insight that engages, and deconstructs, the kind of inane pseudo-theological rhetoric we encountered in Chapter 2. But it also speaks to a rather larger issue too; to moral responsibility.

It is easy to blame the terrorist for the terrorist event. But the experience of terrorism is not so easily ascribed. Again, it is not an inquiry which the advocate of 'realpolitic' would have us embrace. But it is one that must be admitted. As Slavoj Zizek confirms, the 'true ethical test is not only the readiness to save victims' of terror, of all kinds, but also a complementary determination to annihilate those who create the conditions in which they become 'victims'.[29] Ted Honderich agrees. The relationship between the 'bad lives' suffered by others, the violence of their resentment, and us, is irreducible.[30] A credible counter-terrorist strategy must come to recognise the 'agents of wretchedness' as readily as it does the 'agents of violence'.[31] Three thousand died in the Twin Towers on 9/11. On the same day, eight times as many people died around the world of malnutrition and related diseases, and each, Ted Honderich reminds us 'was as individual as each of the 3,000'.[32] We need to see their faces. We need to know more about their lives, and the nature of their suffering. The starved and the diseased live in terror too.[33]

This does not mean that we do not need to know about those who died on that fateful September day, or the maimed lives of those left behind. Our desire to do so, to reach out, to express compassion in 'defiance' of those who sought to wreak their misery, is, as Ariel Dorfman, the one 'dreadful form of hope' to which we can cling.[34] But it does mean that any response to terrorism, to 9/11 and to any other terrorist event, must be rounded. It must aspire to understand the terrorist as well as the terrorised. It must aspire to a 'common humanity', to a sense of inclusiveness, and to a shared compassion that seeks to address the fate of all those who suffer the myriad forms of terror that scar the lives of so many in all corners of the world.[35]

In the days following 9/11, the UN Secretary-General, Kofi Annan, warned:

> We should remember that, in the fight against terrorism, ideas matter. We must articulate a powerful and compelling global vision that can defeat the vivid, if

---

[28] M. Williams, *Empty Justice: One Hundred Years of Law, Literature and Philosophy* (Cavendish, 2002), 218.

[29] S. Zizek, *Welcome to the Desert of the Real* (Verso, 2002), 68.

[30] Honderich, *Terrorism*, 109–11, 147, and *After the Terror* (Edinburgh University Press, 2002), 72–3, 125, 136–7, concluding, at 85, that 'there is among us a responsibility for bad lives'. The same view is taken by Eric Hobsbawn, who locates the terrorism of Islamic fundamentalism within the wider context of economic instability and inequality across the Middle East. See his *Globalisation, Democracy and Terrorism* (Little Brown, 2007), 3, 110.

[31] Honderich, *Terrorism*, 21.   [32] Honderich, *Terrorism*, 23–4, and also 54–6.

[33] Honderich, *Terrorism*, 164–5, and *After the Terror*, 111–15.

[34] Dorfman, *Other Septembers*, 8, and also 11–14.   [35] Dorfman, *Other Septembers*, 8.

extreme, visions of terrorist groups. We must make clearer, by word and deed, not only that we are fighting terrorists, but that we are also standing, indeed fighting, for something – for peace, for resolution of conflict, for human rights and development.[36]

A credible counter-terrorist rhetoric should aspire to the high-ground, politically, morally, emotionally. It should aspire to both compassion and respect. Above all, it must recognise that the seeds of hatred and fanaticism are rooted in perceptions of injustice and indignity.[37] Such a conclusion chimes, very obviously, with those commentators who urge us to comprehend Islamic fundamentalism, and its violent expression, as a post-colonial discourse.[38] Understood in this way, it becomes vital to appreciate that, regardless of how we reconcile the countervailing demands of liberty, equality and security in crafting a credible counter-terrorism strategy, we recognise the primacy of a fundamental principle of 'human dignity'.[39] It is this conclusion that reinvests a belief in international, even cosmopolitan, responses to the challenge of terrorism.[40]

In order to engage such a strategy, we must, as a precursor, first embrace the opportunity to rid ourselves of the pretences of absolute reason, and most particularly the jurisprudential fiction that we need only comprehend an event in order to realise justice. Such a movement, moreover, will be a movement towards sensibility and experience, to something which we might, following Burke, term the 'sublime'.[41] More prosaically, it means that we will at least begin to think like real human beings.[42] This intellectual migration is critical. Again, it underpins the entire aspiration of this book. In these terms, 9/11 was indeed simply one more 'instant', one expression of an ongoing experience.[43] At one level this will not help the lawyer much. The problem with experiences is that they are so variable and subjective. The 'wretchedness of the heart', though familiar, is not consistent. Here again a willingness to embrace the deeper ethical questions is vital.

---

[36] In D. McGoldrick, *From 9–11 to the Iraq War 2003*, (Hart, 2004), 197.

[37] Ignatieff, *Lesser Evil*, x.

[38] See S. Buck-Morss, *Thinking Past Terror: Islamism and Critical Theory on the Left* (Verso, 2003), 2–7.

[39] Ignatieff, *Lesser Evil*, 23–4. Precisely what this means is the subject of Martha Minow's review of Ignatieff's thesis, in 'What is the Greatest Evil?', *Harvard Law Review*, 118 (2005), 2156–62. A subject of immediate relevance here, of course, is torture. For a discussion of the extent to which a respect for 'human dignity' precludes torture, even if it might under certain circumstances permit indefinite incarceration, even death, see Ignatieff, *Lesser Evil*, 142–4.

[40] As articulated, for example, by Ulrich Beck, in 'Terrorist Threat', at 50.

[41] See A. Gearey, '"Tell All the Truth, but Tell it Slant": A Poetics of Truth and Reconciliation', *Journal of Law and Society*, 31 (2004), 49.

[42] For a broad defence of this kind of movement, written within the more immediate context of criminal law, see M. Nussbaum, *Hiding from Humanity: Disgust, Shame and the Law* (Princeton University Press, 2004), particularly 5–12 and 37–45.

[43] See N. Chomsky, *Hegemony or Survival: America's Quest for Global Dominance* (Penguin, 2003), 218.

In defence of stories

And so is a willingness to listen, to acknowledge the experience of terrorism, of terrorist and victim alike. In any war, 'words', as Camus advised half a century ago, are always 'more powerful than munitions'.[44] The 'war against terrorism' is certainly no different.[45] It has been the purpose of this book to argue the case for a jurisprudence of story-telling. Listening to stories, it has been suggested, to testaments of suffering, might just be the best counter-terrorist strategy we have. It is the 'stories of resistance' we need to listen to and try to understand.[46] It is these stories that will challenge our perceptions, make us look and think again. 'Contemplating, literally and figuratively, the faces of the effaced activist and his or her intimates', it has been urged, 'becomes a condition for understanding the inferno of action' that is terrorism.[47]

Such a strategy is poetical and poethical.[48] It urges us to 'keep in view the human fact of the victims of political violence', and to keep in view too, the fact that victimhood can take many forms. 'No breath of apology', Ted Honderich rightly declares, 'is owed to those who may say to themselves that they do not expect to find emotional matter within serious reflection'. It is emotion, far more than cold reason, which takes us 'closer to the reality' of our 'experience' of political violence, in all its forms.[49] Judith Butler agrees. Whilst the language of law, of rights and the like, has a value, it rarely does 'justice to passion and grief and rage, all of which tear us from ourselves, bind us to others, transport us, undo us, implicate us in lives that are not our own'.[50] It is for this reason that we need to invoke alternative strategies, and alternative texts.

The essays which comprise this book have explored three distinct and particular poethical or poetical strategies. First, they have sought to impress the textual nature of terrorism and counter-terrorist responses. It was for this reason that we sought to reconsider the nature of modern terrorist discourse in the particular context of Edmund Burke's *Reflections on the Revolution in France*. It was also for this reason that we read Burke's *Reflections* alongside Shelley's *Mask of Anarchy*. In this way the rhetoric of the counter-terrorist was revealed to be, at precisely the same time, the rhetoric of the potential terrorist too. The nature of this essential and irreducible equivocation was fleshed out

---

[44] Quoted in C. Webel, *Terror, Terrorism and the Human Condition* (Palgrave, 2004), 108.

[45] See Susan Buck-Morss, *Terror*, arguing at 64 that the struggle that matters today is not the war against terror, but the battle for language and expression.

[46] See P. Ewick and S. Silbey, *The Common Place of Law: Stories from Everyday Life* (Chicago University Press, 1998), 234–8.

[47] See Zulaika and Douglass, *Terror*, 217, adding that such a 'confrontation rescues us from obfuscating allegory and representation'.

[48] For the invocation of a more particular jurisprudential 'poetics', see Gearey, 'Poetics', 38–59.

[49] Honderich, *Terrorism*, 4, 13–4. For the same sentiment in his *Terror*, see 33, and 127 concluding that 'we have no need of international law' to remind us of this.

[50] Butler, *Precarious Life*, 25.

still further in Chapter 2, in the textual form of Shakespeare's elusive commentary on the Jesuit scares in *Macbeth*.

The second projected strategy has sought to explore the merits of deploying non-legal texts as a strategic supplement to the bare textuality of those texts to which legalism deigns to ascribe legal validity. Here, in Chapter 3 in particular, but also in Chapters 4 and 6, the case was argued for the inclusion of narrative and poetic supplements. The case is not, of course, exclusive or imperialistic. It is not intended to preclude legalistic texts, or indeed colonise them. Rather it suggests that legal texts which seek to account for terrorist events, the various testaments, expert, juridical, speculative, that constitute court proceedings, must be complemented by further supplementary texts, texts that delve more deeply into the myriad ethical questions that a coherent counter-terrorist strategy needs. For this reason, in the context of the International Criminal Tribunal for Yugoslavia it was argued that there was indeed a strong case for forging the 'kind of public narrative' identified by Richard Jackson as a distinctive contribution to a more literary and literate jurisprudence.[51]

We encountered similar chronicles and similar arguments in the discussion of the so-called 'war on terror' in the last chapter. We noted the aspiration of Brittain and Slovo's *Guantanamo*, just as we also noted that whilst such a text can provide an extra-legal chronicle of this particular juristic 'black hole', so too can it do something more. It can address a second 'black hole', the collateral absence of voice; the attempt, encapsulated in the event of 9/11 and then in the 'war' that has followed, to control our thoughts, constrain our expression and crush our sense of humanity. Most importantly, texts such as *Guantanamo* as well as the novels of McInerney, Sarfan Foer or DeLillo further confirm the juxtaposition of the ordinary and the extraordinary. In doing so they also impel us to reconsider another presumed bipolarity, one that is rather more familiar to legal theorists. They make us think about the fictive boundaries of the public and the private; in the associated context of 9/11, about the higher politics of Guantanamo and the 'war on terror', and the more particular devastation which both the event, and our responses to it, have wrought on the ordinary lives of ordinary people.

The need to cut through the rhetoric, to discern the particular form of suffering which can so easily mutate into violent dissension, was eloquently noted by former US Secretary of State Zbigniew Brzezinski:

> It is a self-delusion for Americans to be told that the terrorists are motivated mainly by an abstract 'hatred of freedom' and that their acts are a reflection of a profound cultural hostility… Terrorists are not born but shaped by events, experiences, impressions, hatreds, ethnic myths, historical memories, religious fanaticism and deliberate brainwashing. They are also shaped by images of what they see on television, and especially by their feelings of outrage at what they

---

[51] See Jackson, *Writing*, 1, 188.

perceive to be a brutalizing denigration of their religious kin's dignity by heavily armed foreigners.[52]

A terrorist is made out of perceptions of injustice, out of individual acts of hurt and suffering, just as he or she is inspired by images of the suffering of others with whom they can all too easily empathise. We must not allow ourselves to be persuaded away from thinking about this.[53]

Here, of course, we encounter the third of our projected 'strategies' of law and literature; poethics. As we have seen from the very beginning, the case for poethical jurisprudence is generally couched in terms of reinvesting ethical debate with a proper sense of its discursive and textual form. It finds an eloquent exponent in Maria Aristodemou, who enjoins us to deploy literature as a critical prelude to reinvesting in us an 'ethics' of 'otherness', or fundamental responsibility for the well-being of all others with whom we engage, however directly or indirectly.[54] Such an aspiration again resonates with post-modern jurists such as Drucilla Cornell and Costas Douzinas. In his *The End of Human Rights*, the latter projects a revitalised jurisprudence at the heart of which is a reinvested ethics of otherness:

> The utopia projected by the human rights imaginary would be a social organ-isation which recognises and protects the existential integrity of people expressed in their imaginary domain. The post-modern utopian hope has ontological importance: it protects the integrity of unique beings in their existential other-ness, by promoting the dynamic realisation of freedom with others. While the individual imaginary helps build an other-dependent identity, the social imagi-nary supports a social organisation in which human relationships will respect and promote the uniqueness of the participants.[55]

Such an 'imaginary' is irreducibly textual. It gestures, not just to a post-modern ethics of deconstruction, but also, perhaps even despite itself, to a poethics. As Douzinas concludes, it will, ultimately, be a jurisprudence of 'love and affection, pity and friendship'.[56] In Chapter 5 we encountered Jacques Derrida making essentially the same claim for his 'politics of friendship', a politics of 'uncondi-tional hospitality'.[57]

A further echo can be found in Richard Rorty's assertion that, in the cause of recasting a jurisprudence of human dignity, 'sentimentality may be the best

---

[52] Quoted in G. Achcar, *The Clash of Barbarisms: The Making of the New World Disorder* (Saqi, 2002), 13–14.

[53] See Buck-Morss, *Terror*, 42.

[54] M. Aristodemou, *Law and Literature: Journeys from Her to Eternity* (Oxford University Press, 2000), 295. See also 2, 225, and also, making the same suggestion, Williams, *Empty Justice*, xviii.

[55] C. Douzinas, *The End of Human Rights: Critical Legal Thought at the Turn of the Century* (Hart, 2000), 341.

[56] Douzinas, *Human Rights*, 33.

[57] See J. Derrida, 'Dialogue' in G. Borradori (ed.), *Philosophy in a Time of Terror: Dialogues with Juergen Habermas and Jacques Derrida* (Chicago University Press, 2003), 120, 128–30, 133, and also J. Derrida, *Politics of Friendship* (Verso, 1997), particularly 8, 100.

weapon we have'.[58] According to Rorty, such a jurisprudence will be enshrined, not in charters of enumerated rights, but in chronicles of 'sentimental stories'. It will embrace 'endless diversity', proclaiming a message of 'human fraternity' and 'romantic hope', whilst triumphing, above all, a poethics of 'compassion'.[59] It is a jurisprudence, of course, which expresses Rorty's deeper belief in an ethics of poetical and metaphorical contingency:

> To see one's language, one's conscience, one's morality, and one's highest hopes as contingent products, as literalisations of what once were accidentally produced metaphors, is to adopt a self-identity which suits one for citizenship in such an ideally liberal state.[60]

The resonance of Rorty's invocation of hope with Douzinas's is immediate. Both project utopias. But in doing so, of course, both seek to counter juristic pessimism; of the kind which presently pervades terrorist and counter-terrorist discourse.[61] And both appreciate the need to reinvest politics and ethics through a proper appreciation of the textual and discursive nature of justice; in Rorty's words a jurisprudence of 'poetry' rather than 'principles'.[62] Of course, as we have seen in previous chapters, there is nothing new about this insight. We encountered the same sentiment of hope in Wordsworth's appeal to a politics of 'warmer love' in Chapter 1, whilst Rorty himself locates a compelling poetic root in Walt Whitman. And the same sentiment can be found in Whitman's contemporary, George Eliot, who affirmed that a proper sense of humanity can only be conveyed through an 'extension of our sympathies', through the 'picture of human life such as a great artist can give'.[63]

The Enlightenment rule of law, however, as we know, was to be a rule of reason, rather than romance, of sense rather than sensibility, and jurists who begged to differ were few and far between. One who did, however, or at least one who sought a better appreciation of the respective value of each, was John Stuart Mill. Mill was a great believer in the 'contagion of sympathy', and the ability of literature to spread it.[64] So too, as Mill readily appreciated, was David Hume.

[58] R. Rorty, *Truth and Progress* (Cambridge University Press, 1998), 172, 177–80. For a discussion of Rorty's writings on human rights and jurisprudence, see I. Ward, 'Bricolage and Low Cunning: Rorty on Pragmatism, Politics and Poetic Justice', *Legal Studies*, 28 (2008), particularly 294–6.

[59] Here he approves Walt Whitman's idea of democracy as a 'poetic agon, in which jarring dialectical discords would be resolved in previously unheard harmonies'. See R. Rorty, *Achieving Our Country: Leftist Thought in Twentieth-Century America* (Harvard University Press, 1999), 18, and also *Philosophy and Social Hope* (Penguin, 1999), 96–7, 122.

[60] R. Rorty, *Contingency, Irony, and Solidarity* (Cambridge University Press, 1989), 61.

[61] See Rorty, *Contingency*, 198, for his express determination to write against democratic 'self-doubt', and also *Philosophy*, 238–9, for similar sentiments couched within the broader need to restore a hopeful 'self-image' of democratic citizenship.

[62] See Rorty, *Philosophy*, 81–3, 99.

[63] G. Eliot, *Selected Essays, Poems and Other Writings* (Penguin, 1990), 110.

[64] J. Mill, 'Utilitarianism' in J. Mill and J. Bentham, *Utilitarianism and Other Essays* (Penguin, 1987), 6.

Writing at the very dawn of Enlightenment, in his *Treatise of Human Nature*, Hume confirmed that:

> No quality of human nature is more remarkable, both in itself and in its consequences, than that propensity we have to sympathize with others, and to receive by communication their inclinations and sentiments, however different from, or even contrary to our own.[65]

The implication of Hume's spectator theory is clear. It demands, above all, that we think in terms, not of law, or at least not just law, but of people. For 'men', as Hume added, 'always consider the sentiments of others in their judgement of themselves'.[66] And when they think about justice, what is fair, what is right, they do so through the faculty, not of reason, but of the 'imagination'.[67]

As we noted earlier, perhaps the most compelling contemporary advocate of the role of literature in nurturing a political imagination is Martha Nussbaum. Appreciating the historicity of this imagination, as well as its literary root, Nussbaum contends that it is literature, rather than law, which can secure the 'good society', quite simply because it can more readily access our 'narrative emotions', and it is these emotions that nurture our capacity to 'love' and which, ultimately, make life worth living.[68] Literature infuses politics with a necessary ethics of compassion, of 'imagination, inclusion, sympathy, and voice'.[69] Understood in this way, 'intelligent' liberal citizenship is defined by an 'ability to think what it might be like to be in the shoes of a person different from oneself, to be an intelligent reader of that person's story, and to understand the emotions and wishes and desires that someone so placed might have'.[70]

In a recent essay on terrorism Nussbaum has reaffirmed that events such as 9/11 confirm the presence of compassion 'in the fabric of our lives'. It is compassion that gives our political morality a necessary 'urgency', even relevance. More than a simple 'warm feeling in the gut', compassion engages our 'thoughts', and the thoughts of others. It transcends boundaries, political or cultural. It enables Americans, she suggests, perhaps rather boldly, to better understand the kind of suffering experienced by victims of terrorism

---

[65] D. Hume, *A Treatise of Human Nature* (Oxford University Press, 1978), 316. A similar statement is to be found in Adam Smith's *Theory of Moral Sentiments*, composed shortly after. Writing about Hume's famous 'spectator theory', Smith suggested that 'pity or compassion' is the most striking form of empathy nourished by our capacity to judge. See A. Smith, *The Theory of Moral Sentiments* (Oxford University Press, 1976), 9.

[66] Hume, *Treatise*, 295–6, 375.

[67] See Hume, *Treatise*, 1–11, 211–12, 319, 385–6, 495, 534. In his *Theory of Moral Sentiments*, Smith again said much the same. See his *Theory* 19, 75, 110–16.

[68] M. Nussbaum, *Love's Knowledge: Essays on Philosophy and Literature* (Oxford University Press, 1990), 53, 75–6, 94–6, 165–6, 190–1.

[69] M. Nussbaum, *Poetic Justice: The Literary Imagination and Public Life* (Beacon Press, 1995), 73–8, 90–1, 115–20.

[70] See Nussbaum, *Cultivating Humanity*, 10–11. This defence of *eudaimonistic* judgement is repeated in *Hiding from Humanity*, 51–4.

elsewhere.[71] It is a matter of nurturing our 'human literacy', our capacity to 'recognise one another'. This is the 'good thing' about tragedy and terror. It can 'awaken a larger sense of the humanity of suffering, a patriotism constrained by respect for human dignity and by a vivid sense of the real losses and needs of others'.[72]

In this she is not alone. Writing alike in the wake of 9/11 Salman Rushdie suggested that it had become ever more obvious that the 'world's stories are no longer separate from each other'. And so, accordingly, we 'can no longer seal our cultures away from each other. We cannot pretend they belong in separate baskets. Everyone's story is everyone else's story, or can become so in a flash or in an explosion'.[73] The same sentiment can be found in Ariel Dorfman's 'dreadful hope' that the experience of suffering, now so acute in America, might nurture a greater sense of 'compassion' for those countless millions who daily suffer terror and deprivation around the globe.[74] 'It is up to writers', Christopher Merrill confirms, 'to redeem the individual from the collective tragedy, to discover the mythic underpinnings of what may seem unimaginable, to bear witness to loss with such empathy and precision that we glimpse how to navigate our way into the future'.[75]

The resolution of any so-called 'war' against terror is far more likely to be achieved by facilitating dialogue, by promoting reconciliation, and inclusion and mutual respect, than it is by invading more and more countries, and slaughtering more and more supposed 'insurgents'.[76] And poetry might help too. In the days that followed 9/11, the internet was inundated with allusions to Auden's poem *September 1, 1939*. The coincidence between the shattering events of that day in New York and Auden's similar invocation, in the same city, of 'blind skyscrapers' that had aspired to 'proclaim / The strength of Collective Man' struck many.[77] As did the sense of millennial foreboding, the feeling of coming uncertainty and darkness; a chronicle of a tragedy foretold, not unlike, in one sense, DeLillo's prophesy in *Mao II*.[78] Auden,

---

[71] She cites the Punjab and Afghanistan; the latter carrying an immediately paradoxical implication, given the role of US forces in 'counter' terrorist activities there. See M. Nussbaum, 'Compassion and Terror' in J. Sterba (ed.), *Terrorism and International Justice* (Oxford University Press, 2003), 231, 234.

[72] Nussbaum, 'Terror', 249–51.

[73] S. Rushdie, 'The Ministry of False Alarms', *Virginia Quarterly Review*, 80 (2004), 7.

[74] Dorfman, *Other Septembers*, 11. It is his 'hope for America: empathy, compassion, the capacity to imagine that you are not unique'.

[75] C. Merrill, 'A Kind of Solution', *Virginia Quarterly Review*, 80 (2004), 70, and also 80–3 despairing of the simplistic alternative, of a political morality founded on 'them' and 'us'.

[76] See Ignatieff, *Lesser Evil*, 82, similarly observing that 'If terrorism is a form of politics, it needs to be fought with the force of argument and not just with the force of arms', and also Minow, 'Evil', 2167 commenting on Ignatieff's essay and agreeing on this particular principle.

[77] See W. Auden, *Selected Poems* (Faber and Faber, 1979), verse 4, at 87, and also M. Williams, 'Then and Now: The Natural/Positivist Nexus at War: Auden's 'September 1, 1939', *Journal of Law and Society*, 31 (2004), 63, 78.

[78] There are immediate echoes of Matthew Arnold's lines in *Dover Beach*, his great muse on England's anticipated demise, the 'melancholy, long, withdrawing roar'. See M. Arnold, 'Dover Beach', line 25, in *A Critical Edition of the Major Works* (Oxford University Press, 1986), 136.

however, a poet whose writing was rooted in a desire for compassion, flirted with hope. For 'no one exists alone', and so, accordingly, 'We must love each other or we must die'.[79]

It was upon this last line in particular that so many alighted in the days and weeks that followed 9/11. It speaks to a greater movement, to a commitment to the very idea of humanity, to what Auden appraised as 'the ethical life', to the supposition that any legal response to acts of extreme violence can only be enhanced by a proper appreciation that we are all products of narrative, the carriers of particular stories and experiences, feelings and emotions.[80] In his review of the film *United 93*, Martin Amis alighted on precisely this possibility. Speaking to the closing scenes of those fated to die seeking to make a last contact with those who mattered most, he concluded, 'Love is an abstract noun, something nebulous. And yet love turns out to be the only part of us that is solid, as the world turns upside down and the screens go black. We can't tell if it will survive us. But we can be sure that it's the last thing to go'.[81] To reject these stories, to ignore these experiences and emotions, to pretend that they have no place in any study of law or politics is, as Nussbaum has recently and rightly supposed, to 'leave out a great part of our humanity'; the greatest perhaps.[82] It is also to deny us that final hope.

The Devil's big day

This realisation matters, always. But it seems to matter more than ever today. 9/11 and the 'war on terror' which it has spawned retains its position at the very forefront of our political and jurisprudential imaginations. Enough of us, it seems, buy into the notion that the events of that day really were apocalyptic, that a war had been declared against the forces of civilisation. Here the image has retained a critical vitality. It consumes us, imprinted indelibly on our minds; as the perpetrators of the horror hoped it would be, and as those who seek to justify our crazed response, our 'war on terror', hope too.[83] As we have suggested already, on more than one occasion, a first step in countering the kind of nihilistic savagery inflicted upon New York on 11 September 2001 is to look beyond the apocalyptic imagery. We must keep our heads, penetrate beyond the equivocation and rhetorical feints, and perceive the human suffering which lies behind.[84] It is this which should hold our attention, and draw our energies.

We should not be surprised that terrorist and counter-terrorist alike should seek to enchant us, to control our gaze. For both share the same critical

---

[79] Auden, *Poems*, verse 8, at 88.   [80] Auden, *Poems*, verse 7, at 88.
[81] M. Amis, *The Second Plane* (Jonathan Cape, 2000), 137.
[82] Nussbaum, *Hiding From Humanity*, 7.
[83] See F. Dallmayr, 'Lessons of September 11', *Theory, Culture & Society*, 19 (2002), 137.
[84] See Ackerman, *Attack*, 169. For an alternative view, dismissing those who mount the 'Panic Theory', as they term it, see E. Posner and A. Vermeule, *Terror in the Balance: Security, Liberty and the Courts* (Oxford University Press, 2007), 59–80.

aspiration, the instantiation of popular paranoia.[85] In his essay simply titled *Murder*, composed on the eve of the 1848 revolutions, the radical Karl Heinzen confirmed that:

> The revolutionaries must always try to bring about a situation where the barbarians are afraid for their lives every hour of the day and night. They must think that every drink of water, every mouthful of food, every bed, every bush, every paving stone, every path and footpath, every hole in the wall, every slate, every bundle of straw, every pipe bowl, every stick, and every pin may be a killer.[86]

The real fear is that we fail to appreciate that Heinzen's strategy is today pursued with just as great an urgency in Washington and London as it is in Helmand and Peshawar. The image of thousands of trained killers walking our streets is ridiculous. It is hard to be sure whether we should be more disturbed by the thought that the man who sought to impress this image knew it was nonsense and said it anyway or that he really believed it. The same can be said of those who pretend to take us on crusade against the fundamentalist infidel. We should be beyond this kind of theological idiocy, the 'quixoticisms' of 'religious chivalry' as Bishop Garnett put it two and a half centuries ago.[87] But are we? The invasion of Iraq, Abu Ghraib, Guantanamo; it is hard to imagine a sequence of events that could be more readily presented as a latter-day 'crusade against Islam'.[88] The leader of the 7/7 bombings in London justified his actions in precisely these terms, as a riposte to crusader imperialism.[89] Whilst such a justification beggars intellectual credence, it is still an absurdity conjured in the corridors of Washington and Whitehall.[90]

The rhetoric is then to be expected. The failure of law, however, has, perhaps, come as a rather greater shock. As we saw in the last chapter, juristic counter-terrorist responses, like the rhetoric of which they are, in large part, the bastard progeny, have been in the main shaming. The patent confusion of the US Supreme Court betokens an apparent bewilderment that borders on the embarrassing, the impotent distaste of the British House of Lords equally so. Guantanamo is peculiarly shaming, the cack-handed attempts of the British government to detain, then tag, and then try to trace the whereabouts of supposed terrorists who simply remove their tags and disappear, the stuff of farce. The law looks to be an ass, our

---

[85] See Scheffler, 'Terrorism', 6–7 and 13–14 on the common instantiation of fear.

[86] In M. Burleigh, *Blood and Rage: A Cultural History of Terrorism* (HarperCollins, 2008), 69.

[87] In J. Sharpe, *Remember, Remember the Fifth of November: Guy Fawkes and the Gunpowder Plot* (Profile, 2005), 112.

[88] Quoted in a message broadcast by the Al-Jazeera network on 1 September 2005, and cited in Achcar, *Barbarisms*, 11. The same conclusion is reached by Richard Norton-Taylor, in J. Pilger, *Tell Me No Lies: Investigative Journalism and its Triumphs* (Vintage, 2005), 557–8.

[89] Something which, Ackerman rightly counsels, should serve as a sober caution. See his *Attack*, 172–3. The testament, recorded on video prior to the mission, declared 'I am directly responsible for protecting and avenging my Muslim brothers and sisters'. Quoted in Achcar, *Barbarisms*, 12.

[90] See Durodie, 'Fear', 429 and also C. Walker, 'The Treatment of Foreign Terror Suspects', *Modern Law Review*, 70 (2007), 456–7.

political leaders alternately simplistic, heartless, and in the case of Britain, supine.[91] This is not how it should be.

Along with their prayers in aid of a sequence of ham-fisted, unwinnable wars against assorted Middle Eastern countries, it is, as we have noted before, reasonable to assume that bin Laden and his henchmen hoped upon hope that the citizens of the US, and their allies, would be so convinced of the terror which they faced, so readily deluded by their political leaders, that they would happily accede to the serial abrogation of their most cherished political and jurisprudential principles. They hoped that we would all buy into the rhetoric of apocalypse and crusade, that we would feel the need to find out if our god really is the biggest. They hoped that we would be cowed by the rhetoric of former British Home Secretary David Blunkett, who, amidst the frenzied atmosphere of autumn 2001, took the opportunity to declaim the 'world' of the 'airy-fairy, libertarian, where everyone does precisely what they like and we believe the best of everybody and then they destroy us'.[92]

And it appears that their prayers have been answered; even if by a more satanic host. For 9/11 does indeed appear to have been 'the Devil's big day'.[93] We have lost our heads, the seeds of 'dread' have been sown.[94] The age of terror, it seems, ushers in an age of judicial 'barbarism'.[95] Guantanamo is representative of precisely such barbarism. It is worth recalling Alexander Hamilton's Letter 84 in *The Federalist*, which advised, 'the practice of arbitrary imprisonments, have been, in all ages, the favourite and most formidable instruments of tyranny'.[96] Now is not the time to abandon law. It is, rather, the time to reinvest the conception of justice which validates law, and which makes it so vital a component of a just society. And it is up to us. Democracy, the rule of law, rights; these are things that must be worked for. As he exited the 1787 Convention, Benjamin Franklin was famously asked what kind of government was being carved out. 'A republic, madam, if you can keep it', was the reply.[97]

In echo of Hamilton, and Franklin, the President of the Israeli Supreme Court, Aharan Barak has rather more recently reminded us that:

---

[91] See Amis's reference to Prime Minister Blair and his government 'helplessly caught up in the slipstream turbulence of George Bush', in *Plane*, at 83.

[92] Quoted in P. Thomas, '9/11: USA and UK', *Fordham International Law Journal*, 26 (2003), at 1202.

[93] See Mailer, *Why*, 111.

[94] B. Barber, *Fear's Empire: War, Terrorism and Democracy* (Norton, 2003), 92, and Ackerman, *Attack*, 169, counselling against the temptation to 'lose our heads' and be persuaded to abrogate our most cherished political and legal principles.

[95] M. Ratner, 'Moving Away from the Rule of Law: Military Tribunals, Executive Detentions and Torture', *Cardozo Law Review*, 24 (2003), 1520, and also M. Ratner and E. Ray, *Guantanamo: What the World Should Know* (Arris, 2004), 92.

[96] The same letter in which he also advised that the writ of habeas corpus was the greatest possible security to liberty and republicanism. See J. Madison *et al. The Federalist Papers* (Penguin, 1987), 474.

[97] In A. Arato, '*Minima Politica* after September 11' *Constellations*, 9 (2002), 50.

Sometimes a democracy must fight with one hand tied behind its back. Nonetheless, it has the upper hand. Preserving the rule of law and recognition of individual liberties constitute an important component of its understanding of society. At the end of the day, they strengthen its spirit and allow it to overcome its difficulties'.[98]

The success or failure of a 'war on terror' will not be gauged in the numbers of cities cleansed of 'insurgents' or fantastical plots foiled. It will be tested by conduct, by the means of its waging.[99] Harold Koh cites former US Secretary of State Albright who, pre-9/11, was keen to remind the world, and more immediately the putatively lawless peoples of Uzbekistan, that:

> One of the most dangerous temptations for a government facing violent threats is to respond in heavy-handed ways that violate the rights of innocent citizens. Terrorism is a criminal act and should be treated accordingly – and that means applying the rule of law fairly and consistently.[100]

Speaking as one who, from personal experience, knows the value of such rights, and how precarious their existence can be, Ariel Dorfman regrets the willingness of millions of Americans to accept that 'an endless and stage-managed war against terrorism, defined in a multitude of ever-shifting and vague forms' can justify not just the abrogation of law, of fundamental juristic principles of human rights or civil liberties, but of our sense of humanity and human dignity.[101]

Law does not exist merely as a tool to inflict upon others. It represents a statement of our collective determination to treat each other justly, humanely, and with compassion. Without this inner belief in a conception of fundamental justice, law is indeed merely a tool of tyranny, a tool of terror indeed. Ultimately, our jurisprudential integrity rests upon the urgent need to reconnect our laws, and our perceptions of justice, with 'basic notions of humanity'.[102] A credible counter to the threat of terrorism will be fashioned around our willingness to comprehend human faces, not executive decrees or legislative statutes. In this we too must resist; for scepticism is a form of resistance, and if the experience of 9/11 has taught us anything it is the urgent need, at all times, to be sceptical of those who would seek to enchant us.

Terrorists, as Michael Ignatieff confirms, 'seek to strip off the mask of law to reveal the nihilist heart of coercion within'. It is for this reason that 'we have to show ourselves and the population whose loyalty we seek that the rule of law is

---

[98] A. Barak, 'A Judge on Judging: The Role of the Supreme Court in a Democracy', *Harvard Law Review*, 116 (2002), 148. A similar statement can be found in the judgement of the Indian Supreme Court in *People's Union of Civil Liberties v Union of India*, which stated that 'If human rights are violated in the process of combating terrorism, it will be self-defeating'. Quoted in Lady Justice Arden, 'Human Rights in an Age of Terrorism', *Law Quarterly Review*, 121 (2005), 618.

[99] See H. Koh, 'The Spirit of the Laws', *Harvard International Law Journal*, 43 (2002), 24.

[100] In Koh, 'Spirit', 30.   [101] Dorfman, *Other Septembers*, 34.

[102] For this appeal, see S. Ratner, 'The War on Terrorism and International Humanitarian Law', *Michigan State Journal of International Law*, 14 (2006), 25.

not a mask but the true image of our nature.'[103] Sadly, he concludes, history reveals that liberal democracies 'consistently overreact to terrorist threats, as if their survival were in jeopardy'.[104] Shelley, once again, would nod his appreciation. He too sought to strip off the mask of tyranny, only in his case the mask was worn not by those presumed to be terrorists, but by those who presumed to cast others in that mould. The fear of terror and the abrogation of legal principle are mutually sustaining. Our present 'war on terror' has become a war on law.[105] It has always been thus.

A liberal constitution is not, as Justice Jackson famously asserted, a 'suicide pact'.[106] Democracy must indeed protect itself. But, as Shelley, and indeed Burke, also appreciated, the threat is various, and the enemy takes many forms. The pretences of national security, so readily and so urgently pressed, must not become a justification for jurisprudential self-immolation.[107] Hysteria must be resisted. There is a point beyond which an executive should not be allowed to go, no matter how great the fear and how great the paranoia.[108] Wherever a state prioritises counter-terrorism over constitutional liberties, we should, as Michael Walzer observes, 'look for tyranny'.[109] Similarly, we should remain minded of the adage that, outwith the realms of utopia, 'suffering' is the 'price of freedom'.[110] It was the same Justice Jackson who, in 1948, famously declared that:

> There is no more effective practical guaranty against arbitrary and unreasonable government than to require that the principles of law which officials impose upon a minority must be imposed generally. Conversely, nothing opens the door to arbitrary action so effectively as to allow those officials to pick and choose only a few to whom they will apply legislation and thus to escape the political retribution that might be visited upon them if larger numbers were affected. Courts can take no better measure to assure that laws will be just than to require that laws be equal in operation.[111]

---

[103] Ignatieff, *Lesser Evil*, 144.

[104] Ignatieff, *Lesser Evil*, ix, and also, at 80, confirming that 'the historical record shows that while no democracy has ever been brought down by terror, all democracies have been damaged by it'. The same assertion is made by Christopher Blakesley, in 'Ruminations', at 1402.

[105] See variously, Minow, 'Evil', 2140; Gearty, 'Terrorism', 383; V. Lowe, 'The Iraq Crisis: What Now?' *International and Comparative Law Quarterly*, 52 (2003), 871; K. Roach and G. Trotter, 'Miscarriages of Justice in the War Against Terror', *University of Pennsylvania State Law Review*, 109 (2005), 1041; and also Ignatieff, *Lesser Evil*, 54, identifying the rhetorical strategy of using 'war' as an excuse for the abrogation of fundamental civil liberties.

[106] See Ignatieff, *Lesser Evil*, 9, 40–4.

[107] See P. Hoffman, 'Human Rights and Terrorism', *Human Rights Quarterly*, 26 (2004), 933–5, 951–2, and also E. Flynn, 'Counter-Terrorism and Human Rights: The View from the United Nations', *European Human Rights Law Review*, 1 (2005), 36.

[108] See L. Zedner, 'Securing Liberty in the Face of Terror', *Journal of Law and Society*, 32 (2005), 22 and also Ackerman, *Attack*, 1–2.

[109] Walzer, *Arguing*, 64.   [110] See Sofsky, *Violence*, 8.

[111] *Railway Express Agency* v *New York* 336 US 106 (1949) at 111–13. Jackson iterated similar statements five years later in *Shaughnessy*, observing 'Fortunately, it is still startling, in this country, to find a person held indefinitely in executive custody without accusation of crime or judicial trial'. See *Shaughnessy* v *US* 345 US 205 (1953), 218. Interestingly, Justice Stevens cited Jackson's observations in *Shaughnessy* in his judgement in *Rasul*.

English law is replete with similar statements.[112]

Periodic terrorist threats are no excuse for the wholesale abrogation, for an indeterminate period, of fundamental civil and human rights.[113] The 'war' against terror, as one German court has recently declared, cannot be a 'wild, unjust war'.[114] Speaking to the British Parliament in 1993, a young British Home Secretary observed:

> If we cravenly accept that any action by the government… must be supported in its entirety without question, we do not strengthen the fight against terrorism, we weaken it. I hope that no Honourable Member will say that we do not have the right to challenge powers, to make sure that they are in accordance with the civil liberties of our country.[115]

Twelve years later in the aftermath of 7/7, and now Prime Minister, the same Tony Blair advised his compatriots that they should not allow their 'normal' lives to be disrupted by terrorism, and nor should they be deluded into abandoning those 'values' which define Britain.[116] But if they accepted the provisions of the Prevention of Terrorism Act that would be nice. The 'rules of the game', he iterated, not for the first time, or the last, had changed.

But have they? Is the threat so desperate, our terror so all-consuming that we have to abandon centuries of jurisprudential evolution? Of course not. Militant Islamic terrorism presents no significant threat to the cohesion and stability of our social and political order, either domestic or international; and nor does any other species of terrorism or political violence.[117] But it sorely hopes that we might be deluded into thinking that it does. And what has changed in our perceptions of humanity, of the fate of others? Is the threat so great, too, that we must close our ears? Is the difference between a terrorist and the rest of us really so great that the former must be cast outside of our legal imagination?[118]

Nothing about terrorism is comforting. We have already encountered Jean-Paul Sartre's Preface to Fanon's *The Wretched of the Earth*, in which he wrote that the violence of the supposed terrorist 'is neither sound and fury, nor the resurrection of savage instincts, nor even the effect of resentment: it is man

---

[112] See for example Lord Scarman's comments in *R v Home Secretary ex p Khawaja* [1984] AC 74, at 111. Interestingly, Scarman's observations were cited, with approval, by Lord Bingham in *A*, at para.48.

[113] So much was admitted by the former British Attorney-General, Lord Goldsmith, who confirmed that 'those suspected of being terrorists are not outside the law, nor do they forfeit their fundamental rights by virtue of that fact'. In P. Sands, *Lawless World: America and the Making and Breaking of Lawless Rules* (Penguin, 2005), 170.

[114] For a commentary on this judgement, provided by a Hamburg court, in a case where the conviction of a suspected terrorist was overturned for failure of process, see Roach and Trotter, 'Miscarriages', 999.

[115] Quoted in Thomas, '9/11', 1233.   [116] Quoted in Achcar, *Barbarisms*, 8.

[117] See Hobsbawn, *Globalisation*, 43, 135–7, 151–3, and also J. Gray, *Black Mass: Apocalyptic Religion and the Death of Utopia* (Penguin, 2007), 180–1, reaching the same conclusion.

[118] Soans, *Talking*, 36. The theme is revisited on a number of occasions in the play. In one such instance, at 59, a British army colonel confesses that he could easily have become a terrorist if he had been raised in Crossmaglen or South Armagh.

re-creating himself'.[119] Nearly half a century has passed, and the lines are little more comforting today. But then they are not supposed to be. They are, however, supposed to be liberating; and this suggestion poses a challenge that is every bit as disturbing. The sentiment belongs to a particular intellectual tradition, of a radicalism that feels the need, in certain circumstances, to justify acts of acute political violence and terrorism. The adage of yesterday's terrorist being today's freedom fighter is a familiar one.[120] And for good reason; history, by and large, has proved it to be right. 'All terrorists', as Hugh Gaitskell once mused, 'at the invitation of the government, end up with tea at the Dorchester'.[121] Those who today laud Fanon, and Sartre, but who presume to loathe bin Laden and the assorted Hizbollah youth of modern Beirut, must reconcile themselves to this paradox.

And they, and we, must once again try to comprehend the sentiments which lie behind Nizar Qabbani's troubling and provocative verse:

> I am with terrorism
> if it is able to free a people
> from tyrants and tyranny...[122]

We could simply choose to ignore Qabbani, just as we might, for reasons of convenience, despatch Fanon and Sartre to the realms of history, just as we might indeed choose to dance around the paradoxes explored in Shakespeare's *Macbeth*, Conrad's *Secret Agent* or Coetzee's *Master of Petersburg*. But that would be a critical mistake. If we fail to address the sentiments of Qabbani, and Fanon and Sartre, and Conrad and Coetzee too, then we really will have lost a 'war' on terror; albeit a rather different war from that which we are time and again assured it is so necessary that we fight.

Such sentiments have a prosaic aspect; of the kind addressed by the German Foreign Minister Joschka Fischer, who observed, in the wake of 9/11, that terrorism will be more likely defeated by making sure everyone has enough to eat than by neo-colonial wars of 'repression'.[123] It is a conclusion which reaffirms the case for an international, perhaps even a transnational, strategy to address a problem the roots of which can be found in global inequalities and resentments. It finds further expression in the words of the Secretary-General of the UN who likewise urged the need to 'articulate a powerful and compelling global vision that

---

[119] Sartre, Preface, 18–19. Walter Lacqueur has recently testified to the extent of contemporary interest in Fanon's book, and Sartre's Preface. See his *War*, 219.

[120] Part of the same 'cycle of hate', as Fanon famously put it. See Fanon, *Wretched*, 68, 70, 73, 165. For further commentaries on this familiar adage, see P. Rees, *Dining With Terrorists* (Macmillan, 2005), xv–vii, xxi, describing the terrorist discourse as one of 'subtle word games', and also S. French, 'Murderers, Not Warriors' in J. Sterba (ed.), *Terrorism and International Justice* (Oxford University Press, 2003), 31–2, and Dershowitz, *Why Terrorism Works*, 8, observing that 'nearly everybody supports some terrorism and opposes other terrorism'.

[121] In Rees, *Terrorists*, 6.

[122] In Tariq Ali, *Bush in Babylon: The Recolonisation of Iraq* (Verso, 2003), 12–13.

[123] In S. von Schorlemer, 'Human Rights: Substantive and Institutional Implications of the War Against Terrorism', *European Journal of International Law*, 14 (2003), 267.

can defeat the vivid, if extreme, visions of terrorist groups'.[124] And at the heart of this vision must be jurisprudence; a belief in the sanctity of the rule of law as a necessary precondition of justice at any level, global, national, local.[125]

But it also contains something more, something rather more metaphysical and elusive, but something every bit as vital. This is the sentiment of human dignity, of care and compassion for the political, cultural and individual integrity of those whom we choose to determine as 'other'. It is captured in John Kenneth Galbraith's plea for a 'coalition of the concerned and the compassionate', and in Robert Falk's equally impassioned injunction that 'only by reconstructing intimate relations on a humane basis can the world move toward the wider public and collective realities of human community'.[126] The prosaic strategy of making sure everyone has enough to eat, of 'draining the swamp' of terrorism as it is commonly termed, must be complemented by the poethical strategy of making sure that the voice of the suffering is heard, and that, on being heard, is addressed.

This appreciation, or the lack of it, defines the success or failure of a counter-terrorist strategy. So, equally, does a willingness to listen, to appreciate the narrativity of terrorism. 'Talking to terrorists', Soans's Northern Ireland Secretary confirms, 'is the only way to beat them'. The most important weapon in any war against terrorism is an 'ear' for listening.[127] 'I never told my story, not before', another of Soans's terrorists comments, 'I'm pleased to tell it. Thank you for listening. Reality cannot hide forever. You might as well try and cover the sun with mud'.[128] We encountered precisely the same sentiments at the close of Chapter 3, in the voice of Hamdo Kharimanovic and that of the young man who testified to the South African Truth Commission. It was the latter who made the striking observation that in simply having the opportunity to tell his story 'it feels like I've got my sight back'.[129]

Inhumanity, like incomprehension, is a contagion. We must guard against it. If we fail to do so, the responsibility and the guilt will be ours. Terrorism expresses a virulent strain of inhumanity.[130] It tempts us to abrogate our

---

[124] In McGoldrick, 9–11, 197.

[125] See Dallmayr, 'Lessons', 139, citing the World Bank report 2000/1 which noted that the average income in the 20 richest countries is 37 times the average in the poorest 20. For similar conclusions, see R. Blackburn, 'The Imperial Presidency, the War on Terrorism, and the Revolutions of Modernity', *Constellations*, 9 (2002), 23–6 and also D. Held, 'Violence, Law and Justice in a Global Age', *Constellations*, 9 (2002), 74–87.

[126] See J. Galbraith, *The Good Society* (Sinclair-Stevenson, 1996), 143, and R. Falk, *On Humane Governance: Toward a New Global Politics* (Polity Press, 1995), 69.

[127] Soans, *Talking*, 28; the voice clearly that of the former Secretary of State for Northern Ireland, Mo Mowlem. Soans agrees with the sentiment, commenting in his Preface, at 5, that 'A huge part of what we call terrorism arises from no one listening'.

[128] Soans, *Talking*, 96.   [129] In A. Krog, *Country of My Skull* (Vintage, 1999), 45–6.

[130] A failure, according to Harold Pinter, of 'our moral sensibility'. See his comments in his Nobel Lecture, in the *Guardian*, 8 December 2005, G2, at 12. See also Steyn's observation, in his 2006 Attlee lecture, that the conspicuous failure of the British government to articulate an opposition to Guantanamo is 'shaming for our country'. At www.attlee.org.uk/Transcript-Styen.doc.

responsibilities to others, and to ourselves. It is the Devil's gambit. In this context, we should indeed ponder, not just the jurisprudential aberrations that are represented in Guantanamo or the rhetorical fancies of 'extraordinary rendition' and the like, but also what they say more broadly about us. Why do we accede to the continued existence of a camp in which the 'worst in human nature' is 'allowed to flourish'?[131] Why do we even ponder the permissibility of torturing other human beings on the off-chance they may know a bit about terrorism?

Small wonder, perhaps, that Soans should leave us with his Bethlehem schoolgirl trying to comprehend the death of her school friend, shot by an Israeli sniper, whilst also expressing her gratification that so 'many thousands' died on 11 September 2001.[132] But he also leaves us with Phoebe, a relief worker, who muses on the subjects of hope and despair:

> Of course so much of it makes you despair, and makes you afraid, for yourself and for humanity, I suppose. But then you sit on the floor, and play with a kid who tells you horrors worse than any nightmare, and yet there he is, sitting there and playing, and behaving perfectly normally to all intents and purposes. Yes, you can absolutely see hope in individuals… enormously…[133]

We can hope. Indeed we must hope. But we must first have courage; to listen and to hold to our own deeper convictions.

---

[131] In Ratner and Ray, *Guantanamo*, xi.

[132] Soans, *Talking*, 96–7. The conclusion resonates with Walter Lacqueur's repeated acknowledgement, that the resentment of Palestinians following the Israeli occupation after 1967 remains a prime catalyst of Islamic 'rage'. See Lacqueur, *War*, 118.

[133] Soans, *Talking*, 95–6.

Index